CULTURAL IDENTITY IN TRANSITION

Contemporary Conditions, Practices and Politics of a Global Phenomenon

CULTURAL IDENTITY IN TRANSITION

Contemporary Conditions, Practices and Politics of a Global Phenomenon

Edited by

Jari Kupiainen • Erkki Sevänen
John A. Stotesbury

ATLANTIC
PUBLISHERS & DISTRIBUTORS

Published by
ATLANTIC PUBLISHERS AND DISTRIBUTORS
B-2, Vishal Enclave, Opp. Rajouri Garden, New Delhi-110027
Phones . 25413460, 25429987, 25466842

Sales Office
7/22, Ansari Road, Darya Ganj, New Delhi-110002
Phones : 23273880, 23275880, 23280451
Fax : 91-11-23285873
web : www.atlanticbooks.com
e-mail : info@atlanticbooks.com

ISBN 81-269-0374-0

Printed in India at
Nice Printing Press, Delhi

Preface

Cultural Identity in Transition is an exploration of both recent and temporally more distant processes involved in the formation of cultural identity. The articles included in this anthology discuss these processes as they have occurred, and continue to occur, in diverse contexts around the world. A contingent emphasis on European — and, in particular, Scandinavian — societies will be found, not the least as a reflection of the ongoing changes in Europe since the latter part of the 1980s, but these processes also have had their counterparts in other parts of a globalising world. In addition, it should also be noticed that the scholars whose work appears here represent a variety of academic disciplines, ranging from literary studies to sociology and from ethnomusicology to anthropology; yet each different analysis invariably finds its own focus in the main topic of this Volume, the construction of cultural identity.

Despite this common focus, it is important to observe that these articles cannot easily be reduced to a single, monolithic standpoint, especially one artificially constructed to present the illusion of a unified approach. On occasion, the articles contradict and differ from each other in ways that may well enhance the ongoing dialogue among different disciplines and perspectives. This is, in fact, a multivocal book, and intentionally so, since we hold the view that this diversity of voices will facilitate the analysis of cultural identity processes within real socio cultural contexts, the ramifications of which, are both local and worldwide. The wealth of agenda and strategies attest to the strength of an underlying pluralism that might otherwise be concealed by a programmatic uniformity imposed by a singular research project.

This Volume is the product of co-operation among several academic departments and research units at the University of Joensuu, Finland, a fact which in itself demonstrates the multi-disciplinarity required to properly address the complexities involved in the formation of cultural identity. The three editors represent three different departments at their home university, all of which have been crucial, the Department of Finnish Language and Cultural Research, the Department of Foreign Languages and the Centre for Media Culture.

Finally, and collectively, we should like to extend our gratitude to the Editorial Board for their assistance, encouragement and support in getting this book into print. Tomi Halonen and Liina Petäjä, students at the Centre for Media Culture, have also been helpful in preparing translations and in dealing with the technical phases of editing this Volume. Thanks are also due to Professor Rajeshwar Mittapalli of the University of Kakatiya, India, whose close connections both with Joensuu and with Atlantic Publishers and Distributors, New Delhi, have facilitated the final preparation and publication of this Volume.

The Editors

CONTENTS

Introduction: From Modernity and Postmodernity to Globalisation

ERKKI SEVÄNEN

Introduction

International intellectual themes have their own special routes and fates, at least in social and cultural research. As long ago as in the 1970s, but especially during the 1980s, social and cultural theorists discussed questions of modernity and postmodernity with considerable passion. Although this discussion took place mainly on the level of social and cultural theory, questions of identity also played an important role in the themes discussed. In those decades the discussion about identity leant heavily on contemporary French thinking. In several cases, the works of Louis Althusser, Jacques Derrida, Michel Foucault, Julia Kristeva, Jacques Lacan and kindred souls offered the basic points of view from which researchers in different disciplines considered questions of identity and theorised about them. And even if many researchers could be dissatisfied with the thinking of the French intellectuals in question, often they also felt an urge to define their stand on those theories. On the whole, those intellectuals then gained a salient position in the theoretical discussion of identity.

In point of fact, the French intellectuals in question had already theorised about identity in the 1960s, but at that time they were almost unknown beyond the French-speaking world. In Great Britain and in the United States, academic departments and intellectual communities began to receive their theoretical ideas only in the 1970s, and in this connection most of them became internationally known as "French post-structuralists". In a precise description this label does not, of course, apply to Althusser, who was "a Marxist structuralist" or "a structuralistic Marxist" rather than a post-structuralist. At any rate, British and American literary critics and art theorists played an active role in the mediation of post-structuralistic theories. Thus, in Great Britain, in developing their theories, the researchers and theorists (Rosalind Coward, John Ellis, Stephen Heath, Colin MacCabe) who accumulated around the journal *The Screen* adopted their central ideas from Althusser, Kristeva and Lacan. Likewise, in the United States the famous group of literary critics, termed "deconstructionists" (Harold Bloom, Geoffrey Hartman, Paul de Man, J. Hillis Miller), presented Derrida's philosophy to a North American academic audience. In addition, in the Anglo-American academic world feminists were actively interested in Lacan's and Kristeva's radical theories of subject and identity, for these theories emphasised that sexual identities are not natural or biological properties of human beings but sociocultural constructions — a view which was being elaborated at the same time by American social anthropologists and feminists themselves. In West Germany, intellectuals and theorists started to receive and evaluate post-structuralist theories at the turn of the 1970s and 1980s, and in Finland, Sweden and other Nordic countries the same process began in the early 1980s.

The above-mentioned thinkers wrote about identities in a particular way in which the identities of human beings were seen as unstable, fluid and incoherent. Human beings, in turn, were understood as de-centered subjects whose true self was, similarly, disintegrated and continuously changing. As a criticism of these notions, many social and cultural theorists pointed out that it was incorrect to deal with the questions of identity in this way, without paying attention to the actual contexts in which people's identities take shape. For example, Stuart Hall (1992), Anthony Giddens (2001: 100), Douglas Kellner (1993: 141-145), and, in their joint article, Scott Lash and Jonathan Friedman (1993: 2-5) laid stress on the cultural differences between historical formations. According to them, in traditional and premodern Western society, people usually had a rather fixed and unproblematic identity which was determined by their place in the social hierarchy and in the Christian system of the world. The process of social and cultural modernisation then sets these old stable orders, these foundation pillars of identities, in motion. As a consequence of this process, in the modern Western world people have become accustomed to ask themselves such questions as "Who am I?", "What should I do with my life?" and "What will I become?" Following Giddens (2001: 74-80), one can say that in the modern Western world identity became a project that an individual needed to realise during the course of his or her life. In this sense the process of modernisation has produced individualisation within Western civilisation.[1] Some theorists of postmodernity have even stated that in contemporary or postmodern society this project has now been condemned to failure, in the sense that it is impossible to form and maintain a fixed and coherent core-identity in a world in which continuous and accelerating change has now been institutionalised as the normal situation. Nevertheless, most social and cultural theorists have regarded this notion as erroneous and oversimplified, although they have been ready to admit that identities have somehow become increasingly complex and flexible.

In the 1990s, particularly in the latter half of the decade, the discussion about modernity and postmodernity was gradually replaced by a new international theme: globalisation. However, this changeover to a new theme was not sharp. In part, the discussion about globalisation has been a continuation of the discussion about modernity and postmodernity. This can be seen, for instance, in the fact that some theorists and researchers have understood postmodern society as a global world society. Likewise, the questions of identity are still important and, quite obviously, more central than several decades ago. Yet these questions have now been posed in a slightly different way than earlier. In the 1980s, identity theorists did not always differentiate between personal and cultural identity. At that time it was, above all, the post-structuralists and their proponents who often theorised, in the first place, about personal and sexual identity, thereby neglecting questions of cultural identity. In a situation like this the concept of cultural identity and its subconcepts (ethnic, national, local identity) were sometimes eclipsed by post-structuralist theorising, although, on the other hand, they were taken up in certain disciplines, for example, in history, sociology and social anthropology. Nowadays, different academic disciplines often focus on questions of cultural identity or, at least, they pay attention to both cultural and personal identity. The basic questions which interest these disciplines can be formulated in the following ways: how does the ongoing process of globalisation affect people's personal and cultural identities? What happens to identities in a globalising world?

Cultural Identity in Transition attempts to deal with these questions. In a variety of ways the book considers different responses. First and foremost, the book concentrates on questions of cultural identity, as its title suggests. Even so, it will not entirely pass over questions of personal identity, even if the volume as a whole has not chosen them as its point of departure. On the whole, it is impossible to keep questions of personal and cultural identity sharply separated. This impossibility seems to be based on two states of affair. From the standpoint of theory, one may state that in reality the difference between personal and cultural identity is vague and therefore we should perhaps regard that difference as mainly conceptual or analytical. From the standpoint of social development, one can add that nowadays we also live in a world characterised by the process of broadening and deepening individualisation — and not only by the process of globalisation. For example, the German sociologist Ulrich Beck (1986; 1995) has pointed out that in our times people are, in Jean-Paul Sartre's words, increasingly "condemned to individualization" (see also Beck and Beck-Gernsheim 1996). That is, when social structures, norms and fixed points tend to change especially rapidly and when collective values and habits no longer regulate people's lives in detail, they are simultaneously both free and obliged to construct their lives for themselves, each in his or her own individual way. Because the current process of globalisation is an important cause of this rapid change and flexibility, in dealing with the theme of globalisation it is relevant to pay attention to both cultural and personal identity.

Personal and Cultural Identity

After the Second World War, the terms "identity", "personal identity" and "cultural identity" gradually emerged in the humanities and social sciences. As this book demonstrates, however, comparable terms had already been in use previously. In the 1950s and 1960s it was, above all, the American psychologist Erik H. Erikson who elaborated the concept of identity and popularized it in his books and articles (Brubaker and Cooper 2000: 2-4). In the Eriksonian tradition (see e.g. Erikson 1959) the theme of identity has been considered primarily from the standpoint of the individual. Thus, in this tradition, a person's identity is that a person's view of the continuity and sameness of his or her own personality. Individuals' sense of their own identity becomes stronger over the years, and in this sense of identity they have a clear awareness of their own aspirations and characteristics (see also Ricoeur 1991).

In the 1960s and 1970s the term "identity" became general in other disciplines within the humanities and social sciences. At the same time these disciplines began to distinguish between personal and cultural or social identity. Although the concepts of personal and cultural identity are nowadays in common use in the humanities and social sciences, they are, as such, rather problematic concepts which are used and defined in different ways. For example, the distinction personal/cultural has often been associated with the distinction individual/social or with the distinction individual/society. On this basis, the personal identity of a human being has been understood to consist of the properties that distinguish him or her from other people and which make him or her a unique person. The cultural or social identity of individuals would then consist of the properties which they share with different groups and collectives (see also Helkama, Myllyniemi & Liebkind 1999: 362-366). It has also sometimes been thought that it is chiefly cultural identity which is a social phenomenon, whereas the personal identity of a human being would take shape during the childhood, before he or she is socialised into society.

In recent theoretical literature this kind of notion is understood as too simple. It is easy to realise that the notion is based on a Western worldview and its tendency to emphasise the antithesis of the individual and society. In certain other cultures the relation between the individual and society is seen differently, and these cultures do not necessarily make a clear-cut difference between personal and cultural identity. In traditional Asian cultures, of which Japan has been a good example, individuals' personal identity is closely dependent on the relationships and ties that they have with different groups and collectives (Friedman 1993: 360-361). In non-individualistic cultures of this kind, people define their "true selves" in relation to the social combinations and associations that are important for them, which means that they do not see their personal selves as isolated from group memberships. These people regard themselves, first of all, as members of their family, professional group and workplace community.

According to these remarks, the proper concept of identity should include people's own subjective interpretations of themselves. When defining the concepts of personal and cultural identity, we have to take into account people's own self-images or self-definitions. As Charles Taylor (1996: 33-34) puts it, the way in which a person sees and defines himself or herself is a constitutive part of his or her identity. The pioneers of social psychology, especially George H. Mead (1962), the founder of "symbolic interactionism", as well as Peter L. Berger and Thomas Luckmann (e.g. Berger and Luckmann 1972) have shown that the self-image of a person develops in the course of social interaction. The ways in which other people — in particular, parents, friends, teachers, marriage partner, colleagues — and social settings see and treat this person have a crucial influence on his or her self-image. Personal identity is, then, a social and cultural phenomenon; it is a product of certain historical, social and cultural factors.

The identity of a person cannot, however, be identical with the self-image or self-definition of this person. It is, in principle and in practice, fully possible that a person has a misconceived self-image. A good example of this possibility is the so-called Napoleon complex. The concept of the Napoleon complex refers to a situation in which an ordinary person seriously overestimates his or her capabilities — and even regards himself or herself as a magnificent hero or heroine. Thus, the self-definitions of a person must also gain support from other people, and these definitions cannot be sharply incompatible with facts and views that are generally held to be valid. The identity of a person is, in this sense, also dependent on other people. Hence, when one uses the concepts of personal and cultural identity, all of these three things — (i) the self-image of a person, (ii) other persons and (iii) facts and opinions — must be taken into account.[2]

Similarly, the cultural self-image of a group might, in some important respects, be erroneous. Ethnic and national identities usually contain fictional and mythical elements, that is, idealised stories about the distant past, and about ancestors stemming from of an ethnic group or a nation (Nairn 1977). Stories like these can be useful for a group or nation, since they increase its self-respect and sense of continuity. But, they are not entirely based on historical facts. Normally, the fictional and mythical elements are by no means dangerous, but in some cases they can be seen to have changed into destructive practices. One example mentioned by many researchers is the Fascist nationalism in Germany in the 1930s and 1940s, where the Fascists created a mystical ideology out of Germanic characteristics, on the basis of which they executed a policy of brutal ethnic cleansing, as it would be termed nowadays.

Despite these observations, the concepts of personal and cultural identity remain rather vague. Because personal and cultural identities are sociocultural phenomena, the difference between them is difficult to define. Hence, many researchers have considered this difference to be mainly analytical; that is, one could not locate it through reality but only through theoretical vocabularies. In this sense those concepts would mainly be tools by which researchers can speak about identity in a differentiated way and focus on certain of its aspects. Nevertheless, it is also possible and more fruitful to consider that a person's identity has different dimensions that are real. On the one hand, identity can be said to have a personal or individual dimension. This dimension consists of how a person differs from other people and how he or she understands his or her individuality. On the other hand, identity also contains a collective dimension. People need security, acceptance and shelter; and partly for this reason they identify with different groups and communities. In the process, these identifications come to form a central part of their cultural identity. We can initially term the first dimension "a personal identity" and the second dimension "a cultural identity".

In general, the writers of this book think that the concept of cultural identity points to a phenomenon that always takes shape within a social and cultural context; and they also tend to think that cultural identities form an integral part of socio-cultural reality. It is useful to divide the cultural identity of a person or a group into different levels or dimensions. Firstly, the cultural identity contains a geocultural dimension (Quijano 2000: 216). In this sense we can, for example, speak about a local, regional, state-wide and continental (European, American, African) identity, and some people may even identify themselves with the whole globe.

In addition, Rien T. Segers und Reinhold Viehoff (1999: 34-35) talk about the following dimensions in people's cultural identity:

(a) A national, ethnic, religious and linguistic dimension.

(b) A dimension that is characterised by people's sexual behavior and self-definition and their roles in social life.

(c) A generation-specific dimension. Members of a single generation have same sort of basic experiences of the world.

(d) People's social positions. This dimension includes people's family and kinship ties and their places in wider social hierachies.

(e) An organisational-corporative dimension. This dimension is determined by people's place in working life and by the co-operation network of their workplace.

Undoubtedly, all these dimensions affect people's identity and their way of life. Nevertheless, one might still ask whether it would be useful, in this connection, to draw a distinction between people's cultural and social identities. Segers and Viehoff do not make use of this sort of distinction, but certain theorists, including Johan Fornäs (1995), have done so. If we commit ourselves to this distinction, then we can perhaps say that the geocultural dimension and dimension (a) clearly belong to the domain of the concept of cultural identity, whereas dimensions (d) and (e) are a parts of a person's social identity. In contrast, dimensions (b) and (c) seem to lie between the cultural and social identities (see also Jacobsson-Widding 1983).

The distinction between the cultural and the social is flexible — and even more vague than the distinction between the personal and cultural identity. Perhaps that is why the former distinction is not widely in explicit use in the articles printed here. Even so, this distinction should not be forgotten, for it is well-known that people who have different social positions and roles may still have adopted a similar cultural (geocultural, national, ethnic, religious, linguistic) identity. Without the distinction between the concepts of cultural and social identity it would be difficult to describe situations of this kind.

Alternative and Complementary Concepts

As the previous section has suggested, the concept of identity has its vague points. On one hand, the relationship between the personal and cultural identity can be understood in different ways, and on the other, it has been suggested that it is fruitful to distinguish between cultural and social identity. Moreover, and in contrast to this, certain theorists have proposed that the concept of identity and its sub-concepts are unnecessary tools in social and cultural analysis. This small group of theorists includes the American scholars Rogers Brubaker and Frederick Cooper. In 2000 they published a joint article entitled "Beyond 'Identity'" in the journal *Theory and Society*, where they present a number of highly critical reservations concerning the concept of identity and its sub-concepts. Brubaker and Cooper speak about a strong and a weak concept of identity. The strong version connects the idea of sameness to the concept of cultural or collective identity:

> Understood as a specifically *collective* phenomenon, identity denotes to a fundamental and consequential *sameness* among members of a group or category. This may be understood objectively (as a sameness in itself) or subjectively (as experienced, felt, or perceived sameness). This sameness is expected to manifest itself

> in solidarity, in shared dispositions or consciousness, or in collective action (Brubaker and Cooper 2000: 7; original italics).

The strong version presumes that there exists a considerable number of objective similarities between persons who share the same cultural identity. Alternatively, it can be said that on the subjective level these persons identify wholeheartedly with their group or community. It is possible that in practice different manifestations of the strong version are based on these two presuppositions. The strong version is foundationalist or even essentialist in the sense that it presumes that people have a solid and permanent core-identity, both in the personal and cultural domain:

> Understood as a core aspect of (individual or collective) selfhood or as a fundamental condition of social being, identity is invoked to point to something allegedly *deep, basic, abiding, or foundational.* This is distinguished from more superficial, accidental, fleeting, or contingent aspects or attributes of the self, and is understood as something to be valued, cultivated, supported, recognized and preserved (Brubaker and Cooper 2000: 7; original italics).

One can easily connect these thoughts with the idea of sameness, at least in the case of personal identity. After making this connection, the strong version suggests, people have a relatively solid and unchanged personal core-identity through their lives. This means that their personal core-identity may remain the same objectively or they have a clear feeling of the continuity and sameness of their personality or personal self.

The strong version is close to the traditional theories of identity and, in fact, Brubaker and Cooper regard Erikson as one of its founders. The weak concept of identity, in turn, mainly originates from post-structuralist thinking, and it is based on the idea that there is no such thing as a solid and unchanged core-identity. On the contrary, the post-structuralists have understood identities as unstable, multiple, fluctuating and fragmented, which means that they have excluded the idea of permanence and sameness from the concept of identity (e.g. Lacan 1966; Kristeva 1980a; 1980b). As mentioned earlier, the post-structuralistic way of conceiving identities has frequently affected those who have theorised about postmodern identities. Furthermore, comparable trains of thought have been presented in "situationist" or "contextualist" accounts of ethnicity, but, for the most part, these less-known accounts have been fairly independent of post-structuralistic influences (Brubaker and Cooper 2000: 8).

When estimating the versions under consideration, Brubaker and Cooper select as their point of departure an analysis of the term "identity". According to them, basically this term means sameness: in a time-dimension it refers to permanence and continuity; and in the context of interpersonal relations it implies group-boundedness and homogeneity. On the basis of their analysis, Brubaker and Cooper conclude that the strong concept of personal identity is too rigid. This concept presumes too much, for it is unrealistic to think that people would remain the same throughout their lives — regardless of how they subjectively experience themselves. The strong concept of cultural identity is also too rigid, since it postulates an incredibly high degree of homogeneity and sameness between the members of a group. The weak concept of identity, in turn, does not deal at all with identity, since it has abandoned the basic meanings of the term identity. Strictly speaking, it is a theory about something other than identity.

Hence, Brubaker and Cooper arrive at the conclusion that the concepts of personal and cultural identity cannot be used as analytical tools in scholarly work:

> Social analysis — including the analysis of identity politics — requires relatively unambiguous analytical categories. Whatever its suggestiveness, whatever indispensability in certain practical contexts, identity is too ambiguous, too torn between hard and soft meanings, essentialist connotations and constructivist qualifiers, to serve well the demands of social analysis (Brubaker and Cooper 2000: 2).

This does not mean that the humanities and social sciences should pass over the phenomenon of identity-talk. On the contrary, a talk about identities is a genuine ingredient in the sociocultural reality. It is, for example, practised by ethnic and national movements as well as by politicians and by representatives of academic disciplines. According to Brubaker and Cooper, the humanities and social sciences should not, however, participate in it. Because a culturally and socially important discussion of this kind cannot have a sufficient preciseness and analytical content, the best thing that those disciplines can do is to analyse it critically from outside.

Brubaker and Cooper (2000: 14-21) propose that the concepts of personal and cultural identity must be replaced by more flexible concepts such as "self-understanding", "social location", "identification" and "connectedness". According to their argumentation, self-understanding is a better concept than personal identity, since it does not presume that people's self-images remain the same throughout their lives. Likewise, in describing the relationships between the individual and his or her groups, Brubaker and Cooper recommend concepts such as "identification", "social location" and "connectedness" instead of cultural or social identity. The former concepts do not imply that there exists a strong homogeneity between the members of the group with which the individual has identified, nor does it claim that the individual identifies with these kinds of groups holistically. People are members in many kinds of groups; they are connected to different groups, with which they have identified themselves to a varying extent. By means of those new concepts, it would be possible to describe differences of degree in people's identifications with groups.

In many items, Brubaker's and Cooper's criticism of the concept of identity seems to be just and appropriate, despite its stringency. As they point out, in the current theoretical and empirical research literature within the humanities and social sciences this concept is often used in an unspecific and obscure way. I would not, however, like to replace the concepts of personal and cultural identity with the new concepts proposed by Brubaker and Cooper. In cultural and social analysis, those new concepts can quite well complete the concept of identity, but they are unable to displace it. There are at least two reasons for this state of affairs.

Even if the new concepts are able to make social and cultural analysis more precise and subtle, the concept of identity has a settled position in the humanities and social sciences. Often it is economical and practical to use this old and somewhat vague concept instead of a more finely-textured conceptual vocabulary that demands additional definitions and extra space. On a theoretical level one can say that Brubaker's and Cooper's thinking is based on rather sharp dichotomies. According to them, the concept of identity includes the idea of sameness, but otherwise it is not at all a question of identity. As an alternative to dichotomies like these, it is fruitful to develop an identity concept in which identities are understood as multi-layered wholes. The core-level or core-layer in identity begins to take shape in early childhood. On the one hand, it contains an individual's basic view of himself or herself, and on the other hand, it includes this individual's view of his or her relationship to other people, in particular, to those people who are called his or her family and relatives. After taking shape, the core-layer usually remains relatively stable, although as an adult person the individual regularly returns mentally to his or her own childhood and interprets it. The layers outside this core consist of the ways in which the individual sees himself or herself, for example, as a school pupil, student and worker or as a possessor of other social roles. The outer layers can change without crucially affecting the core-identity and the basic self-understanding of the individual. In this way the complexity and multi-stratification of the self-understanding of the individual make it possible that in principle the identity of the individual can simultaneously be both stable and variable. This view is congruent with the way Paul Ricoeur (1992) has understood the phenomenon of identity. A rather similar concept of identity has also been presented by Klaus Helkama, Rauni Myllyniemi and Karmela Liebkind (1999: 362-364).

Other Basic Concepts

This, then, is the way in which this book employs the concept of identity and its sub-concepts. Together with the concept of globalisation and its kindred concepts, identity belongs to the central vocabulary of this volume. As for the idea of globalisation, most researchers share the view that globalisation is a real and powerful tendency in culture and society. According to Jens Bertelson, even the constructionists are ready to accept the view that the word "globalisation" points to something real. For this reason Bertelson (2000: 180-181; original italics) writes:

> To my mind, the wide acceptance of globalisation as a fact, is *itself a social fact* worth investigating, especially since it might be argued that this fact is partly constitutive of what globalisation is about: nothing changes the world like the collective belief that it is changing, albeit rarely in directions desired by the believers.

In this respect it might even be dangerous to regard globalisation as a fact. Bertelson does not, however, deny the reality of globalisation. Rather, he wants to emphasise that if globalisation is understood as a natural and inescapable process, then people are willing neither to criticise it nor to act against it. In particular, such people, institutions and corporations that do gain economic profit from globalisation are eager to proclaim it inevitable. Thus, Bertelson has drawn our attention to an important factor. Although globalisation has been a real and ongoing process, it is, at least in part, open as to the ways in which it will come about and continue in the future. In consequence, people have, to some extent, the possibility of influencing and shaping it.

Ulrich Beck has also reminded us of similar problems concerning the discussion of globalisation. For instance, he draws a distinction between globalism and globalisation (see Beck 1997). In his vocabulary "globalism" points to the current new liberalist ideology which declares globalisation a natural and inevitable process. By "globalisation" he means the liberation of capitals, trading and entrepreneurship from taxation, social duties and governmental regulation. It is certainly true that this new liberalist ideology produces globalisation, particularly in the domain of the economy, but the process of globalisation includes other dimensions as well. Moreover, Beck writes that the new liberalist economic policy does not necessarily need to dominate this process — as it happens to do at present — since the process could also be based on values that differ from those of new liberalism. Beck himself hopes that the process of globalisation will continue on a much more democratic basis and in this way level down economic and social inequality in the world.

Globalisation can be defined in different ways. Some researchers see it above all as an economic process. To this group belongs Paul Bairoch (2000: 197): "Globalisation refers to a situation where industrial and commercial companies as well as financial institutions increasingly operate transnationally, in other words, beyond national borders". Other researchers place it in a broader social and cultural context. Göran Therborn (2000: 154) represents this latter group: "It is fruitful to define globalisation as referring to tendencies to a world-wide reach, impact, or connectedness of social phenomena or to a world-encompassing awareness among social actors". What these two definitions have in common is the thought that in the process of globalisation certain phenomena exceed local and national borders and start to influence and operate on a wider geographical scale — in the last resort, on a transcontinental scale. Thus, we can speak about globalisation in the domains of economics, politics, social cooperation, ecological action and cooperation, military action and cooperation, science, communication, cultural production and distribution, sports, tourism and people's mentality and consciousness.

In fact, the study of globalisation did not start recently, even if the word "globalisation" seems to be a new invention — or, at least, this word became popular in the 1990s. In his economic studies Karl Marx was already aware of the fact that the capitalist economic system has a tendency towards continuous growth, besides which he predicted that as a result of this tendency capitalist enterprises would cross local and national boundaries and gradually come to operate world-wide. Lenin later developed these trains of thought in his *Imperialism as the Highest Stage of Capitalism* (1916), and somewhat earlier John W. Hobson published his famous investigation *Imperialism* (1902), which criticises the imperialism of the European states from the standpoint of classical liberal values. Lenin and Hobson defined imperialism as an economic phenomenon; but after the Second World War certain theorists, including Raymond Aron and Hans J. Morgenthau, understood it primarily as a phenomenon of international power politics. In the 1960s and 1970s imperialism and colonialism — which is a special form of imperialism — were often studied on a Marxist or leftist basis, for example, in the works of Harry Magdorff, Ernest Mandel and Paul Sweezy. At the same time, theorists of the world system, in particular Fernand Braudel and Immanuel Wallerstein, developed conceptual and methodic tools for the study of international or transnational formations. In addition to these branches of research, political scientists systematically paid attention to political relationships between states.

Because the above-mentioned branches of research were often critical of modern international economic and political formations, one might ask what has happened to these critical aspects. Is the concept of globalisation devoid of any critical meanings? As a preliminary answer to this question we may say that unfortunately this concept is quite often used in a manner that pays no attention to economic oppression and power politics. In this kind of use, the current process of globalisation is described as some kind of inevitable natural phenomenon or force, independent of human control. Yet, as the Finnish political scientist Raimo Väyrynen (2001: 20-21) writes, the economic and social benefits of the current process of globalisation are not distributed evenly, since, so far, at least two thousand million people have been left outside it. Mostly these people live in the "Third World", but in Western countries there are also groups of poor people who have no possibility of gaining any benefit from the process of globalisation. In this respect the sharp criticism that the Attac-movement has levelled against the concept and process of globalisation may be just.[3]

Globalisation is not new. Fernand Braudel (1985a; 1985b) places its first steps in the late fourteenth century, when a new and wide trading area emerged in the Mediterranean region. Immanuel Wallerstein (2000: 250), in turn, regards its starting point as the late fifteenth century, when Europeans became increasingly aware of other continents and began to exploit them. On the other hand, according to Therborn (2000: 158-164), in the history of humankind there have been six globalisations:

(1) *The diffusion of world religions and the establishment of transcontinental civilizations.* Roughly speaking, this phase took place between the 4th and 7th centuries. During this time, Christianity became dominant in Europe through its establishment and officialisation in the Roman Empire; Hinduism spread to Southeast Asia from the southern parts of the Indo-Chinese peninsula; Buddhism went from India to China and spread from there to Korea and Japan; and by the beginning of the eighth century Islam ruled Spain, the Arab world and certain regions in Africa and Asia.

(2) *At the turn of the sixteenth century, European states started their colonial conquests and expansion.* Portugal, Spain, Holland, France and England led this expansion and also competed with each other.

(3) *In the eighteenth century and at the beginning of the nineteenth century there was a series of power struggles between certain European states, especially between France and England.* These battles were fought both in Europe and in the colonies of the European states.

(4) *The heyday of European imperialism. This wave lasted from the mid-nineteenth century to 1918.* The aftermath of the First World War established the first global organisations of states, the League of Nations, the International Labour Organization, and a set of ambitious but completely ineffective global norms.

(5) *Cold War globalization after the Second World War.* In this phase the world was divided into two political-economic blocks; the USA ruled the liberal or capitalist block, and the Soviet Union ruled the socialist block. Nearly all of the continents were involved in this division. This phase ended in the 1980s.

(6) *The current wave of globalization.* This wave started in the late 1980s. So far, this phase has been, in the first place, financial and economic, since among its key words has arisen the term new liberalism. Since the collapse of the socialist bloc, the idea of governmental regulation has increasingly been seen as old-fashioned. The characteristics of this new wave are also the

prevalence of the English language, new modes of communication, tourism, mass migration and refugees.

Obviously, this list has been constructed from the standpoint of the Western world, partly for the reason that Western countries have dominated the world system since the late fifteenth century. Therefore the list provides only a narrow picture of the globalising processes within the non-Western world. According to Therborn, globalisation has not been an evenly progressing process in the history of humankind. On the contrary, there have also been phases of deglobalisation. For example, the period from the twelfth century to the sixteenth century can be understood in this way, in Europe as well as in Asia, since it was especially during these centuries that national written languages and early nation-states started to develop on both of these continents. Similarly, the short period between the two world wars in the twentieth century was a time of national particularism. Therborn (2000: 165) does not, however, talk about cyclical repetition of the phases of globalisation and deglobalisation, for in part these waves have been simultaneous processes. The waves of globalisation have also been multidimensional processes involving political-military, economic and cultural forces.

Therborn sees the ongoing wave of globalisation primarily as an economic and financial process. Compared with this, Arjun Appadurai, in his *Modernity at Large. Cultural Dimensions of Globalisation* (1996), defines globalisation in terms of five flows: (i) the flow of people (immigrants, refugees, asylum-seekers, tourists), (ii) the flow of machinery and corporations, (iii) the flow of money and currencies, (iv) the flow of images and information and (v) the flow of ideologies and ideological images. All of these flows are certainly culturally relevant, but flows (i), (iv) and (v) seem to have the most to do with culture. In his book Appadurai also deals with the question of whether it is accurate to equate the current phase of globalisation with the Westernisation or Americanisation of the world. For him, the Westernisation or Americanisation of the world is an important aspect in the current phase of the globalisation process. In particular, this aspect is visible in the production and distribution of information, life-styles and cultural products. However, he does not share the pessimistic view that the whole world is developing into "a macdonaldized world village" or "a global Disneyland" (see also Beck 1997). In general, the question as to what extent the ongoing process of globalisation produces Westernisation and Americanisation of the world is an important and disputable theme in current research literature on globalisation. It is also a question which the articles in this volume do not answer in a single, uniform way.

Culturally speaking, what else could be characteristic of the ongoing wave of globalisation? Certain theorists have thought that, in the present phase, geocultural dimensions or factors are, in a rather unusual way, closely connected with each other. For instance, Ronald Robertson (1992; 1995) has emphasised that in the current situation a close interaction between the global and the local (regional, state-wide) produces something that might be called "the glocal". Glocal factors would be combinations of former global and local factors. As far as globalisation, in cooperation with certain other processes, has produced glocalisation, people's old local identities and consciousness have been replaced, or they will be replaced, by new or glocal identities and consciousness. The concept of glocal identity refers to a state of mind in which a person's consciousness of the rest of the world genuinely shapes his or her old local identity and gives to it new qualitative ingredients. And conversely, in this state of mind local people increasingly understand themselves as citizens or members of the whole globe (see also Wang 2000: 109, 111).

The concept of glocalisation has been elaborated not only by theorists but also by certain important institutions and organisations. For example, the European Union has represented glocalisation as a suitable developmental strategy for regions and local units belonging to the Union. According to the Union, these regions and local units can no longer be closed areas, but they must open themselves to the rest of the world and let this world shape them. In the same vein industrial, financial and commercial enterprises have regarded glocalisation as a successful strategy in a globalising economic life. Although these collective actors have to operate increasingly in the world market, they must simultaneously and everywhere adapt their activity to local circumstances, that is, they should operate glocally.

It has been said that today this sort of interaction is typical of cultures and cultural identities in general. Stuart Hall (1992) remarks that in recent decades, chiefly from the 1960s on, the population of Western Europe has changed radically. Huge numbers of people have moved from North Africa to France, Belgium and Italy; Germany has large Turkish and North African minorities; Holland has received people, in particular, from East and West India and from Surinam; and Great Britain has considerable Caribbean, Indian, Pakistani and African minorities.

These changes in population are, to a certain extent, repercussions of the European colonial systems, because in part the immigrants have come from the former colonies of European states. In addition, in the Nordic states, which had no colonies of their own, there are also communities of immigrants and refugees. Thus, West European states are increasingly multi-cultural, just as the United States and many South American countries have already been for a long time. Therefore, Hall concludes, many people nowadays have a dual or hybrid identity that contains elements and ingredients from different cultures. Salman Rushdie has often been seen as a particular example of this phenomenon, because as a child this Indian-born author had an Islamic upbringing and he was taught to speak both a local Indian language and English. Later he moved to Great Britain, gave up his Islamic faith and received a university education at Cambridge. His identity is, then, truly rooted in two cultures, and he himself accepts this situation wholeheartedly.

The concept of creolisation, introduced by the Swedish social anthropologist Ulf Hannerz in the late 1980s, is to some extent similar in meaning to the concept of hybridisation. According to Hannerz (1987; 1992), under certain conditions a close and continuous interaction between different cultures may produce a situation in which these cultures shape each other strongly and create new sorts of cultural combinations — like the creole languages in South America, for example, and Creole French in Haiti and the so-called Negro Spanish in the Dominican Republic, which started as mixtures of European and local languages. For these sorts of phenomena Hannerz has created the concept of creolisation. Originally, he applied this concept mainly to small and peripheral cultures outside the Western world. He wanted to understand what would happen to such cultures in a globalising world, and in answer to this he elaborated his understanding of the concept. Hence, this concept has not been meant as a universal analytical tool (see Hannerz 1996). Secondly, it is useful to note that those cultures participating in the process of creolisation were not necessarily pure or closed before this process. Usually, cultures such as these had already adopted elements from other cultures and, to a certain extent, they were also, as such, products of different sources.

In certain respects the concept of Europeanisation bears a resemblance to the concepts of glocalisation and hybridisation. The latter concepts imply that people's commitment to one geocultural unit and to one national unit is in the process of weakening. A single commitment like this will increasingly be replaced by multiple commitments to cultural units. Richard Münch (1999: 233-239) predicts that the process of Europeanisation, of which the development of the European Union is the most clear-cut instance, will produce similar effects within Europe. On the one hand, this process will reduce the relative importance of national identification; on the other, it will — in part due to the politics of the Union — increase the relative importance of local, regional and European identity (see also Reese-Schäfer 1999: 259-260). This change in cultural identity concerns not simply Western Europe, for many former socialist countries in Central and Eastern Europe are on their way into the European Union. As such, part of Germany, the former East Germany is, in fact, already a member of the Union. If the intended plans are realised, Estonia, Hungary, Poland, Slovenia, the Czech Republic, Bulgaria, Latvia, Lithuania, Rumania and Slovakia — together with Cyprus, Malta and Turkey — will also become members in the near future.

This volume has a somewhat ambivalent relationship to the fashionable concepts of globalisation, glocalisation, hybridisation, creolisation and Europeanisation. Not all of the writers published here accept these terms without question. Some writers describe the current situation by means of these concepts, while others have a critical attitude to the thinking that underlies them — or rather, they utilise concepts of a different kind. It is mainly the concepts of glocalisation and hybridisation that can be called into question here. As Manuel Vasquez and Mario F. Marquardt (2000: 124) point out, the interaction between the local and the global is not a new phenomenon; it has also occurred previously, although today it is more intensive and visible than before. Therborn's list of the waves of globalisation shows that before the current wave there has also been hybridisation between cultures. In earlier periods different cultures were not pure or closed, either. Hence, the concepts of glocalisation and hybridisation have their own dangers: they may produce and maintain erroneous images suggesting that different cultures have not affected each other until recently. Thus, if we decide to utilise them, we should make clear that we are not referring to something that is totally new in the history of humankind. On the other hand, we have good grounds for asking whether the concept of creolisation is too pessimistic. This concept seems to presume that in a globalising world small and peripheral cultures are too weak to resist the influence of Western culture. Yet we know that today we are also living in a phase of "ethnic revival", that is, a phase when a huge number of indigenous peoples and ethnic groups have founded cultural and political organisations in order to protect their own culture.

Practices and Politics of Cultural Identity

Practices and politics of cultural identities nowadays occur in a world that has been said to be increasingly globalising, localising, hybridising, creolising and, from a more local perspective within Europe, Europeanising. Actually, it is difficult to make a clear distinction between the practices and politics of cultural identities. Intuitively, it should be easy to grasp this difference, since the practices of cultural identities are something that people are making daily. These practices consist of the ways in which people understand and define themselves, and with what they identify themselves. Identity politics, in contrast, often seem to be maintained by social, ethnic and national groups and by organisations of states. When an indigenous or aboriginal people begins to demand its rights, when an ethnic group maintains its own cultural institutions (language, traditions, schools, newspapers); and when a national minority seeks autonomy or independence, they all practise identity politics. Similarly, when a state cherishes its national symbols and when it permits or forbids the cultural action of its ethnic minorities, it practises identity politics.

In this sense the difference between the practices and politics of cultural identities is, no doubt, clear. Nevertheless, one needs to keep in mind that the cultural identities of individuals also contain a political aspect. When an individual identifies with a collective, this identification is often, at least potentially, politically significant. As Thomas Hylland Eriksen (1993: 76-77) writes, "Identity processes are fundamentally dual and comprise aspects of meaning as well as politics in a wide sense.... People are willing to die for their nation (or ethnic community) but not usually for their social class or city". The collective mobilisation of people often requires a successful identity politics. Before people are ready to act together, a feeling of togetherness or a sense of common interests must, in many cases, have arisen between them (Huiskamp 2000: 399-400). That is why people's cultural identifications and their feelings of loyalty have always interested those in power.

As far as cultural identities are concerned, the concept of identity politics refers to different endeavours to arouse and maintain feelings of togetherness within a group or within a whole society, and conversely, this concept also points to situations in which different institutions and actors try to prevent endeavours and feelings of this kind. Thus, the concept of identity politics includes attempts to affect people's cultural identifications. As we noted earlier, in their cultural identifications people see and feel themselves as members of certain kinds of collectives or communities. Usually, there is a strong sense of mutual solidarity between the members of collectives or communities like these. In short, one can characterise identity politics as a particular branch of cultural politics.

It should be borne in mind that people's identities are not determined solely by their daily practices and by the identity politics of different groups and institutions. These determining factors belong to the conditions of identities, but people's identities are also shaped by economic, social and political structures, which are largely independent of individuals and which cannot be entirely controlled by means of consciously practised identity politics. In this sense, for instance, the globalisation of the economic activity and communication as well as new kinds of labour market and employment opportunities affect people's lives and their self-images. In the same vein the economic and political cooperation within the European Union creates new social structures that may influence people's cultural identities in the various European countries.

In the first place this volume deals with the processes of globalisation, glocalisation, hybridisation, creolisation and Europeanisation from the standpoints of culture and cultural politics. Other standpoints will, therefore, be secondary here. As far as globalisation is concerned, Therborn (2000: 151-153) has talked of about five major discourses involved in its make-up:

(a) a discourse of economic competition

(b) a discourse of social criticism

(c) a discourse that stands for the standpoint of the states

(d) a discourse of cultural flows and changes

(e) a discourse of planetary ecology

This is not, of course, an exhaustive catalogue of the possible and actual discourses concerning the process of globalisation. Yet, it gives us a useful overview of the different ways in which we can talk about this process, and it also serves well the needs of this collection of papers. Let us therefore briefly comment on the list and explicate it.

(a) Since the turn of the 1980s and the 1990s, the new liberalist discourse and its doctrine of free economic competition have spread throughout the world. After the collapse of the Soviet Union and the socialist bloc, the idea that states should regulate economic life has begun to look old-fashioned, mainly, however, in the eyes of world's economic and political leaders. In particular, large multinational and transnational companies and certain powerful international organisations such as the government of the United States, IMF (International Monetary Fund), WTO (World Trade Organisation), the World Bank and the European Union have promoted the principles of free trade and free competition. (b) In contrast to this, many popular and civil movements around the world have accused these companies and organisations of economic exploitation, social irresponsibility and ecological shortsightedness. In recent years, some of these movements have also challenged the current wave of globalisation through street demonstrations in Seattle, Gothenburg, Prague and Genoa. (c) On the other hand, representatives of traditional nation-states and political parties have worried about the diminishing ability of states to control economic action and digital flows of currency and information (Sassen 2000: 19). (d) After the terrorist attacks against the World Trade Center in New York and against the Pentagon in Washington on September 11th, 2001, it became evident that the ongoing wave of globalisation is not a mere economic-financial phenomenon. Everywhere in the world, but especially outside the Western hemisphere, there is a huge number of people who are afraid that this wave is threatening to change their way of life — that is, in the wide sense of the word, their culture. (e) Finally, a discourse of planetary ecology discusses humankind and global society as parts of the planetary ecosystem. The proponents of this discourse share an awareness of the globe as a whole in attempting to define the requirements for "reasonable and sustainable social development".

This book represents mainly discourses (c) and (d). Here discourse (c) must, however, be understood in a wide sense. It refers not only to the level of the states but to other political phenomena as well. Today, there is a strong connection between cultural and political discourses. Everywhere in the world indigenous and aboriginal peoples have begun to demand political guarantees for the survival of their culture. In Europe, in particular, the growing multiculturality of societies has produced racism and extreme right-wing political movements. The process of Europeanisation, in turn, has stimulated regionalism in the regions that are afraid of this process or that can gain no profit from it. Moreover, the current wave of globalisation seems to have come true mainly on conditions imposed by the United States and the Western hemisphere, which has provoked counter-movements such as anti-capitalist demonstrations and religious fundamentalism. These examples show that discourses (c) and (d) concern not only the process of globalisation but also the processes of glocalisation, hybridisation, creolisation and Europeanisation.

The authors of this volume represent different academic disciplines: literary studies, musicology, linguistics, folkloristics, ethnology, anthropology, religion studies, sociology, social policy and political history. What they have in common is an interest in culture and cultural politics. They come from Finland, Norway, Estonia, Russia, the Netherlands and Great Britain. The collection considers these topics from a Northern European standpoint in the sense that the writers will unavoidably bring their own cultural backgrounds into their articles and into their points of view on the theme of globalisation. Nevertheless, the book exceeds its own cultural backgrounds in the sense that the articles will also pay attention to cultural situations outside the west. Finally, it should be mentioned that the writers do not share one and the same view of the theme and process of globalisation. In consequence, each writer is personally responsible solely for his or her own article, and not for the views presented in the others.

NOTES

1. According to Kellner (1993: 142-143), certain philosophers, especially Friedrich Nietzsche, Martin Heidegger and Jean-Paul Sartre, have also emphasized that identity must be seen as an existential project which an individual has to reach or form in his or her life. This is obviously an accurate remark, but it is equally important to see that there is, in this respect, no historical dimension in Nietzsche's, Heideggers's or Sartre's thinking. For them, identity has always been a project. On the other hand, Nicholas Rose (1996: 306-309) has remarked that individualisation is not peculiar to the modern world. On the basis of historical research, Rose presumes that the same kind of process was also, for example, ongoing in Rome during the first and second centuries.

2. I am indebted to Professor Rien T. Segers for his presentation of this three-part classification in his lecture "On Cultural Identity" at the University of Joensuu in September 2000.
3. The letter combination Attac is an appreviation of the whole name "L'Association pour la taxation des transactions financières pour l'aidre aux cityons" (The Association for the Taxation of Financial Transfers with the Purpose of Helping the Citizens). This long name tells us that the Attac-movement wants to tax capital transfers in the interest of ordinary people.

REFERENCES

Appadurai, Arjun 1996: *Modernity at Large. Cultural Dimensions of Globalizations.* Minneapolis: University of Minneapolis Press.

Bairoch, Paul 2000: The Constituent Economic Principle of Globalization in Historical Perspective. Myth and Reality. *International Sociology.* 15:2. 197-214.

Beck, Ulrich 1986: *Risikogesellschaft. Auf dem Weg in eine andere Moderne.* Frankfurt am Main: Suhrkamp.

Beck, Ulrich 1995: *Eigenes Leben. Ausfluge in die unbekannte Gesellschaft, in der wir leben.* München. C.H. Beck.

Beck, Ulrich 1997: *Was ist Globalisierung? Irrtümer des Globalismus — Antworten auf Globalisierung.* Frankfurt am Main: Suhrkamp.

Beck, Ulrich and Elisabeth Beck-Gernsheim 1996: Individualization and 'Precarious Freedoms': Perspectives and Controversies of a Subject-Oriented Sociology. In Paul Helas, Scott Lash and Paul Morris ed.: *Detraditionalization. Critical Reflexions on Authority and Identity.* Cambridge, Massachusetts and Oxford UK: Blackwell.

Berger, Peter L. and Thomas Luckmann 1972 (1966): *The Social Construction of Reality. A Treatise on the Sociology of Knowledge.* Harmondsworth: Penguin.

Bertelson, Jens 2000: Three Concepts of Globalization. *International Sociology.* 15:2. 180-196.

Braudel, Fernand 1985a: *Civilization and Capitalism 15th — 18th Century. Volume One: The Structures of Everyday Life. The Limits of Possible.* Translated from the French by Sian Reynolds. London: Fontana Press.

Braudel, Fernand 1985b: *Civilization and Capitalism 15th — 18th Century. Volume Two: The Wheels of Commerce.* Translated from the French by Sian Reynolds. London: Fontana Press.

Brubaker, Rogers and Frederick Cooper 2000: Beyond 'Identity'. In *Theory and Society.* 29:1. 1-47.

Eriksen, Thomas Hylland 1993: *Ethnicity and Nationalism. Anthropological Perspectives.* London and Sterling, Virginia: Pluto Press.

Erikson, Erik H. 1959: *Identity and the Life-Circle: Selected Papers*. Psychological Issues Monograph Series. 1:1. New York.

Fornäs, Johan 1995: *Cultural Theory and Late Modernity*. London, Thousand Oaks and New Delhi: Sage.

Friedman, Jonathan 1993 (1992): Narcissism, Roots and Postmodernity. In Scott Lash and Jonathan Friedman ed.: *Modernity and Identity*. Oxford UK and Cambridge USA 1993: Blackwell.

Giddens, Anthony 2001 (1991): *Modernity and Self-Identity. Self and Society in the Late Modern Age*. Cambridge: Polity Press.

Hall, Stuart 1992: The Question of Cultural Identity. In Stuart Hall ed.: *Modernity and Its Futures*. Cambridge: Polity Press and Open University.

Hannerz, Ulf 1987: The World in Creolization. *Africa*. 57: 4. 546-549.

Hannerz, Ulf 1991: Scenarios for Peripheral Cultures. In Anthony D. King ed.: *Culture, Globalization and the World-System. Contemporary Conditions for the Representation of Identity*. New York: Macmillan.

Hannerz, Ulf 1996: *Transnational Connections. Culture, People, Places*. London: Routledge.

Helkama, Klaus, with Rauni Myllyniemi and Karmela Liebkind 1999: *Johdatus sosiaalipsykologiaan* [Introduction to Social Psychology]. Helsinki: Edita.

Huiskamp, Gerard 2000: Identity Politics and Democratic Transitions in Latin America. (Re)organizing Women's Strategic Interests Through Community Activism. In *Theory and Society*. 29:3. 385-424.

Jacobsson-Widding, Anita ed. 1983: *Identity: Personal and Socio-Cultural*. Uppsala: Almquist & Wiksell.

Kellner, Douglas 1993 (1992): Popular Culture and the Construction of Postmodern Identities. In Scott Lash and Jonathan Friedman ed.: *Modernity and Identity*. Oxford UK and Cambridge USA: Blackwell.

Kristeva, Julia 1980a (1997): *Desire in Language. A Semiotic Approach to Literature and Art*. Translated by Thomas Gora, Alice Jardine and Leon S. Roudiez. Oxford.

Kristeva, Julia 1980b: *Pouvoirs de l'horreur. Essai sur l'abjection*. Paris.

Lacan, Jacques 1966: *Ecrits*. Paris: Seuil.

Lash, Scott and Jonathan Friedman 1993 (1992): Subjectivity and Modernity's Other. In Scott Lash and Jonathan Friedman ed.: *Modernity and Identity*. Oxford UK and Cambridge USA: Blackwell.

Mead, George H.1962: *Mind, Self and Society. From the Standpoint of a Social Behaviorist*. Chicago, Illinois: University of Chicago Press.

Münch, Richard 1999: Europäische Identitätsbildung. Zwischen globaler Dynamik, nationaler und regionaler Gegenbewegung. In Reinhold Viehoff und Rien T. Segers Hrsg.: *Kultur. Identität. Europa. Über die Schwierigkeiten und Möglichkeiten einer Konstruktion*. Frankfurt am Main: Suhrkamp.

Nairn, Tom 1977: *The Break-Up of Britain. Crisis and Neo-Nationalism.* London: New Left Books.

Quijano, Anibal 2000: Coloniality of Power and Eurocentrism in Latin America. In *International Sociology.* 15:2. 215-232.

Reese-Schäfer, Walter 1999: Supranationale oder transnationale Identität. Zwei Modelle kultureller Integration in Europe. In Reinhold Viehoff und Rien T. Segers Hrsg.: *Kultur. Identität. Europa. Über die Schwierigkeiten und Möglichkeiten einer Konstruktion.* Frankfurt am Main: Suhrkamp.

Ricoeur, Paul 1991: Narrative Identity. In David Wood ed.: *On Paul Ricoeur. Narrative and Interpretation.* London: Routledge.

Ricoeur, Paul 1992: *Oneself as Another.* Translated by Kathleen Blamey. Chicago: University of Chicago Press.

Robertson, Ronald 1992 (1993): *Social Theory and Global Culture.* London, Newbury Park and New Delhi: Sage.

Robertson, Ronald 1995: Glocalization: Time-Space and Homogeneity-Heterogeneity. In Mike Featherstone, Scott Lash and Ronald Robertson ed.: *Global Modernities.* London: Sage.

Rose, Nikolas 1996: Authority and the Genealogy of the Subjectivity. In Paul Helas, Scott Lash and Paul Morris ed.: *Detraditionalization. Critical Reflections on Authority and Identity.* Cambridge, Massachusetts and Oxford UK.

Sassen, Saskia 2000: Digital Networks and the State. *Theory, Culture and Society.* 17:4. 19-33.

Segers Rien T. und Reinhold Viehoff 1999: Die Konstruktion Europas. Überlegungen zum Problem der Kultur in Europa. In Reinhold Viehoff und Rien T. Segers Hrsg.: *Kultur. Identität. Europa. Über die Schwierigkeiten und Möglichkeiten einer Konstruktion.* Frankfurt am Main: Suhrkamp.

Taylor, Charles 1996: *Sources of the Self. The Making of Modern Identity.* Cambridge: Cambridge University Press.

Therborn, Göran 2000: Globalizations. Dimensions, Historical Waves, Regional Effects, Normative Governance. *International Sociology.* 15:2. 151-179.

Wallerstein, Immanuel: Globalization or the Age of Transition? A Long-Term View of the Trajectory of the World-System. *International Sociology.* 15:2. 249-265.

Wang, Horn-luen 2000: Rethinking the Global and the National. Reflections on National Imaginations in Taiwan. *Theory, Culture and Society.* 17:4. 93-117.

Vasquez, Manuel and Mario F. Marquardt 2000: Globalizing the Rainbow Madonna. Old Time Religion in the Present Time. *Theory, Culture and Society.* 17:4.

Väyrynen, Raimo 2001: Markkinavoimin rakennettiin rauhaa. [The Peace Was Constructed With the Help of Market Forces]. *Tiede* [Science]. 8. 18-23.

PART ONE
Theoretical Perspectives

1

The Study of Cultural Identity: Development and Background of a Multi-Disciplinary Field of Research

ERKKI SEVÄNEN

Introduction

In their joint paper "Beyond 'Identity'" the American scholars Rogers Brubaker and Frederick Cooper (2000: 28-29) point out that in recent decades the concepts of identity and cultural identity have become popular in the humanities and social sciences. Although Brubaker, a sociologist, and Cooper, a historian, speak chiefly about the situation of the academic world in the United States, their remarks are obviously applicable to several other countries. To a great extent, what they say is true, at least, of the academic world in North America and West Europe. In consequence, Thomas Hylland Eriksen's generalisation seems to describe the research situation in Western universities accurately. This Norwegian social anthropologist writes that concepts such as "ethnic group", "ethnicity" and "ethnic conflict", all of which belong — together with "nationality" and "cultural identity" — to the same family of concepts, are today part of the common vocabulary used in the humanities and social sciences. Eriksen presumes that these concepts in particular have been used in sociology, social anthropology, political science and history, but obviously they have also been important in other disciplines within the humanities and social sciences. Different disciplines continuously produce studies and anthologies that analyse and elaborate these concepts and describe the contemporary cultural scene by using them.

This paper deals with the study of cultural identity and the position of the concept of cultural identity in the humanities and social sciences within the Western academic world. By the "Western world" I mean primarily Europe and North America. No doubt definitions like these are slightly problematic, for one may ask whether, for example, Russia belongs to the Western world. In answer to this question one may say that Russia is, in part, a member of Europe and the Western world, but large areas of it belong geographically and/or culturally to Asia. On the other hand, Australia can be said to belong to Western civilisation, although geographically it is situated close to Asia. Despite this kind of vagueness, the expression "Western world" is a useful tool in cultural theory and research. My paper cannot, of course, take into account the study of cultural identity in every Western country in detail, for this kind of task would be impossible to realise within a short article. Instead, the paper outlines certain central development trends in the study of cultural identity and in the position of the concept of cultural identity. In doing so I must often overlook the differences between single countries and concentrate on the trends that those countries have had in common.

This metatheoretical article is divided into four parts. After the introduction, it outlines the previous situation in the humanities and social sciences. In particular, it explicates the position which the study and the concept of cultural identity has previously had and the kinds of ideological and philosophical presuppositions which have underlain them. Secondly, the article considers the present situation and its ideological and philosophical presuppositions, and at the end I present certain generalisations concerning this development. The article shows that the study of cultural identity has been closely related to identity politics, and that this dimension is still included in it. A study like this has been, at least potentially, politically significant, because it has participated in the construction of cultural or collective identities.

Cultural identity is a wider phenomenon than ethnic and national identity, which are subspecies of it. The concept of ethnicity usually refers to a group or community whose members believe that they descend from the same tribe or from the same ancestors; in brief, they stem from a common origin (Eriksen 1993: 1-17; Smith 1991: 51). This type of belief is not necessarily based on facts, with the consequence that it is often difficult to prove it. For this reason, one could label it a myth. Nevertheless, it can provide members of an ethnic community with a firm collective identity, their own ethnic identity. National identity, in turn, can be based on ethnic bonds, but this is not always the case, since some nations include ethnic minorities. For example, there is in the United States a large number of ethnic communities, most of which have adapted to North American society, feeling themselves to be parts of the nation led by the central government in Washington. We can therefore say that a nation is the kind of community whose members find that they belong together, and this view often provides them not only with a feeling of togetherness but also with a sense of mutual solidarity. Feelings and senses like these can be based on common traditions, habits, values and rights of citizenship, besides which a common language and religion and ethnic bonds may function as a basis of national identity (Sevänen 2000: 17-18).

Roughly speaking, the concept of cultural identity gained its present position in the 1980s and the 1990s. Previously, certain aspects of national identity were also objects of research in disciplines such as literary studies, philology, folkloristics, ethnology and history, even if in these disciplines the term "national identity" probably did not emerge until after the Second World War. Before that time those disciplines preferred to use terms like "national character", "national characteristic", "national spirit", "national feeling", "national consciousness" and "national peculiarities", which, in many respects, had a meaning rather similar to the concept of national identity. In practice, the disciplines in question were already studying national identity before the Second World War. From the nineteenth century onward, they had focused on the phenomenon of national identity, paying attention also to the needs of national identity politics, with the result that they largely ignored other subspecies of cultural identity. At the same time, social and cultural anthropology concentrated on studying small cultures outside the Western world. In describing them, anthropologists used concepts such as culture, nation, race and tribe, whereas specific questions of identity hardly interested them at all. Generally speaking, they did not systematically take into account the self-definitions and self-understanding of the peoples they investigated. It was not until the 1960s that the concept of ethnicity and kindred concepts such as ethnic group and ethnic identity took firm root in social anthropology (Eriksen 1993: 4).

Before the 1980s, the humanities and social sciences had, in the first place, taken into account national and ethnic identity when dealing with the phenomena of cultural identity, although after the Second World War they also displayed a growing interest in the study of local and regional cultures and identities. This dominance may explain why the concept of cultural identity is still sometimes associated mainly with ethnic and national identity.

Because the above-mentioned disciplines, apart from social anthropology, often choose their objects of research from the domestic culture, they could, as a whole, be termed national studies. Particularly in Finland, the study of Finnish literature, language, folklore and history has traditionally been referred to in this way, but as such the idea of national study or national science has not been Finnish in origin.

Particularism, universalism and evolutionism in traditional humanities and social sciences

In Europe, the idea of national studies began to take shape in the sixteenth and seventeenth centuries, that is, in the early phase of the development of modern centralised states, when, especially in England, the processes of state-building, the Reformation and the dissolution of the medieval Roman Catholic Church created a need to consider history from a national standpoint (see Greenfield 1993, ch. 1). In this phase it was largely only the elite groups who had an active interest in the national standpoint, whereas the great majority of ordinary people or, as they were called, "the mob" usually had a strong local or regional identity and a weak or nonexistent national consciousness. The idea of national study did not become popular and important until the turn of the eighteenth and nineteenth centuries. At that time, traditional European states (England, France, Prussia,

Sweden) began to transform into nation-states, the ideal of nation-state became widely accepted in Europe and, finally, nationalism and national consciousness gradually developed into mass phenomena.

An attempt to realise the ideal of the nation-state was not sought solely with the aid of political arrangements, although they were important in this realisation. From the very beginning, emergent nation-states and the different forms of nationalism contained, simultaneously, both political and cultural dimensions. In the political sense, nation-states and nationalisms laid stress on the principle that political units should coincide with national units; state and nation should correspond to each other, as far as possible, and thereby in an ideal situation each nation would have its own political unit, usually a state or an autonomous region. Moreover, democratic forms of nationalism and national consciousness were based on the idea that political power must gain its legitimisation from the people; that is, the use of political power should be accepted by the common people. Both conservative and democratic forms of nationalism and national thinking shared the view that, on one hand, it was necessary to build ties of loyalty between the rulers and the common people; and, on the other hand, it was important to stimulate feelings of togetherness and solidarity among the common people. In short, nationalistic movements and proponents of national thinking wanted to transform the population of their state into a nation; they wanted, in effect, to provide this population with a new type of collective identifying that is nowadays usually termed national identity.

Shared political institutions and symbols as well as common traditions and ethnic bonds were important in the building of nation-states. Despite this, it was popular education, compulsory school attendance and the school system that were perhaps the most effective arrangements by means of which the cultural homogeneity of the population could be developed. Arrangements like these provided the people with a common language and with common national representations and patriotic sentiments (Schudson 1994: 27-32). From the late eighteenth century literature, painting, music and the other arts also proved to be important in this respect. Literature produced the stories and myths of the nations and their past, painting created visual representations of national events, heroes and landscapes, and music expressed people's collective experiences and sentiments (Smith 1995: 47-50, 62-67).

Timothy Brennan (1994: 52-53) has pointed out that, in general, national identities have to a greater or lesser extent been based on mythical stories and representations produced by the arts. One may add to this the observation that the creation of national myths by means of the arts was exceptionally important in the case of the nations that lacked their own state and political independence. Often these nations could not freely make use of the university system and develop their identity on the basis of research, with the consequence that, for them, the arts were invaluable tools of nationality politics. Until the beginning of the twentieth century, nations such as Estonia (a part of Russia), Finland (an autonomic part of Russia), Norway (a part of Sweden) and Poland (which Russia, Germany and the Austrian-Hungarian Empire had divided up between themselves), belonged to this group. These nations did not possess a glorious political past, but their artists provided them with fascinating mythical traditions with which they could identify. In the nineteenth century, the writers Elias Lönnrot (the author of the *Kalevala*, Finland) and Felix Kreutzwald (the author of *Kalevipoeg*, Estonia) as well as the compositors Edward Grieg (Norway) and Frédéric Chopin (Poland) were typical examples of these kinds of artists. On the whole, most of the non-independent nations in question existed in Central, East and Southeast Europe — in an area that was ruled by three bureaucratic multinational states, namely the Russian Empire, the Austrian-Hungarian Empire, and the Ottoman Empire (Turkey). In practice, these three Empires had divided up that area between themselves. By possessing their own cultural traditions, nations that lived in the area in question showed the rest of the world that they had the right to political sovereignty.

Especially in the traditional European states, but also in countries like Finland and Norway, the elaboration of national identities was also widely promoted by certain academic disciplines that were often based on the romantic philosophy of nationality, in particular, on the writings of the German philosophers. According to this philosophy, the spiritual characteristic or mentality of a nation finds its clearest expression in the culture of this nation: in its language, literature, traditions and habits. Experts in literary history, philology, folkloristics, ethnology and history now began to consider the world with the aid of this principle: on the one hand, they classified the social-cultural reality into national cultures, and, on the other hand, they regarded cultural artefacts as the expressions of these cultures (Brennan 1994: 52-53; Giesen 1991: 11-12). Art history and musicology, which were instituted in European universities somewhat later, often in the late nineteenth century, also adopted this principle, even if they arguably had a slighter relation to nation-building than the above-mentioned disciplines had (King 1993: 1-6).

Thus, the general concept of cultural identity was not important in the traditional humanities, whereas the study of national identity occupied a central position. This study had two important functions. Firstly, in the humanities terms such as "national spirit", "national characteristic" and "national peculiarities" were analytical concepts by means of which different disciplines described and interpreted cultural artefacts. Secondly, these terms also functioned as tools of identity politics, since the above-mentioned disciplines not only investigated national identity but also produced it. For example, in Germany a discipline called "Germanistik" had a political function of this kind from the early nineteenth century to the 1960s, since it studied German literature, language and cultural history as expressions of the German spirit, and in this way, it produced definitions and images of German nationality (Abels 1989: 270; Lämmert 1971: 10). Likewise, in Great Britain and Finland the study of domestic literature — British or Finnish, respectively — served, in part, the needs of nation-building. In both countries this kind of bond between literary studies and nationality politics lasted, roughly speaking, from the late nineteenth century to the 1960s (e.g. Eagleton 1984; Varpio 1990).

National identity politics have represented particularism or a conscious particular viewpoint on social-cultural reality, and it was, above all, in this sense that cultural particularism occupied a firm position in the traditional humanities. However, there were also clear-cut elements of universalism in these disciplines. Perhaps this universalism was at its strongest in the domains of art theory and philosophical aesthetics. In his massive and detailed investigation *Kritik der Urteilskraft* (Criticism of the Judgment, 1790) Immanuel Kant, one of the founders of modern philosophical aesthetics, defined the aesthetic experience as a universal sphere of the human mind (see Kant 1975). By this definition he meant that the aesthetic experience can be aroused in the human mind only under the condition that the human being gives up his or her personal and narrow interests and, in their place, adopts a more general perspective on the world. In other words, by possessing the aesthetic experience the human being rises, in Kant's theory, to the level of the human species and considers the world from the point of view of humanity itself. Because art has been one of the main sources of aesthetic experience, the proponents of Kantian aesthetics thought that works of art express themes and sentiments that have universal applicability. Thus, in Friedrich Schiller's *Über die ästhetische Erziehung des Menschen in einer Reihe von Briefen* (1975, On the Aesthetic Education of Man in a Series of Letters, [1793-94]) and in Matthew Arnold's *Culture and Anarchy* (1969, [1869]) literature and the other arts are seen as channels which guide people to universal truths and values — or to "humanity". From time to time, this view of art has also been included in the concrete study of art. In practice, the object of this concrete study was usually Western art, which means that the traditional humanities glorified Western art and, more generally, Western high culture.

The ideology that underlay traditional humanities was a mixture of particularism and universalism. At first glance these two elements seem incompatible, but in practice this was not necessarily always the case. At least the proponents of the idea of national studies were apt to see a dialectical relationship between the national and the universal. As Anthony D. Smith (1979: 2) states, they thought that humanity or the universal culture is, in a natural way, divided into national cultures and each national culture has something to give to the universal culture. Hence, provided that thinking of this kind is correct, a particular nation can best enrich humanity simply by cultivating its own culture. For example, in the nineteenth century "Finland's national philosopher" Johan Vilhelm Snellman defined the relationship between the national and the universal in precisely this way. He explained that a particular culture can have universal dimensions only on the condition that it is deeply rooted in national traditions, meanings and mentalities (e.g. Karkama 1989).

As in the humanities, universalism was a salient element in the old European and Western social philosophy and social sciences, but here it was more explicitly connected to evolutionism. The American-Swedish social anthropologist Jonathan Friedman (1996: 5, 50-51) writes that evolutionism emerged most forcefully in France and England during the eighteenth century and was developed throughout the nineteenth century as a dominant ideology of European or Western identity. In social philosophy John Locke, David Hume, some French Encyclopedists and Auguste Comte elaborated it; the pioneers of political economy, that is, Adam Smith, David Ricardo and Karl Marx, shared this doctrine, which was furthermore accepted in social anthropology, among others, in the studies of Edward Taylor, Edward Westermarck and Lewis Henry Morgan.

Classical evolutionism was an ideology that, according to Friedman (1996: 5), "ordered the different areas of the globe on a scale of progress leading to the industrial civilisation of Europe". In its early phase, evolutionism was materialistic insofar as it located the origin of the progressive development in economic and technological growth. Yet it was during the nineteenth century that the combination of evolutionism and materialism found its strongest manifestations, especially in Marx's theories, which reduced social progress to the developmental logic of productive forces. In an optimistic way, classical evolutionism saw, Europe and Western civilisation as the highest stage of world civilisation. Even so, this ideology had its opponents. As early as in the eighteenth century Jean-Jacques Rousseau, a spokesman for "primitivism", elaborated the concept of the "noble savage" which pointed to "original" and "uncorrupted" civilisations outside Europe. Thoughts of this kind were also formulated in the nineteenth century, but they could not dethrone evolutionism.

The later phases of evolutionism are quite well-known. During the twentieth century evolutionism lost a considerable part of its former status in the European social sciences. In the early twentieth century, evolutionism was, for example, criticised by the British social anthropologist Bronislaw Malinowski, whose thoughts dominated European anthropology from the 1920s to the 1960s. Malinowski's works represented a moderate cultural relativism, since he thought that each particular culture is a functional whole that should be understood in itself — and not with the help of universalising models (e.g. Söderholm 1994: 124-127, 129-132 and 134). In the United States it was Franz Boas, in particular, who abandoned the Western-centric picture of the world and brought elements of cultural relativism into American anthropology. Boas's influence in America was at its strongest in the 1910s and 1920s, and he also had successful successors — among others, Margaret Mead and Ruth Benedict, who were still active in the decades after the Second World War. However, regardless of this continuity, in the 1930s evolutionism returned to American anthropology in which it was a strong and, according to Friedman (1996: 53), the dominant way of thinking until the 1960s. At the same time evolutionism was also a salient feature of American sociology, especially of the "structural-functional school" launched by Talcott Parsons. In his theory of the process of sociocultural modernisation, Parsons regarded Western society as the most progressive civilisation in the world. For him, the leading force in Western civilisation of the twentieth century was, self-evidently, the United States (e.g. Parsons 1966; 1971; Alexander 1983). To a certain extent, French structuralism and Marxism can also be seen as a continuation of this type of thinking. In the 1960s and 1970s, these two schools gained wide popularity among the new academic generation both in North America and in Europe, and even if they criticised "conservatism in science", they did not, in fact, abandon the evolutionistic social philosophy and the Western-centric picture of the world (Larrain 1994: 7-8). In fact, the European or Western proletariat was for Marx and his proponents the most advanced force in the progressive development of humanity.

As far as universalism is concerned, the founders of modern social philosophy and sociology attempted to formulate generalisations that would hold true for every human society. They wanted to explicate the general nature and development logic of human societies, with the consequence that they often had only a slight interest in particular societies. Thus, the theoretical works of Auguste Comte, Karl Marx, Herbert Spencer and, to a certain extent, Émile Durkheim and Max Weber contain these kind of universalising elements. The language of classical sociology was universalising in the sense that even when the classical sociologists studied concrete phenomena and national societies, they could easily draw universalising conclusions and generalisations on the basis of their studies (Therborn 2000a: 149-150; Turner 1994: 343). However, according to Martin Albrow (1990: 6), the situation changed during the twentieth century when sociology achieved a more professional status and was institutionalised as a distinct academic discipline. In this phase it focused more on national phenomena and societies. Albrow's remarks are obviously fairly correct, because during the twentieth century departments of sociology in various countries produced a huge number of studies on national phenomena and problems. Nevertheless, one should not forget that the universalising mode of theorising about society did not end in the twentieth century (Robertson 1993: 16). In particular, it was continued by the Parsonsian structural-functional school, Marxism and French structuralism. This being the case, Claude Lévi-Strauss (1963: 630), the leading figure in French structuralism in the 1950s and 1960s, understood structuralistic ethnology "as a transformation of the Kantian investigation in the domain of ethnology". In his epistemology Kant was interested in the principles by which the human mind operates; similarly, structuralists wanted to discover how the human mind structures reality and its own experiences with the help of language and other cultural systems of signs.

Both in the humanities and in the social sciences the term "identity" emerged and became general in the decades after the Second World War. Although in the humanities certain aspects of national identity had been objects of research since the early nineteenth century, now researchers in these disciplines started to speak explicitly about national identities — in fact, at a time when this kind of study and the nationality politics based on it were losing their former unquestioned status. In the decades after the Second World War, sociologists were interested in people's class identity and political consciousness, and social anthropologists started to use the subconcept of ethnic identity, which some of them could equate with the concept of cultural identity. However, apart from these instances, the general concept of cultural identity did not otherwise belong to the central vocabulary of these disciplines.

The term identity was, above all, introduced and popularised by the American psychologist Erik H. Erikson (e.g., Erikson 1959), who defined it by pointing to the self-understanding of a person or an individual. In the Eriksonian tradition the identity of a person consists of how this person understands the continuity and sameness of his or her own personality. In this sense, the Eriksonian use of the concept of identity lays stress on the subjective self-definitions of a person. However, if this concept is used in a methodologically correct way, one should notice that the identity of a person cannot be sharply incompatible with facts and views that are generally held as valid; and neither can it be sharply incompatible with how other persons see the person in question. If these preconditions are not valid, other people can point out that the person in question has a distorted self-image. Therefore, considering that these kinds of preconditions are relevant in the study of identities, we can say that social anthropologists practised identity politics before the Second World War, even if in those days they were not explicitly interested in questions of identity and people's self-definitions. The early classics of social anthropology published studies on the institutions, rituals, kinship networks, habits and belief systems of non-Western communities and in this way they produced definitions and images of foreign peoples or cultures — just as modern states have been accustomed to classify, name and label their populations. Foreign cultures did not, of course, always accept these outsider definitions or this kind of colonial use of definition power, but it does not refute the fact that the classics of social anthropology practised identity politics with regard to non-Western cultures.

Furthermore, even in the 1960s and the 1970s, in the humanities and social sciences there were still long-term evolutionist and universalistic elements which often, explicitly or implicitly, contained a faith in the superiority of Western civilisation. The proponents of these elements tended to think that the object of their studies was not, in the last resort, a particular culture or a particular society, but culture or society as such. This thought was often associated with the assumption that the concept of cultural identity expresses only a particular identity — that is, the identity of some group — and therefore it would not be applicable to phenomena that are universal. Hence, the proponents of universalising thinking of this kind could understand the concept in question as unnecessary from the standpoint of their own studies. Theorists of the world system, imperialism and colonialism were critical of the Western-centric point of view in question, but at the same time Marxist theories of imperialism, almost paradoxically, regarded Western industrial civilisation as the most progressive phase in the history of humankind. Theories of the world system, imperialism and colonialism were developed in disciplines such as economics, sociology, political science and history. Although the younger generation in social anthropology was also fairly critical of the Western-centric thinking and "anthropology's colonialist past", it did not develop its own theory of colonialism and imperialism. Instead, it started to reflect more upon its own theories, methods, concepts and social functions, just as Clifford Geertz did in his influential work *The Interpretation of Cultures* (1993, [1973]). Later reflexive thinking of this kind was continued, for example, by James Clifford and George E. Marcus in their *Writing Culture. The Poetics and Politics of Ethnography* (1986) and by James Clifford in his *The Predicament of Culture. Twentieth-Century Ethnography, Literature, and Art* (1988).

The Rise of Multiculturalism and Cultural Relativism

It is in the last two decades that the concept of cultural identity and its subconcepts have gained massive popularity in different disciplines. As Brubaker and Cooper (2000: 2-3) remark, during that period the whole conceptual vocabulary surrounding identity has penetrated the foreground of theoretical and empirical research in the humanities and social sciences. Concepts such as identity, personal identity, sexual identity, cultural identity, national identity, ethnic identity, geocultural identity, regional identity and local identity have been discussed and utilised in numerous books, publications, seminars and congresses. To be sure, most of these concepts had been used previously, but they are now often used in a new way. It might be accurate to say that in the last two decades many, if not most, theorists of identity and cultural identity have defined these phenomena as constructions. In other words, according to this new way of thinking, people's personal and cultural identities are not innate human properties, but they always take shape in some socially, culturally and historically specific context. To a great extent, they are products of various social, cultural and historical factors or determinants. In the 1960s and 1970s French post-structuralists elaborated this kind of view with regard to personal and sexual identity, and at the same time Peter L. Berger and Thomas Luckmann formulated it in their *The Social Construction of Reality* (1972, [1966]), and somewhat later theorists working on nationalism also began to adopt a constructionistic idea of national identity. Today, within academic research, constructionism and its different versions undoubtedly form a widely accepted way of thinking about identity. As we shall see later, however, for certain reasons its position seems to be firmer in West Europe and North America than in East and Southeast Europe.

Brubaker and Cooper content themselves with stating the popularity of the research on cultural identity, without attempting to explain it. How, then, could one explain it? I think that in any explanation we have to take into account two main things, namely (i) the collapse of traditional theories of modernity and (ii) the growing multiculturality of present-day societies. Thomas Hylland Eriksen (1993: 2), among others, has pointed to these factors when explaining the current interest in ethnic and national identity:

> An important reason for the current academic interest in ethnicity and nationalism is the fact that such phenomena have become so visible in many societies that it has become impossible to ignore them. In the early twentieth century, many social theorists held that ethnicity and nationalism would decrease in importance and eventually vanish as a result of modernisation, industrialisation and individualism. This never came about. On the contrary, ethnicity and nationalism have grown in political importance in the world, particularly since the Second World War.

Formerly it was, indeed, thought that people's identification with ethnic groups and national communities would gradually weaken in the process of sociocultural modernisation. For many reasons, classical social theories ignored the questions of ethnicity and nationality, even if they tended to divide social reality up into national — British, French, German — societies. This ignoring was, in part, due to the evolutionism and universalism of these theories, but usually they also held that ethnic and national identification is an old-fashioned social bond, belonging to premodern ties of loyalty that can no longer have a firm position in the modern world. For example, Marx and his successors often thought that ties of loyalty like these would sooner or later be replaced by class identities based on people's "objective" economic interests. Although other classics used different conceptual vocabularies, the concepts of ethnicity and nationality did not gain a constitutive part in their theories, either.

Throughout the long period since the Second World War, nation building has been on the political agenda in many parts of the world, especially in the "Third World" in which ethnic and national movements have often been the results of colonial policies. In the earlier phases of the process of globalisation, European colonial powers created administrative territories highhandedly, without respecting local circumstances and tribal or ethnic boundaries. In consequence, these territories first gained their independence and only then did they go on to recognise the fact that they were composed of multiple ethnic and national groups. Usually this kind of situation resulted in armed conflict between different groups or tribes, and even today there are ethnic and national movements in the "Third World" which seek to establish their own state or autonomic region. To these groups belong, for instance, the Kurds, Palestinians, Sri Lankan Tamils and certain groups in Indonesia, in addition to which several African states have suffered from serious disagreements and armed conflicts between different tribes or ethnic coalitions. Thus, we may conclude that the feeling of ethnic or national togetherness still provides a basis for state building or, at least, for movements seeking to establish their political own unit.

Nowadays the nation-state also seems to be one of the norms for state building. Not only the situation in the "Third World" but the development in post-socialist Europe confirms this generalisation. Since the turn of the 1980s and 1990s, the former Soviet Union has split into about fifteen ethnically or nationally based states, and during the 1990s a similar ethnic or national split occurred in the former Socialist Federal Republic of Yugoslavia. Eriksen (1993: 2) has calculated that at the beginning of the 1990s thirty-five of the thirty-seven major armed conflicts in the world were based on ethnic or national juxtapositions. Even if the situation in post-socialist Europe is more peaceful today, ethnicity and nationality are still real and powerful forces in the world.

As for the phenomenon of multiculturalism, there are in the states of Europe and North America a growing number of ethnic and national minorities. These states were, of course, also previously multicultural wholes, although in Europe most of them usually presented themselves as nation-states. In this case the word "nation-state" was not a completely accurate expression, since there have been ethnic and national minorities in European states, with the consequence that the populations of these states have not been as homogenous as the concept of nation-state requires (Connor 1991: 39-41; Finer 1975: 85-86; Tilly 1994: 35, 48). This concept includes the idea that the population of the state which calls itself "nation-state" consists of only one and the same nationality; in this case the whole population of this state would have adopted a similar national identity. In practice, the idea of the nation-state was an ideal that has hardly come true anywhere, for virtual states usually comprise different ethnic and national groups. The idea of nation-state was also an ideal whereby states sought to integrate and even assimilate different groups into societies led by ethnic majorities. After the Second World War, it gradually became evident that states in West Europe contain minorities that attempt to preserve their own culture and perhaps also establish their own political unit. The best known of these movements have been the IRA in Northern Ireland, Scottish nationalism in Great Britain, Corsican separatism and the Bretons in France, and the Basque movement in Spain. In addition to these groups, since the 1960s Asian, Arabic, African and Caribbean immigrants, refugees and asylum seekers have made the ethnic and national situation in West Europe increasingly complex. Partly as a result of these changes, states in West Europe have recently defined the principle of multiculturalism as a new norm for their identity politics. The current popularity of racist parties, organisations and movements everywhere in West Europe shows, however, that this policy, like the phenomenon of multiculturalism itself, has not yet achieved sufficient approval among the populations of these societies.

Several present-day states in Central, East and Southeast Europe also have their own ethnic and national minorities. Most of these states were already previously multicultural units, but before the 1990s, ethnic and national contrasts usually remained latent in them — mainly for the reason that they were dominated by socialist parties and the imperial Soviet Union or the Central Government of the Socialist Federal Republic of Yugoslavia. In the late 1980s and the early 1990s, these centralised systems dissolved, their constituent states and units were liberated and their political power was restored to national institutions. In this sense the political revolutions in the states and units at issue were national revolutions; and, of course, they were also revolutions on the level of economic policy, for at the same time those states and units were opened up to the rest of the world and to the capitalist world market — or to the global capitalist economy (Leggewie 1999: 191-192). Each of these states or units has usually tried to build a nation-state and national symbols on the basis of the dominant ethnic group, and some of them have even attempted to discourage or suppress their ethnic minorities. No wonder, then, that serious ethnic contrasts and conflicts emerged in them during the 1990s. The warlike events in the Balkan Peninsula form another story completely, but there have also been tensions between different ethnic groups in certain other countries. For example, each Baltic country — that is, Estonia, Latvia and Lithuania — has a notable Russian minority which mainly took shape during the era of the Soviet Union, as a consequence of the Russification politics of the Soviet government. Owing to these kinds of historical events and memories, the dominant ethnic groups in the Baltic states have not been willing to give their Russian minorities full rights of citizenship, which has aroused dissatisfaction both amongst these minorities and in the Russian government.

For the above-mentioned reasons, many states in Central, East and Southeast Europe have not accepted the principles of multiculturalism and ethnic pluralism as eagerly and widely as governments in Western Europe and North America have. It can even be said that the new states in the Balkan Peninsula have mostly been openly hostile to these principles. On the whole, the nationality politics of the new states in Central, East and Southeast Europe have often been too one-sided and monolithic for the European Union, which has asked and demanded that those states ought to adopt a more tolerant stance toward their ethnic and national minorities. Another important difference between those states and West Europe can be seen in that in the former ones the intelligentsia has actively participated in the building or renewing of national institutions and symbols, whereas West European intelligentsia has, to a great extent, become estranged from active national movements (see also Delanty 1999). In the 1990s, Lennart Meri, a highly respected writer and essayist, was elected President of the republic of Estonia, and at the same time Vaclac Havel, also a writer, acted as the first President of the Czech Republic. Compared with this, in Western Europe writers and artists seem to have left active political participation many decades ago. Moreover, in this connection it is relevant to point out that in the former socialist countries constructivist theories of identity have aroused certain doubts and suspicions among researchers, who favour a more essentialist concept of identity (see Talvet in this volume).

In Western Europe and North America in particular, the popularity of research on cultural identity is connected with the above-mentioned interlocking phenomena: the collapse of the traditional theories of modernisation and the growing multiculturality of present-day societies. With these two phenomena, the background ideology or underlying world picture of the humanities and social sciences has changed considerably. Friedman (1996: 196-197), Robertson (1993: 41-42, 99-100) and Seung (1982) have suggested that these disciplines have gradually adopted a more relativistic picture of the world and cultures. This cultural relativism takes diverse forms, of which the following two are worth noticing:

> (Version One) According to Robertson (1993: 99-100), cultural relativism of today often includes a refusal to make any universalising generalisations about different cultures. In its extreme form this kind of relativism is based on the belief that there is no such thing as a universal culture; the only thing we have is a huge diversity of different cultures.
>
> (Version Two) The humanities and social sciences can no longer start from the assumption that a particular culture would, *a priori*, be superior to other cultures. When this principle is applied to Western culture, one has to say that the traditional evolutionist presuppositions concerning this culture are inaccurate. Western culture is only one particular culture among the cultures of the world, and as such, one cannot regard it as a privileged representative of humanity and humankind.

In the first place these principles represent the world picture of researchers within the humanities and social sciences in Western Europe and North America. It is difficult to say to what extent other social groups in those countries have adopted a similar way of thinking. As noted earlier, at least in Europe certain signs — xenophobia, the spread of racism and extreme right-wing movements — tell us that in most European countries there are serious obstacles to a genuine cultural pluralism and tolerance, although the majority of the population of these countries might be willing to approve a relatively wide cultural diversity. Within the humanities and social sciences a more or less relativistic picture of the world usually underlies new research trends such as post-structuralistic philosophy, postcolonial criticism in literary research, postcolonial studies, study of "the Other", or foreign cultures and research on multiculturality. All these trends express the mental landscape of the academic intelligentsia in the humanities and social sciences.

As a specification to this, one can say that, on the whole, post-structuralists have praised human instincts and drives, which they have given preference to over rational reasoning and organised society. In Lacan's (1966) and Kristeva's (1980) works, the latter remain somewhat vague, whereas, for example, in Gilles Deleuze's and Felix Guattari's work *L'Anti-Oidipe. Capitalisme et schitsoprénie* (Anti-Oidipus, Capitalism and Schizoprenia, 1972) the concept of society points to modern Western capitalism; and in Michel Foucault's *Histoire de la sexualité* (History of Sexuality, 1976-84) society means, more generally, Western civilisation.

Furthermore, it should be borne in mind that academic Western femininists have often criticised the "hegemonic Western culture", which they have characterised as "white, middle-class and male". Certain feminists have also spoken about the possibility that they could shake this order by allying with radical social and political movements in the "Third World".

Along with the new research trends, the long-term evolutionist, universalist and Western-centric world picture of the humanities and social sciences has been called into question. Actually, this kind of questioning began to emerge in the 1970s. According to Friedman (1996: 54), after the Second World War the Western world experienced an economic upswing until the years of the "energy crisis" in the mid-1970s, when it suddenly had to realise that economic growth and technological development have their limits. Since that time phenomena such as ecological problems, the world population explosion and the collapse of socialism and leftist utopias have also shaken the optimism of Western intellectuals and undermined their evolutionistic and Western-centric world picture. Following Friedman, one can say that since the Cold War, Western countries undoubtedly form the strongest bloc in the world, definitely representing the hegemonic military position nowadays, but in other respects the power of this bloc proved to be vulnerable many decades ago. Friedman's conclusion is that factors such as these have produced a crisis in the traditional self-image of Western intellectuals, which, in part, explains the current interest in cultural identity. In addition, he thinks that in the last resort the crisis at issue concerns the basic premises of classical Western modernity, this ideology, with its roots in the seventeenth and eighteenth centuries, has been based on a faith in the progress of individuals and societies.

However, Friedman does not connect the concept of crisis solely to Western intellectuals. This is a crisis that is more general:

> The crisis of identity in the center [that is, in the West] is expressive of a more general global crisis.... The crisis consists in the weakening of former national identities and the emergence of new identities — especially the dissolution of a kind of membership known as "citizenship" in the abstract meaning of membership in a territorially defined and state-governed society, and its replacement by an identity based on "primordial loyalties", ethnicity, "race", local community, language and other culturally concrete forms (Friedman 1996: 86).

The world is simultaneously experiencing two seemingly opposite or contradictory processes: on one hand, the number of ethnic and national movements has been on the increase, and on the other, nation-states are in the process of weakening. The latter process has been the result of economic and political development. In the present-day globalising economy, nation-states have no effective means of controlling digital flows of capitals, currencies, investments and information, with the result that their ability to regulate economic activities has declined. This, in turn, has strengthened transnational as well as local and regional units at the expense of traditional nation-states, whose officials and members have often regarded it as a crisis. In this sense the latter process has somewhat problematised and relativised former cultural identities and made the questions of identity topical (e.g. Delanty 1999; Eder 1999; Münch 1995; 1999; Telò 2001).

Owing to the above-mentioned changes, researchers have become more careful when using the categories of evolution and universality. For example, from the 1970s onwards Niklas Luhmann developed the concept of social evolution, but in his theory of social evolution he did not, at least explicitly, speak about the superiority of Western civilisation. For him, social evolution meant such things as the growth of society's internal differentiation and complexity and the increase of its regulation capacities (see Luhmann 1997a; 1997b). Similarly, Jürgen Habermas (1987a; 1987b) has partly equated sociocultural evolution with differentiation, besides which he has stated that in modern society economic and political-administrative systems have increasingly penetrated people's life worlds and daily life and, in this way, limited the independence of these social spheres. Luhmann's and Habermas's concepts of social evolution seem to be Western-centric chiefly in the sense that they are rather monolithic; that is, these concepts have not sufficiently taken into account the possibility that there might be several ways of evolution. Implicitly, Luhmann and Habermas have theorised about evolution on the basis of Western experience, in this way neglecting non-Western developmental trends.

As far as the concept of universality is concerned, researchers' present-day fears of using this concept are not unproblematic. Within the Western academic world, these fears have, of course, been welcome because they indicate that during recent decades Western researchers and intellectuals have learnt some sane self-criticism. This social group now understands that it can no longer speak and write as if Western civilisation were self-evidently the best representative of the whole of humankind. At the same time it is obvious that the principle of cultural relativism and tolerance has its limits — as the following tragic event that occurred in Sweden, in the city of Uppsala, exemplifies, provided that it is interpreted properly.

In January 2002 a Kurdish father killed his daughter Fadime Sahindal, a twenty-six year old woman who had lived in Sweden since the early 1980s and had been going steady with a Swedish man. His father, an unlearned and unemployed man, demanded that his daughter should end the courtship and instead get married to a Kurdish man — an order which his daughter could by no means accept. The young woman also told about her painful situation and her father's order on a television programme but, according to her father, by doing this she disgraced him in public.

Eventually, the father went and shot his daughter, who was living away from her parents. After the shooting the father claimed to have committed the murder as an attempt to protect the family honour, and appealed to the customs of Kurdish culture — a claim that the Kurdish community in Sweden later refuted and condemned. However, his attempt at this defence indicates that, by killing their disobedient female relatives, men like him believe that they can preserve their self-respect and the honour of their family in the Kurdish community. The Swedish court also discredited the father's claims about the "murder of honour" and in April 2002 sentenced the father to life imprisonment for the murder.

Most researchers in the Western academic world can express understanding and can explain the sociocultural background of these acts, even though they regard them as morally wrong and incompatible with basic human rights. On a more general level we may say that multicultural societies need some common juridical and moral rules that different groups and subcultures would be able to share in. In many cases it is the ethnic or national majority group in a society that has defined such rules, while minority groups have been unable to do anything but adapt themselves to such rules. In a truly multicultural society, however, the majority ought to take into account the needs of minority groups and negotiate with them on such rules, otherwise the situation may very well result in serious conflicts between different groups. In a well-functioning multicultural society different groups must then have some common norms, values and communicative means to prevent and regulate such conflicts.

The need for common rules and norms is an urgent problem in the present-day world. The process of globalisation forces different continents, countries, and regions into increasing interaction with each other — whether or not these units are happy about this situation. The interaction between different units has its negative by-products that contain misunderstandings and conflicts, for example, in the domain of moral behaviour and religious values. However, it is interaction in the field of a global economy that may be the main source of social and cultural problems, since the global economy is dominated by the new liberalist economic policy. New liberalism, in turn, can easily lead to a situation in which powerful mega-corporations ruthlessly exploit national and regional resources. In order to prevent such threats, the world needs common rules and norms which will regulate interaction on a global scale and which could also provide poor nations and peoples with a sufficient standard of living. Beck (1997) writes that, in the present-day world, there is also an urgent need to form by democratic means a world state or a world government — an advanced version of the United Nations — that would guarantee the validity of those common rules and norms (e.g. Held 2000; Meyer 2000; Patomäki 2000; Therborn 2000a; 2000b).

Even if these kinds of thoughts may sound idealistic, their underlying message is clear: the globalising world needs a sufficient amount of common or shared culture, which means that in practice the strong form of cultural relativism (Version One) must somehow be overcome. Cultural tolerance is really a virtue and a desirable state of affairs in the multicultural world, but the strong version of cultural relativism is a problem rather than a solution, since the interaction between different cultures cannot be based simply on it alone.

Version One is also problematic in the sense that it refuses to make any universalising generalisations. However, in the present situation social and cultural theorists must speak about the world as a whole. They have, at least to start from the assumption that a generalising or universalising talk is not entirely nonsensical. Robertson (1993: 100), who supports this stand himself, calls it "Worldism" and formulates it in this way:

> [Worldism] is based upon the claim that it is possible and, indeed, desirable to grasp the world as a whole analytically; to such an extent that virtually everything of sociocultural or political interest which occurs around the globe — including identity presentation — can be explained, or at least interpreted in reference to, the dynamics of the entire 'world-system'.

Worldism has not a licence to be geographically and culturally blind. Therborn (2000b: 169) remarks that the present phase of globalisation is a worldwide process, but its effects vary in different regions and continents. For example, in Western Europe it has forced the states to cooperate actively with each other and to form the European Union, by which those states try to compete effectively with the United States and Japan. After opening themselves up to the rest of the world, the states in Eastern and Southeast Europe have participated in the ongoing phase of globalisation, but in the economic sense they have, so far, lost a great deal in this process. In Asia, South America and Africa this phase has meant a liberalisation of national economies — an event that has often come true by following the advice of the International Monetary Fund and the World Bank, with the consequence that globalisation has also encountered sharp criticism and bitter resistance in those continents.

These examples show that Worldism differs crucially from traditional evolutionism and universalism, even if this stand desires to overcome the strong form of cultural relativism — a value principle that has been expressed in Version One. However, Worldism is compatible with Version Two, because it does not start from the assumption that some civilisation — in particular, Western civilisation — is inherently superior to other civilisations. However, the proponents of Worldism cannot entirely deny the fact of cultural determination, which means that their own cultural background may affect the standpoints from which they consider the world. In this sense they are also sometimes unavoidably guilty of Western-centrism.

Conclusions

In the Western context, the study of cultural identity emerged at the turn of the eighteenth and nineteenth centuries, when in the humanities certain aspects of cultural identity became objects of research. At that time researchers in the humanities began to divide the sociocultural reality up into different national cultures, and they also became interested in the peculiarities and "spiritual" characteristic of nations and national cultures. In particular, researchers considered their own domestic national culture. By publishing studies on this culture they produced definitions and images of the nationality in question, and in this sense they practised nationality politics, that is a special form of identity politics.

From the very beginning, the study of national identity was closely related to political phenomena on a wider scale. To a great extent, it can be seen as a part of the nationality politics of the states or national movements. By arousing feelings of a common nationality among their populations, traditional and established states (Great Britain, France, Prussia) attempted to integrate different social and regional groups into society and to make these groups loyal to those in power. In short, in this way the states in question partly developed towards the ideal of the nation-state. National movements, on the other hand, attempted to mobilise their proponents by appealing to the nationality of these people. In both cases, studies devoted to "a common national culture" provided nationality politicians with useful "scientific evidence".

In the social sciences and social philosophy, the study of cultural identity was not important in the nineteenth century and the early twentieth century, although of these sciences it was social anthropology that was closest to the study of cultural identity. By publishing studies of foreign cultures, this discipline produced definitions and images of those cultures as well. In their research practice social anthropologists even took into account the self-definitions and self-understanding of the representatives of non-Western cultures, which can as such be understood as an implicit act of identity politics. Social anthropologists also exercised identity politics explicitly. Namely, by classifying and defining — or by "identifying" — foreign cultures and peoples from the outside, they applied conceptual power to non-Western cultures.

The traditional humanities, social sciences and social philosophy more or less shared a universalistic and evolutionist way of thinking based on a Western-centric view of the world. On the whole, these three traits were characteristic of European and Western ideology and cultural identity in the nineteenth century. However, in the twentieth century there were also periods of cultural relativism (the Boas school: Mead, Benedict, Herskovits) in the above-mentioned disciplines, particularly in cultural anthropology. In the United States the present-day boom in the study of cultural identity has lasted a good two decades, and its social background contains interlocking processes such as globalisation, the weakening of the position of the traditional nation-states, the diminishing of Western-centrism and the growing multiculturality of present-day societies. As a result of processes like these, the background ideology in the humanities, social sciences and social philosophy has changed in the sense that the criticism of Western-centrism and the principles of cultural relativism and pluralism have been more or less characteristic of the new research tendencies in the disciplines in question. To be sure, these tendencies have been strong in West Europe and North America, both among the intelligentsia and the governments, whereas the states, especially the new states in Central, East and Southeast Europe, have exercised a more monolithic nationality politics.

The above-mentioned shift to a more relativistic picture of the world and cultures has not been the result of a logical development, but neither has it been the outcome of a purely internal theoretical development in the humanities, social sciences and philosophy. The traditional background ideology of these disciplines has not been refuted or falsified. On the contrary, the reason for the shift in question can rather be found in researchers' life worlds: the old ideology no longer corresponds to researchers' experiences of sociocultural reality. Hence, one might say that this shift seems to verify Thomas S. Kuhn's famous theoretical model of scientific revolutions — a model according to which a shift in science to a new paradigm is largely a non-logical or irrational process.

In the present-day globalising world researchers in the humanities and social sciences must, however, overcome their fears of universalism. When constructing a picture of ongoing social and cultural processes researchers have to be ready to speak about the world as a whole — without forgetting the differences between societies. The strict cultural relativism must be overcome in social practices as well. Multicultural societies and multicultural world need such value principles and norms of a kind that different nations and groups can share; a common culture of this kind and a sufficient standard of living can best guarantee societies' peaceful development, insofar as it is possible at all. Undoubtedly, the common culture at issue should come into being as a result of conversation and interaction, and not as a result of political and military coercion.

REFERENCES

Abels, Kurt 1989: Deutschunterricht vor und nach 1848 im Widerstreit pädagogischer, politischer und konfessioneller Interessen. *Bildung und Erziehung*. 42:3. 269-282.

Albertin, L. 1999: Regionale kulturelle Identität. Selbstgenügsames Refugium oder europäischer Handlungselement. In Reinhold Viehoff und Rien T. Segers Hrsg.: *Kultur, Identität, Europa. Über Schwierigkeiten und Möglichkeiten einer Konstruktion*. Frankfurt am Main: Suhrkamp. 321-332.

Albrow, Martin 1990: Globalization, Knowledge and Society. In M. Albrow and E. King ed.: *Globalization, Knowledge and Society*. London: Sage.

Alexander, Jeffrey C. 1983: *Theoretical Logic in Sociology. Volume Four. The Modern Reconstruction of Classical Thought: Talcott Parsons*. Berkeley and Los Angeles: University of California Press.

Arnold, Matthew 1969 (1869): *Culture and Anarchy, With Friendship's Garland and Some Literary Essays*. Cambridge: Cambridge University Press.

Beck, Ulrich 1997: *Was ist Globalizierung? Irrtümer des Globalismus — Antworten auf Globalisierung*. Frankfurt am Main: Suhrkamp.

Berger, Peter L. and Thomas Luckmann 1972 (1966): *The Social Construction of Reality*. Harmondsworth: Penguin Books.

Brennan, Timothy 1994 (1990): The National Longing for Form. In Homi K. Bhabha ed.: *Nation and Narration*. London and New York: Routledge.

Brubaker, Rogers and Frederick Cooper 2000: Beyond 'Identity'. *Theory and Society*. 29:1. 1-47.

Clifford, James 1988: *The Predicament of Culture. Twentieth-Century Ethnography, Literature and Art*. Cambridge, Massachusetts, and London, England: Harvard University Press.

Clifford, James and George H. Marcus ed. 1986: *Writing Culture. The Poetics and Politics of Ethnography*. Berkeley, Los Angeles and London: The University of California Press.

Connor, Walker 1994 (1978): A Nation is a Nation, is a State, is an Ethnic Group, is a.... In J. Hutchinson and A.D. Smith ed.: *Nationalism*. Oxford and New York: Oxford University Press. 36-46.

Delanty, G. 1999: Die Transformation nationaler Identität und die kulturelle Ambivalenz europäischer Identität. Demokratische Identifikation in einer postnationalen Europa. In Reinhold Viehoff und Rien T. Segers Hrsg.: *Kultur, Identität, Europa. Über Schwierigkeiten und Möglichkeiten einer Konstruktion*. Frankfurt am Main: Suhrkamp. 267-288.

Deleuze, Gilles and Felix Guattari 1972: *L'Anti-Oedipe. Capitalisme et schizoprénie*. Paris.

Eagleton, Terry 1984: *The Function of Criticism from The Spectator to Post-structuralism*. London: Verso.

Eder, K. 1999: Integration durch Kultur? Das Paradox der Suche nach einer europäischen Identität. In Reinhold Viehoff und Rien T. Segers Hrsg.: *Kultur, Identität, Europa. Über Schwierigkeiten und Möglichkeiten einer Konstruktion*. Frankfurt am Main: Suhrkamp. 147-179.

Eriksen, Thomas Hylland 1993: *Ethnicity and Nationalism. Anthropological Perspectives*. London and Sterling: Pluto Press.

Erikson, Erik H. 1959: *Identity and the Life-Circle: Selected Papers*. Psychological Issues Monograph Series. 1:1. New York.

Finer, S.E. 1975: State- and Nation-Building in Europe: The Role of the Military. In Charles Tilly ed.: *The Formation of National States in Western Europe*. Princeton, New Jersey: Princeton University Press. 84-163.

Foucault, Michel 1976-84: *Histoire de la sexualité*. Paris: Editions Gallimard.

Friedman, Jonathan 1996: *Cultural Identity and Global Process*. London, Thousand Oaks and New York: Sage.

Geertz, Clifford 1993 (1973): *The Interpretations of Cultures. Selected Essays*. London: Fontana Press.

Giesen, Bernhard 1991: Einleitung. In Bernhard Giesen Hrsg.: *Nationale und kulturelle Identität. Studien zur Entwicklung des kollektiven Bewusstseins in der Neuzeit*. Frankfurt am Main: Suhrkamp. 7-18.

Greenfeld, Liah 1993 (1992): *Nationalism. Five Roads to Modernity*. Cambridge, Massachusetts and London, England: Harvard University Press.

Habermas, Jürgen 1987a (1981): *Theorie des kommunikativen Handelns. Band 1. Handlungsrationalität und gesellschaftliche Rationalisierung*. Frankfurt am Main: Suhrkamp.

Habermas, Jürgen 1987b (1981): *Theorie des kommunikativen Handelns. Band 2. Zur Kritik der funktionalistischen Vernunft*. Frankfurt am Main: Suhrkamp.

Held, David 2000: Regulating Globalization? The Reinvention of Politics. *International Sociology*. 15:2. 394-408.

Helkama, Klaus with Rauni Myllyniemi and Karmela Liebkind 1999: *Johdatus sosiaalipsykologiaan* [Introduction to Social Psychology]. Helsinki: Edita.

Kant, Immanuel 1975 (1790): Kritik der Urteilskraft. In Immanuel Kant, *Werke. Band 8. Kritik der Urteilskraft und Schriften zur Naturphilosophie.* Darmstadt: Wissenschaftliche Buchgesellschaft.

Karkama, Pertti 1989: *J.V. Snellmanin kirjallisuuspolitiikka* [The Literary Politics of J.V. Snellman]. Helsinki: Suomalaisen Kirjallisuuden Seura.

King, Anthony D. 1993 (1993): Spaces of Culture, Spaces of Knowledge. In Anthony D. King ed.: *Culture, Globalization and the World-System. Contemporary Conditions for the Representation of Identity.* London: Macmillan. 1-18.

Kristeva, Julia 1980 (1977): *Desire in Language. A Semiotic Approach to Literature and Art.* Translated by Thomas Gora, Alice Jardine and Leon S. Roudiez. Oxford.

Kuhn, Thomas S. (1962): *The Structure of Scientific Revolutions.* Chicago: The University of Chicago Press.

Lacan, Jacques 1966: *Ecrits.* Paris: Seuil.

Larrain, Jorge 1994: *Ideology and Cultural Identity.* Cambridge: Polity Press.

Leggewie, C. 1999: Erneuter Griff nach der Notbremse oder: Revolution als Restauration. In Reinhold Viehoff und Rien T. Segers Hrsg.: *Kultur, Identität, Europa. Über Schwierigkeiten und Möglichkeiten einer Konstruktion.* Frankfurt am Main: Suhrkamp. 180-200.

Levi-Strauss, Claude 1963: Réponse à quelques questions. *Espirit.* 31. 628-653.

Luhmann, Niklas 1997a: *Die Gesellschaft der Gesellschaft.* Zwei Bände. Band 1. Frankfurt am Main: Suhrkamp.

Luhmann, Niklas 1997b: *Die Gesellschaft der Gesellschaft.* Zwei Bände. Band 2. Frankfurt am Main: Suhrkamp.

Lämmert, Eberhard 1971 (1967) : Germanistik — eine deutsche Wissenschaft. In *Germanistik — eine deutsche Wissenschaft.* Beiträge von Eberhard Lämmert, Walther Killy, Karl Otto Conrady und Peter von Polenz. 5. Auflage. Frankfurt am Main 1971: Suhrkamp. 7-42.

Meyer, John B. 2000: Globalization. Sources and Effects on National States and Societies. *International Sociology.* 15:2. 233-248.

Münch, Richard 1995 (1993): *Das Projekt Europa. Zwischen Nationalstaat, regionaler Autonomie und Weltgesellschaft.* Frankfurt am Main: Suhrkamp.

Münch, Richard 1999: Europäische Identitätsbildung. Zwischen globaler Dynamik, nationaler und regionaler Gegenbewegung. In Reinhold Viehoff und Rien T. Segers Hrsg.: *Kultur, Identität, Europa. Über Schwierigkeiten und Möglichkeiten einer Konstruktion.* Frankfurt am Main: Suhrkamp. 223-252.

Parsons, Talcott 1966: *Societies. Evolutionary and Comparative Perspectives.* New Jersey: Prentice-Hall.

Parsons, Talcott 1971: *The System of Modern Societies.* Englewood Cliffs, New Jersey: Prentice-Hall.

Patomäki, Heikki 2000: The Tobin Tax. A New Phase in the Politics of Globalization. *Theory, Culture and Society.* 17:4. 77-91.

Robertson, Ronald 1993: *Social Theory and Global Culture.* London, Newbury Park and New Delhi: Sage.

Schiller, Friedrich 1975 (1793-94): Über die ästhetische Erziehung des Menschen in einer Reihe von Briefen. In Friedrich Schiller: *Über Kunst und Wirklichkeit.* Leipzig: Reclam.

Schudson, Michael 1994: Culture and the Integration of National Societies. In Diana Crane ed.: *Sociology of Culture. Emerging Theoretical Perspectives.* Oxford, UK and Cambridge, USA: Blackwell.

Seung, T.K. 1982: *Structuralism and Hermeneutics.* New York: Columbia University Press.

Sevänen, Erkki 2000: The Post-National Condition. On the Relationship between the State, Nation and Nationalist Policy in the Present-Day Western World. *Interlitteraria.* 5. 15-36.

Smith, Anthony D. 1979: *Nationalism in the Twentieth Century.* New York University Press.

Smith, Anthony D. 1991: *National Identity.* London: Penguin Books.

Smith, Anthony D. 1995: *Nations and Nationalism in a Global Era.* Oxford, UK and Cambridge, USA: Polity Press.

Söderholm, Stig 1994: Antropologinen kulttuurintutkimus [Anthropological Study of Culture]. In Jari Kupiainen and Erkki Sevänen ed.: *Kulttuurintutkimus. Johdanto* [Cultural Research. An Introduction]. Helsinki: Suomalaisen Kirjallisuuden Seura. 119-142.

Telò, Mario ed. 2001: *European Union and New Regionalism. Regional Actors and Global Governance in a Post-hegemonic Era.* Aldershot, Burlington USA, Singapore, Sydney: Ashgate.

Therborn 2000a: Introduction: From the Universal to Global. *International Sociology.* 15:2. 149-150.

Therborn 2000b: Globalizations. Dimensions, Historical Waves, Regional Effects, Normative Governance. *International Sociology.* 15:2. 151-179.

Tilly, Charles 1994 (1993): *European Revolutions, 1492-1992.* Oxford: Blackwell.

Turner, Bryan S. 1994 (1990): Two Faces of Sociology: Global or National. In Mike Featherstone ed.: *Global Culture. Nationalism, Globalization and Modernity.* London, Newbury Park and New Delhi: Sage.

Varpio, Yrjö 1990: *The History of Finnish Literary Criticism 1828-1918.* Helsinki: Societas scientiarum Fennica.

2

The Underestimated Strength of Cultural Identity between Localising and Globalising Tendencies in the European Union

RIEN T. SEGERS

Introduction: A Nursery Rhyme for Scholars and Students

At the annual meetings of the World Bank and the International Monetary Fund in Washington in September 1999 Wole Soyinka, the Nigerian writer and Nobel laureate, said:

> Culture is a matrix of infinite possibilities and choices ...from which we can extract arguments and strategies for the degradation or enoblement of our species, for its enslavement or liberation, for the suppression of its productive potential or its enchantment, for the stagnation of social existence or its renewal.

Soyinka's quotation will function as a background against which I would like to introduce the concept of cultural identity. I think there are at least two reasons for devoting a paper to questions concerning cultural identity.

The first reason can be found in the immense popularity of the concept of cultural identity itself. The scholarly, journalistic and popular press is filled with references to the field of cultural identity and its related themes, national and corporate identity. You often feel that you are encountering a huge container concept which has lost its specific semantics due to the abundant use of that very concept. Scholarship's task is to look at the specificity of semantics, especially if it concerns such an important social concept. That is exactly what I am trying to achieve here: to look for the lost semantics of the concept of cultural identity and to frame it within its natural context.

The second reason is concerned with demonstrating the validity of the concept of cultural identity. I strongly believe that insight into cultural identity will result in a deeper insight into the European integration process, when viewed from a contemporary social perspective. Let us focus briefly on a simple but intriguing nursery rhyme:

> The Germans live in Germany, the Romans live in Rome,
> the Turkeys live in Turkey; but the English live at home.

We could ask a number of questions here. For instance:

- Which nation invented this nursery rhyme?
- When was it invented?
- To what extent is it justified?

It is the last question which will be the specific focus of this paper. In other words, the focus will be on the question of what situation the cultures and nations of the EU in particular find themselves today. Should this situation be characterised by the concept "localisation" or by the concept of "globalisation"? Is it correct to define "localisation" — as some do — as a predominantly nineteenth-century concept and globalisation as a predominantly late twentieth-century concept?

These are simple questions but with complicated answers. I shall explain and deconstruct the current Great Millennium Myth, which implies a belief that the structure of contemporary society or even "the world" can only be characterised by the concept of globalisation, globalisation as a mythical construction of post-industrial European society. There is a caveat here: my argument denotes a specific set of Western assumptions concerning concepts such as culture, nation and cultural identity. I shall mainly concentrate on cultural identity here, since this concept is not only *en vogue* in many scholarly circles around the globe, but also because to a great extent this concept determines other concepts which are of crucial importance to the discourse of our time: globalisation, localisation, multiculturalism, ethnicity, nation state, ideology.

Insight into cultural identity implies at the same time a partial insight into all the tricky container concepts I have just mentioned.

My guiding principle is the systemic theory of culture (Even-Zohar, Luhmann, Maturana, Varela; for a bibliography see e.g. Tötösy de Zepetnek 1992; for a recent critical analysis see Sevänen 2001). This theory considers culture as a system consisting of a number of subsystems, such as economic, educational, religious, technological and artistic subsystems. Each subsystem is based on all activities as performed by participants, people active within that subsystem. This means that a systemic approach is interested in all the "actions", in all the "activities" as performed by the participants within a particular subsystem.

How can you recognise a culture when you see one: an attempt at a definition

Before its anthropological incarnation, culture predominantly meant refinement. The nineteenth-century humanist Matthew Arnold, for instance, considered culture to be a study of perfection, an inward condition of the mind and spirit. He regarded cultured people as drawing ever nearer to "the beautiful" and "the graceful". Culture in his view was the best that has been thought and said. This conception of culture still remains very much *en vogue* today.

Cultural anthropologists have reworked this accepted concept of culture to apply it not only to a learned and sophisticated few, but to *all* human beings. As Clifford Geertz (1980) notes: "Culture...is not just an ornament of human existence, but...an essential condition for it.... There is no such a thing as a human nature independent of culture." This implies that as human beings we are *all* cultured. Culture in this sense has become a value-free concept as opposed to the value-laden Arnoldian concept. The question whether this concept of culture is needed seems to be justified, since there are so many other words seemingly describing more or less the same anthropological concept, such as a set of norms, value systems, behaviour patterns, rituals and traditions. The organisational psychologist Edgar H. Schein (1992: 10-11) correctly answers this question as follows. Unlike all the other words just mentioned, the concept of culture adds two relevant critical notions.

First of all there is the implication of structural stability in a community or group of people. Cultural elements are elements that are not only shared but are also stable and "deep", which means less conscious, less tangible and less visible. Cultural elements also bind together into a coherent whole; they reveal a certain pattern at a deeper, invisible level. Secondly, culture denotes the accumulated shared learning of a given group, covering behavioural, emotional and cognitive elements of the group's members total psychological functioning. Schein (1992: 10) correctly observes: "For shared learning to occur, there must be a history of shared experience, which in turn implies some stability of members in the group." The implication behind the above points of departure is the constructive nature of culture. Culture is not a set of innate or ontological characteristics which have a static nature, but rather a set containing a great number of actions performed by those who participate in that (sub)culture. These actions are performed on the basis of more or less conventional schemes.

My understanding of culture is influenced by Geert Hofstede's (1994: 5) ideas about it. I subscribe to his view because his definition unites three important elements: the decisive value of culture, the importance of cultural relativism and the constructed character of culture.

Hofstede (1994: 5) distinguishes two meanings of the word culture. There is culture one, which refers to civilisation, a refinement of the mind which can be found in education, art and literature. This is not a description of culture I would like to refer to. I shall select Hofstede's culture two, which

> ...deals with much more fundamental human processes than culture one; it deals with the things that hurt.
>
> Culture (two) is always a collective phenomenon, because it is at least partly shared with people who live or lived within the same social environment, which is where it was learned. It is *the collective programming of the mind which distinguishes the members of one*

> *group or category of people from another* (Hofstede 1994: 5; original emphasis).

According to Hofstede, culture is learned, not inherited. It derives from your social environment, not from your genes. He distinguishes culture from human nature based on the following reasoning: as a human being you can feel fear, anger, love, joy, sadness, etc. All these feelings are part of human nature. However, the way these feelings are expressed is modified by culture. Culture is the software of the mind. It is also distinguished from the personality of an individual. The latter is described as a unique personal set of mental programmes he or she does not share with any other human being. Hofstede's description of "personality" is somewhat naive, but his concept of culture is extremely useful.

An example of this is the Lewinsky affair in the United States, or perhaps we should say the Clinton affair. In many cultures, no wife, children or even an entire nation wants the husband, father or political leader to engage in adultery, perjury, or bribery. It does not fit the image you construct of a husband, a father, or a president. Even the supposition of adultery, perjury or bribery gives rise to the same human feelings of anger, sadness and disgust in many cultures. It would result in the same headlines in the media and in the same criticism from the media in most cultures, since this is the level of human nature: violation of confidence, a central human value in most cultures. But the way those feelings of violation of confidence are expressed is culturally bound, dependent on "the programming of the mind" in that particular culture.

The programming of the Dutch political mind in this respect would be such that a Dutch political leader in a similar position to Mr. Clinton would have resigned immediately on his or her own initiative, not necessarily out of respect for the people of the country or for his or her relatives, but out of fear of the Dutch House of Representatives. It would mean the definitive end of a political career. After a year of silence the fallen Dutch leader would become Chairman of the Association of Cheesemakers or Tulip Growers and would be out of public sight forever. The programming of the Dutch mind is still heavily Calvinist.

The programming of the Japanese political mind is quite different. A Japanese political leader in similar circumstances would step down immediately out of shame, since he would think that he had lost face. At the press conference he would bow very deeply, apologise and take all responsibility, even for things he could not be held responsible for. Recently, a new phenomenon has been added to this traditional programme: the leader must weep and cry. After a year of silence, the Japanese political leader re-enters politics through the back door of the Lower House, where he could direct his faction again and significantly influence Japanese politics as if nothing has happened. The programming of the Japanese mind is heavily based on the Japanese version of Buddhism.

Hofstede has a systemic (*in sensu* Niklas Luhmann) conception of culture. He does not see culture as a vast unspecified domain, but rather as an entity consisting of different levels, which are interrelated. At the same time, a person always belongs to a number of the following levels, or indicators of identity, for instance: a national level according to one's country; a regional/ethnic/religious/linguistic affiliation; a gender level; a generation level; a social class level; and an organisational or corporate level for those who are employed. The implication is that it is impossible to speak about "the" identity of a person or of a group; it may vary according to circumstances.

Hofstede undertook a large-scale intercultural research project which revealed the following five dimensions, on the basis of which cultures can be classified:

1. Social inequality, including the relationship with authority.
2. The relationship between the individual and the group.
3. Concepts of masculinity and femininity; the social implications of having been born as a boy or a girl.
4. Ways of dealing with uncertainty, relating to the control of aggression and the expression of emotions.
5. A long-term orientation in life versus a short-term orientation.

Hofstede's conception of culture has a number of advantages.

In this conception, culture is an ever-changing entity not a static one; culture is learned not inherited; there are no criteria on the basis of which culture A is "intrinsically" better than culture B (with exceptions such as a culture that deliberately and seriously violates human rights); "culture" is a mental construction rather than the innate property of a certain community. This implies that Hofstede's view of culture is more useful with respect to its application in actual research than many other definitions of culture, which base themselves on ontological or essentialist conceptions.

What is Cultural Identity: Just another Container Concept?

A weak aspect of Hofstede's book (1994), however, is that the very concept of cultural identity is not used. Yet this concept is needed to discuss questions whenever two cultures come into contact with each other or — on an academic level — are compared with each other. A key question such as "How can the distinctiveness or the specificity of this culture be determined?" is in fact a question concerning the *cultural identity* of a particular community. The extent to which a certain culture can be said to have distinctive *and* common traits can only be determined on a comparative basis. As the American sociologists Jepperson and Swidler (1994: 368; italics added) recently stated: "The essential strategy for making the invisible visible is *of course* comparative research. And that is exactly why disciplines which have a comparative basis should take the lead in research in this domain."

Giving a description of cultural identity is clearly linked to important other concepts such as ethnicity, nation and nation-state. I take here the guidelines given by Adrian Hastings to define those terms. Hastings considers ethnicity to be a group of people with a shared cultural identity and spoken language. He correctly considers ethnicity to be the major distinctive element in a pre-national society, but ethnicity — he adds — "may survive as a strong subdivision with a loyalty of its own within established nations" (Hastings 1997: 3). Hastings (ibid.) defines a nation as follows:

> A nation is a far more self-conscious community than an ethnicity. Formed from one or more ethnicities, and normally identified by a literature of its own, it possesses

> or claims the right to political identity and autonomy as a people, together with the control of specific territory, comparable to that of biblical Israel and of other independent entities in a world thought of as one of nation-states.

This clears the way to a description of a nation-state:

> ...a state which identifies itself in terms of one specific nation whose people are not seen simply as 'subjects' of the sovereign but as a horizontally bonded society to whom the state in a sense belongs. There is thus an identity of character between state and people. ...In [the state], ideally, there is basic equivalence between the borders and character of the political unit upon the one hand and a self-conscious cultural community on the other. In most cases this is a dream as much as a reality. Most nation-states in fact include groups of people who do not belong to its core culture or feel themselves to be part of a nation so defined. Nevertheless almost all modern states act on the bland assumption that they are nation-states (Hastings 1997: 3).

Books discussing the cultural identity of a particular nation or nation-state often refer to certain "special features", "characteristics" and "traits" of that nation-state or its people. Often these observations are principally based on impressions, introspections, myths and — not to be forgotten — jokes rather than on factual evidence or empirical research. Obviously, I do not want to deny, for instance, that the thousands of jokes concerning national and cultural stereotypes may highlight particular aspects of the cultural identity of a particular community or nation, but they are simply indicators and no more than that. Consider, for instance, the following two jokes. The first originated in New York, the second in Tokyo.

In a New York hotel, an American and Japanese engineer met for the first time and introduced themselves to each other. Obviously the American went first: "Hello, my name is John, John Smith. Nice to meet you. I am an electrical engineer and — by the way — at the moment I am working for Kodak".

After two minutes of silence the Japanese says: "Hello, I am Toyota and my name is nobody". This joke may serve as an indicator of the American self-image as individualistic, self-confident and successful. The joke also implicitly constructs an image in which Japanese professionals are not individuals, and are neither self-confident nor successful.

Obviously, the Japanese in their turn have a pagoda full of jokes about Americans, such as this one. An American and a Japanese meet each other on a safari trip in the Kruger National Park (South Africa). They take a walk together, somewhat outside the safe tourist path. All of a sudden they are confronted by a hungry-looking lion. The American immediately starts running and running. But the Japanese does not move and carefully opens his black leather briefcase in order to take out a pair of running shoes. Looking back at the Japanese the American starts shouting: "Come on, run for your life, leave those running shoes behind; you don't have a chance anyhow to run faster than the lion does." The Japanese thinks, waits a bit and says politely: "The one I have to outrun is not the lion, but you." This joke may serve as an indicator of the Japanese self-image as smart, civilised and competitive, whereas the American is seen as impulsive, thoughtless and pushy.

These jokes not only demonstrate the well-known fact handed down to us by social psychology that the image of a neighbouring people is constructed as a negative counterpart of one's own image, on the basis of which the in-group people can identify themselves more easily with their own self-image (Fink 1991: 453). But the jokes should also show that the construction of cultural identity involves at least two parts: the in-group and the out-group, the perception of oneself and the perception of the other (*Selbstwahrnehmung* and *Fremdwahrnehmung*). The Japanese looks at the American from a Japanese perspective, and *vice versa*.

In our times, it is of great importance to have an adequate, well-balanced insight into the cultural identity of a particular nation. A distorted view can significantly hamper understanding and adequate communication with citizens of that nation. Very often political conflicts and wars find their deep origin in distorted visions of one's own and the foreign identity.

In his latest collection of essays, Ernest Gellner (1994: 45) asks for serious attention to be paid to cultural identity:

> [It] is not a delusion, excogitated by muddled romantics, disseminated by irresponsible extremists, and used by egotistical privileged classes to befuddle the masses, and to hide their true interests from them. Its appeal is rooted in the real conditions of modern life, and cannot be conjured away, either by sheer goodwill and the preaching of a spirit of universal brotherhood, or by the incarceration of the extremists. We have to understand those roots, and live with their fruits, whether we like them or not.

Much scholarly research and journalistic writing about cultural identity takes as its point of departure well-established stereotypes, which sometimes do not exceed the level of the type of jokes mentioned above. These writings are normally based on an ontological belief in the specificity of a certain community. What alternative can we offer which would make it possible to overcome the old essentialist approach to identity and to by-pass the new extreme relativism which says that identity escapes every attempt at definition?

In order to understand the roots of cultural identity we need to understand the semantics of this very concept. For this, we do not have to go through the work of Sigmund Freud, George Herbert Mead, Erik Eriksson, Talcott Parsons, Jürgen Habermas and others to come up with a well-grounded description of identity. William Bloom (1990: 53) offers an elegant summary of current thinking, concluding that

> ...identification is an inherent and unconscious behavioural imperative in all individuals. Individuals actively seek to identify in order to achieve psychological security, and they actively seek to maintain, protect and bolster identity in order to maintain and enhance this psychological security which is a *sine qua non* of personality stability and emotional well-being. This imperative works from infancy through adulthood and old age. Moreover, identifications can be shared, with the result that individuals who share the same

> identification will tend to act in concert in order to protect or enhance their shared identity.

These are beautiful words with which one can easily agree. But the problem arises when we try to describe somebody's personal identity or the cultural identity of a particular people. Talking about personal and cultural identity can be tricky, especially if wishful thinking, stereotypes and a strong belief in the overstressed uniqueness of a particular person or country are the only guidelines.

For the concept of cultural identity, this implies that the cultural identity of a particular group or people is only partly determined by their national identity. Cultural identity is a broader concept than national identity. In this respect I subscribe to the views of E.J. Hobsbawm (1990: 182), who emphasises that belonging to a particular state "is only one way in which people describe their identity among many others which they use for this purpose, as occasion demands". Whether it is justified to conclude on the basis of that argument that the power of nationalism is receding around the globe, as Hobsbawm does, is another matter and seems to be wishful thinking. The struggle between localisation and nationalisation on the one hand and globalisation on the other is not yet decided. Based on recent political developments in some parts of the world — on the wars, fighting and severe discussions which are going on — my forecast would differ from that of Hobsbawm. I shall return to this point in the next section.

Often, cultural identity is seen as a range of characteristics that are unique for a particular culture and "innate" to a specific people. The Japanese scholarly tradition of *Nihonjinron* (Studies about Japaneseness) is a typical example of this approach (for a critical survey see e.g. Dale 1986; Yoshino 1992; Segers 1996). But in other cultures, too, many examples of this type of thinking can be found, and in many cases not only practised long ago but even nowadays, and not only primarily in the periphery of scholarship, either. Another view suggests that cultural identity has a structuralist character where a particular culture is seen as consisting of a set of characteristics which are all related to each other, more or less independently of the people who produce that culture.

The alternative to the conception of "identity" as a set of unique or structural characteristics is the idea of identity as a *construction.* Within such a constructive framework, the cultural identity of a particular nation or of a certain ethnic group within that nation can be attached to three factors: (1) the statistics concerning that nation or group at a given time in history, (2) the programming of the mind within a particular community on the basis of which the cultural identity by the in-group is being constructed, (3) the way in which people from outside conduct a process of selection, interpretation and evaluation concerning the specificity of the in-group, in other words: the outside image of the cultural identity of a foreign nation or group. The relationship between these three elements is a dynamic one. Ideally, the (scholarly) construction of identity should be based on all three actors (for a more extensive explanation, see Segers 1992).

What are statistics with respect to cultural identity? They are "facts," figures, which can be found in statistical handbooks concerning a particular country or ethnic group and which determine to a great extent the programming of the mind of a given society, and *vice versa.* For instance: they list the total number of citizens of a country, the size of the country, the gross national product, average income, percentage of unemployment, the number of museums, or the number of books produced.

Since we do not have direct access to the way in which peoples' minds are programmed, we have to resort to visible indicators thereof. We have to look at the style of conduct and communication in a particular community, to use Gellner's (1983: 92) more pragmatically oriented definition of culture. This style of conduct and the communication of the citizens of a state or the members of a particular ethnic group is their visible cultural identity. This visible cultural identity can be suppressed or thematised by opinion leaders (individuals and institutions) within that particular community. It is impossible to talk about cultural identity without taking into consideration which spokesmen/spokeswomen are defining it and along which lines this happens.

The third element of the identity triangle consists of the constructions made by people, usually opinion leaders or important institutions from outside, concerning the conduct and communication of the people inside.

It would be somewhat misleading to think that the idea of considering national or cultural identity as a construction originated in system theory (from Ludwig von Bertalanffy to Niklas Luhmann). Scholars working outside this domain have arrived at more or less the same conclusion. An interesting example is Benedict Anderson, who coined the term "imagined community." In an attempt to define the concept of nation, he states:

> ...it is an imagined political community — and imagined as both inherently limited and sovereign. It is *imagined* because the members of even the smallest nation will never know most of their fellow-members, meet them, or even hear of them, yet in the minds of each lives the image of their communion (Anderson 1983: 15; original emphasis).

I am not saying that Anderson's "imagination" is equivalent to Luhmann's "construction". The similarity is to be sought in the emphasis on the mental processing of a particular object. To consider cultural identity as a construction means that it is a mental conception which may vary according to the constructor, the time and place of construction. This implies that it is impossible to speak about *the* cultural identity of a community. In theory there are as many cultural identities of a given community as there are times, places and people that construct those identities. This should not prevent scholars from undertaking the necessary task of describing and systematising the common characteristics based on those several existing identities. Moreover, in reality we are usually confronted with only one *dominant* construction of the cultural identity of a particular country.

The most recent development concerning the concept of cultural identity has been the addition of the prefix "post" as an attempt to resolve the paradox between globalisation and nationalisation. The term "postnational identity" is coined in a book by Dewandre and Lenoble (1994). It implies the paradox between the necessity of the construction of one political European identity based on the development of the European

Union as against the promotion of the cultural distinctiveness of the several European nations and regions: one political identity versus many distinctive cultural identities, all living under the same roof of a house called postnational identity. This concept of postnational identity seems rather utopian, prompted by wishful thinking "from Brussels with love" (for more extensive criticism, see Picht 1994; for an extensive discussion on European cultural identity, see Segers and Viehoff 1999b).

There is, however, yet another caveat to be considered, one which in particular applies to cross-cultural or comparative studies concerning cultural identity. Richard Handler (1994: 27) has formulated the following reasonable objection in this respect: "Identity has become a salient scholarly and cultural construct in mid-twentieth century, particularly in social-scientific scholarship in the United States. Its prominence in that context, however, does not mean that the concept can be applied unthinkingly to other places and times."

Western notions of collective identity are grounded in individualist metaphors. Attributes of boundedness, continuity, uniqueness, and homogeneity which are ascribed to human beings are ascribed to social groups as well. This leads Handler (1994: 33) to the following conclusion: "Thus it seems to me that if other cultures imagine personhood and human activity in terms other than those we use, we should not expect them to rely on Western individualistic assumptions in describing social collectivities."

Clifford Geertz (1980: 24-25) tells an anecdote which reveals a completely different approach to boundaries and the essence of a community. It concerns the Balinese state, where the rulers did not compete for boundaries (territory) but for the allegiance of men:

> The Dutch, who wanted...to get the boundary between two petty princedoms straight once and for all, called in the princes concerned and asked them where indeed the borders lay. Both agreed that the border of princedom A lay at the farthest point from which a man could still see the swamps, and the border of princedom B lay at the point from which a man could

> still see the sea. Had they, then, never fought over the land between, from which one could see neither swamp nor sea? "Mijnheer," one of the old princes replied, "we had much better reason to fight with one another than these shabby hills."

Cultural Identity Squeezed by Globalisation? Concerning the Vitality of the Local: The Cultural Turn

The scholarly focus on cultural identity is confronted with two serious objections. First of all, there is the fear that research into the specificity of a particular culture invokes nationalistic tendencies. Research into cultural identity could reinforce "old-fashioned nationalism," based on the fact that it could result in determining the "unique" characteristics of a certain community or people. I am not so sure about whether this objection is justified. The outcome of a research project is strongly dependent on the status of the research methodology employed. If the methodology is based on an ontological understanding of the innate characteristics of a particular culture, the research results will reveal the true colours of this metaphysical basis. However, if the methodology is based on the idea that cultural identity should be defined by the triangle of characteristics explained above, then the danger of stressing the innate uniqueness of a culture is absent. In addition, the fact that we consider cultural identity to be a construction rather than a given adds to the rejection of the imminent danger involved.

A second objection which is levelled against the concept of cultural identity concerns the idea that the current globalisation tendency in the world will destroy most parts of the specificity of a particular local culture. It is the famous adage concerning the big unknown world becoming a small familiar village. From a superficial point of view, the village theory looks good and it has strong advocates, starting with its guru Marshall McLuhan. But let us take a more refined look at the globalisation problem.

If we examine the interrelations between cultures now, at the beginning of a new millennium, we can perceive two contradictory but strong tendencies:

> ...on the one hand, there is the search for cultural authenticity, the return to origins, the need to preserve minor languages, pride in particularisms, admiration for cultural self-sufficiency and maintenance of national traditions; on the other hand, we find the spread of a uniform world culture, the emergence of supranational myths and the adoption of similar lifestyles in widely different settings. Modern technological societies have generated a transnational, composite, mass culture with its own language whose linguistic imprint is already universally evident (OECD 1989: 16).

This paradox between localisation and globalisation can be found in many parts of the world and in many different ways. Concerning European unification, for example, Philip Schlesinger (1994: 325) has aptly described this paradox as follows:

> On the one hand, the difficult search for a transcendent unity by the EC — one which must recognise component differences — throws the nation-state into question from above, arguably contributing to crises of national identity. The political and economic developments in the integration process, however, are out of phase with the cultural: what European identity *might be* still remains an open question. On the other hand, the ethno-nationalist awakenings in the former communist bloc and current developments within western Europe — whether neo-nationalist separatisms or racist nationalisms — tend to reaffirm the principle of the nation-state as a locus of identity and of political control.

Schlesinger correctly points the finger at the ultimate paradox of the last decade of the twentieth century: the clash between the indigenous, inner culture of a particular community, on one hand, and the global outer culture of a certain constructed *ensemble* of a number of communities, on the other. On a programmatic level, this paradox goes under different catchwords and slogans, including: localisation or nationalisation versus globalisation, "small is beautiful" versus "big is necessary and inevitable," or individual responsibility versus centralist efficiency. On a pragmatic level, these slogans relate to conflicts at several distinctive levels: between an individual and his or her direct working environment (say, a university department), between a department and a new faculty structure, between the faculty and the development of a new government system, between a national government and the regulations of the European Union.

The paradox between localisation and globalisation has appeared under a great number of different labels. William Butler Yeats long ago said that our world is caught between the two eternities of race and soul. Race: reflecting the tribal past, and soul: anticipating the cosmopolitan future. Closer to our time, Benjamin Barber in a well-known book (2000: 21) has labelled both sides of this paradox "Jihad" and "McWorld", respectively.

The Jihad trend, named after the Islamic fundamentalist movement, stands for extreme localisation: the Balkanisation of nation states in which culture is pitted against culture, people against people, tribe against tribe. It is a movement against interdependence, against integrated markets, against modernity and against modern globalised technological developments.

On the other side, McWorld, according to Barber, paints the future in shimmering pastels,

> a busy portrait of onrushing economic, technological and ecological forces that demand integration and uniformity and that mesmerise peoples everywhere with fast music, fast computers, and fast food — MTV, Macintosh and McDonalds — pressing nations into one homogeneous global theme park, one McWorld tied together by communications, information, entertainment, and commerce (Barber 2000: 31).

Barber notices that the Jihad tendency pursues a bloody politics of identity, while McWorld strives for a bloodless economics of profit. With regard to the latter movement (McWorld), Barber sums up in a bleak observation:

> Music, video, theatre, books and theme parks — the new churches of a commercial civilisation in which malls are the public squares and suburbs the neighbourless neighbourhoods — are all constructed

> as image exports creating a common world taste around common logos, advertising slogans, stars, songs, brand names, jingles and trade marks. Hard power yields to soft, while ideology is transmuted into a kind of videology that works through sound bites and film clips. Videology is fuzzier and less dogmatic than traditional political ideology; it may as a consequence be far more successful in instilling the novel values required for global markets to succeed (Barber 2000: 25).

It is clear that Barber holds an extremely negative view of a future in which localisation and globalisation will go hand in hand and reinforce each other constantly. But is it all that sombre? Need it be all that pessimistic? Let us first consider what is really understood by globalisation, this fashionable container concept.

Arjun Appadurai (1990: 6-7) has suggested that globalisation consists of five dimensions, five cultural flows which cross each other at various levels in many parts of the world:

> Firstly, there are *ethnoscapes* produced by flows of people: tourists, immigrants, refugees, exiles and guestworkers. Secondly, there are *technoscapes,* the machinery and plant flows produced by multinational and national corporations and government agencies. Thirdly, there are *finanscapes,* produced by the rapid flows of money in the currency stock exchanges. Fourthly, there are *mediascapes,* the repertoires of images and information, the flows which are produced and distributed by newspapers, magazines, television and film. Fifthly, there are *ideoscapes,* linked to flows of images which are associated with state or counterstate movement ideologies which are comprised of elements of the Western Enlightenment world-view — images of democracy, freedom, welfare, rights, etc.

It is tempting to speculate on the question: What will be the strongest force in the near future: localisation or globalisation, Jihad or McWorld? Obviously, the question is too tricky to be answered in a couple of pages. In any case, both tendencies with their completely opposite aims exist in the same place and at the same time. It is difficult, however, as has been attempted in a number of publications, to come up with convincing arguments implying that the globalisation tendency will be a much stronger force than the localisation tendency in the near future.

The well-known Japanese economist and consultant Kenichi Ohmae could be mentioned as a representative of the globalisation movement. His recent book *The End of the Nation State. The Rise of Regional Economies* (2000) has become an international global academic bestseller. In this book Ohmae advocates the theory that nation states have already lost their role as — in his words — "meaningful units of participation in the global economy of today's borderless world." What are his arguments for his theory? He comes up with four reasons, which I shall give in his own words:

> First of all, the uncomfortable truth is that, in terms of the global economy, nation states have become little more than bit actors. They may originally have been, in their mercantilist phase, independent, powerfully efficient engines of wealth creation. More recently, however, as the downward-ratcheting logic of electoral politics has placed a death grip on their economies, they have become — first and foremost — remarkably inefficient engines of wealth distribution.
>
> Secondly, and more to the point, the nation state is increasingly a nostalgic fiction. It makes even less sense today, for example, than it did a few years ago to speak of Italy or Russia or China as a single economic unit. Each is a motley combination of territories with vastly different needs and vastly different abilities to contribute.
>
> Third, when you look closely at the goods and services now produced and traded around the world, as well as the companies responsible for them, it is no easy matter to attach to them an accurate national label. Is an automobile sold under an American marque really a US product when a large percentage of its components comes from abroad?
>
> Finally, when economic activity aggressively wears a national label these days, that tag is usually present neither for the sake of accuracy nor out of concern for the economic well-being of individual consumers. It is

> there primarily as a mini-flag of cheap nationalism — that is, as a jingoistic celebration of nationhood that places far more value on emotion-grabbing symbols than on real, concrete improvements in quality of life (Ohmae 2000: 207-208).

Another example frequently used to prove the supremacy of globalisation is what has come to be called Americanisation. Many scholars and journalists go so far as to suggest that those two concepts are synonymous. By Americanisation is meant the spreading of American culture (or what is regarded as such) into all corners of the world: Hollywood films, American TV soaps, American Bestsellers, American cars, Americanised food. There are two main problems with substituting globalisation with Americanisation. First of all, you could question the extent to which the elements just mentioned really are representative of the culture of the U.S.A. It is altogether possible that, in constructing these art forms, parts of the value system and some of the artistic norms of the so-called non-American global periphery were seriously involved. As far as I know, no serious research has yet tackled these or similarly structured questions. Secondly, it should be stated that the reception of these so-called American cultural products might differ according to the specificity of the receiving culture. Important conventions which make up that specificity structure the direction and the depth of Americanisation. I would venture the hypothesis that Americanisation has been carried out differently in every member state of the EU.

Ralf Dahrendorf (1994) may be introduced as a representative of the localisation theory. After his fine analysis of the future of the nation state, he remarks:

> Auf absehbare Zeit wird der Nationalstaat der Rahmen individueller Rechte und die Aktionseinheit der internationalen Beziehungen bleiben. Das gilt auch in und für Europa. Der Nationalstaat wird hier und da angenagt und angekratzt, bleibt aber in seinem Kern durch neuere Entwicklungen unberührt. Er ist auch der Raum, in dem Menschen Zugehörigkeitsgefühle empfinden können. Einstweilen haben wir noch nichts besseres erfunden als den heterogenen Nationalstaat.

To phrase this in other well-known German words: "Europa ist ein Kopfgeburt und die Regionen sprechen das Herz an."

Thus, localisation and globalisation are two sides of the same coin. On the one hand we can observe that "nationalism is back today with a vengeance all over the world" (Radhakrishnan 1992: 83), from Canada to India, from the former USSR to Iraq, from Japan to Turkey. For the time being, I am one of those who believe that nationalisation or localisation will dominate globalisation, at least for the foreseeable future, and not only outside western Europe, as some critics want us to believe, but also to a considerable extent in the countries that belong to the key group members of the EU. In this context Helmut Dubiel (1994: 896) points to new forms of German nationalism: "sei es des inszenierten Lobs des Vaterlandes, der wahlkampfstrategischen Instrumentalisierung nationaler Ressentiments und des besoffenen Rufs 'Deutschland den Deutschen'". But similar tendencies are alive and well in many other countries of the EU.

On the other hand, we can see the severe impact of the five cultural flows of globalisation. Globalisation will persist as an extremely strong tendency and its strength may even increase. But in the decades to come the nationalisation tendency will be able to adopt and adapt many global trends. Globalisation will be nationalised to a great extent. Let me add here that the threat to the nation, to nationalisation or localisation, does not primarily consist of globalisation tendencies, but rather the threat comes also from within the nation itself. We could think here of several well-known ruptures, such as in Canada, Belgium, Spain, or in former countries such as the USSR, Czechoslovakia and Yugoslavia, and in a way, we could add paradoxically the unification of Germany, where the following joke could be heard shortly after the unification: an East German says to a West German: "We are one people now!" The West German replies: "We too!"

Understanding the complicated paradox contained within localisation *versus* globalisation is an object that is highly interesting and rewarding for a number of scholarly disciplines. Understanding this paradox, however, can only be achieved through the central concept of cultural identity. This very concept represents the ultimate reason for the serious conflicts between the smaller community and the larger constructed *ensemble* or between two or more smaller communities.

When applying the concept of cultural identity, another fallacy should be deconstructed: The old opposition between the West and the Rest. This opposition is in many cases the hidden, invisible basis upon which many theories are being based. This fallacy of cultural imperialism considers — consciously or not — the West (which often simply means the United States) to be the centre and "the rest" to be the periphery. Localising movements are performed on the periphery, globalising trends are realised in the centre, such as the Newconomy network and successful and appealing TV programmes.

In order to avoid cultural imperialism, the simplistic centre-periphery oppositional geography should be replaced by a more realistic model of regions. Sinclair *et al.* (2000: 301) present a more realistic scenario, that of creolisation:

> Instead of the image of "the West" at the centre dominating the peripheral "Third World" with an outward flow of cultural products, we see the world as divided into a number of regions which each have their own internal dynamics as well as their global ties. Although primarily based on geographic realities, these regions are also defined by common cultural, linguistic, and historical connections which transcend physical space. Such a dynamic, regionalist view of the world helps us to analyse in a more nuanced way the intricate and multi-directional flows of television across the globe.

We could now ask why there is this focus on culture and cultural identity. In a moment of unsophisticated generalisation, you could say that half the Library of Congress consists of books which more or less deal with this very topic. But there are at least two reasons that make it necessary to concentrate systematically on these topics and to reinterpret them according to ever-changing social circumstances. The scholarly reason is — as we have seen — that culture is still too often conceived of as an ontological concept, which leads directly to unjustified claims of superiority, dominance and ultimately atrocious wars. These wars and other evil developments immediately lose their *raison d'être* and their justification if culture is seen within a systemic and constructivist context.

The second reason is based on the socio-political relevance of the concept of culture around the turn of the millennium. A recent book by Samuel P. Huntington (1997), an academic bestseller in the United States since 11 September 2001, convincingly argues for the central role which cultures play now and will play in the next decades. His general thesis is that the communist world collapsed in the late 1980s, which meant the end of the Cold War, the end of a world divided by ideological, political and/or economic principles. Obviously, the end of the Cold War does not mean either eternal or temporary peace, as some utopian voices said right after the fall of the Iron Curtain in 1989. Another distinction quickly arose: the cultural distinction. This implies "...that culture and cultural identities, which at the broadest level are civilisational identities, are shaping the patterns of cohesion, disintegration, and conflict in the post-Cold War world.... The most important groupings of states are no longer the three blocs of the Cold War but rather the world's...major civilisations" (Huntington 1997: 20-21).

Huntington distinguishes nine different cultures: Western, Latin American, African, Islamic, Sinic, Hindu, Orthodox, Buddhist and Japanese. We can, of course, disagree with Huntington about the number of civilisations he distinguishes or about his definition of each civilisation. This boils down to questions such as why is Japan recognised as a distinct civilisation and Korea is not? Is it justifiable to define "African civilisation" as sub-Saharan including the country of South Africa? Regarding this question, Huntington sums up some of the problems himself:

> The north of the African continent and its east coast belong to Islamic civilisation. Historically, Ethiopia constituted a civilisation of its own. Elsewhere European imperialism and settlements brought elements of Western civilisation. In South Africa Dutch, French, and then English settlers created a multifragmented European culture. Most significantly, European imperialism brought

> Christianity to most of the continent south of the Sahara. Throughout Africa tribal identities are pervasive and intense, but Africans are also increasingly developing a sense of African identity, and conceivably sub-Saharan Africa could cohere into a distinct civilisation, with South Africa possibly being its core state (Huntington 1997: 47).

Whatever the justification for the number and specificity of the several civilisations may be, the message is clear: the most important distinctions between peoples are no longer ideological, political or economic, but cultural. To quote Huntington once more: "In this new world the most pervasive, important, and dangerous conflicts will not be between social classes, rich and poor, or other economically defined groups, but between peoples belonging to different cultural entities" (ibid.: 28). And Vaclav Havel (1994) stated along the same lines: "Cultural conflicts are increasing and are more dangerous today than at any time in history".

Conclusion: The Cultural Turn

Looking at the contemporary world, be it a region, a nation-state or an ethnic group within that nation, implies looking at a complicated wrestling game between globalisation and localisation. In order to understand the fact that in many cases localisation will be the winner, we should pay attention to a neglected force: the importance of the cultural factor which is like a home crowd, always in favour of the local wrestler. Whereas the globalisation tendency is a force mainly driven by technological and economic flows in one form or another, the localisation tendency is based on cultural identity. In many cultures globalising tendencies are being localised to a certain degree, as we have seen above. To what extent? That depends on the strength of a particular cultural identity.

The fact that cultural identity is the decisive factor in constructing the specificity of a certain society could be called the "Cultural Turn." This means, among other things, that contemporary political and social developments, and also economic and technological developments, whether they have a global or rather a local nature, can only be understood via the concept of cultural identity as it has been defined above.

Without an interest in and an understanding of the major differences and the striking similarities between cultures, no adequate construction can be made of modern civilisations or of groups of people within those civilisations.

In most parts of today's world, cultural borders no longer coincide with national borders; cultural diversity within one nation-state is more the rule than the exception. To give just one example, until the late 1960s the Netherlands was a state with hardly any ethnic diversity, a rather homogeneous state despite its international history, like many others in Western Europe at that time. On 1 January 1991, the four largest cities in the country (Amsterdam, Rotterdam, The Hague and Utrecht) had a total population of almost two million. Of those two million people, more than 400,000 (21%) were people of non-Dutch descent (i.e. mainly Turks, Moroccans and people of Surinam and Netherlands Antilles ethnic origin) (OECD 1992: 71).

All over the world, a growing number of severe political and ethnic conflicts have arisen, originating in an imbalance in the relationships between the three cultural factors in the triangle, as explained above. The nature of this imbalance may vary from place to place: it may be a wrong, one-sided selection of the material statistics, an inadequate and too strong self-image or a distorted look at the foreign partner. The nature of the imbalance may be different, but the result is always the same: cultural relativism gives way to cultural absolutism.

It goes without saying that the current political situation in many parts of the world implies that the study of culture and of cultural identity has become an important item for scholarship. Issues related to culture and cultural identity seem to be and will stay *the* issues of the coming decades of the new millennium. The "Cultural Turn" will continue to bare its teeth. In one of its many reports now more than fifteen years ago, the OECD (1987: 43) wrote:

> Awareness of an ethnic or regional identity, or of a minority status, can be hidden for many decades by the myth of national unity and identity, of ethnic homogeneity, of mass culture or planetary culture. It

> can also be hidden by an analysis in terms of social groups or the evocation of proletarian internationalism. Today, ethnic or racial claims, nationalist or regionalist movements, and movements for independence or autonomy, have broken up communities which were merely a facade.

This process of breaking up seemingly homogeneous communities and the consequent struggle for identity will undoubtedly continue for a number of years in many parts of the world. To study this process from a literary and cultural point of view offers as many challenges as possibilities for literary and cultural studies in the years to come.

I have been trying to demonstrate in this article that the English in the following *English* nursery rhyme:

> The Germans live in Germany, the Romans live in Rome,
> the Turkeys live in Turkey; but the English live at home.

can be substituted by any other nation or any ethnic group living in a particular nation. As Hofstede (1994: 235) has observed:

> Everybody looks at the world from behind the windows of a cultural home and everybody prefers to act as if people from other countries have something special about them (a national character) but home is normal. Unfortunately, there is no normal position in cultural matters. This is an uncomfortable message, as uncomfortable as Galileo Galilei's claim in the seventeenth century that the Earth is not the centre of the Universe.

To conclude with a variation on Hobsbawm (1990: 183): the owl of Minerva which brings wisdom flies out at dusk. It is a good sign that it is now circling around cultural and literary identity.

REFERENCES

Anderson, Benedict 1983: *Imagined Communities. Reflections on the Origin and Spread of Nationalism.* London: Verso.

Appadurai, Arjun 1990: Disjuncture and Difference in the Global Cultural Economy. In Mike Featherstone ed.: *Global Culture, Nationalism, Globalization and Modernity.* London: Sage.

Barber, Benjamin 2000: Jihad vs. McWorld. In Frank J. Lechner and John Boli ed.: *The Globalization Reader.* Malden, Mass. and Oxford: Blackwell.

Bloom, William 1990: *Personal Identity, National Identity and International Relations.* Cambridge: Cambridge University Press.

Dahrendorf, Ralf 1994: Die Zukunft des Nationalstaates. In *Merkur: Zeitschrift für Europäisches Denken.* 48:9-10. 751-761.

Dale, Peter 1986: *The Myth of Japanese Uniqueness.* London: Croom Helm.

Dewandre, Nicole and Jacques Lenoble ed. 1994: *Projekt Europa. Postnationale Identität: Grundlage für eine europäische Demokratie.* Berlin: Schelzky & Jeep.

Dubiel, Helmut 1994: Über moralische Souveränität, Erinnerung und Nation. *Merkur: Deutsche Zeitschrift für Europäisches Denken.* 48:9-10. 884-897.

Featherstone, Mike ed. 1990: *Global Culture. Nationalism, Globalization and Modernity.* London: Sage.

Fink, Gonthier-Louis 1991: Das Bild des Nachbarvolkes im Spiegel der deutschen und der französischen Hochaufklärung (1750-1789). In Bernhard Giesen: *Nationale und kulturelle Identität. Studien zur Entwicklung des kollektiven Bewusstseins in der Neuzeit.* Frankfurt/M: Suhrkamp.

Geertz, Clifford 1980: *Negara. The Theatre State in Nineteenth-Century Bali.* Princeton: Princeton University Press.

Gellner, Ernest 1983: *Nations and Nationalism.* Oxford: Blackwell.

Gellner, Ernest 1994: *Encounters with Nationalism.* Oxford: Blackwell.

Giesen, Bernhard 1991: *Nationale und kulturelle Identität. Studien zur Entwicklung des kollektiven Bewusstseins in der Neuzeit.* Frankfurt/M: Suhrkamp.

Handler, Richard 1994: Is "Identity" a Useful Cross-Cultural Concept? In John R. Gillis: *Commemorations. The Politics of National Identity.* Princeton, N.J.: Princeton University Press.

Hastings, Adrian 1997: *The Construction of Nationhood. Ethnicity, Religion and Nationalism.* Cambridge: Cambridge University Press.

Havel, Vaclav 1994: The New Measure of Man. *New York Times.* 8 July.

Hobsbawm, Eric 1990: *Nations and Nationalism Since 1780. Programme, Myth, Reality.* Cambridge: Cambridge University Press.

Hofstede, Geert 1994 (1991): *Cultures and Organizations. Software of the Mind.* Hammersmith, London: HarperCollins.

Huntington, Samuel P. 1997: *The Clash of Civilizations and the Remaking of World Order.* New York: Touchstone.

Hutchinson, John and Anthony D. Smith ed. 1994: *Nationalism.* Oxford and New York: Oxford University Press.

Jepperson, Ronald L. and Ann Swidler 1994: What Properties of Culture Should We Measure? *Poetics.* 22. 359-371.

Lechner, Frank J. and John Boli ed. 2000: *The Globalization Reader.* Malden, Mass. and Oxford: Blackwell.

Luhmann, Niklas 1988 (1984): *Soziale Systeme. Grundriss einer allgemeinen Theorie.* Frankfurt/M: Suhrkamp.

OECD 1987: *Multicultural Education.* Paris: Organisation for Economic Co-operation and Development; Centre for Educational Research and Innovation.

OECD 1989: *One School, Many Cultures.* Paris: Organisation for Economic Co-operation and Development; Centre for Educational Research and Innovation.

OECD 1992. *Trends in International Migration.* Paris: Organisation for Economic Co- operation and Development; Centre for Educational Research and Innovation.

Ohmae, Kenichi 1995: *The End of the Nation State. The Rise of Regional Economics.* New York: Free Press.

Parker, Andrew, Mary Ruso, Doris Sommer and Patricia Yaeger 1992: *Nationalisms and Sexualities.* New York and London: Routledge.

Picht, Robert 1994: Europa — aber was versteht man darunter? Aufforderung zur Überprüfung der Denkmuster. *Merkur. Deutsche Zeitschrift für europäisches Denken.* 48:9-10. 850-866.

Radakrishnan, R. 1992: Nationalism, Gender, and the Narrative of Identity. In Parker et al.: *Nationalisms and Sexualities.* New York and London: Routledge.

Rusch, Gebhard 1991: Zur Systemtheorie und Phänomenologie von Literatur. Eine holistische Perspektive. *SPIEL. Siegener Periodikum zur Internationalen Empirischen Literaturwissenschaft.* 10. 305-339.

Schein, Edgar H.1992: *Organizational Culture and Leadership.* San Francisco: Jossey-Bass.

Schlesinger, Philip 1994 (1992): Europeanness: A New Cultural Battlefield? In John Hutchinson and Anthony D. Smith ed.: *Nationalism.* Oxford, New York: Oxford University Press.

Segers, Rien T. 1992: Research into Cultural Identity: A New Empirical Object. The Case of Japanese "Uniqueness" Between East and West. *SPIEL. Siegener Periodikum zur Internationalen Empirischen Literaturwissenschaft.* 11. 149-162.

Segers, Rien T. 1994: Japanese Cultural Identity and Reading Behavior. *The Japan Foundation Newsletter.* 22:1. 15-20.

Segers, Rien T. 1996: *Sleutelboek Japan.* Amsterdam: Balans.

Segers, Rien T. & Reinhold Viehoff 1999a: Die Konstruktion Europas: Überlegungen zum Problem der Kultur in Europa. In Rien T. Segers & Reinhold Viehoff hrsg.: *Kultur Identität Europa. Über die Schwierigkeiten und Möglichkeiten einer Konstruktion.* Frankfurt/M: Suhrkamp.

Segers, Rien T. & Reinhold Viehoff hrsg. 1999b: *Kultur Identität Europa.*

Über die Schwierigkeiten und Möglichkeiten einer Konstruktion. Frankfurt/M: Suhrkamp.

Sevänen, Erkki 2001: Art as an Autopoietic Sub-System of Modern Society. *Theory, Culture & Society.* 18:1. 75-103.

Sinclair, John, Elizabeth Jacka and Stuart Cunningham 2000: Peripheral Vision. In Frank J. Lechner and John Boli ed.: *The Globalization Reader.* Malden, Mass. and Oxford: Blackwell.

Tötösy de Zepetnek, Steven 1992: Systemic Approaches to Literature: An Introduction with Selected Bibliographies. *Canadian Review of Comparative Literature / Revue Canadienne de Littérature Comparée.* 19. 21-93.

Yoshino, Kosaku 1992: *Cultural Nationalism in Contemporary Japan. A Sociological Enquiry.* London and New York: Routledge.

PART TWO

Europeanisation and Globalisation in Northern Europe

3

Changing Images of Europe and the Preconditions for Cross-Border Cooperation on the External Borders of the European Union

ILKKA LIIKANEN

Introduction

The end of the Cold War has dramatically changed the image of Europe and its borders. The re-conceptualisation of borders and cross-border interaction has been particularly profound in the case of Finland and its eastern borderline. In terms of international politics the border has lost its meaning as a dividing line between two rival social and political systems, the communist and the capitalist — or as a "Finlandised" gray zone between them. But this has not meant that the Finnish-Russian border has been stripped of its supranational definitions. Since 1995, the Finnish eastern border has been the only land border between the European Union and the Russian Federation. In consequence, the border has become the object of a considerable range of "Europeanisation", and cross-border interaction has been re-conceptualised in terms of European integration and EU politics. This, in turn, raises the question: What kind of preconditions for cross-border co-operation do the new rivalling conceptualisations of Europe hand down for local actors on the external borders of the EU?

Throughout the post-war period the Finnish eastern border was heavily guarded on both sides. Co-operation and trade across the border between Finland and the Soviet Union was administered by bilateral agreements between the two states. After the collapse of the Soviet system the border is still heavily guarded but the forms of cross-border co-operation have changed and the scale of interaction has expanded considerably.

On one hand, new regional and local actors have taken an active role in cross-border co-operation. Nowadays, regional administrative units, economic enterprises and organisations of civil society co-operate directly with one another across the border. On the another hand, the co-operation across the Finnish-Russian border has become part of a broader dynamic of international relations (Eskelinen, Liikanen and Oksa 1999: 1-3). European integration and the reformation of the Russian state apparatus have turned Finnish and Russian Karelia into a field of experiment, and possibly even into an institutional model of co-operation between the European Union and the Russian Federation. The agreements and arrangements adopted on the Finnish-Russian border are today seen as part of the Northern Dimension of EU politics and as part of the renewal of Russian foreign and regional politics.

These changes have affected especially the formation of Euregio Karelia, the joint initiative of the Finnish border counties and the Karelian Republic. In connection with the EU's eastern enlargement, the initiative of building joint administrative structures for co-operation is gaining a broader European significance. The institutional forms adopted will generate a model or a set of experiences that will be carefully reviewed when European border policies and policies towards neighbouring areas are reorganised as the eastern enlargement proceeds (Cronberg 2000: 170-183).

Whatever the fate and schedule of the enlargement process will be, regional co-operation across Finnish-Russian border will be increasingly seen within a broader European framework. Consequently, it is becoming of the utmost importance for the regions involved to analyse and recognise the ways in which this European frame is defined and understood within the political and scientific discussion concerning European integration. The different patterns of conceptualising European integration will designate different approaches to security and co-operation and thus will have far-reaching consequences for elaborating new models of regional cross-border co-operation (Paasi 2001: 7-28). Regardless of our attitude towards the so-called linguistic turn in social sciences, it seems quite clear that in this case the conceptualisations of Europe (and Russia) are powerful agents in the construction of the preconditions for regional cross-border co-operation on the Finnish-Russian border. In the following, an attempt is made to review and to comment on Western scholarly discussion of European integration and to analyse the varieties of attitudes towards Russia and cross-border co-operation with the different concepts of integration represent.

Federalism and Functionalism

My starting point is a critical stand on both the idealistic Euro-histories and the functionalist explanations which see the European Union as the logical and inevitable product of the large processes of economic and social change. In the present-day, public discussion and popular literature are often dominated by federalist Euro-histories, which present the process of integration as the advancement of peace and democracy and the fulfilment of the federalist thoughts of Monnet and Schumann, whom we are gradually recognising as the "great men" of the Union (Pinder 1995). Starting from the constitutive Schuman declaration of 1950, European economic integration has been accompanied by a visionary rhetoric of peace and democracy. But what actual role has been played by federalist ideas in the course of European integration?

There is some truth in the collegial joke often recounted by historians that the placing of the federalists at the centre of Euro-historiography results not from the significance of the group but from the fact that the clique has been so small and so insignificant that it has been the easiest target for historians to gather material on and to construct interpretations of. It is, indeed, quite obvious that the history of European federalism tells very little about the forces and strategies that have been advancing integration inside the national political communities. The federalists have never had any connection with mass politics and consequently they have played no role on the level at which the political will and the legitimation of the integration process has been achieved.

Aside from idealistic federalism a second popular pattern

in the conceptualisation of the integration process can be characterised as economic functionalism or even economic determinism. As already mentioned, the institutional development of European integration easily encourages us to think of the process in economic terms. And in everyday political discussion this may well be the most common way of looking at the development of the European Union — among both the proponents and the opponents of the integration process. There are the functionalists who see the EU as the logical response to the internationalisation of the economy and the formation of a "European common market". And there are the critics of globalisation, who see the EU as the grand agent of a globalising economy and the highest stage in the development of a faceless capitalist machine. (Milward 1997a).

According to Alan Milward, the origins of the Union have had little or nothing to do with either the functional imperatives of economic interdependence or the visions of a handful of federalist worthies. The post-war integration of Western Europe has not been a straightforward or smooth path leading to supranational sovereignty, but rather a means of reinvigorating national power and, indeed, a part of the programme aimed at "the rescue of the nation-state". It was within the framework of the nation-state that welfare politics were developed and the legitimacy of power re-established after the disaster of the Second World War. Even the supranational agreements and institutions that have been established were in the first place a means of promoting the post-war reconstruction of the nation-state. In Milward's vision the European Economic Community was essentially born out of the autonomous calculations of national states that the prosperity on which their domestic legitimacy rested would be enhanced by a customs union (Milward 1997b; Anderson 1997).

What kind of role is then left for cross-border cooperation in the federalist and functionalist visions of integration? Clearly, neither variety leaves any significant room for regional cross-border co-operation. The federalist vision tends to promote a top-down approach which does not encourage the role of regional actors, while functionalist views often bear traces of economic determinism which do not leave much room for politics in general or regional politics in particular.

European Values and European Identity

Today, the preconditions for European integration are often discussed in terms of identities and mental borders. It is argued that the weakness of the European Union lies, most of all, in the fact that the Union has not been successful in generating a common European identity, mythology, symbols, solidarity or devotion which might strengthen Europe as a community of values and encourage people to identify themselves as Europeans. Ethnic origins and nationalism are considered to be a stronger basis for identification — and the main obstacle to deepening integration and future enlargement.

Most recently, the view that there exists a conflict between national and European identity has been contested in at least two ways. According to the much discussed scenario described by Joseph Weiler, a deepening integration and a future enlargement of the European Union require the construction of a new kind of supranationalism. Supranationalist thinking subscribes to the idea that nations and nation-states will remain the principal bases of identification and identity construction. This means that European citizenship cannot be constructed by attempting to create a uniform identity for a single European community. Even in the future, European citizenship will be based on a diversity of national identities. Instead of an alternative European identification, its main essence will be founded on a commitment to "common European values." Instead of symbols such as flags, anthems and monuments, European citizenship will be based on common values such as human rights, the social ethos that has generated the welfare state, tolerance, and respect for minorities (Weiler 1999).

Supranationalism evidently provides a neat solution to the problem of overcoming the contradictions between a deepening European integration and the persistent legacies of national identification. It has, however, been noted that the concept of European values is more problematic than has been assumed in supranationalist thinking. European values can hardly be presented as a fixed set of ethical norms applicable to all times and places. The heritage of the European spirit should rather be understood by means of conceptual history as a tradition of constant redefinition, criticism, self-criticism and discussion concerning the adoption, modification and revision of common values according to the circumstances at hand (Sihvola 1998). As Bo Stråth puts it: "In short, Europe as a set of values, or as a region of shared history, has no clear demarcation. There are many competing claims to constitute its historical core, while the values inscribed in the concept are contested and contradictory" (Stråth 1999).

The idea that European political culture is based on contested norms and values turns on its head the vision that sees European boundaries as frontlines in the clash between fixed civilisations, the Western and the Eurasian. It reveals how the idea of a European community of values does not simply integrate people into a common European home: this idea also constructs new mental borders between us — the Europeans, and the others. Similarly, theories in which the enlargement of the EU into Eastern Europe is conceptualised as a return to Europe or to the West (Lauristin and Vihalemm 1997) represent a discourse where belonging and identification are largely based on the exclusion of the other. Belonging to a certain civilisation is understood as a given that can only seldom be changed. In this view the boundaries of Europe are to be accepted as the pre-given result of a centuries-old clash of cultures.

Considering the future of the European Union in terms of identity and as a struggle between national, European and Eurasian identification inevitably leads to more or less pessimistic prognoses concerning a deepening European integration and cross-border cooperation. At worst, the idea of a community held together by common values turns into a vision of a sharp-edged Europe that looks at cross-border cooperation through the prism of security risks.

Nation-building and Integration as Redefinitions of Political Space

A nightmare has been posed for the missionaries of European values and identity by the rise of nationalism and national movements in the Eastern European countries. They are seen as representing archaic and pre-modern "Eastern" traditions which constrast sharply with the idealised picture of modern Western society. In recent literature on European nation-building; this model of ideal modernisation and its enemies has been seriously challenged by the notion of the common roots of national movements, modern civil society and mass politics (Furet 1981; Hunt 1984). This interconnection between nationalism and political culture opens up a new perspective on the preconditions for cross-border cooperation in the European north.

John Breuilly has argued strongly in favour of the view that nationalism should primarily be considered in terms of politics and political modernisation. For Breuilly, nationalism does not mean only "civic religion" in the sense of legitimating the boundaries and power structures of a certain state. National movements have also functioned as oppositional forces striving to establish an alternative political community or to challenge the dynastic power structures in an existing one (Breuilly 1996; c.f. Anderson 1983). In regard to European integration this would mean that the heritage of nationalism does not necessarily imply maintaining pre-ordained ethnic and cultural boundaries but, on the contrary, may represent a readiness to act politically within an alternative framework and to mobilise in order to challenge the domestic power structure.

In the peculiar context of Finland it is obvious that the national and the political have been fused and that the national movement has fulfilled the dual mission of, on the one hand, legitimating and defending the autonomy of the political space and, on the other, challenging the power structure in this arena. How, then, will EU membership affect this political legacy of Finnish nationalism? In the latest European parliamentary elections the Finnish electorate was not highly interested in having their voice heard in the EU. This, however, was not necessarily due to the persistent legacies of nationalism in the sense of agreement over locating politics solely within a national frame. In contrast, it may express frustration deriving from the perception of the EU as a functioning political space in which power-holders can be challenged by hegemonic blocs that actualise the battle over representing the will of the people. Consequently, with regard to the EU we may conclude that, if nationalism is understood in terms of political modernisation, the major obstacle to European integration is not so much the persistent legacies of national identification. It is, rather, that the impartial development of EU-level political institutions prevents the formation of a functioning political space where rival hegemonic bloc can be incorporated; if this were to be the case, it would inspire identification with the European political community (cf. Tiilikainen 1998).

In a sense, the construction of the Northern Dimension of EU politics which Finland has advocated addresses the same questions. If we take seriously the argument put forward by Geoffrey Hosking that Russia is in fact for the first time going through the process of nation-building, it is evident that nationalism in post-Soviet Russia cannot simply be labelled as a struggle between "archaic" forces opposing modernisation and Western "civic" values (Hosking 1998: 482-486). Even in the case of Russia, the rise of nationalism can be understood as a form of political modernisation. Since the collapse of the Soviet Union, Russia has been struggling to construct a functioning political community (Liikanen 1999). In international relations there is no reason to exclude Russia *a priori* from the community of European values or to view it as an archaic Empire with an Eastern heritage. As a country of the European north, Russia, too, can be seen to be tackling the same problems of redefining the boundaries of national and multi-national political space. The elaboration of the Northern Dimension of EU politics makes it possible to see Russia as a partner in the process of redefining the mental borders of the political community called Europe.

The future of cross-border co-operation is, of course, equally dependent on how the broader frame is understood on the Russian side, and on how European integration and Russian nation-building are defined in the media and in official documents. The construction of Euregio Karelia and the way in which it is understood in the public debate will provide a unique chance to study this problem in concrete terms on both sides of the border.

REFERENCES

Anderson, Perry 1997: Under the Sign of the Interim. In Peter Gowan and Perry Anderson eds.: *The Question of Europe*. London: Verso.

Breuilly, John 1996: Approaches to Nationalism. In Gopal Balakrishnan ed.: *Mapping the Nation*. London: Verso.

Breuilly, John 1999: Nationalism and Modernity. In Johannes U. Müller and Bo Stråth (eds.), *Nationalism and Modernity*. EUI Working Paper HEC No. 99/1. Florence: European University Institute.

Cronberg, Tarja 2000: Euregios in the Making. The Case of Euregio Karelia. In Pirkkoliisa Ahponen and Pirjo Jukarainen eds.: *Tearing Down the Curtain, Opening the Gates. Northern Boundaries in Change*. Jyväskylä: Sophi.

Dann, Otto 1999: Modernity and the Project of Modern Nation. In Johannes U. Müller and Bo Stråth (eds.), *Nationalism and Modernity*. EUI Working Paper HEC No. 99/1. Florence: European University Institute.

Dann, Otto 1978: Nationalismus und sozialer Wandel in Deutschland 1806-1850. In Dann, Otto Hrsg.: *Nationalismus und sozialer Wandel*. Hamburg: Hoffmann und Campe.

Eskelinen, Heikki, Ilkka Liikanen and Jukka Oksa 1999: Introduction. In Heikki Eskelinen, Ilkka Liikanen and Jukka Oksa eds.: *Curtains of Iron and Gold. Reconstructing Borders and Scales of Interaction*. Aldershot: Ashgate.

Furet, F. 1981: *Interpreting the French Revolution*. Cambridge: Cambridge University Press.

Hobsbawm, E.J. 1997: An Afterword: European Union at the End of the Century. In Jytte Klausen and Louise A. Tilly eds.: *European Integration in Social and Historical Perspective*. Boston: Rowman and Littlefield Publishers.

Hosking, G. 1998: *Russia. People and Empire 1552–1917*. London: Fontana Press.

Hunt, L. 1984: *Politics, Culture and Class in the French Revolution*. London: Methuen.

Huntington, S.P. 1993: The Clash of Civilizations? *Foreign Affairs*. 72:2. 22-28.

Lauristin, M. & Vihalemm, P. eds. 1997: *Return to the Western World. Cultural and Political Perspectives on the Estonian Post-Communist Transition*. Tartu: Tartu University Press.

Liikanen, Ilkka 1995: *Fennomania ja kansa. Joukkojärjestäytymisen läpimurto ja Suomalaisen puolueen synty* [Fennomania and the People. The Breakthrough of Mass Organization and the Birth of the Finnish Party]. Historiallisia Tutkimuksia 191. Jyväskylä: Suomen Historiallinen Seura.

Liikanen, Ilkka 1999: The Political Construction of Identity. Reframing Mental Borders in Russian Karelia. In Heikki Eskelinen, Ilkka Liikanen and

Jukka Oksa eds.: *Curtains of Iron and Gold. Reconstructing Borders and Scales of Interaction.* Aldershot: Ashgate.

Milward, Alan S. 1997a: The Social Bases of Monetary Union. In Peter Gowan and Perry Anderson eds.: *The Question of Europe.* London: Verso.

Milward, Alan S. 1997b: The Springs of Integration. In Peter Gowan and Perry Anderson eds.: *The Question of Europe.* London: Verso.

Paasi, Anssi 2001: Europe as a Social Process and Discourse: Considerations of Place, Boundaries and Identity. *European Urban and Regional Studies.* 8:1.

Pinder, John 1995: *Euroopan Unioni. Erään yhteistyön historia* [The European Union. History of a Cooperation]. Helsinki: Tammi.

Sihvola, Juha 1998: *Toivon vuosituhat: eurooppalainen ihmiskuva ja suomalaisen yhteiskunnan tulevaisuus* [A Millenium of Hope: The European Image of Humankind and the Future of Finnish Society]. Jyväskylä: Atena.

Stråth, Bo 2000: *EU Efforts at Creating a European Identity: 1973 and beyond in a Historical Light.* Conference paper, EUR/68. 1999-2000 European Forum, IDNET Conference "Europeanization and Multiple Identities".

Tiilikainen, Teija 1998: *Europe and Finland. Defining the Political Identity of Finland in Western Europe.* Aldershot: Ashgate.

Weiler, Joseph 1999: *The Constitution of Europe. "Do the New Clothes Have an Emperor?" and Other Essays on European Integration.* Cambridge: Cambridge University Press.

4

Marginality and the Renewal of Independence in Estonia

REIN VEIDEMANN

Introduction: History as a Crossword

The history of the Estonian people and Estonia raises more questions than answers. It is like solving a crossword. There has recently been stress laid on dialogism (question-answer-new question) as the main mode for "a universal description of the historically developing life practise" (Kivimäe 2000: 33). In this article I will concentrate on the culmination of the narrative of self-fixation, on the factual and interpretative factors of the 1991 resumption of the Estonian independence process. Firstly, until the middle of the nineteenth century Estonian history was a history written by others, its conquerors. In that history, the Estonian people were either mute or backstage voices. Secondly, the Estonian people's history is a "secondary history". In this context, secondarity needs to be considered in two ways. The history of the Estonians has been the co-product of European history, the result of the first enlargement of Europe at the end of the twelfth and at the beginning of the thirteenth centuries (Hvostov 1999: 9-57), but this also means a secondarity of the sources. These have been written about the Estonians before the Estonian people started to write about itself as a nation and country. Thirdly, the history of Estonia is a paleo-romantic history born within the canon of Romanticism. The historic philosophy of J.G. Herder accepted the possibility of reconstructing a Golden Era and this has directly influenced the first generation of Estonian intellectuals and their developed national ideology

(Undusk 1995). In consequence Estonian history has been shadowed by a national mythology (Annus 2000), the prerequisite of Estonian identity. However, national identity itself is a questionable phenomenon, and the history of the Estonian nation and Estonia itself is a narration of the local collective consciousness and self-fixation (Veidemann 2000).

Magic and/or Logic

The twentieth century has passed into world history with its two self-destructive wars (the First and Second World Wars), and with the genesis and collapse of the German Reich and the Soviet Union. The destiny of European nations, including Estonia, has been directly or existentially affected by these super phenomena. Contemporary historical study concentrates on the conditions and causes of the origins of totalitarian countries and wars in an attempt to find their evolutionary logic composing "the lessons of history". In the case of Estonia and the Estonians, an extra question has been added to the investigation of this evolutionary logic. How was it possible for a small nation like Estonia to survive the monstrous social and political cataclysms of the century? The Estonian case is also remarkable for the way that in a single century a small nation has managed to create its state, then lose it after twenty years of sovereignty, and restore it finally after nearly fifty years of occupation. What then are the social, political and cultural factors that have determined such a scenario, and how much do these conditions include legitimacy, how much chance?

In *End of Millennium* (1998) Manuel Castells has dealt thoroughly with the collapse of the Soviet Union. The expansionism and totalitarianism of the Soviet Union regime derived its energy in the first half of the twentieth century from the limitless exploitation of natural and human resources, from economic industrialism and from state-controlled (i.e. Communist Party) terror. The lives of citizens and of the entire society were controlled by a paradigm of fear and by paradigms of a fanatical religious personality and power cult. Castells has summarised this in the concept of "statism": "By statism, I understand a social system organized around the appropriation of the economic surplus produced in society by the holders of power in the apparatus, in contrast with capitalism, in which surplus is appropriated by the holders of control in economic organizations" (Castells 1998: 7). Statism was accompanied by international isolation, militarisation of the economy, and a chronic budget deficit (ibid.: 21).

By the mid-1970s the Soviet economic and social structure was incapable of meeting the challenges raised by the beginning of the transition to the information society in the West. The reforms initiated by Mikhail Gorbachev in the mid-1980s — like Stolypin's reforms at the beginning of the twentieth century — were aimed at modernising and revitalising the system, but they led to the crash of the system itself: "And history has shown that once Russian society comes into open political ground, because it has so long repressed, it refuses to mold the pre-packaged state policies, takes a political life of its own, and becomes unpredictable and uncontrollable" (Castells 1998: 8).

Castells (1998: 8) claims that nationalism, including Russian nationalism, developed as an expression of the conflict between society and the state. The formation of the Soviet Union in 1922 proceeded from the Russian substratum, although the 1924 constitution specified the Soviet Union as a multinational and federal state. According to the constitutional law, entering and leaving the federation was free, but in reality the Soviet Union was from the very beginning controlled by the party and power structures, a strictly hierarchical unitary state characterised by the domination of political-administrative power within the state and the totalitarian character of the latter (Titma 2001: 9).

The expansionism of the Soviet Union determined its destiny. The Soviet Union as a state consisted of five concentric circles, each marking also the expansionist waves of Russianism: Russian language, ideology, Russian Orthodox religion and mentality. The geopolitical centre was the Russian Empire, surrounded by a network of autonomous satellite republics (the Russian Federation). This was considered to be the heart of Soviet rule. However, there was a paradox in the fact that the Russian Federation was the only republic without its own national Communist Party. The first defence zone of this central power consisted of the non-Russian republics. This zone was formed conclusively during the years of 1939-40, when the Soviet Union annexed and incorporated the independent Baltic States. The third concentre and also the third expansion wave of Russianism was connected with the republics of people's democracy outside the Soviet Union, which despite their juridical independence were subject to the territorial and military control of the Soviet Union. The fourth concern was formed by vassal states such as Cuba, Vietnam and North Korea. The fifth circle came into being as a result of an international communist movement, where organisations presented themselves as the embryos of the Soviet statehood and ideology (Castells 1998: 41-42). This kind of mixture of ahistoricism, class combat ideology and geopolitics in the genesis of one empire could produce only schizophrenic results on the basis of economic, social and national politics. The paradox was that "Russian imperialism", on which the Soviet regime was based, deformed and even repressed the cultural source of Russian nationalism itself (ibid.). Next to the ethnicity in the Soviet periphery the reawakening of the cultural self-consciousness of the Russian nation itself plays a crucial role in the collapse of the Soviet Union.

The Estonian sociologist Marju Lauristin approaches the reasons for the collapse of communism differently. Lauristin proceeds from the basis of Samuel Huntington's conception on the conflict of civilisations as the "developing mechanism" of history, and confirms that "[t]he most decisive role in the collapse of the Soviet Union was played, not by ethnic nationalism...but precisely by the civilizational conflict between the Russian-Soviet Empire, the "New Byzantium" of the 20th century, and the Baltic and other East-European nations, representing the Western traditions of the individual autonomy and civil society" (Lauristin et al. 1997: 29). The surviving strategy of the Baltic nations was based on the preservation of Western traditions, mentality and socio-political experience (political liberalism, democracy and market economy) in their cultural consciousness. The struggle to restore statehood was treated as an unconventional return to home — Return to the Western World, Return to Europe (ibid.).

From at least the beginning of the twentieth century, Europe has played a leading role in Estonian culture. The renewal of the Estonian society, the creation of the Republic of Estonia in 1918, and the explosive economic and cultural development ran under the dictates of the famous intellectual generation known as the *Noor-eestlased* ("the Young Estonians") and their slogan devised by the Estonian poet Gustav Suits: "Let us be Estonians but also become Europeans" (Tuglas 1936: 16-20). In this call one can already see the binding of one ethnic cultural collective with a broader cultural entity, under what Huntington defines as civilisation (Huntington 1999: 167-168). At the same time Huntington has warned about overestimating the impact of Western civilisation (here: European) that has emerged within the euphoria accompanying with the fall of the Soviet Empire and also the fall of the false impression of Western universalism and expansionism guaranteeing global stability; this may lead to a new war between civilisations (ibid.: 395). The years 1980-1990, which saw Estonia regaining its independence, can also be considered to be the result of the first wave of European integration, which began in 1958 with the establishment of the European Economic Association (Jaanson 2000: 42). Yet, the integration based on the growth of a European political identity presupposed the existence of the nation-states because "only truly independent nation states can unite" (ibid.).

Estonia's (and the other Baltic States') economic and geopolitical logic in the independence process echoes the more formidably definable factors that accumulate around ethnos and national identity. It is even difficult to decide which of these in this process is more decisive: political logic or ethnos, the appearance of "passionarity" (see Gumiljov 1988 Vol. II: 71). But there seems to be good reason to regard nationality as the *primus motor* of this process. National self-determination was transmitted as the self-determination of the state.

Multidimensionality of National Identity

National self-determination is also a question of national identity and these, in turn, culminate in the national question. Nationalism can be defined as a system of views, value orientations and judgments, and it has two modes of occurrence: civil nationalism and ethnic nationalism. The criteria of civil nationalism are loose, incorporating individuals who belong under one government policy and use mutual franchises from a certain nation (Dann 1991: 57-58). Under ethnic nationalism only those individuals are accounted as belonging to a single nation who regard themselves as deriving from mutual ancestors and who are strongly bound together by a collective identity (Scheff 1994: 277-303; Sevänen 1999: 27-28). If civil nationalism characterises Western civilisation, then ethnic nationalism describes the Eastern phenomenon (Kohn 1994: 163-165). However, such a classification can appear useless when categorising the national phenomena, "usually the national ideologies have been a mixture of civil nationalism and ethnic nationalism" (Sevänen 1999: 29). It was thought that during the 1980s and the 1990s ethnic nationalism dominated in the East-European national movements (Sevänen 1999: 36). In the case of Estonia and Latvia the reason is seen to be the presence of powerful foreign elites — Germans during the nineteenth century, and Russians during the second half of the twentieth century — on native territory, which has given rise to the clear opposition of "us and them" (ibid.).

Next to civil nationalism and ethnic nationalism the formative story of the Estonian nation refers to yet another mode of classification, that of cultural nationalism (Karjahärm & Sirk 1997: 212-214). The cornerstone of the Estonian national ideology, national identity and national movement both during the second half of the nineteenth century and during the 1980s was Estonian culture, and especially Estonian literature. This means that, unlike government-powered civil nationalism and ethnic nationalism based on kinship or religious grounds, cultural nationalism is by its very nature an open nationalism. The "openness" is already determined by the concept of culture, which itself is amorphous and can be interpreted in many ways (Deane 1995: 361). Unlike state, law, and party institutionalism, culture represents superstructure and is an easy subject for various idealisations. It is possible to oppose culture to political and economic power, while leaving at least an initial impression of cultural nationalism as harmless to the ruling power. Cultural nationalism was an important factor for Ireland during that country's determination as an independent country (Deane 1995: 363-368). In that process, the writers (W.B. Yeats, J. Joyce) played an important role, and so, too, have the Estonian writers in the key positions of Estonian cultural nationalism. National myths and ideological concepts are significant in cultural nationalism — nation as an imagined community — as the handiwork of people's beliefs, attachments and inclinations (Anderson 1983; Gellner 1994: 22-27). If culture is treated as a "self-sufficient universe" (J. Lotman 1999: 419) or a semiotic monad, then dialogism, self-description, interpretivity, adaptivity and other such characteristics will start to be accented. All of these also appear in the Estonian nationalism summarised under the concept of marginality.

From the point of view of cultural nationalism, the ideal of a national identity (including Estonian national identity) also obtains a broader meaning. The concept of identity is being taken as the birth product of modernism. "Descartes' cogito is a crucial index of the novel stress on identity", Craig Calhoun (1994: 10) claims. Identity is self-evident but also a fiction. As there can be many such fictions or self-narratives, we should talk about the plurality of identities. In every identity — national, political or cultural — being in a relationship with the other is projected onto the self: every identity bears traces of others. More specifically, identity, like the self-narrative, also bears traces of an ideal other because "our identities are always rooted in part in ideals and moral aspirations that we cannot realize fully" (Calhoun 1994: 29). Even national identity is at the same time a self-narrative and contains reflections of another subject and ideal in the self. The genesis of Estonian national identity follows all three of the aspects mentioned above, whereby intellectuals have played a decisive role in the formation of identity. During the first decades of the nineteenth century, local Baltic Germans were the first to start constructing an Estonian nation. This has recently given Ea Jannsen (1998: 12) reason to question whether the Estonian nation might even be regarded as the fantasy or invention of Baltic German intellectuals.

In the mid-nineteenth century, the earliest elite of the Estonian intelligentsia metaphorically took over the baton.

This involved individuals such as Fr. R. Faehlmann, Fr. R. Kreutzwald, J.V. Jannsen, C.R. Jakobson and J. Hurt, for whom the Estonian nation primarily meant intellectual equality with the German colonists (Annus 2000: 12; Jannsen 1993: 295). They weighed their uniqueness — an old and rich culture, the Estonian language, a rural mentality — against the ruling minority, i.e. the colonists, and finally turned towards the idea of the nation state (Veidemann 2000: 98). Yet at the beginning of the twentieth century there was no anticipation of the creation of an Estonian nation-state, and the idea was limited to applying for autonomy within the Russian state (Karjahärm 1998: 98). In other words, people were aware of the ideal — for example, the proclamation of Gustav Suits (2002: 12): "We want our free homeland and free social order" — but could not foresee any realistic chances of fulfilling the ideal.

The same thing occurred again in the second half of the twentieth century. At the end of the 1960s the hope emerged of restoring the Estonian statehood that had been destroyed in 1940, and the nation's opinion leaders begun to pursue autonomy. This was based on the understanding that Estonian "cultural progress has been fast and almost constant during the last century and is still continuing at the moment" (Taagepera 1988: 41; 1995: 21). In the addresses and manifestations (Jõgi 1988: 223; Kogumik MRP-AEG Infobülletään 1987-1988: 254-257; Rahvakongress 1988: 183-185) that introduced the "singing revolution", the Estonian version of the peak of social and political activity was comparable to the "Velvet Revolution" in Czechoslovakia. This was triggered in 1988 and was expressed in terms of historical correction, justice and the right of a nation's self-determination. Nevertheless, the discursive background of this was the (national) culture. The Estonian and Baltic experience of a sovereign state saw the nation-state as the only possible guarantee of the durability of cultural creativity and the identity of the nation. This was vividly summarised by a Lithuanian culture philosopher, Antanas Maceina, in the *Nation and State* published in 1939: "The objectivity of the nation is the state. Only within the state, does a nation obtain a perceptible form, only within the state can it organise, only within the state does it obtain the authority and power to arrange its public existence. The state is formed by the voice of nationality or the personification of nationality" (Maceina 1990: 75).

A leading Estonian ethnologist, Oskar Loorits, has thoroughly linked the destiny of Estonian statehood with the quality of its cultural elite (Loorits 2000: 208-259). At the end of the 1930s, culture as a concept of Estonian existentialism obtained a special place in the writings and studies of intellectuals (Karjahärm & Sirk 2001: 229-234). The common scholarly opinion is that culture is like a religion for the Estonians (ibid.). It is no wonder that in 1980 forty Estonian intellectuals addressed a public letter to the Soviet authorities. It was never published owing to its subsequent repression but it testified to the suppression of the Estonian language and culture under the Russian oppression as a "symbol of dignity" for Estonians (Neljakümne kirja lugu 1990: 6).

Culture has been interpreted as a tense dialogue or even an opposition between folk tradition and Western culture (Loorits 2000: 216-217). Dichotomies and antithetical classifications have also characterised both the debates over Estonian culture at the beginning of the twentieth century and the approach to culture in the middle of the century (Karjahärm & Sirk 2001: 249-250). This has created the internal dynamics of Estonian culture and produced a certain sense of openness in Estonian nationalism. Although "Estonian intellectuals have always dreaded being cast aside from the mainstream of Western civilisation and to becoming marginal and inconspicuous in Europe" (Karjahärm & Sirk 2001: 333), there are signs of an element of self-creativity.

Marginality and/as the Ideological Code of Culture

In the terms used by Estonian intellectuals to express their fear of remaining marginal, marginality has been understood to have a negative and pejorative meaning. This kind of approach has been generated in social psychology, when the behaviour and operating possibilities of a subject are specified by its belonging to a group, by its relationship with the norm and by its correspondence with the "outline". In this, marginality is linked to the same terminological locus where "deviation", "status inconsistency" and "periphery" also belong. For example, it has been common to call a person marginal if the person at the same time belongs to two or more different or even opposite groups or cultures. It is said that marginality creates a role conflict when a person cannot choose between controversial demands, expectations and values. The long-standing status of marginality is said to cause a split in personality. In the main, marginality is transmitted from the level of personality to a group — marginal groups, sub- and contra-cultures, and we may loosely speak of marginal cultures, nations and states. The cognitive basis of the sporadically *ad absurdum* classification consists of spatial and evaluative oppositional pairs: system/outside the system; centre/periphery; equivalent/ambivalent; obligatory/redundant (J. Lotman 1990: 248-271). Marginality, derived from the Latin stem *margo, inis* (verge, border, periphery, frame), loses its pejorative character when one interprets the forming texts within these oppositional pairs as an "active semiotic transformer" (M. Lotman 2001: 220).

Marginality is also a part of a semiosphere (e.g. text as a "semiotic universe"), "because the constituents of the semiosphere are not time and causality, and the semiotic space is not constructed for the physical world, but for the proper mechanisms of the sign system...primarily communication and interpretation" (M. Lotman 2001: 226). Juri Lotman has reckoned the concept of boundary to be the most important functional and structural position that "determines the essence of the semiotic mechanism of the semiosphere". "The boundary is a bilingual mechanism which translates the external messages into the internal language of the semiosphere and vice versa", Lotman claims (1999: 14).

In every culture it is possible to distinguish centres, peripheries and boundaries, but in the Estonian culture and national identity the problems of boundaries are doubled. The reason is that territorially and geo-culturally Estonia itself has lain on the European periphery and simultaneously at the point of transition and contact between Eastern and Western Christianity, marking the openness and uncertainty of the Eastern side of Europe (Undusk & Rein 2001: 42, 51). The Estonian topos is an intermediate, median and marginality. This is confirmed by a circumstance that within the various positionings of Estonia — a Baltic province, Warägische Grenzraum, Pribaltiiski krai, deutsche Ostsseeprovinzen Russlands, Randstaat or Baltoscandia (Kant 1999: 292) — a certain boundary to their intersection appears. The Estonian economic geographer Edgar Kant has described this in the following way:

> This is the zone between the great nations, where a range of small nations have been determined mostly by the struggle for the great internal border of the Western peninsula of Eurasia, combat for areas, for space: for some because of the markets of the hinterland, for others because of the seascape or of the urge for conquest, but for the small nations because of the struggle to be themselves (Kant 1926: 175).

This strife could only originate from the geopolitical reality which the growing Estonian nationality had to take into account in the nineteenth century and which has influenced the ideological code of Estonian culture, both synchronically and diachronically. In the semiotics of ideology the ideological code is defined as "a system of signs capable of expressing discursively the basic principles of a specific ideology, subordinating its functioning to syntactical and representational strategies which blend with the aesthetic-verbal condition of the literary discourse which frames it" (Reis 1993: 30). The essence of the ideological code is an integrated phenomenon of the culture (Kõnno 2001: 55) — and in the case of Estonia, it is marginality.

Understandably, during the formation process of the national culture this was not brought into consciousness — even less, it was not manifested at all — and the question about the genuine "self" or Estonianism withdrew in the face of functionality and of pragmatic concerns. At the end of the eighteenth century and until the middle of the following century, the enlightenment texts translated from German and published in calendars, the adaptations of German popular literature (Vinkel 1966) and Estonian mythology (Fr. R. Faehlmann's *Estonian Folk Tales*) based on the memory of Greek mythology and practically taken as an intertext, all gained their "Estonian sign". The publication of Estonia's own folk tales occurred in the 1880s (Vinkel 1966: 298) and the problematic of authenticity or marginality was focused in the Estonian national epic *Kalevipoeg*, written by Fr. R. Kreutzwald (1853-1862). Although during the period of publication the work was mainly known indirectly, usually through presentational writings, it was still accepted as a "national creative text" (Undusk 1994: 148). *Kalevipoeg* was "the direct poetic echo of the formation process of Estonian nationalism" (Nirk 1975: 269) and elevated to be "the countersign of the national movement" (Nirk 1975: 271).

On the other hand, in 1908 Friedebert Tuglas polemically stressed that: "Because this work is only marginally national in its theme and purpose, its aesthetic essence is not national but German, and therefore contrary to Estonian nationalism" (Tuglas 1919: 105). Later academic approaches (Annist 1944; Oinas 1994; Undusk 1990) have thoroughly opened up the intertextuality and composition of the "kernel text of Estonia". This has somewhat narrowed the canonical entity of *Kalevipoeg*. Throughout recent history, marginality has been silently recognised as a sub-code of the national ideology. This applies to the 120-year-old tradition of Estonian song festivals, established among the circles of the fraternities which spread at the end of the eighteenth century in South Estonia (Põldmäe 1969: 9) and through the nineteenth century adaptation of the culture of choir-singing from Switzerland and Germany (Kahk 1998: 58). The *liedertafel* repertoire was set as the example for the development of choirs by J.V. Jannsen, and it has influenced the national oriented works of Estonia's own composers (Põldmäe 1969: 65). The fact that the first Song Festival held in 1869 was dedicated to the 50th anniversary of the liberation of the peasantry from serfdom speaks for the recognition of marginality (ibid.: 76).

The address given in 1899 by Jakob Hurt, the leader of the national awakening period, which was inspired by cultural tolerance, can be taken as an essential recognition of marginality:

> We the nationalists honour German education and highly appreciate the value of German culture. We do this more preferably and happily because our own education and culture — if we can be permitted to talk about it amongst ourselves — is mainly German in nature and

> we are protected from "slavification" through "co-knowledge" of your education and culture. But you, Germans too, should also respect our nation and recognise our national pursuits, and in return you will get our backing against "slavification". Only mutual recognition and respect of this kind will make us strong and enable us to achieve productive co-operation (Karjahärm & Sirk 1997: 214).

The development of Estonian culture during the twentieth century has been radically affected by the *Noor-Eesti* ("Young Estonia") movement and their slogan "Let's be Estonians but also become Europeans". If we approach this from the aspect of marginality, it reveals not a goal of identification but rather a call for syntheticism and universalism (Karjahärm & Sirk 1997: 306). This is one of the emphases of marginality as a dynamic dialogue. Marginality can also be interpreted as a synonym for glocality, provided it is understood as "any locus in the interactive context of a world-system" (Riggs 1998).

In the 1990s the paradigm of marginality has — indeed without immediate recognition — gained a more influential position in Estonian texts and Estonian discourses. Yet as long ago as in 1971 Rein Taagepera dreamed about the kind of Estonia "to whom it is said that here the Eastern and Western Europe started to merge into one, here lies the heart of Europe" (Taagepera 1988: 41; 1995: 21). We can also point out the historic studies by Lennart Meri (e.g. *Hõbevalge*) and the historic prose by Jaan Kross (*Keisri hull, Vastutuulelaev, Mesmeri ring*), where Estonia and its people are notional in the West-East context.

Marginality in the 1990s, as the ideological code of Estonian culture, has gained new dimensions. First of all, people started to recognise the Baltic-German culture as an inseparable part of Estonian culture and as an initiator of the metatext of an Estonian national consciousness (Jansen 1993; 1998: 802; Paul 1999; Undusk 1992; 1995; 1997). Germans were even acknowledged as the creators of the Estonian written language (Paul 1999: 77). Another important change was that the Estonian language as the basis of an Estonian national discourse was subjected to debate. On one hand, this meant the abandonment of the long-dominant concept of the Finno-Ugric language tree (e.g. Künnap 1996; Sutrop 1999; Wiik 1996) and its replacement by the concept of junction (Saari 1999). On the other hand, the Estonian language as a sign system was bound up with the German context (Ross 2002: 229). This did not mean the abandonment of Estonian culture or the uniqueness of the Estonian language (Ross 2002: 230), but an understanding that the structures of marginality and boundaries can in themselves generate uniqueness and be sources of mental energy and identity. For example, it has been thought about Estonian history that precisely because of the geopolitical inter-medium of the Baltic government it was possible for Estonia to gain its independence in 1918 (Medijainen 1995: 304). The experience of Estonian "marginality" holds a more global meaning: we can see here exactly what kinds of existential roles can be played by openness, transparency, polylogic and syntheticism (Talvet 2002: 999-1000).

Conclusion: The Power of Marginality

Juri Lotman (1999: 16) has written: "The border has an additional function in the semiosphere — it is a zone, where semiotic processes descend more rapidly; these happen more actively in the periphery of cultural wholeness, in order to rush into the kernel structures and to reject previous ones." The renewed independence process of Estonia began immediately after Mikhail Gorbachev's proclamation of *perestroika* in 1985 and was first manifested as a discursive turn (the tuning of the press, television and the radio into the *perestroika* wave, and in its shadow creating the Estonian Cause). This continued with the genesis of public politics and ended with the re-establishment of Estonian independence on 20 August 1991. Such developments tend to prove Lotman's thesis.

Signals (*perestroika* and *glasnost*) from Moscow, the centre of the empire, were reconstructed with the aid of the code of social and cultural memory, which was adapted to the local and regional conditions and then channelled into the "kernel structure" — the totalitarian regime — against itself. This was first attempted 16 November 1988, when the Soviet Estonian Supreme Council (a quasi-parliament of the Soviet system) passed the Estonian Declaration of Independence. This triggered a constitutional crisis in the Soviet Union. The periphery (Estonia) challenged the centre (Moscow) for the second time on the 30 March 1990, when the Supreme Council of Soviet Estonia set forth a transition period towards the renewed-independence of Estonia. In practice, this indicated liberation from the centre. The third resolution — the re-establishment of the independence of Estonia on the 20 August 1991 by the Supreme Council of the Republic of Estonia — began to draw the kernel structure of the Soviet power system away from the "Estonian semiosis". This triggered the reconstruction of the kernel structure through the collapse of the Soviet Union.

In the case of Estonia, we are dealing with the power of marginality. It was as a result of this power that the process of renewed independence unfolded as a flexible, step by step operation of re-establishing democracy and reconstructing the Estonian national state. Throughout the whole process the local (the Estonian national state), the regional (the Baltic States, Nordic Countries) and the global (the Soviet Union versus the United States) dimensions remained in balance. As emotional border markers in this process, I should like to underline two statements. The first comes from the prominent Estonian theatre director, Mikk Mikiver, who, during a meeting of the Estonian creative communities on 1-2 April 1988, said:

> The problems of this land cannot be solved from a distance.... I also have nowhere to leave to. I would never leave to anywhere else. The problems of this country are the same as if they were my personal problems; there can be no hiding from them. This is where we belong. Even when death strikes (Jõgi 1988: 213; translation R.V.).

The second statement was made just a few minutes before the declaration of Estonian independence on the evening of the 20 August 1991, in the Estonian Supreme Council:

> Yes, tonight we are standing face to face with history. We are standing face to face with the question of whether to let ourselves to be swept away by the current stream or to justify ourselves in that current as a subject, a

> nationality, and a state. It is true that for others this can only be a passing moment, a fact from somewhere in Europe; for some of us here it is a fact from the periphery of the empire. But we have to accept that this is all we have. For us there can be no other way, because history has destined us to live here and our duty, as the representatives of the nation, is to guarantee the possibility of life here (Kaks otsustavat päeva Toompeal 1996: 60; translation R.V.).

It is of no importance that the latter statement came from the author of this text. The important thing is that both underline the power of marginality, where the inevitable is bonded with hope and duty. What was felt as a miracle at the beginning of the 1990s has now turned into a sense of national obligation: "We have to remain as a periphery, but a more self-conscious and audacious one; not regretting what we are going to lack from the centre but emphasising the cognitive advantages that a periphery has to offer" (Undusk 2002: 13-72; translation R.V.).

REFERENCES

Anderson, Benedict 1983: *Imagined Communities. Reflections on the Origins and Spread of Nationalism*. London: Verso.

Annist, August 1944: *"Kalevipoeg" kui kunstiteos* ["Kalevipoeg" as art]. Tartu.

Annus, Epp 2000: Kiigelaual mineviku ja tuleviku vahel: rahvuslikust mütoloogiast [On the seesaw between the past and the future: about national mythology]. *Looming*. 1. Tallinn: Perioodika.

Annus, Epp 2000a: Kirjanduskaanon ja rahvuslik identiteet [Literature canon and the national identity]. *Keel ja Kirjandus*. 1. Tallinn: Perioodika.

Calhoun, Craig 1994: Social Theory and the Politics of Identity. In Craig Calhoun ed.: *Social Theory and Politics of Identity*. Cambridge, Massachusetts: Blackwell Publishers.

Castells, Manuel 1998: *The Information Age. Economy, Society and Culture. III. End of Millennium*. Oxford: Blackwell Publishers.

Dann, Otto 1991: Begriffe und Typen des Nationalen in der frühen Neuzeit. In Bernhard Giesen ed.: *Nationale und kulturelle Identität. Studien zur Entwicklung des kollektiven Bewusstseins in der Neuzeit*. Frankfurt am Main: Suhrkamp.

Deane, Seamus 1995: Imperialism/Nationalism. In Frank Lentricchia and Thomas McLaughlin ed.: *Critical Terms for Literary Study*. Chicago and London: University of Chicago Press.

Eesti NSV loominguliste liitude juhatuste ühispleenum 1.-2. aprillil 1988. [Plenary meeting of directors of the creative council of the Soviet Republic of Estonia 1-2.4.1988.] Tallinn: Eesti Raamat.

Gellner, Ernest 1994: Rahvused ja rahvuslus [Nations and nationalism]. *Akadeemia.* 10 -12. Tartu.

Gumiljov, Lev 1988: Mõtteid etnosest [Some thoughts about tribes]. *Vikerkaar.* 1-3. Tallinn: Perioodika.

Huntington, Samuel P. 1999: *Tsivilisatsioonide kokkupõrge ja maailmakorra ümberkujunemine* [The clash of civilizations and the remaking of world order]. Tartu: Fontes.

Hvostov, Andrei 1999: *Mõtteline Eesti* [The ideal Estonia]. Tallinn: Vagabund.

Jaanson, Kaido 2000: *Geopoliitiline seisund. Eesti uue aastatuhande lävel* [The geopolitical situation. Estonia at the threshold of the new millennium]. Tallinn: TEA.

Jannsen, Ea 1993: Veel kord ärkamisaja kulturimurrangust. [One more time about cultural break of the era of national awakening]. *Keel ja Kirjandus.* 5. Tallinn: Perioodika.

Jannsen, Ea 1998: Muinaseesti panteon: Faehlmanni müütide roll eestlaste rahvusteadvuses. [The ancient Estonian Pantheon: The role of Faehlmann's myths in Estonian popular thinking]. *Keel ja Kirjandus.* 12. Tallinn: Perioodika.

Jõgi, Mall ed. 1998: *Eesti NSV loominguliste liitude juhatuste ühispleenum 1.- 2. aprillil 1988* [The Plenary meeting of directors of the creative council of the Soviet Republic of Estonia 1-2.4.1988]. Tallinn: Eesti Raamat.

Kahk, Juhan 1998: Kuidas sündis Euroopa ja mis eestlastel sellega pistmist on [How Estonia was born and what the Estonians had to do with it: The White Dwarf star in the dispersing universe]. In R. Veidemann ed.: *Valge kääbustäht hajuvas kõiksuses.* Tallinn: Perioodika.

Kaks otsustavat päeva Toompeal (19.-20. august 1991) [Two significant days in Toompea (19-20 August, 1991)] 1996. Tallinn: Eesti Entsüklopeediakirjastus.

Karjahärm, Toomas 1998: *Ida ja Lääne vahel. Eesti-Vene suhted 1850-1917* [Between East and West. The relationship of Estonia and Russia between 1850 and 1917]. Tallinn: Eesti Entsüklopeediakirjastus.

Karjahärm, Toomas & Väino Sirk 1997: *Eesti haritlaskonna kujunemine ja ideid 1850-1917* [The emergence of the Estonian intelligentsia and its ideas from 1850 to 1917]. Tallinn: Eesti Entsüklopeediakirjastus.

Kant, Edgar 1999: *Linnad ja maastikud* [Cities and environments]. Tartu: Ilmamaa.

Kiin, Sirje, Rein Ruutsoo & Andres Tarand 1990: *40 kirja lugu.* [The story of 40 letters]. Tallinn: Olion.

Kivimäe, Mart 2000: Ajaloomõtlemise kolm strateegiat ja nende dialoogisuhted minevikuga [Three strategies of historical thinking and their dialogical relationships with the past]. In R. Koselleck, J. Rüsen, E. Nolte ed.: *Historismi muutumise, arendamise, ületamise probleemid* [Overcoming the problems of historicism with change and development]. Tallinn: TPÜ kirjastus.

Kohn, Hans 1994: Western and Eastern Nationalisms. In John Hutchinson and Anthony D. Smith ed.: *Nationalism.* Oxford and New York: Oxford University Press.

Kogumik MRP-AEG Infobülletään [Kogumik MRP-AEG information bulletin] *1987-1988.* Tallinn.

Kull, Anu 1990: Eesti geograafilisest kuluvusest [About the geographical erosion in Estonia]. *Vikerkaar.* 11. Tallinn: Perioodika.

Kõnno, Andres 2001: Ideoloogilise kirjelduse semiootika [The Semiotics of ideological accounts]. *Acta Semiotica Estica.* I. Tartu: Tartu Ülikooli Kirjastus.

Künnap, Ago 1996: Mea culpa, aga omakeelsed Eesti põlisasukad oleme olnud ehk juba 12 000 aastat [Mea culpa, but the first Estonian aboriginal native language speakers may have lived already 12 000 years ago]. *Keel ja Kirjandus.* 8. Tallinn: Perioodika.

Lauristin, Marju, Peeter Vihalemm, Karl Erik Rosengren and Lennart Weibul 1997: *Return to the Western World. Cultural and Political Perspectives on the Estonian Post-Communist Transition.* Tartu: Tartu University Press.

Lias, Pärt 1985: *Eesti nõukogude romaan* [The Soviet Estonian novel]. Tallinn: Eesti Raamat.

Loorits, Oskar 2000: *Meie, eestlased* [We, the Estonians]. Tartu: Ilmamaa.

Lotman, Juri 1990: *Kultuurisemiootika* [Cultural semiotics]. Tallinn: Olion.

Lotman, Juri 1999: *Semiosfäärist* [About the semiosphere]. Tallinn: Vagabund.

Lotman, Juri 2001: *Kultuur ja plahvatus* [Culture and explosion]. Tallinn: Varrak.

Lotman, Mihhail 2001: Paradoksaalne semiosfäär (Järelsõna) [The paradoxical semiosphere (epilogue)]. In Juri Lotman: *Kultuur ja plahvatus.* Tallinn: Varrak.

Maceina, Antanas 1990: Rahvus ja riik [Nation and state]. *Vikerkaar.* 5. Tallinn: Perioodika.

Medijainen, Eero 1995: Kas Balti riikide iseseisvumine oli kangelastegu? [Was it a heroic act for the Baltic states to become independent?] In J. Blomstedt, M. Lõhmus & E. Tarasti ed.: *Ajalaval.* Tallinn & Helsinki.

Nirk, Endel 1975: Eesti rahvuseepos "Kalevipoeg" [The Estonian national epic "Kalevipoeg"]. *Kalevipoeg.* Tallinn: Eesti Raamat.

Oinas, Felix 1994: Surematu Kalevipoeg [The immortal Kalevipoeg]. *Keel ja Kirjandus.* Tallinn: Perioodika.

Paul, Toomas 1999: *Eesti piiblitõlke ajalugu* [The history of Estonian Bible translation]. Tallinn: Emakeele Selts.

Põldmäe, Rudolf 1969: *Esimene Eesti üldlaulupidu 1869.* [The first Estonian song festival in 1869.] Tallinn: Eesti Raamat.

Rahvakongress 1988 [Public congress 1988]. Materjalide kogumik. Tallinn: Perioodika.

Reis, Carlos 1993: *Towards a Semiotic of Ideology*. Berlin and New York: Mouton de Gruyter.

Riggs, Fred W.1998: Globalisation. Key concepts. *http://webdata.soc.Hawaii.edu/FredR/glocon.htm*

Ross, Kristiina 2002: Baltisaksa pastorid ja eesti keel [Baltic German pastors and the Estonian language]. *Keel ja Kirjandus*. 4. Tallinn: Perioodika.

Row, Carlos 1995: *Structure. Critical Terms for Literary Study*. Chicago and London: The University of Chicago Press.

Saari, Henn 1999: Kolm refleksiooni Urmas Sutropile [Three reflections of Urmas Sutrop]. *Keel ja Kirjandus*. 11. Tallinn: Perioodika.

Scheff, Thomas J. 1994: Emotions and Identity: A Theory of Ethnic Nationalism. In Craig Calhoun ed.: *Social Theory and the Politics of Identity*. Cambridge Massachusetts: Blackwell Publishers.

Sevänen, Erkki 1999: Nationalismi ja kansakuntien muodostuminen luokittelevasta, vertailevasta ja historiallisesta näkökulmasta [Nationalism and the formation of nations as seen from classificatory, comparative and historical perspectives]. In Tero Koistinen, Piret Kruspere, Erkki Sevänen & Risto Turunen ed.: *Kaksi tietä nykyisyyteen. Tutkimuksia kirjallisuuden, kansallisuuden ja kansallisten liikkeiden suhteista Suomessa ja Virossa* [Two roads to the present. Studies on the relationships between literature, nationality and national movements in Finland and Estonia]. Helsinki: Finnish Literature Society.

Suits, Gustav 2002: *Vabaduse värval* [The recruiter of freedom]. Tartu: Ilmamaa.

Sutrop, Urmas 1999: Eesti keele vanimatest perioodidest [About the oldest periods of the Estonian language]. *Keel ja Kirjandus*. 9. Tallinn: Perioodika.

Taagepera, Rein 1998: Variant kujutlusele Eesti tulevikust "30 aasta plaan" [An alternative version for the Estonian future: "the 30 years plan"]. *Vikerkaar*. 10. Tallinn.

Taagepera, Rein 1995: *Homme nägin ma Eestimaad* [Tomorrow I saw Estonia]. Tallinn: AS Arhitekturibüroo Ignar Fjuk.

Talvet, Jüri 2002: Lääs ja süntetismi väljakutsed. [The West and the challenge of syntheticism]. *Akadeemia*. 5. Tartu.

Titma M. 2001 ed.: *Sõjajärgse põlvkonna elutee ja seda kujundanud faktorid* [Factors describing the lives of post-war generations]. Tartu: Tartu Ülikooli Kirjastus.

Tuglas, Friedebert 1919: *Kriitika* I. Tartu: Noor-Eesti.

Tuglas, Friedebert 1936: *Kriitika* V. Tartu: Noor-Eesti.

Tõnisson, Ilmar 1997: *Emajõe ääres* [By the river Emajõgi]. Tartu: Ilmamaa.

Undusk, Jaan 1990: Kalevipoeg ja Prometheus: Friedebert Tuglase "Põrgu värvas" ja selle koht rahvaluleteaduses. [Kalevipoeg and Prometheus:

Friedebert Tuglas's "Hell's Gate" and its place in folklore] *Keel ja Kirjandus*. 10-12. Tallinn: Perioodika.

Undusk, Jaan 1994: Rahvaluuleteksti lõppematus: Felix Oinas, soome meetod ja intertekstuaalne "Kalevipoeg" [The never-ending text of folklore: Felix Oinas, the Finnish method and the intertextual "Kalevipoeg"]. Oinas, Felix: *Surematu Kalevipoeg* [The immortal Kalevipoeg]. Tallinn: Keel ja Kirjandus.

Undusk, Jaan 1995: Hamanni ja Herderi vaim eesti kirjanduse edendajana: sünekdohhi printsiip. [Hamman's and Herder's spirits as promoters of Estonian literature: the principle of synecdoche]. *Keel ja Kirjandus*. 9-11. Tallinn: Perioodika.

Undusk, Jaan 1997: Kolm võimalust kirjutada eestlaste ajalugu: Merkel — Jakobson — Hurt [Three alternative ways to write the history of Estonians: Merkel — Jakobson — Hurt]. *Keel ja Kirjandus*. 11-12. Tallinn: Perioodika.

Undusk, Jaan 2002: Kas meist savad Balti baskid ehk kuidas olla esindatud? [Will we become the Baltic Basques and how are we presented?] *Looming*. 9. Tallinn: Perioodika.

Undusk, Rein 2001: *Topos. Kohakujutelm müüdist mõisteni* [Topos. The mind map of place from myth to concept]. Tallinn: Underi ja Tuglase Kirjanduskeskus.

Veidemann, Rein 2000: The Formation of the Estonian Nation from a Semiotic Aspect. *Interlitteraria*. 5. Tartu: Tartu Ülikooli Kirjastus.

Vinkel, Aarne 1966: Eesti rahvaraamat [The Estonian national book]. Tallinn: Eesti Raamat.

Wiik, Kalevi 1996: Põhja-Euroopa rahvaste ja keelte päritolu küsimusi [Questions about the origin of Northern European nations and languages]. *Keel ja Kirjandus*. 9. Tallinn: Perioodika.

5

Nation, Glocality, and the Estonian (Baltic) Literary Discourse at the Turn of the Millennium

JURI TALVET

Introduction: A Constructionistist view of the Nations

In recent decades, with the Cartesian-Kantian idea of the "world contained in the thinking head" strongly prevailing in the world outside the human brain, semioticians, constructionists (structuralists) and deconstructionists have been more interested in mental structures than in vital, existential or historical processes. It is but natural that, as Monica Spiridon (2000: 76) in referring to Confino (1997) and others has observed, that nation "has been downgraded to a mere cultural artefact". The idea of nation as an intellectual construct, often supported by exaggerated cultural myths (of an ideal past and a perfect future, and not so much dealing with the present) (Spiridon 2000; Annus 2000) — a brilliant target for de-constructionist de-heroisation, de-sacralisation, parody and pastiche — can be seen in several essays (Kruuspere 2000; Èakare 2000; Fernández 1999) published in the most recent issues of the Estonian journal *Interlitteraria*. At their worst, especially when applied by some powerful super-nations like Hitler's Germany or Stalin's Soviet Russia, such myths can lead to human tragedies of terrifying dimensions. Thus, the postmodern deconstructionistic effort, widely echoed in cultural manifestations not only in the West but also in the post-socialist countries and, to some extent, even in some of the largest Eastern cultural areas such as China and India (Li Xia 1999; 2000), can be seen as something historically justified. The information-technological and economic process of globalisation seems to support the present processes of de-nationing, an observation which has led several scholars to suggest that we may be fairly close to the last phase of the existence of nation-states and their concomitant national cultures, which also includes national literatures (see Sevänen 2000).

One would like to remind these scholars that Karl Marx and Friedrich Engels wrote a lot about nation as a mere invention — or in postmodern terms, as an "intellectual construct" — of the bourgeoisie, and also that Vladimir Lenin wrote several treatises about the extinction of the state under communism, not to mention his article on a "European United States" in which he foresaw some of the ideas of Joschka Fischer, the present-day German foreign minister. And as for the Baltic, at the end of the nineteenth century Ernesto (Ernst) Bark, an important Baltic-German essayist and bohemian who was born near Tartu, fled from the Tsarist persecutions to the West and finally settled in Spain where he published some fifty books in Spanish in the best vein of modernity and Euro-socialism, and dreamed about an independent Baltic Federal State, something Western politicians would gladly welcome in the present day.

Nations as Cultural Deep Structures

None of these noble ideas has come true, not because the bourgeoisie is still here, not because the attempt to build a perfect communist world has for the time being failed, and not in the least because the Baltic peoples would like the return of the Soviet empire. It is, rather, because nations are never merely mental discourses or cultural artefacts but something much deeper than that. Nation has to do with a wide complex of internal dynamics, between the process of human consciousness, on the one hand, and biological-psychological-linguistic-social-economic-political and historical processes, on the other hand. It is no wonder that in the last phase of his work Juri Lotman became especially interested in the frontier area between the anthroposphere and the biosphere or, as he called it, the "semiosphere". It is in the semiosphere where any culture or nation realises itself. Any frontier — border or liminal — area, according to Lotman, is dialogical in essence. The greatest human tragedies occur when the dialogical semiosphere is disrupted and distorted by dogmatic-monologic structures or discourses, which in history, enhanced by economic and political ambitions, have nearly always emerged from the great centres of power.

Nation is a collective reality because it comprises a great number of individuals. However, in many respects it is itself comparable to an individual. Its origin is generally connected with a determined patch of the earth which by its geographical-physical characteristics provides certain psychological propensities, differences and idiosyncrasies. Any language can efficiently participate in the interpretation of basic signs. Thus, the Estonian equivalent for "nation", *rahvus*, cannot be used to denote "state" (*riik*); it is derived, instead, directly from "people", "folk" (*rahvas*), thus meaning a collective reality devoid of governmental and official connotations that "nation" may easily have in the major Western Indo-European languages.

Travellers in all times have been busy trying to define the contours of these differences and idiosyncrasies. Another important source has been reading and relying on various myths circulating in a society about the peoples of other countries. Thus the Spanish Baroque philosopher and writer Baltasar Gracián never crossed the Spanish borders but in his allegorical-symbolist novel *El criticón* (1651-1657) provided a fairly comprehensive view of the psychology of different nations (peoples) of Europe and the world at the start of the Modern Age.

Linguistic community is not an exclusive precondition of a nation, but nonetheless it has been one of the decisive factors in the formation of a nationhood and also of a nation-state. Even though Latin America and the Arab-speaking world both comprise a number of nations and states, their community of psychological, cultural and even political attitudes, based on the Spanish, Portuguese and Arab languages, respectively, is undeniable. Attempts that have been made to found an Arab Union of states have failed, and the dream of Simón Bolívar of a United States of South America has not become a reality because both geographically and ethnically these areas are too vast and varied. The deeper ethnic-cultural substrata, prior to the Arab expansion and the Spanish and Portuguese conquests, have had their basic say in these differences. Compared with South America, the less numerous indigenous peoples of North America could be suppressed and socially ousted, to create to a certain extent equal preconditions for European settlers (colonists, immigrants) to establish a multinational and multicultural society. However, in this new century the traditional hegemony of English may easily be threatened, as the Mexican indigenous people are with the process of repopulating vast areas of the south-western United States, making Spanish rival English in all public spheres.

Other vast multicultural areas tell different stories. Large states comprising a number of smaller ethnic groups are reluctant to confer on them the title of nation. For historical reasons — which have seldom shown justice to ethnic minorities — and above all in the political and economic interests of the centres, at least initially dominated by ethnic majorities, the notion of nation has been identified with that of state. Even though the linguistic and cultural idiosyncrasy of the Catalans, the Basques and the Galicians has been recognised, there is a considerable unease in the Spanish official-centralist circles when speaking of the Catalan or the Basque nation. The political self-government of minor nationalities within a larger nation state is tolerated only up to a certain point. As soon as that point is transgressed by the national aspirations of the minority, it immediately becomes a source of hostilities and serious conflicts, which generally are declared to be an "internal affair" by the central structures of the large state. Some minorities surrender peacefully to the "historical inevitability" of submitting their destiny to central political structures, while others try, often by violent and desperate means, to continue their struggle for political liberty, thus defying the "construct of nation" launched by the central power and tacitly approved by other political centres in the world. The case of Chechenia, in our days, can be seen as the most vivid epitome of these tendencies.

Estonia and the other Baltic States

Even the most recent history, however, proves that nations and national cultures are part of the everlasting changes and dynamics taking place in larger semiospheres. Only a little more than ten years ago nobody could even dream of the Baltic states regaining their political independence and being re-conferred the title of nation. Now this has become an internationally accepted reality. Overnight, Estonians, Latvians and Lithuanians were turned from peripheral minorities into political majorities in their respective countries, while the sizable Russian populations there, traditionally considered as a part of the majority, were suddenly reduced to the position of a minority. This gave rise to socio-psychologically conflicting situations, which now are being gradually toned down. Nevertheless, as a result of forty years of Russian occupation and systematic Russification directed by the former centre, especially Latvia and Estonia are at present among Europe's most multi-ethnic and multicultural societies, their difference from West European societies being in their lack of social welfare, which in the case of the latter has been the first premise in integrating the non-autochthones. With an unprecedented number of Russian citizens (about 100,000) living at present in Estonia (whose autochthones scarcely number a million), this small country is facing a challenge that has few precedents in Europe. Whereas in the case of larger nations even a large-scale immigration can hardly hope to endanger the culture and language of the native population, Estonians have lived and continue to live under a constant existential threat. There would appear to be a great deal of truth in the Spanish philosopher Miguel de Unamuno's suggestion a century ago, about the will and desire to survive — as the basic passion of all human existence — not only in individual people, but also in collective bodies of people, or nations. Small nations are especially vulnerable in this sense, as their daily existence and search for identity is realised in a permanent "liminal situation".

With the above-mentioned examples I wished to stress the great variety of individual cases in formation and existence of nations. No nation can be too secure about its future, as the future will always be submitted to complicated processes of change. That is why any mental construct or cultural conception about nation can offer only a temporary perspective or comfort. As Estonia and other Baltic peoples have now been enjoying their renewed political independence, the existential tensions have in some senses relaxed. Younger generations of Balts may not be willing to share the existentially formed creeds of their parents, because their borders with the outer world are no longer being watched over by Soviet soldiers and the KGB. Their worry about the survival of their language and culture is apparently less grave than amongst the older generations. They are more open to Western-directed globalising processes and share increasingly in the belief of Westerners that individual welfare is the highest value, while collective realities, such as nations' destinies and identities, are more or less mere myths or "cultural artefacts". An influential part of postmodern literature reflects this change in attitudes by parodying and laughing at the idealising beliefs which even in the 1980s still seemed to be deeply rooted in the native population. Nothing can be done about this. Any pedagogical or moralising effort to teach existential attitudes would fail, simply because existentialism does not mean living exclusively by means of mental and cultural constructs but by existential experience or living *per se*.

Cultural and Economic Aspects of Globalisation

To expand on the theme of globalisation, it would be useful to differentiate between its cultural and economic aspect. Information technology operates here as all techniques can operate: simply as a mediator, while the postmodern computer technologies do not mean a greater revolution than the invention of book-printing, for instance, in the fifteenth century, or the invention of alphabets in more ancient times. When the German romantics, with Herder, Goethe and Friedrich Schlegel in their vanguard, introduced the notion of historicity in interpreting cultural values and started to appreciate the cultural creation outside the syntagmatic (rationally centred) patterns powerfully impelled by the Enlightenment, it was a huge leap towards cultural globalisation unparalleled in previous history. It is sometimes thought that Goethe, by introducing in 1827 the notion of *Weltliteratur*, envisaged a kind of universal literature that would replace the hitherto existing national literatures. This is certainly not the case. Goethe was perfectly aware of the artificiality of such a project and the hollowness of universality when deprived of its national roots. He repeatedly stressed that universality does not contradict nationality and that a national literature, when entering into contact with other literatures, should by no means abandon its idiosyncrasy. *Weltliteratur* meant for him the openness of a national culture to the values of the cultural creativity of other nations of the world, a willingness to enter into a dialogue with the other, enriching itself whenever possible, but never abandoning a search for national identity. He also believed that in this way the peoples of the world could learn to understand each other better, though he never idealised that difficult process, admitting that even if they were incapable of loving each other, they could at least become more tolerant.

Such a fundamental revolution in dealing with the other, in fact an immense leap towards cultural globalisation, did not emerge from Western centres but from the European periphery — Germany, which up to those times had never been united as a nation. It should be remembered that Herder was formed intellectually in the Baltic area — in Köningsberg, and later in Riga — while Goethe died without ever having visited Paris or London. That fact, if we were to follow Lotman's understanding of "borders" as "mechanisms of dialogue", could provide the "romantic globalisation" with a premise of a genuinely dialogical nature.

The globalisation of which we speak at the turn of the third millennium, on the contrary, has been first and foremost an economic enterprise directed by Western "centralist" values and attitudes. The Peruvian writer Mario Vargas Llosa, who in recent years has been an outspoken critic of nationalism and has advocated globalising processes as something intrinsically connected with democracy, speaks in one of his essays about the new advantages for the spread of world's linguistic — and consequently, cultural — diversity under globalisation. He asks: "How many millions of young people of both sexes, worldwide, have started to learn, thanks to the challenges of globalization, Japanese, German, Mandarin, Cantonese, Arab, Russian or French?" (Vargas Llosa 2000: 13).

Nevertheless, the learning of Russian, contrary to Vargas Llosa's claim, has rather declined in the recent decade, at least in Eastern and Central Europe, while in the growing business contacts with Japan and China, Western languages, above all English, firmly hold their own. Vargas Llosa does not mention the earlier colonisation and imperialist processes which, indeed, in times when nobody knew anything about globalisation, produced a revolutionary expansion of the Western languages in today's Third World countries — not too differently from the way in which the Russian Soviet occupation produced a miraculous spread of the Russian language in all of the peripheries of the communist empire. Thus, we can ask, has globalisation really favoured the learning and the spread of the native languages — kitché, náhuatl — of Vargas Llosa's own home area, Latin America, to enable the autochthons to enter into a genuine dialogue with the postcolonial power structures? I am afraid Arturo Casas (2000: 62) is right in observing how Vargas Llosa tends to fight minor nationalisms from the platform of major nationalisms and especially, as far as the Spanish cultural situation is concerned, from that of Spanish pan-nationalism.

As one of the individuals who after Estonia's regained independence introduced Spanish studies at Tartu and Estonia, I might add that the foundation of the first centre for Spanish studies in the Baltic area could become reality first and foremost thanks to the happy situation of the Estonian national euphoria of openness to the world after the long Soviet occupation. Under the latter it would have been impossible simply because it was not *polozheno* (not considered necessary) by the educational and ideological administrators of Moscow, the supreme centre. After the ten short years of Estonia's independence, with globalising processes ever more influencing the country, English has completely replaced Russian as the first language of communication between the outer world and Estonia, and in some cases, even between Estonians and Russians. As direct economic incentives are weak, the spread of Spanish will mainly be restricted to the cultural sphere, as before, with some expansion in the field of tourism.

In the saddest situation, however, is the inter-Baltic cultural communication. Very few literary works are at present being translated from one Baltic language into another, as the reading public is becoming increasingly orientated towards Western or Anglo-American mass literature. Without the hope that

Baltic books might sell, no editor ventures to publish them. Even the work of the most influential Baltic writers of today, such as Jaan Kross, which after long delays and despite a number of complications has been introduced in the West, is virtually unknown in the other two Baltic countries.

Examples of this kind, unfortunately, abound on a worldwide scale, within the present globalisation. One-sidedness, distorting and simplifying views on culture, a shameless submission of the cultural market to the trends manipulated by the economic and commercial centres of the world, have become commonplace in all parts of the globe. The main trends in present-day multiculturalism itself reveal deep claws, as the Chinese writer Li Xia (2000) has succinctly pointed out in her critical essay.

The Estonian and Baltic Literary Discourse

What could be said about Estonian and Baltic literary discourse at the present time? I should place "Baltic" in brackets, because my first-hand access to it is, naturally, restricted. From the writing of my Latvian and Lithuanian colleagues I can still deduce that the processes are approximately analogous, though with some insignificant shades of difference.

As a relatively liberalised periphery of the Soviet empire, Estonia managed to accumulate an important cultural potential, especially starting from the 1960s — a fact that is often ignored by people in the West. Elsewhere I have tried to describe three aspects of that accumulation process: (1) language, (2) cultural media and (3) translations (Talvet 1998). To summarize them in a few words: Estonia managed to conserve and develop its native language despite the harshness of Stalinism and the subsequent restrictions and Russification. In this, Estonian cultural media, and the media in Estonian in general, played a decisive role; translations of top world literature, both old and new (although the latter were subjected to considerable delays and restrictions) prepared for the Estonian cultural openness to the world after the regained independence.

These aspects of cultural-literary activity revealed a spectacular intensification on the eve of the new independence: new literary magazines were founded, Moscow could no longer control or forbid the introduction of Western modernist literature. From long being on the defensive, the native Estonian language moved onto the offensive: from the first years of independence the knowledge of Estonian became the decisive differentiating factor between those who were accepted as "own", and those who were declared "foreigners", the other inhabitants of Estonia. A central Language Office was founded to guarantee the use of the state language, Estonian, in all public spheres.

In the most recent years this cultural intensity has not diminished, though there are some signs that should make us cautious. The central cultural weekly *Sirp* and a number of literary-cultural monthly magazines — *Looming, Vikerkaar*, and the more academic *Akadeemia* and *Keel ja Kirjandus* — all continue to do admirable work, probably unparalleled in the whole of Europe, bearing in mind Estonia's smallness as a nation, but they depend almost exclusively on state subsidies and they are experiencing increasing financial difficulties. An attempt to publish an alternative cultural weekly *Kultuurimaa*, based on private capital, however, has failed after appearing for approximately a year. Estonia's largest newspapers, which all traditionally have their cultural pages, are suffering gravely from the dictates of their Scandinavian owners, being forced to adapt themselves more and more to a rather vulgar publicity style and taste. As a result, at present only two main daily newspapers in Estonian that can be taken seriously have remained (*Postimees* and *Eesti Päevaleht*), whereas in Soviet times there were three. The future of the recently founded literary supplement of *Eesti Päevaleht* seems to be insecure, while *Postimees* has almost ceased to include literary criticism in its cultural pages, being increasingly orientated toward the visual and mass arts.

In the field of translation, it is especially fictional narratives rendered from other languages that are flooding the bookshops, but as already mentioned, under economic globalisation mediocre Anglo-American literature has become dominant, while even important translations from other languages, which from time to time do still appear, are considerably less visible than they were in the 1970s or the 1980s, when Western mass literature was practically absent in Estonian translation.

Finally, as for the Estonian language, some Estonian academic scholars have recently come to doubt whether the use of Estonian, as far as the universally acceptable and publishable "serious science" is concerned, has any value at all, while all of these goals can be much more effectively reached in English, the only true Latin of globalisation.

Against this background, the state and the future of Estonian literary creation seem to be becoming rather vague. Here I would like to comment briefly on the context of locality/globality which has been bent into the term "glocality". In fact, I know few examples of ancient and modern literature, generally recognised as having the quality of "world literature", that could not be described in terms of glocality. James Joyce's Dublin is local and concrete to an extreme, as is William Faulkner's Yoknapatawpha or García Márquez's Macondo. At the same time, they are universalised by a powerful mythification that transgresses any local or national limits. Have we now, in postmodernity, stepped into a phase of literary discourse that would cancel the validity of this observation? I doubt it. On the contrary, I am convinced that the best guarantee of some permanence in value for Estonian literature at present and in the future would be its glocality or, to be more precise, its ability to comprise the dynamics between the planes of locality and globality. Different manifestations of such a glocality are present in all major Estonian literary works that have attracted national and, in some cases, international attention in the last thirty years.

Thus, in the field of fiction, Jaan Kross has majestically, and against the ample background of European and world history, reflected Estonia's long and dolorous path towards becoming a nation, as well as its aspirations — which at the same time can be interpreted as the goals of any minor nation that has become conscious of its individuality — of liberty and a free search for identity. The mythical dimension is constantly present in the novels of Mats Traat, who has centred his novel saga on rural life in Soviet Estonia. Relying on a complicated symbolism and, in many cases, a highly ambiguous grotesque, Vaino Vahing and Arvo Valton have revealed in their narrative work the falsity of the universality imposed by the centre, that is, the Soviet regime, and have sought instead to disclose universal patterns in the behaviour of the individual in restricted social circumstances, like those of the recent Soviet Estonia (e.g. Tootmaa 1997). Mati Unt followed a similar path up to his novel *Sügisball* ("Autumn Ball") (1979). In his later fiction he has anticipated some trends that coincide with the precepts of Western postmodernism, such as an extreme fragmentation of the narrative plot, almost abandoning any "sujetisation", and essential irony. However, judging by the work of some internationally known authors (Milan Kundera, Umberto Eco) who have been recognised as epitomising the postmodern novel discourse, a plot or "sujet" still seems to be something essentially inherent in the fictional genre. Fragmentation and mosaic intertextuality may be more successfully adapted to the theatre. In fact, Unt's latest creation belongs to the theatrical genre, where he, with Madis Kõiv, another master of de-mythologising intertextualisation and fragmentation, has become well-known both as a scene director and as an experimenting adapter of literary works (e.g. Kruuspere 2000).

The suffering rural environment of the post-war Stalinist years are depicted, with great sensivity to nature and the surrounding concrete everyday world, in Viivi Luik's novel *Seitsmes rahukevad* ("The Seventh Spring of Peace") (1985), which has been translated into a number of Western languages. Here the universal or global plane is provided by the deeply sensitive contact of the narrating protagonist with nature and the concrete material world around her. The same is true of the novels of Tõnu Õnnepalu, alias Emil Tode, who, starting from his first novel *Piiririik* (1993) and the Prize of the Baltic Assembly conferred on it, has attracted considerable international attention. The difference with Luik, however, is that Luik wrote her novel under strongly restricted circumstances, in an ideological sense. Even if she had wished to, she could not go any further in her scrutiny of universal or global values. In contrast, Õnnepalu has no limitations in analysing (and rejecting) as false and insufficient both Soviet and Western universality. In fact, he goes even further and casts doubts on some of the "universal truths" traditionally connected with nature itself, as for the first time he has introduced into Estonian literature the theme of homosexual marginality. A similar "border situation" of the narrating protagonist can be discovered in Ene Mihkelson's novel *Nime vaev*, the title of which has been translated as "The Labour of Naming" by Tiina Kirss in her comprehensive "postcolonial" analysis of the novel (Kirss 2000). Mihkelson's protagonist, too, vacillates in accepting the truths of any centre, either old or new, and clings instead to introspection into her own self. Once again, Lotman's conception of dialoguing borders has been proved, though not because Mihkelson or Tode or Kross would have followed Lotman's "frontier" theory or that of Khomi Bhabbha about liminal hybridisation. Theoretical and artistic responses always emerge from certain existential situations, and are never merely intertextual. The border situation of Lotman, Kross, Mihkelson and Õnnepalu, in every individual case, has favoured a dialoguing tendency in their work — in contrast, for instance, to the overwhelmingly "centralist" thinking of Samuel Huntington in his influential *The Clash of Civilizations and the Remaking of the World Order* (1996).

I could well demonstrate the validity of these observations in what I consider the most significant part of Estonian poetry in the last thirty or thirty-five years of the twentieth century. Even the most "cosmopolitan" of modern Estonian poets, Jaan Kaplinski, is in his poetry deeply rooted in the Estonian soil, in the Estonian nature that he cherishes in such detail as few Estonian poets have been able to do. In the same way, the poetry of Hando Runnel, generally considered as epitomising a truly nationalist tendency, in antipodal contrast to the universalist Kaplinski, hides in its depth a global concern for the human ecology unbalanced and violated by the world power centres. There is a dynamic and a tension between the global and the local in the poetic work of Paul-Eerik Rummo, Andres Ehin, Ene Mihkelson, the late Juhan Viiding, as well as Mari Vallisoo, despite the differences in their individual poetics and world perception. I will analyse their work in greater detail in another article. Here it will do to conclude that the mainstream of Estonian and, I hope, Baltic literary discourse has entered the third millennium with a double sensibility — an openness to both the locality and the globality of the processes that surround us.

REFERENCES

Annus, E. 2000: National Mythology: Past and Present. *Interlitteraria*. 5. 115-130.

Èakare, V. 2000: Postmodern Emancipation from Meaning in the Discourse of Post-Socialist Latvian Literature. *Interlitteraria*. 5. 268-272.

Casas, A. 2000: Problemas de historia comparada: la comunidad interliteraria ibérica. *Interlitteraria*. 5. 56-75.

Confino, A. 1997: *The Nation as a Local Metaphor. Wurtemburg Imperial Germany and National Memory 1871-1918*. Chapel Hill and London: University of North Carolina Press.

Fernández, A. 1999: Globalización y transculturación en el lenguaje de la postmodernidad: angustia y ansiedad en la poesía actual. *Interlitteraria*. 4. 115-131.

Kirss, T. 2000: Falling into History: Postcolonialism and Fin-de-Siècle in Ene Mihkelson's *Nime vaev*. *Interlitteraria*. 5. 131-151.

Kruuspere, P. 2000: The Role of National Theatre at the Turn of the Millennium: Estonian Theatre Interpreting Estonian Literature in the 1990s. *Interlitteraria*. 5. 186-199.

Li Xia 1999: Confucius, Playboys and Rusticated *Glasperlenspieler*: From Classical Chinese Poetry to Postmodernism. *Interlitteraria*. 4. 41-60.

Li Xia 2000: In Search of New Paradigms: Signposting Multiculturalism and Comparative Literature for the New Century. *Interlitteraria*. 5. 37-55.

Sevänen, E. 2000: "The Post-National Condition": On the Relationship between the State, Nation and Nationalist Policy in the Present-Day Western World. *Interlitteraria*. 5. 15-36.

Spiridon, M. 2000: Inventing Romania. Nationalism and Literature in the Twentieth Century. *Interlitteraria*. 5. 76-86.

Talvet, J. 1998: The State of Estonian Literature Following the Reestablishment of Independence. *World Literature Today*. l. 72:2. 307-312.

Tootmaa, R. 1997: Fixing Anti-Values and Creating Alienating Illusions. *Interlitteraria*. 2. 313-326.

Vargas Llosa, M. 2000: Las culturas y globalización. *El País / Opinión*, 16. IV.

PART THREE

Identity Processes Among European National and Ethnic Minorities

6

Ethnic Identities in Global and Local Discourses: Contested Narratives of Sámi Ethnic Heritage

STEIN ROAR MATHISEN

Introduction

One of the things which the present postcolonial situation has brought us is a new kind of global awareness of the situation of indigenous populations throughout the world. As a result of this development, it may be observed that conflicts not only divide but also unite humankind (Nederveen Pieterse 1995: 52). From this perspective, conflicts of a global nature, such as colonialism and imperialism, can be seen as the origins of a postcolonial awareness of the common fate of indigenous populations all over the world. This has led to various ethnopolitical movements that work on a global scale to improve the situation for indigenous peoples. The feeling of a common situation has also led to global similarities in ethnopolitics, and in some ways to the advancement of a "common" indigenous culture, where the symbolic value of cultural elements, politics, and heritages can be transported interculturally and sometimes mutually substituted for each other. The global focus on indigenous peoples has led to ethnopolitical organising, but also to a focus on these matters in other fields worldwide, such as in business and tourism. This development has again influenced local ethnopolitical movements that work to improve their situation in specific local areas. Much weight is placed on the relationship between cultural heritage and cultural identity.

Cultural Heritages and Cultural Identities

Large economic, social and cultural changes often bring about a demand for a cultural heritage, a sort of basic foundation in culture and society that may eventually serve as a point of departure for future actions. As we shall see, this point of departure is in some way constructed culturally, but at the same time the impression is created as something stable, nature bound or natural. It is often described as the roots of a people and accorded importance on the basis of such statements. The use of biological metaphors is common in this kind of cultural construction.

This development has been specific to the whole process of modernisation in most Western countries, and it has played an important role in the development of individual nations. Each nation has had to acquire its own national history, and the sense of national unity has been communicated through symbols derived from such a constructed common background. The whole idea of a nation was crucial for guiding the nation into the process of modernisation. To obtain the unity of a nation, the gaze was shifted to the shared, common background of the people, the historical monuments, the ways of the forefathers, ancient myths, folktales and songs of the ordinary peasants, and so on. This constituted the heritage that made the people into one people, consistent with the ideas of romantic nationalism and Herder.

It is easy to see that similar processes of heritage politics are continuing today. This can be observed both in young nations, for example in Eastern Europe, who want to manifest themselves as sovereign states, and also amongst many of the indigenous peoples who seek a greater political freedom than they may obtain as cultural minorities in a majority culture. These ethnopolitical movements are often countered by the expression of views among representatives of cultural research in the majority cultures claiming that the whole idea of a people or a nation is simply something that is constructed, and even false. Such "deconstructionist" points of view often strike the representatives of those fighting for cultural and political freedom among the new nations or ethnic minorities as utterly arrogant and provocative. After all, the representatives of majority cultures have already obtained political freedom and power on the basis of simply emphasising their common heritage and background, but now they do not want to permit others to do the same.

The problem is, however, that constructions of heritages in majority cultures also implicitly influence the constructions of heritages in minority or subordinate cultures. Domination in cultural politics, and hegemonic power structures, may influence what is eventually considered to be the "authentic" culture of an indigenous people. The deep historical roots of such descriptions of the minorities may reveal how structures of domination are inherent in contemporary presentations of indigenous people, even when they are presented by the representatives of the indigenous population themselves.

The tendency to heritage-building and the cultural construction of identity must also be seen in relation to another, in many ways opposite, tendency connected with globalisation. The movement of peoples, by force or by their own will, has led to the development of what is generally referred to as multiculturalism, or the hybridisation of cultures in many areas. For many cultural researchers, this describes the typical result of globalisation, and it is also seen as something that is eventually going to change the ethnic landscape and turn the old ethnic, indigenous groups into something new and different. Culture is seen as flow and development, and not as essence and stability. The implications of this development are not necessarily moving in the direction of cultural standardisation and uniformity, as criticism of globalisation often maintains. Rather, it leads towards hybridity and global mixing, if we look at it in terms of cultural forms and expressions.

But different analytical angles point us towards different focuses, standardisation and hybridisation, and globalisation and localisation. The currents move in both directions. The solution seems to be to analyse this as a relation and not as a stream, flow or one-directional movement. It is appropriate to focus on power relations between cultural minorities and cultural majorities. In this way, the relation must also be understood as historically created and historically established, and hence a historical perspective is also necessary. Only in this way will it be possible to establish an insight into what is often missing from the different concepts describing these processes: the historical conditions of such relations, the acknowledgment of the unevenness, asymmetry and inequality of global relations (see also Nederveen Pieterse 1995: 54). The historical roots of the focus on essentialism and the movement towards hybridity should re-direct attention to cultural relations rather than to cultural elements.

The Case of the "Natural" Sami

To demonstrate this, I want to take as a point of departure some of the narrative discourses connected with relations between the Sami, the indigenous population of the Scandinavian north and the Kola Peninsula, and the so-called "majority" population of this area, with particular reference to the Norwegians. The focus will be on narrative discourses referring to the indigenous population as being in a particularly close relationship with nature. Traditionally, the Sami have earned their livelihood from nomadic and semi-nomadic hunting, fishing and reindeer herding. Today, the Sami find their occupations in most areas of modern society. However, reindeer herding continues to enjoy great cultural symbolical prominence, as it is considered the most typical Sami way of life.

Descriptions of indigenous or aboriginal people as nature bound, living in a special harmony with nature, understanding the deep-ecology of nature, having a special knowledge of the powers in nature, and so on, proliferate today. This is part of a narrative which has a global distribution, and it occurs within many different fields (Krech 1999). It can be in political fields, such as ethno-politics and the struggle for land rights, or it may be in commercial fields such as the television, Hollywood movies and tourism, or in advertising and commercials. But it is also easy to see how this global image of indigenous populations influences the lives of these indigenous populations at a local level. While the image of the indigenous population as nature bound is nearly univocal in the globalised discourse, it is certainly to a much greater degree questioned by some people in their local contexts. While the question of the relation between nature and indigenous population is referred to in more essentialising terms in the global discourse, the question of conflicts and instrumentalism is more often raised in the local context.

The narratives of the Sami and their relation to nature have been changing throughout history. These discourses concerning the Sami and their relation to nature can be analysed by starting from different categories of narrative material: folklore, fiction, travel accounts, research reports, newspaper presentations, and other such texts. This kind of narrative is generally about the "other" and implies ethnic categorisations. When the narratives are analysed from a historical perspective, however, it turns out that there are changes in the discursive fields that become relevant at different moments time. These changes are closely connected with the dominant ideologies in majority politics. In this way, ethnic boundary-making and ethnic categorisations must be studied as parts of dynamic inter-ethnic processes where the questions of power and hegemony must also be afforded attention.

The Sami as "Witches": Bestiality

In narratives from a pre-modern period, the view of the Sami as "natural" was understood partly in a geographical sense, as living in the wilderness: in the forests and in the mountains, and at the margins of civilised areas. But the Sami were also understood as marginalised in a religious sense, where the supernatural powers they were believed to control resided in nature. In the writings of the missionaries who were sent out to Christianise the Sami during the eighteenth century, these supernatural powers were dichotomised in relation to Christianity, and consequently they were seen as representing evil or demonic powers. The Sami were thought to be particularly able in sorcery, and they were thought to be able to influence the elements of nature by these means. It was, for example, an old European belief, documented from as early as around the twelfth century, that the Sami possessed the power to unloose storms, and that it would be possible for sailors to buy winds from the Sami (Moyne 1981).

In this connection another motif that was prevalent in the folklore about the Sami is of interest. In legends documented until at least the 1930s, it was a common belief that some of the Sami who were versed in witchcraft could change themselves into wild and dangerous animals, such as bears and wolves. In this disguise they would hurt or kill the domestic animals of the Norwegian farmers. The reason for this would typically be that a poor Sami begging for meat was refused and in this way took his revenge on the domestic animals. In these narratives, the relationship between the domestic animals and the wild and dangerous animals symbolically relates to the relationship between the Norwegian majority population and the indigenous Sami population. In this way, the ethnic boundary between the Norwegians and the Sami was related to the opposition between animals and human beings, and to the opposition between nature and culture. The juxtaposition of the Sami and the wild animals tended to place the Sami closer to the animals and nature, while Norwegian ethnicity came to represent what was human and cultivated.

This tendency is also obvious in a legend of pseudo-biblical, etiological character: God did not create the Sami like other people. Once upon a time, Adam had sexual intercourse with a dog, and the result of this relationship was the Sami. There is also a Norwegian proverb, which says: "The dog and the Sami are related" (Qvigstad 1922: 228). This may also have something to do with the wish to keep the Sami a subordinate group. The ambivalence of the metaphor of the Sami/dog is striking. Although the dog is an animal, it lives in homes together with people.

The answer to what was described as a wild and dangerous semi-animal, versed in witchcraft, was missionary activity, with the destruction of the "stone gods" in nature, the neutralisation of the Sami shaman, the *Noaidi*, and the destruction or "collection" of his most vital instrument, the shaman drum. In this connection, I would stress the importance of the missionaries' demonisation of the supernatural powers that the Sami found in nature. This had a profound influence on the way people understood the Sami and their religion. Besides their demonic and heathen religion, key concepts in the description of the Sami in this period are "wildness" and "bestiality". The picture painted is that of a threatening being, and forces in nature are transformed into demonic and evil powers. But already by the end of the nineteenth century the view of the Sami as a people of nature was developing into something different, inspired by the great discoveries in natural science, the general modernisation of society, and the rise of industrial society in Norway.

The "Primitive" Sami: A Child of Nature

In the early period of modernisation, the Sami's closeness to nature is often understood and related to as a primitive trait, placing the Sami on a lower step in cultural evolution, in the spirit of the dominant social Darwinist ideology of the time. Hence, from around 1870 there was a significant change in the way in which government officials reported about the Sami people. While missionaries, officers, clergymen, schoolmasters and sheriffs had earlier praised the Sami for their capability and competence, they now reported on them in terms of their laziness and dirtiness, their immorality and their drunkenness (Gjessing 1973: 78). The folklore material of this period also relates to the Sami as "primitive", and tells of low standards in housing and low hygienic standards for both humans and domestic animals. As a consequence, the Sami were described as dirty and louse-ridden. The supernatural danger that they had represented as being versed in witchcraft was partly substituted by the risk they were thought to represent in infecting Norwegians with tuberculosis or other diseases (Mathisen 1989: 112). A life in close contact with nature was now interpreted as threatening to both civilization and health.

The answer to the recognition that "primitive" people existed within the boundaries of the nation-state met, however, with different political solutions. In Norway, the result was the politics of "Norwegianisation", which was ultimately intended to lead the Sami people into the modern world as "first-class" Norwegian citizens, by "cleansing" them of everything that could be connected with Saminess, which meant their language, habits and traditions. In Sweden, on the other hand, the Sami were considered to be on such a low step in cultural evolution that it was not considered possible to civilise them. They would only be fit to herd reindeer herd, and to safeguard their reindeer herding culture; they should be protected from "civilisation". This eventually led to the policy of *Lapp-ska-vara-lapp* (Sami shall stay Sami). Among other things this implied that Sami children received a primary school education of lesser quality than that received by the rest of the Swedish population, so that they "should not be tempted to leave the Lapp (Sami) way of life". While attending school, Sami children had to stay in cold and draughty *skolkåtor* (school turf-huts) to be hardened up for their hostile natural conditions (Broberg 1982; Kvist 1995).

Both these policies practised in relation to the indigenous populations can be interpreted as representing a common view of the time: a paternalistic view of a primitive people that was much in need of guidance and support, summed up in Kipling's famous words about "The White Man's Burden". In this way the Sami was understood as a kind of "nature's child", but with a double implication. From one point of view, the Sami represents the authentic and unaltered picture of man living in close contact with nature; "the noble savage". On the other hand, however, they also represented the irresponsible "children of nature", much in need of paternalistic guidance.

The "Ecological" Sami: Conservation or Modernisation?

Since the 1980s, a global ethno-political movement has been claiming that the indigenous peoples of the world have a special position in relation to nature and resources; and that, accordingly, they should have a greater moral right to use nature and its resources. The relatively broad international acceptance of such political ideas can be understood as a kind of moral cure for the injustice that colonialism created for so many indigenous peoples of the world. But this principle is also based on the idea that indigenous peoples live in closer contact with, also in equilibrium with, nature itself, compared with people in the modern and industrialised world, and they are therefore entitled with greater moral right to nature's resources. Of course, this general idea has many positive aspects, but it also tends to establish a cognitive division between "us" in the modern and rational world, and "them" in a traditional and pre-modern world. They are considered to have their own separate "cultures", in some way not belonging to the same global reality as modern developed societies. An implied belief is in other words created, which argues that their reality should be subject to other laws of development and modernisation than those enjoyed by the rest of the world.

In the present age of late modernity, many of the uncontrolled negative consequences of modernisation are becoming apparent: the impoverishment of natural resources, pollution, and radiation are all threatening the very basis of our existence. At the same time, however, a romantic notion exists that indigenous peoples possess a knowledge and wisdom that is going to make us capable of living in a true balance with nature again. This has generated the idea of the "ecological" Sami, where the Sami are understood as a "people of nature" close to nature and living in ecological harmony (Schanche 1993: 59).

During the latter years of the 1990s the Norwegian mass media, and especially the regional newspapers in the Finnmark area, were filled with debates and letters to editors discussing the question of whether the Sami should have any special rights to use nature and its resources. This was the result largely of the fact that the Sami Rights Commission presented its proposals after nearly twenty years of work. The Sami Rights Commission was established in 1980 as the result of bitter conflicts over the decision to dam the Alta River and the subsequent hunger strike outside the Norwegian Parliament by seven young Sami in a *lávvu* (traditional Sami herding tent). The commission had the mandate to prepare recommendations to the Norwegian Parliament concerning the Sami population's land rights and their rights to the natural resources in the Sami region. The first part of their proposal was presented in 1984 and the second in 1997. In this document there also exist apparent references to indigenous people as possessors of a more "ecologically-friendly" or balanced view at the use of natural resources. It says (in my own translation):

> Generally, indigenous people have kept their knowledge of an ecologically safe use of nature. This knowledge will be useful for world society in its work to safeguard survival prospects on the earth, among other things by making use of their traditional knowledge of the systems of relations in nature, and by making their way of life

> an object of inspiration and a model for further work (NOU 1997: 4:63).

To judge from the debates in the regional newspapers referred to above and in what people generally say on the topic, certainly not everyone supports this viewpoint. It is claimed that today's intensive reindeer herding means overgrazing of this arctic environment and that this is a serious threat to the ecological balance of the Finnmark tundra. Likewise, the extensive use of motorised transportation by reindeer herders is said to be a hazard to the environment, and it is maintained that reindeer herding will ultimately change the Finnmark tundra into a desert. The leader of *Norges Miljøvernforbund* (the Norwegian Environment Association) declared in a newspaper interview that he was ready to take action against the reindeer herders (*Altaposten* 4/6 1997). Besides the factors mentioned above, the general background for this was, that a substantial number of reindeer had starved to death because of extreme snow conditions during the winter in question (1996-97). It was also claimed that it was a myth that the reindeer herders were living in harmony with nature:

> There is no use in pretending that the majority of the Sami people are ecological keepers of an ecological business. They are no more a people of nature than Kurt Oddekalv [meaning himself]. He has no problem seeing the reasons for this change in reindeer herding. Modern technological remedies and a modern way of life have become a natural part of Sami society as well. But knowledge of and attitudes to the use of nature is not left unaltered. Motorized transportation is expanding, the tundra is subject to overgrazing, and nature is destroyed. We cannot allow this to continue, he maintains (Altaposten: op. cit.; translated by S.R.M.).

In this way, the position that the Sami way of life today should be ecological is contested by many researchers, politicians, environmental organisations and ordinary people. This creates a discursive field where the descriptions of the ecological and natural Sami are brought to question. The Sami are often faced with demands to document their genuine naturalness and authenticity, and to reject everything in their culture that might be related to modernity or that can be interpreted as loans from the majority culture.

The ethno-political appropriation of the idea of the "natural" Sami by some Sami groups may be seen as a kind of strategic essentialism that has proved effective in dialogues with the majority population. But it is also a problematic strategy, as it then radically limits the possibilities of Sami self-identification in a modern world. Young Sami people today are often met with claims that they should act "more traditionally" correctly as they try to construct a modern version of what it could be like to be Sami in modern society. This attitude can be found both within the Sami political world and as a demand from the external majority society (Stordahl 1996: Hovland 1996).

One may also see examples of how the dominant, majority culture is actually defining what the indigenous culture should be, and not the indigenous peoples themselves. The majority culture has hegemonic control over educational systems, research and political organisations and institutions. When elements of indigenous culture are revitalised in this way, they are also placed in new contexts. One can often see that specific conditions or demands are made by the central governments as to how these elements of one indigenous culture should be incorporated in legislation. A normative view of what should be considered "genuine" Sami is often established: some cultural elements are interpreted as traditionally Sami, while others are considered to be modern and Norwegian.

This is also the case in heritage politics where the way of life of the indigenous peoples becomes part of the conservation issue. The result may well be that lifestyles and cultures are objectivised or reified as closed cultural forms. Thus, they become part of a setting in which the indigenous population is supposed to live as they did "once upon a time" (or perhaps as they may actually have never done, but as it has once been described by an outside ethnographer); as in a living museum, and sometimes as objects for the gaze of modern tourists, from "our" world.

There is a risk that this will only perpetuate the old paternalistic attitudes that were so manifest in the wake of social Darwinism. Again it becomes "The White Man's Burden" to be responsible for the "primitive" cultures, only this time for their preservation. This tendency can also be seen in one of the Sami Rights Commission's suggestions; this is the area where the proposition is most concrete and detailed. It concerns the reestablishment of a reindeer herding *siida* (local group) among the Skolt (East) Sami. It must be acknowledged that the history of the Skolt Sami is quite special regarding injustice and suppression of their rights, and that in the course of history they have been deprived of the possibility to practise reindeer herding. However, it is proposed that the reestablishment of reindeer herding should be organised according to the old traditions of the Skolt Sami (as described by the Finnish ethnographer Väinö Tanner in 1929), with relatively small herds under collective ownership, intensive herding with the milking of reindeer, and the use of reindeer for transportation. It should be mentioned that none of these activities are presently practised in reindeer herding in the Norwegian Sami area. The only "modern" aspect of this reestablishment is, ironically, that it is suggested that it could be a part of the tourism industry (NOU 1997: 4:365), so that people from "our" modern culture may come and visit this "old" and "authentic" Sami culture.

Another paradoxical consequence of this proposed re-establishing of a Skolt Sami *siida* is that the group of Sami is using this area for reindeer herding today has to be put out of business. In this way, a "living" and active, modern reindeer herding unit is to be replaced by a "constructed" reindeer herding culture, to better respond to the majority culture's demands for a genuine and authentic Sami culture. This may fulfil an apologetic function on behalf of the majority population, but the result is rather confusing in terms of ethnic self-determination.

In this way, questions of ethnic heritage are revealed as being deeply rooted in hegemonic structures. Within such structures, the whole idea of an "authentic" Sami culture also becomes normative and radically limits the room for action for the members of an indigenous population. When it is established which kind of culture is considered to be the *right* kind of culture for the indigenous Sami population, there seem to be only two options. People may either live up to that image, which may not be too easy in modern society, or they may choose to live otherwise. But then they are not considered to be "authentic" Sami any more. They may be described as Norwegianised, and in this context this has a moral implication, because the impression is given that they have betrayed their real Saminess. The truth is that Sami culture in the heritage-making process has been homogenised in a way that it never was in real life. This also raises the question of the role of cultural research, which surely bears some responsibility in this connection (Bruner 1986).

Preservation of Cultural Heritage as Ethnic Marginalisation

This paper has focused on narratives, myths, media presentations and research presenting the Sami as bound to nature. This is surely not the only element carrying significance in the inter-ethnic relation between the Sami and the majority populations. Although one may speak of different periods containing different specific narratives of the relation between Sami and nature, it is also possible to see how many of these ideas continue to emerge in the current discourse on the Sami. Each of these narrative constructions — the Sami as "witches", the Sami as "primitive", and the "ecological" Sami — may still be activated in current discourses, but they may appear in new forms and new combinations. The historical perspective and the focus on narrative formations helps to reveal some of the thinking that is concealed behind the contemporary discourse.

It is important to understand how ideas of cultures, cultural heritage and, in this case, also "nature" are constructed in specific cultural contexts. Closeness to nature in Sami everyday life is essentialised in the descriptions of the Sami culture and then defined as the decisive factor for identifying a genuine Sami culture. But it is important to identify who is actually defining the "authenticity". Renato Rosaldo is one of the anthropologists who have pointed out the significance of who is actually defining what culture is in an ethnographic sense. The cultural researchers veil their own cultural backgrounds but emphasise what is different and exotic in the culture they are studying. But in this way they are also hiding a power relation:

> Thus they conceal the ratio's darker side: the more power one has, the less culture one enjoys, and the more culture one has, the less power one wields. If "they" have an explicit monopoly on authentic culture, "we" have an unspoken one on institutional power (Rosaldo 1989: 202).

One aspect of this is that those who are defined as representatives of ethnic minorities are given very limited space for action in our modern, contemporary society. They continuously run the risk of being faced with sanctions when their actions are seen as not complying with the expectations that are held (among the majority population) concerning the ethnic minority in question. In the case of the Sami, we have seen that this can be seen in connection with the century-long construction of the Sami as a people of nature. But the norms for how a "people of nature" should behave in a society are by no means stated as objective facts. Rather, the norms are created as a result of relations between different ethnic groups. In this case, one of the groups is also hegemonic in relation to the other.

The narrow frames for action that are presented for an ethnic group in this way can be seen as a special form of suppression or marginalisation. Demands for authenticity, homogeneity and genuinity in a culture can, of course, be seen in relation to the ideas of romanticism and nationalism. But they gain a specific significance in the relation between a hegemonic majority and a cultural and ethnic minority. It is interesting that the exhibition of cultural heritage is made at an important meeting-point between a majority and a minority, where the minorities are seemingly given an opportunity to make their voice heard. What in reality is actually happening is that they are forced into a situation where they can only speak in the voice of the majority and are forced to use the majority's categories. The Norwegian anthropologist Tord Larsen (1996) has discussed this and maintains that this is the last remnant of the civilisation process, which can be seen in relation to colonialism. In the contemporary globalised situation, historically created structures of power obstruct a communication that is not at the same time influenced by these structures.

This eventually leads to a standardisation and homogenisation of Sami culture which in reality is shaped by categorisations derived from the majority culture. In this way, the whole idea of an "authentic" Sami culture becomes normative, and this implies limitations for future development. Since it is established which version of Sami culture should be considered the "real" and the "authentic", this version may be so narrow that it in fact excludes the majority of just that indigenous population. Those trying to adjust to life in a modern, contemporary society become marginalised. This marginalisation is typically taking place on a double scale; both in relation to their "more indigenous" fellows and in relation to the majority population of the dominant culture, yet they for some reason do not quite fit in either. In reality it is, of course, the culturalisation and essentialisation of the cultural heritages *per se*, and not the actual way that people are living their lives, that leads to this kind of marginalisation. The idea of a single Sami heritage makes Sami culture seem more homogeneous than it has ever been.

Focus on Hybridity or Ethnic Relations?

The claim to authenticity and genuineness that is made with regards to ethnic minority cultures may be just another side of the same complex that leads to skepticism towards studying the mixture of ethnic cultures or hybrid cultural forms. From this perspective, there is always the danger that "mixture" is automatically interpreted as "disintegration" (Mathisen 2000: 187f.). On a local level, the ethnic mixture is, however, more likely to be the rule rather than the exception, and different aspects of the identity can be used in different contexts (Canclini 1995). It is also a political tendency that many of those who have a Sami background choose to call themselves *Finnmarkinger* (people from Finnmark, a region with people of Sami, Kven or Finnish, and Norwegian ethnic background), thereby placing weight on their mixed descent. In this way it is possible to escape the limited frames for action attached to being categorised as a "genuine" Sami. But paradoxically enough, there seem to be several processes leading to the essentialisation and culturalisation of the multicultural as well. Faced with a hegemonic majority culture, the multicultural is often turned into an exotic cultural heritage, as there are many examples to refer to (for example, Creole or Cajun). It is, therefore, important to demonstrate how the hegemonic structures create discourses that carry meaning far outside the actual local contexts, where the actual narratives of ethnic authenticity are taking place.

As has been pointed out by several authors writing in the postcolonial tradition, a celebration of hybridity and multiculturalism without constructing links with the processes of domination and with situations of hegemony runs the risk of also celebrating the violence and hegemonic power that have led to the situation observed. The other implication is, of course, that the mere cultural description of a multicultural, hybrid situation would implicitly categorise it as "something", and thereby in some strange way essentialise it, as has already happened in certain commercial presentations of Creole and Cajun cuisine, world music, and other such phenomena. On the other hand, it is easy to see that the focus on hybridity, as for example in religions, can serve to question and challenge institutions that have become too powerful. But all of this points towards the importance of the analytical strategy proposed in this paper: the historical investigation of the ethnic relations that are behind the cultural forms and expressions which we can observe today.

REFERENCES

Altaposten 4/6 1997: Kurt Oddekalv frykter økologisk katastrofe. Vil aksjonere i Finnmark. [Kurt Oddekalv fears ecological catastrophe. Wants to take action in Finnmark.]

Broberg, Gunnar 1982: Lappkaravaner på villovägar. Antropologin och synen på samerna fram mot sekelskiftet 1900. [Lappish groups on false trails. Anthropology, the public and Sami exhibits at the turn of the century.] *Lychonos. Lärdomshistoriska Samfundets Årsbok* 1981-1982. Stockholm: Almqvist & Wiksell International. 27-86.

Bruner, Edward M. 1986: Ethnography as Narrative. 139-155 in: Victor W. Turner and Edward M. Bruner ed.: *The Anthropology of Experience.* Urbana and Chicago: University of Illinois Press.

Canclini, Néstor García 1995: *Hybrid Cultures: Strategies for Entering and Leaving Modernity.* Minneapolis: University of Minnesota Press.

Gjessing, Gutorm 1973: *Norge i Sameland.* [Norway in Sami-land.] Oslo: Gyldendal.

Hovland, Arild 1996: *Moderne urfolk — samisk ungdom i bevegelse.* [Modern

Indigenous People — Sami Youth in Motion.] Oslo: Cappelen Akademisk Forlag.

Krech; Shepard 1999: *The Ecological Indian: Myth and History.* New York: Norton.

Kvist, Roger 1995: Det rasistiska arvet i svensk samepolitik. [The racist heritage in Swedish Sami Politics.] *Politologen: organ för statsvetenskapliga förbundet* nr. 1995/1. Stockholm. 22-34.

Larsen, Tord 1996: Den globale samtalen: Modernisering, representasjon og subjektkonstruksjon. [The global conversation: Modernization, representation and the construction of subjects.] I: Siri Meyer og Morten Steffensen red.: Norge: Museum eller fremtidslaboratorium? [Norway: Museum or a Future Laboratory?] *Kulturtekster* 8, Bergen; Senter for europeiske kulturstudier. 117-146.

Mathisen, Stein R. 1989: Den etniske grensen mellom samer og nordmenn. [The ethnic boundary between Sami and Norwegians.] *Norveg. Tidsskrift for folkelivsgransking* 32. Oslo: Universitetsforlaget. 105-115.

Mathisen, Stein R. 2000: Travels and Narratives: Itinerant Constructions of a Homogenous Sami Heritage. In Pertti Anttonen et al. ed.: *Folklore, Heritage Politics and Ethnic Diversity. A Festschrift for Barbro Klein.* Botkyrka: Multicultural Centre. 179-205.

Moyne, Ernest J. 1981: *Raising the Wind: The Legend of Lapland and Finland Wizards in Literature.* Newark: University of Delaware Press.

Nederveen Pieterse, Jan 1995: Globalization as hybridization. In Mike Featherstone, Scott Lash and Roland Robertson ed.: *Global modernities.* London: Sage. 45-68.

NOU 4:1997: Naturgrunnlaget for samisk kultur. [The nature foundation of Sami culture] *Norges offentlige utredninger.* Oslo: Statens forvaltningstjeneste.

Qvigstad, J. 1922: Lappische Sprichwörter und Rätsel. *Kristiania (Oslo) Etnografiske Museums Skrifter* 1. Kristiania. 137-251.

Rosaldo, Renato 1989: *Culture and Truth: The Remaking of Social Analysis.* Boston: Beacon Press.

Schanche, Audhild 1993: Kulturminner, identitet og etnisitet. [Cultural heritage, identity and ethnicity.] *Dugnad* 19 (4/1993). 55-64.

Stordahl, Vigdis 1996: *Same i den moderne verden: Endring og kontinuitet i et samisk lokalsamfunn.* [Being Sami in the modern world: Change and continuity in a Sami local community.] Karasjok: Davvi Girji O.S.

Tanner, Väinö 1929: Antropogeografiska studier inom Petsamo-området 1. Skolt-lapparna. Helsingfors. [Anthropo-geographical investigations in the Petsamo area. 1. The Skolt Sami.] *Fennia.* 40:4.

7

Performing Ethnicity Among the Nenets and the Veps Peoples in Russia

KAIJA HEIKKINEN

Introduction

Post-colonial critics have put an end to any naiveté in the social and cultural sciences, if any still existed, and have brought the scholar's position into the very centre of such studies. This particularly concerns the ethnic, national, social and cultural aspects and while it is the focus of the present research, it is only secondarily an epistemological question of objectivity. Ethnology and anthropology have from the very beginning dealt with "others". In a contemporary world full of actualised ethnic and national movements we have nevertheless to ask: In whose name is the ethnologist speaking?

This has been one of the central issues in a paper by S.R. Mathisen.[1] He elaborates an majority and minority relationship on the basis of the Sami case in Norway. But scholars are not the only actors in the field of defining, manipulating and — perhaps — taking advantage of ethnicity. A variety of individuals and institutions (official agents, the media, public opinion) is involved in this issue, who can be regarded as representatives of the majority people (outsiders). But are the majority people's images of minorities really homogenous? Insiders have created institutions of their own, some of which are ethno-national organisations which may have a semi-official position in the structure of the state.

There has long been a continuous negotiation over how to interpret ethno-cultural heritage and whether it is "right" or not to emphasise ethnic features that are individualising or unifying. In the contemporary globalising world this kind of negotiation has intensified. The right to represent and define ethnic groups and their culture is a very concrete and highly political issue.

In this article it is my intention to address the question of representativeness through two cases involving the Nenets and the Veps peoples in Russia. More concretely, I will examine how different institutional identifiers produce ethno-cultural identity, and what ethnic, political and social results can be observed on the basis of a particular ethno-cultural identification.

The most general framework here consists of contemporary globalisation. As a result of the collapse of the socialist system and the end of the Cold War, the former socialist countries have started participating in global world economics and in the related political structures. Among the resultant consequences are ethnic revival movements and new types of immigration from Russia and other parts of the former Soviet Union. In the case of ethnic minorities, globalisation produces concrete and fundamental changes in the political context. International legislation increases the pressures on the majority populations to observe internationally accepted norms and cross-border cooperation has started in a less formal way.

In elaborating the development and changing positions of minority groups in Russia, the economic, political, ethno-national and cultural contexts have to be taken into consideration. These contexts began to change during perestroika in the late 1980s, and there is no stability yet to be seen. As a result, ethno-national movements have needed to react to many, often quite unexpected changes in legislation, political demands, contemporary regional-political plans, the formation of a new market system and other ethno-national actions. Unlike the former socialist countries, Western countries have maintained a more or less stable political, economic and social structure. This makes it difficult to compare the ongoing ethno-cultural processes in Russia with those in the Western countries. It also creates problems and extra difficulties for any international cooperation which attempts to deal with ethno-national and ethno-cultural issues.

The Ecological Aspect as a Part of Ethno-cultural Identity

It is well-known that in the process of nation-building such phenomena as common history, language, special traditions, way of life and mentality have all played a significant role. Different features have been underlined in different periods of history. In practice, however, certain characteristics of national culture are shared only by the (national) majority people, who regard it as a sort of collective culture. But as Mathisen emphasises, the construction of heritage in majority cultures has also had some influence on the construction of heritage in subordinate cultures (see Mathisen in this volume). Even if national majorities are politically dominant and have the power to produce ethno-national images, they are not living in isolation but are connected with minorities in numerous ways. This means that both minorities and majorities reflect each other's "otherness".

Mathisen is also concerned with another theme which is becoming more significant in the contemporary world, namely, the ecological factor in people's ethno-cultural identity. He analyses the ways in which the Sami people's relationship with nature has been interpreted in different periods: the Sami as a witch, i.e. bestiality, the Sami as a child of nature, and the "ecological" Sami (Mathisen 2001). In the last image the Sami people have been seen as transmitters of ecological values.

We can regard the Sami case as a good example of contemporary environmentalism. The ecological aspect has become impossible to ignore either ideologically or in practical social activities. It is no wonder that it is also one of the most powerful factors in ethno-national movements. Representatives of nomadic or semi-nomadic cultures and a pre-industrial, traditional economy and way of life tend to emphasise the ecological "health" of their cultures. In particular, one special category of peoples is active in using this argumentation: Peoples who are indigenous. The convention (169) Concerning Indigenous and Tribal Peoples in Independent Countries was adopted by the ILO in 1989, although Norway is the only Nordic country to have ratified it, which it did in 1990 (Anttonen 1999: 140-142). The law on the status of the indigenous minorities of Russia was ratified in 1999. The stated criteria are: (1) the small size of the population (less than 30,000); (2) the traditional form of livelihood; and (3) the ancient settlement in the region (Granberg 1999: 250; Kodima 1999). Furthermore, questions over which ethnic groups are living a natural way of life or, for example, whether contemporary reindeer herding is really "natural", result in both practical and ideological consequences.

Case 1: The Nenets

I return now to the question of the Sami people's ethno-cultural identity in order to elaborate on it in the context of the Barents Region, where they encounter another indigenous people, the Nenets, who live in the Nenets Autonomous Region in the Archangel District. According to statistics, the ethnic composition in the Nenets Autonomous Region in 1989 was: Russians 35,489 (65.8%); Nenets 6,423 (11.9%); Komi 5,624 (9.5%); Ukrainians 3,728 (6.9%); White Russians 1,051 (2%); and Tatar 524 (1%) (Tuisku 1999: 192). The total number of Nenets in Russia in 1989 was 34,655 (Lallukka 1992: 5).

The Barents Region is a new multinational region which was established in 1993 to focus common interest and facilitate cross-border contacts. The Barents Region is a European region that is engaging in increasing cross-border cooperation. It provides a good example of the increasing popularity of the idea of a "Europe of Regions". It is composed of Scandinavian and Russian regions with sparse populations and rich natural resources, which are located in territories where high value is placed on military strategy (Granberg 1998: 232-233).

Granberg brings an interesting aspect into the discussion of the Barents Region. According to his interpretation, even if there were major economic resources (such as large oil and gas finds) and political needs for starting collaboration in the North, these reasons are not really enough to develop cooperation. Something more is needed, something culturally and mentally important. Granberg talks about the myth of the Barents Region, which consists of two stories. One concerns the centuries-old trade connections which were said to have been established by the so-called Pomori. The other tells about the similar pattern of life, culture and identity of two indigenous peoples, the Sami and the Nenets (Granberg 1998: 235-236).

Granberg points out how mythologised history in this way simply excludes many ethnically, culturally and politically important facts. For instance, there are nationalities like the Karelians, whose age-old trade with the Finns is well-known at least in Finland; Russians other than the Pomori, and other minorities as well, have been swept way (Granberg 1998: 236). In addition, since this picture is drawn mostly by the Norwegians,[2] it is first and foremost Norway-centred and serves their own interests.

Even if in reality the way of life of the Nenets and the Sami in Russia differs profoundly from that in Scandinavia, there exists the ideology "invented" and supported by political activists and scholars alike to the effect that there is a common origin, history and way of living to be found for all these people. The unifying factor seems to be reindeer-herding.

Indigenous peoples in the Barents Region have organized themselves, and, in particular, political activists, ethnologists and members of civil organisations have been active there. The Committee of Indigenous Peoples of the Barents Region has a mandate to develop an action programme for the indigenous peoples in the region. This includes detailing the status of the present cooperation, highlighting forms of organisation for the indigenous peoples in their respective countries, proposing improvements in the living conditions of the indigenous peoples and their cultural and industrial development in the region, proposing the way in which the Regional Council could best make their contribution to positive development, and indicating the economic and organisational consequences of such a proposal (Granberg 1998: 232, 250).

In this way the Western countries — in this case, generally Norway — extend themselves and gain access to the Russian region to co-operate with, and manipulate, people there. But the Nenets have an ethno-political setting of their own. They do not live in isolation in Russia, but belong to the category of the so-called small peoples of the North. This categorisation has brought them some government subsidies (for instance, centralised consumer-goods suppliers and some social security benefits; see Slezkine 1994: 376).

Like other non-Russian peoples, during perestroika the Nenets started organising themselves and in 1989 they founded an ethnic organisation, Jasavei. Its aim is to safeguard the rights and interests of the small peoples (in practice, the Nenets) and give them help and counselling in solving their economic and social problems. Like the Sami Parliament in the Nordic countries, the Jasavei has the right in the Nenets Autonomous Region to participate in legislation concerning the indigenous peoples and to make proposals for legislation. But in reality, according to Tuula Tuisku, this does not work (Tuisku 1999: 193, 213).

A variety of conflicts seems to exist between the authorities at the local level in the Archangel District and Nenets Autonomous Region and the central political leadership in Moscow. For instance, some actions and programmes for supporting reindeer herding have been accepted at the central level, but they have not been implemented in the Nenets Region. As a result of this situation, Tuula Tuisku believes that the Nenets (in the Nenets Region) consider the government their protector, in particular where natural resources are concerned (Tuisku 1999: 213). By placing their trust in the central power Nenets activists have positioned themselves in the midst of contradictory tendencies. They seek protection, social security, subsidies and benefits from the government, and at the same time they demand more economic freedom.

From the very beginning the Jasavei organisation was criticised by different interest groups. First, it was thought to be too closely tied to the official structure and thus too bureaucratic. Secondly, it was criticised for tending only to the interests of one small group, namely, the Nenets, and by operating in this way the organisation was said to be engaged in divisive politics (Kalabanov 1997: 194-196). Critics have defined one typical dilemma: should institutional organisations underline regionalism (develop regional identity) or should they develop ethnicity?

In addition to its local, regional and Moscow-centred relations, the Jasavei also has to handle other ethnic associations. In the Archangel District these include the Association of the Pomori Renaissance, alongside the ethno-cultural organisations of Poles, Germans, Estonians and Tatars (Kalabanov 1997: 201).

Case 2: The Veps

The Veps are a small linguistically Finno-Ugrian minority group living in Russia. According to the latest statistics from 1989 they number about 12,000 (see Heikkinen and Mullonen 1994). Their ethno-cultural and administrative situation is in many ways similar to that of the other minority peoples of Russia. Administrative reforms have been demanded which seek economic independence and a strengthening of the national culture. Like most of the non-Russian peoples in the former Soviet Union, the Veps founded their ethno-cultural organisation, the Vepsian Culture Society, in 1989. The leaders of the Society are scholars from the Karelian branch of the Academy of Sciences and the university (Birin 1996: 28-32; Klementjev 1996: 142-145). The main purpose of the Society is to preserve, cultivate and develop the Vepsian language and ethno-cultural traditions — as they are modified by the activists, and mostly with the help of researchers.

Some elementary goals concerning language and ethnic culture have been achieved. A literary language has been created and linguistic primers and other elementary books published. In 1992, the Petrozavodsk Centre for National Cultures was opened; Karelian and Vepsian newspapers have been founded; and the "national" languages have been approved as school subjects in a number of schools in the Karelian Republic and the Leningrad district. In 1993 the Faculty of Baltic-Finnish Languages and Cultures at the University of Petrozavodsk was established; and in 1994 new Departments of Karelian and Vepsian Languages and Cultures were created at the University of Petrozavodsk and the Pedagogical University of Petrozavodsk. National folklore festivals have been organized. Television and radio programmes and novels and poetry have been published in the newly developed national languages, though with very limited circulation. Vepsian and Karelian national administrative units have been formed in the Karelian Republic. Vepsian (like Karelian) ethnic administrative units have been formed in the Karelian Republic (Birin 1996: 34; Heikkinen 1994: 287-288; 2001: 103-104).

In the area of ethno-national culture, organisational and financial support originating from Finland has been important. A part of this has been channelled through the government budget and the rest organised by individuals and groups. To some extent this might also have influenced the role that the movements have played in the renewal of the political system.

The Vepsian activists have been successful not only in the field of linguistic politics but also in general internal politics. They managed to get the Veps recognised as an indigenous people — in Russia the status of indigenous peoples is of the utmost importance. It brings some guarantee — at least in theory — of a developing economy, which is defined as traditional, in addition to cultural matters, and the status is the object of clear political and national policies. From a practical point of view, it provides access to the cooperation organised by the Committee of Indigenous Peoples in the Barents Region, as has been observed in the Nenets case. However, it is still too early to assess how effective this new status actually is for the Veps. Thus far, the Secretariat of the Barents Region has supported the Vepsian cultural programmes financially.

After being recognised as an indigenous people the Vepsians noticed in 1999 that they were in somewhat unfamiliar company. This happened in Moscow at a congress titled "The Small Indigenous Peoples in Russia in the Beginning of New Millennium: Problems, Perspectives and Priorities" where most of the participants arrived from the North, Siberia and the Far East. The chairman at one session referred to the Veps as "this nomadic people — the Veps" (Kodima 1999). Even if this slip of the tongue was laughed at by the Veps themselves, and even if no one expects them to start leading a traditional nomadic way of life, this remark makes quite visible the strangeness of this category in which the Veps have been classified.

Performing Ethnicity

I have dealt here with the Nenets and Veps cases only from an institutional point of view. The actors are either semi-official or non-governmental organisations and pressure groups, and their ethno-cultural politics underline the practical and instrumental side of ethnic existence. In the post-socialist countries every group and organisation (be it ethnic, local, religious, gender, professional, business, etc.) attempts to collaborate with Western partners. In this cooperation ethnicity is only one instrument, but it is, in fact, a good marker of the contemporary globalising world.

It is too easy to interpret these cases only as examples of how the economic factor affects ethnic movements. Such an aspect has been emphasised by many scholars, most of whom have studied ethnicity as a process in Western countries, where ethnic groups have a fixed niche inside a nation-state (e.g. Roosens 1989; Verdery 1994; Anttonen 1999). It is possible that the increasing importance of the instrumental aspect of ethnicity has led Western scholars to overestimate the situated, voluntary side of (ethnic) identity. On the other hand, many scholars warn against extreme individualism. Richard Jenkins is one of these. He underlines the importance of circumstances: "actors may make their own identities, but they do not do so in circumstances of their own choosing" (Jenkins 1997: 142). A realistic comment of this kind reminds us of certain limits and frames in the process of negotiating ethnicity.

It is tiresome to read paternalist explanations of the unexpected re-appearance of ethnic movements and feelings. It is easy to find interpretations in both popular and academic texts of how ethnic identity is a place of escape for people in the rapidly changing global world (e.g. Roosens 1989: 16; Anttonen 1999: 245). This kind of ethnicity concept is mostly used by scholars who themselves represent some majority people. By identifying in this way they more or less unconsciously represent the interests of their nation-state. This makes their scepticism both arrogant and destructive.

The individual side of ethnic identity and more personal images have not been discussed here. It is, however, possible to estimate the character of ethnic identity among the Veps and the Nenets. Even if only 14 per cent of the Nenets population in the Nenets Autonomous Region are really reindeer breeders, most of them regard reindeer-herding as one of the strongest factors for constructing an ethnic identity (Tuisku 1999: 12). Among the Veps, knowledge of the Vepsian language is the basic feature, even if a certain segment of the population identifies themselves as Veps even without this linguistic knowledge (see Strogal'šèikova 1989: 40-41).

In Russia this type of scepticism is reflected in a specific line of thinking that has brought destructive consequences. The empathy which previously existed with ethnic minorities has now diminished. Briefly before the collapse of the Soviet regime, ethnic anti-governmental activity was welcomed by many ethnographers both in the former Soviet Union and abroad. Today, many commentators underline the negative and destructive nature of ethno-national movements (see Heikkinen 2000: 105-112). The main idea concerns saving the Russia that still remains, and consequently we can observe a more openly pro-Russian atmosphere. This will produce dramatic implications for sociocultural studies.

Since the mid-1990s astonishing attacks on ethnography have been published in Russian ethnographic journals, stating that ethnic and social disorder has been caused by ethnographic studies. One of the most extreme representatives of such an ideology is S.V. Eeško, who has written in the authoritative and traditional *Etnografièeskie Obozrenija* [Ethnographic Review], that "ethnology in its politicised and populist variant has become one element of the ideological mechanism ruining society, one of the means of justifying ethnic violence" (Èeško 1994: 36).

This is a very strong accusation in a country where there exist enormous economic, political and social crises in addition to ethnocultural problems. His statement is just one of many similar arguments that have appeared in recent years in Russia. The rhetorical tone of the statement is familiar: to be "politicised" or to "politicise" is a concept which appeared after the collapse of the Soviet scientific canon. This argument has been, and still is used to devalue both Soviet science and — with regard to certain situations — contemporary sociocultural studies.

Among Russian ethnographers there are "opponents" who define themselves as representatives of "radical" and "critical" science. Their critical attitude sometimes tends to oppose the old Soviet science and sometimes to favour it. In fact, in many cases contemporary theories of the extreme constructivist character of ethnicity, which have been developed under totally different national and political circumstances in the postmodern Western world, seem to have become tools for making small ethnic minorities "unreal" in Russia, that is, their existence has been made suspect. Tiškov[3] puts this very clearly when he accuses ethnographers of producing a product such as ethnic group and ethnicity as a whole, and thus creating ethnic conflicts (Tiškov 1996: 35).

Argumentation of this kind does not offer small ethnic groups (more concretely, agents of ethnic movements) many possibilities for building up their own ethnic consciousness and, through it, any ethnic identity politics of their own.

NOTES

1. The core of this article consists of my comments given on Mathisen's presentation at the "Cultural Identity and Its Global Manifestations" Congress, September 14-16, 2000, in Joensuu.
2. At an International Scientific Symposium in Archangel in 2001 I observed that this picture of the past in the Archangel area has gained support from many Russian scholars and political activists.
3. V.A. Tiškov is the director of the Russian Academy of Sciences and one of the most respected ethnographers and historians in the country.

REFERENCES

Anttonen, M. 1999: *Etnopolitiikkaa Ruijassa. Suomalaislähtöisen väestön identiteettien politisoituminen 1990-luvulla* [Ethnopolitics in Ruija. The politicisation of identities among the Finnish-origin population in the 1990s]. Helsinki: Finnish Literature Society.

Birin, V. 1996: Kansalliset liikkeet Karjalan tasavallan yhteiskunnallisessa murroksessa. [National movements amidst the social transformation of the Karelian Republic] In I. Liikanen & P. Stranius ed.: *Matkalla kansalaisyhteiskuntaan? Liikettä ja liikkeitä Luoteis-Venäjällä* [On the road to civil society? Moves and movements in the Northeast Russia]. Joensuu: University of Joensuu, Karelian Research Institute.

Èeško S.V. 1994: Èelovek i etniènost [Man and ethnicity]. *Etnografièeskie Obozrenija* [Ethnographic review]. No. 6. 35-45.

Granberg, L. 1998: Constructing the Barents Region: The Play and the Audience. In L. Granberg ed.: *The Snowbelt. Studies on the European North in Transition.* Helsinki: Aleksanteri Institute and Kikimora Publications.

Heikkinen, K. & I. Mullonen ed. 1994: *Vepsäläiset tutuiksi.* [Learn to know the Veps] Joensuu: University of Joensuu, Karelian Research Institute.

Heikkinen, K. 1994: Mahtuvatko vepsäläiset kansalaisyhteiskuntaan? [Can the Veps fit into the civil society?] In T. Hämynen ed.: *Kahden Karjalan välillä, kahden Riikin riitamaalla.* [Between the two Karelias] Joensuu: University of Joensuu, Faculty of Humanities.

Heikkinen, K. 2000: Ethnicity and Nationalism in Contemporary Russian Ethnography. In C.J. Chulos and T. Piirainen ed.: *The Fall of an Empire, the Birth of a Nation. National Identities in Russia.* Aldershot: Ashgate.

Heikkinen, K. 2001: The Ethnic Movements of the Finno-Ugrian People in Russia — Their Reflections on the Ethno-National Situation in Finland. In *Etnièna Istorija Narodov Jevropi. Istoriko-Etnologièni Doslidzhennja i Naèional'na Ideja* [The ethnic history of European peoples. The historical ethnological research and the national idea]. Publication 9. Kiev: Kiev National University. 100-106.

Jenkins, R. 1997: *Rethinking Ethnicity. Arguments and Explorations.* London, Thousand Oaks, New Delhi: Sage.

Kalabanov, A. 1997: Etnopolitièeskaja situacija v Arhangels'skoj oblasti i Respublike Komi i razvitie federalism av Rossii [The ethnic situation in the Archangelskij district in the Komi republic and the development of federalism in Russia]. In *Na putjah politièeskoj transformacii (politièeskie partii i politièeskie elity postsovetskogo perioda)* [On the road to political transformation (political parties and the political elite of the post-soviet period)]. Publication 8. Part 1. Moscow: str. 184-206.

Klement'ev, Y. 1996: Formation of a Civil Society and National Movement in the Republic of Karelia. In K. Heikkinen and E. Zdravomyslova ed.: *Civil Society in the European North. Concept and Context.* St. Petersburg: Centre for Independent Social Research.

Lallukka, S. 1992 ed: *Venäjän uralilaisten kansojen tilastoa.* [Statistics about the Uralic peoples in Russia] Julkaisusarja A. Helsinki: Venäjän ja Itä-Euroopan instituutti.

Roosens, E.E. 1989: *Creating Ethnicity. The Process of Ethnogenesis. Frontiers of Anthropology. Vol. 5.* Newbury Park, London, New Delhi: Sage.

Slezkine, Y. 1994: *Russia and the Small Peoples of the North.* Arctic Mirrors. Ithaca and London: Cornell University Press.

Strogal'šèikova, Z.I. 1989: Ob etnodemografièeskih tendencijah v social'no-ekonomièeskom i kul'turnom razvitii vepsskoi narodnosti [Ethno-demographic tendencies in the socio-economical and cultural development of the Vepsian people]. V.V. Pimenov, Z.I. Strogal'šèikova & J. Surhasko ed.: *Problemy istorii i kultury vepsskoj narodnosti* [Problems of history and culture of the Vepsian people]. Petrozavodsk: The Karelian Department of the Academy of the Soviet Union.

Tiškov, V.A. 1996: O nacii i nacionalizme [About nations and nationalism]. *Svobodnaja Mysl* [The free thought]. No. 3. 30-38.

Tri dnja v Moskve [Three Days in Moscow]. *Kodima* [Homeland]. 11-12. Dec. 1999.

Tuisku, T. 1999: *Nenetsien ankarat elämisen ehdot tundralla ja kylässä. Poronhoidon sopeutumisstrategiat ja delokalisoitumisprosessi Nenetsiassa* [The harsh living conditions in the tundra and the village. The adaptation strategies of reindeer-herding and the process of delocalisation among the Nenets]. Rovaniemi: University of Lapland.

Verdery, K. 1994: Ethnicity, Nationalism, and State-making. Ethnic Groups and Boundaries: Past and Future. In H. Vermeulen and C. Govers ed.: *The Anthropology of Ethnicity. Beyond "Ethnic Groups and Boundaries"*. Amsterdam: Het Spinhuis.

8

From Local to National and Back: Finnish Music and the Construction of Minority Identity in Sweden

PEKKA SUUTARI

National identity politics are not simply directed from above and mediated to the people through folk education. Local activities and individual experiences are important elements in unifying communities, and thus the identification processes may be studied at a grass-roots level as well as in the wider national discourses. Many cultural theorists have pointed out how difficult it is to study cultures and identities which are in a state of constant change. A commonly offered solution to this dilemma is to "stop the process" and to draw a kind of still picture of the culture in motion (e.g. Hall 1996b: 117). The result is, however, very complex and the analyses need phenomenological and empirical surveys in order to make sense of the historical contexts (McRobbie 1994: 27). "The levels of micro and macro, local and global, are dynamically interrelated and inseparable", as Sarah Cohen has written (1993: 133).

The case of the Finnish music scene in Sweden is interesting for the way in which the identification process has started at the local level, and how national politics has only later reacted to the popularity of the dance music practices. The discovery of the value of local music-making has formed a basis for the development of a musical profile in national institutions, and this in turn has accelerated music production. In this article I will present some of the results of my dissertation work which dealt with the Finnish-Swedish dance music scene in

Gothenburg (*Göteborg*), and the music publicity of the Finnish-Swedish recording and broadcasting industries. In my research I tried to connect local ethnography with the analysis of national media. The final goal was to view the construction process of identity from two directions, through empirical and discourse analyses. As the theoretical basis I combined the face-to-face experiences of identity (e.g. Berger and Luckmann 1994) and the articulation theory of cultural studies (e.g. Hall 1996a).

Between the years 1990 and 1998 I spent two years altogether doing ethnomusicological fieldwork among the Finns in the Gothenburg region. In two separate chapters (Suutari 2000) I wrote textual analyses of dancing and music. Besides music I was interested in the roles played by the audiences, as well as the functions of the bands. In short, the entire interplay as a whole was examined, between the participants, musicians and dancers alike, through participatory observation. Then from 45 thematic interviews these observations were analysed in detail. The study of music in local context also provided essential information about the dynamics of and changes in cultural practices. There may not be a causal relation between culture and particular performances, but the historical construction of identity can be observed (see Grossberg 1995: 208-209).

Ethnomusicologists have talked at great length about the definition of music, not solely as a score — according to the romantic ideal of musicology — but as sound in actual performances (e.g. Will 1998; Nettl 1983). I think, however, that we need to go further and take the physical experiences of music into account, and not only its sound quality, when we are making participatory observation and interviews. In my research this was made concrete through the ambiguity of dance music aesthetics and its function as an accompaniment to dance. Music may seem awkward, square or old-fashioned if regarded from outside the dance floor only (see also Keil and Keil 1992: 3), but it becomes meaningful at another level if the researcher places himself in a situation to play and to try to dance, for example. In this situation, the functions of music are ideal, and the scholar also will simultaneously receive significant ideas for the forthcoming interviews (Thornton 1995: 5). How would he or she otherwise be able to ask the central questions about dancing experiences? Musical activities are important vehicles for constructing a sense of Finnishness and for embodying its cultural features. With music people can immediately experience otherness (Frith 1996a).

Identities of the Finns in Sweden

Local cultural practices strongly affect present-day national Finnish-Swedish identity. Earlier sociological suggestions about the eventual acculturation of immigrants have proved to be untrue (e.g. Sintonen 1999), and so cultural research has taken the mutual activities of immigrants seriously, along with, or instead of, earlier subjects such as adaptation and cultural confrontation. Social activities construct identities (ibid.: 121), and narratives of difference may influence people's behaviour (Berger and Luckmann 1994: 200). In spite of their supposed acculturation, the Finns in Sweden have maintained their present cultural traditions since the 1950s, and the history of Finnish culture throughout Sweden dates back to the Middle Ages. The Finns received official status as a national minority from the Swedish parliament in June 2000 on the grounds of the relatively large number of members in the group, its long history and its distinctive language and culture (SOU 1997: 51-52).

Most Finns in today's Sweden have moved, or their parents have moved, from Finland as industrial workers after the Second World War. This immigration grew because Swedish industry underwent strong growth hindered only by a constant shortage of labour. The reasons for emigrating from Finland were the shortage of housing, low income levels compared to Sweden, and the undeveloped educational system in Finland (Reinans 1996). Immigration continued in relatively large numbers until 1980, by which time a total of half a million Finns had settled permanently in Sweden. Nowadays, the number of Finnish-Swedes is estimated to be 445,000, and this number consists only of immigrants and their children, that is, people born in Finland or whose mother or father was born in Finland (SOU 1997). To this number we may also add 50,000 aboriginal people in Northern Sweden (*Tornedalen*) who speak a local variant of Finnish (*Meän kieli*).

In Gothenburg there live an estimated 30,000 Finnish-Swedes (six per cent of the total population), and Gothenburg is the second largest Finnish centre in Sweden after the Stockholm region, where most of the national Finnish-Swedish institutions are located. The biggest immigrant waves came to Gothenburg relatively late, in the 1960s and 1970s, but currently the Finnish language and other cultural features are common phenomena in the city and especially in its northern suburbs.

The official position of the Finnish-Swedes has improved, but the everyday practices of administration and education have changed more slowly, and the cultural situation is still far from stable. Consciousness of the advantages of the language has spread among the younger members of this group, but the general attitude and self-identification vary from person to person (Skutnabb-Kangas 1994). Earlier, being a Finn was considered a stigma (Barth 1971), but alongside the rising level of education among the second generation their status has also risen considerably (Wande 1988; Lainio 1996). However, nobody knows how many individuals actually speak Finnish, participate in various Finnish-Swedish cultural activities, or would like to have services provided in their own language. A strong decline has occurred in the amount of bilingual teaching, and nowadays only about 1,800 pupils (4% of the age groups) attend bilingual schools in grades 1-9 (Municio 1993; Salmela 1999). This number is alarming especially when we think about identification as a constant process and not based on primordiality or cultural uniformity within a group. The reasons for the low proportion of education in Finnish are partly the lack of supply and partly the feeling of uncertainty and the lack of self-esteem among the Finns. Knowledge and awareness of the history and active participation in cultural events, such as dances, are thus important elements in identity politics. Face-to-face interaction is needed because Finnish-Swedish cultural institutions and media can satisfy only a small segment of the cultural consumption.

The Dance Venues and the Audience

Finns have organised dances for themselves in Gothenburg since the early 1960s. In the early days they were arranged within the Finnish Associations, but as soon as the population grew, some of the restaurants outside the city centre started to offer a dance programme, often inviting star performers from Finland. The dance music scene became comparably lively by the end of the 1960s, and later, even if the international musical trends changed, the Finns (of all age groups) in Sweden kept on doing social dancing in pairs. During the 1980s, when the leading stars in the Finnish mainstream increasingly came from outside the field of dance music, the importance of local bands grew at the live venues in Gothenburg. Curiously, Finnish rock remained relatively unknown to the Finnish-Swedish adolescents, who were enculturated in Finnish music through their homes.

The Finnish dance music scene in the city was at its height during the 1970s, when as many as two thousand guests attended the dance venues every weekend. Since the early 1990s, the number has remained stable at between 300 and 500 clients per week. This means that the Finnish dance music has become a subculture, while it still was mainstream music for expatriate Finns 25 years earlier. I have estimated that in the 1970s 10-15 per cent of Finns went dancing at the Finnish places, and interestingly this portion is the same among the majority population in Sweden (Larsson & Svensson 1992).

The age-groups in the dance restaurants (such as *Kangaroo*, *Johans krog* or *Hisinge hus*) were rather mixed, though the youngest clients (18-25) were fewer than the people in their middle ages (during my field work). At the Finnish Associations' dances the public is less diverse and often older than in the restaurants or nightclubs. The young and the seniors had different motivations for going dancing. One woman of the first generation said to me that "dancing gave her back her lost Finnishness" (she had lived in Sweden since the early 1960s). One of the active participants among the young (she was 18 and was born in Gothenburg) said, on the other hand, that "it shows that we are Finns". Yet all recognised the

Finnish music as clearly different from the respective Swedish dance music (*dansbandsmusik*): "I have always loved to dance in Finnish" as one woman said, admitting, however, that she visits the Swedish places nowadays more often than the Finnish ones.

Despite the importance of stardom in the popular music industry, the audience members did not talk much about the performers or about the music itself. The role of the dancers themselves was much more central, and most interviewees were eager to analyse the dance as well as the interplay with a dancing partner. The most common way of learning to dance was to imitate others (to do it "naturally" or "by ear" by listening to the rhythm of music, as the interviewees put it). Dance courses were also arranged, and these often gave people the courage to try their skills in "real situations". On the dance evening everyone is supposed to be able to ask anyone to dance. Ideally, a new partner is looked for after each dance, which consists of two songs of similar types. The gendered customs are followed, such as the gentleman will lead a woman into the dance and to her table after dancing. Everybody has an individual choreography to use, so a lot of collaboration and adaptation are needed to make the dance with a new partner a pleasing experience. At its best, dancing is exciting and creative, and a lot of improvisation is required to adjust the bodily movements between the pair and with the music. People dance close to each other, which means a very extraordinary communication between the pair, though open sexuality is not normally present. Such dancing is not "art", and not performed for others (as in Hanna's dance definition; 1992), but it is a personal relationship to traditions and socially acceptable bodily movements (Hoppu 1998).

Various styles are performed throughout the evening, and the most common dances among the Finns are the foxtrot, slow fox, tango, waltz, humppa (a Finnish fusion of folk music and jazz from the 1920s), jenka, polka, samba, cha cha and jive. A Swedish style, bugg, is also used by a few competent dancers. In some of the musical styles, such as discohumppa (techno) or rock and roll, people often choose between several different dance steps including the bugg or dancing without contact between partners. All these styles are rather common to all Finnish evenings, and the multitude of dance types is one way of demonstrating at grass-roots level the Finnish traditions of the dance music scene. People at the dance events are also very conscious of the peculiarities of Finnish music, and the common feeling of otherness is clearly symbolically performed in the dances. Finnish dance music and dancing are one of the most obvious ways of showing that "we are not Swedes, but we have our own cultural traditions".

Music-making in a Live Context

During the fieldwork I interviewed eighteen dance bands that frequently played at the Finnish venues in Western Sweden. Some of the musicians had been active since the 1970s, although music-making is a hobby for them in addition to their day-to-day jobs. At the beginning of the 1990s, most bands had drums and bass, plus guitars and keyboards (or an accordion) in their line-up, while some also had wind instrumentalists. During the following seven years, more than half of the bands had started to use the sequencer technology and at the same time the number of musicians became smaller in most of the bands. The most common line-up was now a duo: a keyboard and a guitar. Sometimes a vocalist (male or female) also belonged to a group. Thus, the keyboardist was responsible for playing the bass and the drums by pressing chords by means of the keys. The sequencer in the control of the player repeated the pre-programmed patterns or other parts of the arrangement.

There were many reasons for the introduction of the sequencer technology. First of all, it followed the aesthetics of necessity because it was cheaper to employ smaller groups, and while audiences had diminished, the duos or trios could still offer a suitable musical programme at a reasonable price. At the same time the musicians could continue playing for the Finnish audience, and, in fact, there were more professional musicians in 1997 than earlier — and fewer amateurs. Secondly, skilful use of the sequencers made it easier to adapt new songs for the repertoire and to play a larger variety of different styles, ranging from disco and samba to traditional polkas. The best musicians made an effort to keep the sound lively and dynamic, even if it was produced with machinery. In consequence, preparatory work in home studios became an essential part of the actual performances, and this, of course, paved the way for home recordings and CD publications produced by the musicians themselves.

Some members in those bands that did not use the sequencers heavily criticised their colleagues, claiming that operating "the machines" was cheating people or that it was more fun to employ friends than the apparatus. In other words, the problems of using sequencer technology did not relate that much to music, but were principally visual and mental. Some of the dancers thought it unpleasant if you could not see the saxophone solo or the drum beat, but as long as there were "live" musicians on the stage (you can never see what the keyboardist does with his fingers), this shortcoming was generally a minor one. The players could still communicate with the audience and could vary their repertoire according to requests from the dancers. For this interplay, it was also important that the musicians were able to change their playing style, nuances, arrangements, or the length of the piece in response to the reactions of the audience (this is considered to be "high resonance", according to Shield 1980: 116). Hence, the music was still at least partially live, even if the accompaniment was realised with the automatic drum and bass figures. Of course, the new equipment also set up musical challenges in their users. The most difficult styles to play with the sequencers were the so-called old Finnish dance music, especially, humppa, jenka, polka, tango and waltz, because the variation, nuances and rhythmic accentuations were so important in the drums' part. Steady beat or shuffle was much easier to play on the keyboard. Anyhow, more than half of the actual repertoire consisted of the old dance music, and on average one-third was modern beat, according to my field recordings (see the table in Suutari 2000: 168).

The main thing from the point of view of the audience was to hear a variable programme that was easy for them to dance. The musicians and the dancers were similarly enculturated in the Finnish popular music, which they had listened to since childhood, and even if they practised a variety of other styles (such as classical, jazz, rock or other international genres), the dance music represented Finnishness to them. This music played different roles for individual players. One claimed that it "saved him" from loneliness, misery and destructive identity problems, because it gave him a reasonable and creative free time activity, and he could now be proud of his cultural heritage in the midst of his strange and oppressive cultural surroundings. Another young man said that he had always (he was eighteen years old) listened to Finnish dance music, and that was why it was so dear to him. The interviews showed that especially for the younger generation this music seemed to remind them of home, while rock or other styles belonged to other circles (like friends or the school).

For musicians and dancers alike, it was important that they all had a kind of common language and a general repertoire which had prominent Finnish origins and mentality. The music changed quite a lot during the fieldwork periods and new styles even emerged. Despite the changes in the repertoire, the deep structures of Finnish music were increasingly important. By this I mean that new songs and innovations followed the customary functions of music and were seen as continuously reminiscent of the Finnish traditions. The new songs that were preferred were the ones which had some melodical, harmonious or other distinctive stylistic traits that created the mood of Finnish music.

Macro Level and the Role of Music in National Minority Policy

In this section I will discuss the meaning of the music at the national level. By "Finnish-Swedish music" I mean in the first place the music made by the Finns in Sweden for their compatriot listeners. This premise conforms with the idea of the Finnish-Swedish literature, journals and electronic media which are published for the Finnish audience in Sweden (e.g. Pynnönen 1989; Jokinen 1996). In my dissertation (Suutari 2000) I have included a discography appendix including 238 published Finnish-Swedish record titles (LPs, CDs, singles and cassettes). This list still deliberately excluded some of the most famous Finnish artists from Sweden whose music is not in the first instance identified with the Finnish minority (such as the Harmony Sisters, Jukka Tolonen, Jari Sillanpää, Markoolio, or the three members of the Kent).

The Finns in Sweden have had an ambiguous relationship to popular music. Music and dancing have formed very important parts of their meetings, social life and even the funding of other functions at Finnish Associations. Nevertheless, they were underrated, ignored or even mocked from the 1960s to the 1980s, for example in the journal *Ruotsin Suomalainen*, published by the National Association of Finns in Sweden (*NAFS*). NAFS also organised cultural competitions (later "musters", *kulttuurikatselmus*), in which a separate category was also formed for the "light music singing" from 1966 onwards. This came to be the most popular among dozens of different events, and according to the Finnish newspapers of the time, also of the highest standard in the 1970s, when a total of more than 500 people participated in the competitions and thousands of people were watching. "Light music" was like a young cuckoo, to whom a small role was given, but who soon attracted the greatest interest.

To begin with, politicians and researchers were also critical of the popular music, and the dances were often described as a misery or even as in a state of decay. For example, the researcher Kari Tarkiainen described the Finnish-Swedish Associations' dances in 1971 as having the stagnant and isolated atmosphere of the rural community houses in the Finnish countryside (Tarkiainen 1996: 178). Osmo Hormia, the leader of the NAFS, for his part complained (according to the newspaper *Aamulehti* 2.3.1973) that the Finns "only want entertainment", and "they do not have a thirst for higher culture". Many other writers mentioned paradoxically that the Finnish-Swedish dance music at grass-roots level was common, though it rarely exceeded the local contexts and therefore had little artistic impact on the Finnish-Swedish culture (e.g. Gronow 1980; Muukkonen 1980; Gronow & Tingander 1983).

The printed political programme of the NAFS (1972), for example, mentioned that their target group consisted mainly of labour workers and that the cultural activities had to touch the masses instead of the cultural elite. However, the concrete efforts during the 1970s were made more often in support of established art: to put up a professional theatre group, to finance literature, and to develop the Finnish-Swedish media (e.g. Laakkonen 1982). Folk dance activities were also encouraged (Jaakkola 1983). The Finns seemed to be unable to create their own meaningful popular music (Kurkela 1983). Anyhow, NAFS also published one of the first Finnish-Swedish LPs in cooperation with the Finnish company Love Records in 1973. It was only in 1995, that popular music was released again with the support of public funding.

FINNISH-SWEDISH RECORDINGS

The first Finnish-Swedish recordings appeared in 1973. They were the compilation *Siirtolaisen tie* [The way of an Immigrant] and Esa Niemitalo's *Alla Slussenin siltojen* [Under the Bridges of Slussen]. The titles of both pointed out clearly that it was a question of a new category, "Finnish-Swedish music" (The Bridges of Slussen indicate a place in the central Stockholm where the homeless Finns would hang out). Some years later a record company, *Swe-Finn Records*, also started up production, which included some 15 albums before it closed down in 1983. Needless to say, their production was also made by and directed at the Finnish-Swedes.

In many different recordings, the songwriters have described the life of the Finns in Sweden. To begin with, this group was clearly subordinated and so the stories were often ironical, comic or even surrealistic. A new subject in artistic form is easiest to approach realistically or with humour. "Sweat smells and the accordion is playing" is one very symbolic narrative of the Finnish-Swedish life written by Rolf Berg and Urpo Salo (Love Records 1973). This story is a good example of a pertinent parody which covered the setting of the Finnish dance music scene in Sweden. Other albums which told about the same subject, but with less humour, were made by Esa Niemitalo, Pentti Kumpulainen and Paavo Niva, for example.

By the end of the 1990s more records were produced, and they also touched more often on the situation of the immigrants. At the same time the picture broadened and the contradictions became milder. Life in Sweden was no longer always miserable, but the stories included other elements as well. Sometimes people felt loneliness or rootlessness, which was described metaphorically (e.g. *Koivupuu* [Birch Tree] by Kai Tapani on the *Musalista* cd 1995). A sign of adaptation was, on the other hand, the praise of the natural beauty of the new homeland (e.g. *Maahanmuuttajan valssi* [Immigrant's Waltz] by Merja Wivolin on *Musalista* 1997 sounds like a national anthem). A couplet singer, *Hallstan Hilta* (her real name is Tuula Sirjonen), has described in detail the different sides of Finnish-Swedish life, from the quarrels at the Finnish Associations to the success of young urban immigrants, on her first CD-album *Kaksi vanhaa finniämmää* [Two Finnish Old Women] (2001). Humour has a therapeutic function in her music, where difficult subjects such as acculturation or language problems are touched on.

A new trend in the lyrics of the records was also to figure out how the next generation would identify itself with the Finnish minority. For example, Olavi Niemisalo has written (*Syntynyt Suomessa* [Born in Finland] 1989) about the pain of losing contact with the children, because the narrator was unable to speak proper Swedish while the children never learned Finnish. Later on, the identification of the second generation was treated as more complex and the parents wanted to understand bilingualism, multiculturalism and generally mediate some of the elements of their own background to their children (e.g. *Billingin kevät* [Spring in Billing] by Lokarit 1999).

The members of the second generation saw themselves very differently in their relationship to the minority culture and the Finnish heritage. Some handled the subject humorously, pointing out the peculiarities of the Finnishness (e.g. *Markoolio sticker hårt* [Markoolio Sticks Hard] 1998), while others reflected the harshness and difficulties in being a Finn in Sweden (e.g. Paskofobia's *Vi är jävla Finnar* [We are Bloody Finns]; my field recording 1997). Most of the singers in the first and second generations had songs about Finland in their repertoire, its landscape and its people (e.g. *Karjalan kuningas* [King of Karelia] by Tarja Holappa in *Musalista* 2000; *Elina* by Esa Rautiainen 1998; *Koillismaan valssi* [Koillismaa Waltz] by Kimmo Tuomaala on *Musalista* 1995).

Despite these noticeable features, very typical of the Finnish-Swedish recorded lyrics is that they do not locate themselves in any recognisable landscape, but are neutral or anonymous in their settings (compare Lilliestam 1995: 42). This is because the implied market for the songs is partially in Finland — very many songs have already been recorded in Finland by famous artists — and descriptions of the Swedish landscape would possibly turn Finnish record producers off.

The wide variety of genres in the Finnish-Swedish recordings represent well the different musical activities within the Finnish community. Primary is dance music, which is performed in restaurants (ideal listening situation; see Frith 1996b: 250). Some of the recordings are typically traditional in their repertoire (e.g. Pentti Kumpulainen, Jorma Käkelä and Niina & Duo's) though some others are rock-influenced or otherwise modern in their image and sound (e.g. Kai Tapani and Kicke Paananen). Besides the dance records, Finns have also produced religious music, folk, accordion albums, music for children, choirs, singer-song-writers, classical, blues-rock, Christmas carols and poems. It is interesting how an increasing number of record releases is resulting from the Finnish-Swedish activities, even though at the same time the number of these events and participants in the Finnish Associations have decreased strongly. When the stories of the social life become a subject in the CDs, they become crystallised in a way which symbolises the everyday practices of the local history.

On the other hand, some of the Finnish artists outside the Finnish-Swedish context have now and again managed to produce very unconventional types of music which have sometimes shown the way for the success of new styles such as Swedish rap (written by Markoolio), low-fi pop (played by Kent) or, for example, multimedia art performances (planned by Tuomo Haapala). Furthermore, the music and art which tell about the life of the minority to the majority population often create their story with humour, exoticism and exaggeration, as in the recent novel *Populärmusik från Vittula*, by Mikael Niemi (2000). Despite their artificial parody, this discourse and method of representation form as important a part of the identification project as do the face-to-face interaction and culture at grass-roots level.

Musalista and The Role of Music in Finnish Broadcasting

Since 1995 the Swedish Broadcasting Company (*Sveriges radio, SR*) has provided powerful support for music production in the form of a song contest, *Musalista* (Music List), which is broadcasted on Saturdays five or six times a year. The original idea of the programme was to produce material in a suitable format for the forthcoming Finnish radio channel — *Sisuradio P7* was established in 1997. The producer Eija Björstrand called for digital dat-tapes (home recordings) from the musicians and dance bands, and, to begin with, she also obtained some tapes from the record producer Pirjo Hanhineva, who had collected music for an anthology which she was not, however, able to publish for monetary problems (interviews with Björstrand 1995; Hanhineva 1996). It soon turned out that the right form for the programme was a song contest in which the radio listeners could select the winners by means of telephone-voting. Radio producers, musicians and listeners alike were more than astonished at the immediate success of the programme. Musalista has received as many as 3000 telephone calls, which makes it the most popular interactive programme of SR in proportion to the respective population.

It also came as a surprise to all that so much music was being recorded in home studios, and that so many musicians composed their own material, which was unknown on the dance music scene. The Finnish-Swedish records had remained relatively unknown because the record companies would not accept Finnish-Swedish music and the self-financed production suffered from the lack of the record distribution and public marketing. Not only has the radio programme Musalista achieved an enormous popularity, but its annual CD anthologies have also been relatively successful despite their noncommercial nature. The first eight Musalista records (1995-2002) include 179 pieces. Most of the songs belong to the genre of dance music, in which old and new styles are used equally, from waltz and jenka to beat and discohumppa. Most of the material has been recorded in home studios with the help of keyboards and computers and the sequencer programmes. Thirteen pieces have also been selected and recorded in a special troubadour competition at the cultural festival *Axevallan kesä* [Axevalla Summer]. There are more than eighty artists singing in eight compilations. Most of these are well-known singers at live venues, and the troubadours are also popular performers. A relatively large proportion of the singers (some thirty) belong to the second generation. For the songwriters the Musalista in particular has provided a springboard for more compositions and for the production of CDs. At the same time, the reputation and importance of the Finnish-Swedish dance music have increased considerably.

Musalista, and the *Sisuradio* in general, have encouraged musicians to make more music, while the costs of producing records are also considerably lower nowadays. At the same time the radio plays a dual role in both sponsoring and controlling the music that receives a hearing (e.g. Frith 1983: 92). Thus, Sisuradio is both a producer and a marketer of music, but also a supervisor whose duty it is to be critical in selecting the music for the audience. The aim has been to create a kind of "general" Finnish-Swedish musical style which is suitable for representing the Finnish community. This kind of music should also be suitable for different performance situations — live, recorded and mediated. In fact, the educative and national symbols of music are in common use everywhere (see also Kurkela 1989: 98).

In order to suit the demands of the general national style, the music has had to be normative, generally applicable, established, and able to shift from one medium to another (Kurkela 1989: 99). Dance music was suitable for this purpose because it was so commonly and regularly at an everyday level and the recordings made in home studios were of a relatively high sound quality and made in digital format. The media became also interested in this kind of music: records were marketed and sold, and in the late 1990s the Finnish-Swedish press also started to write about dance locales and about the artists. The dance music especially shaped the features of the general style which became normatively accepted when radio started to select the music for their programmes. Musalista also affected other programmes on Sisuradio, because the songs for the forthcoming competition had to be presented during the five days before each actual contest, and the winning pieces received more playing time later on. The *Musalista* albums are also commonly played elsewhere in the prime-time programmes of Sisuradio, where according to the programme planning a Finnish-Swedish song has to be played once every hour.

Conclusion: Music and Multicultural Identity

Local and national levels are interconnected in complex ways in the case of Finnish identity and culture in Sweden. The origins of its meanings are to be found at the grass-roots level and in local dance activities, whereas in the media dance music was underrated until the 1990s. However, a lively music scene first penetrated the radio in 1995 and then also the other media. This happened partly because social dancing gained respect internationally, and partly because the communal public image needed a concrete content and contact with to the everyday life of the Finns in Sweden. In addition, the official situation of the Finns has improved and one consequence has been increased time resources of the Finnish programmes on the digital radio since 1997.

Popular music has now become an essential part of Finnish-Swedish identity. It gained a public — though with no significant monetary support — and thus encouraged local music-making and attracted new audiences to live music events. Moreover, the new public supported the changes in technology and the willingness to write their own material in addition to the normal cover songs of the live dance music performance. Recorded music has widened the artistic image of the minority culture, and Finnish music in Sweden has changed considerably during the past decade. It differs from the mainstream music of both Sweden and Finland, and at the same time it has been open to the process of hybridisation and musical change without losing its Finnish-Swedish character.

My research has concentrated on the public performances and discourses of music as signifying practices, and thus it tells little about the multicultural identification in the private sphere. In the public sphere the occasions that are labelled as Finnish and organised for the Finnish-Swedish audience do not consciously strive to combine Finnish and Swedish traditions. Instead they survive on the condition that they succeed in creating a dynamic Finnish atmosphere which is interesting for young and old people in the audience. The elements in the music are recognised geographically as belonging to Finland, or more rarely to the Finnish minority in Sweden, but other aspects of music culture, such as dance choreographs, social life and language, are important as well.

At the same time, the international features of contemporary Finnish music are not so important as the clearly articulated elements.

Music is a powerful medium for a listener in its embodiment of the identity and in giving a content to the cultural categories (Frith 1996a). The experience of music is immediate and relies on the systematic use of national musical symbols. Music in itself may change, but the everyday practices of listening and playing make its meanings authentic. It is not just notes on papers, but music raises bodily sensations that are associated with cultural histories. Face-to-face interaction provides an immediate experience of how it feels to belong to a group and become its member (see also Berger and Luckmann 1966). At the wider national level of identity, music gives a sense of dynamics and constant change, where signs of modernity are articulated trough stories of the past. A sense of identity may lead to active participation in society and to individual empowerment which facilitate the expression of national self-esteem and feeling of community. Music is not tied to national categories, and it may not represent all the individuals of the group in question, but it can raise narratives of the communal history and reality — the symbolic construction of identity.

The anxiety and even shame experienced by the Finnish population has turned to optimism and a willingness to act for the dynamic bilingualism and multiculturalism, which would benefit both the minority and the majority. A lot of effort is needed, however, to maintain and develop the use of language, tradition and education, which are in many ways related to the practices of Finnish music in Sweden. The people whom I studied in Gothenburg had many different musical interests and activities, which was a proof that double (or multiple) identities were in use on an everyday level. Among these several styles the prestige of Finnish music has increased, and this may allow Finnish music to gain new arenas in the future.

REFERENCES

Barth, Fredrik 1971: Minoritetsproblem från socialantropologisk synpunkt. [Minority problems from the viewpoint of social anthropology.] In David

Schwarz ed.: *Identitet och minoritet. Teori och politik i dagens Sverige.* [Identity and minority. Theory and politics in contemporary Sweden.] Stockholm: Almqvist & Wiksell.

Berger, Peter L. and Thomas Luckmann 1994 (1966): *Todellisuuden sosiaalinen rakentuminen.* [The Social Construction of Reality. A Treatise on the Sociology of Knowledge.] Translated by Vesa Raiskila. Helsinki: Gaudeamus.

Cohen, Sara 1993: Ethnography and Popular Music Studies. *Popular Music.* 2. 123-138.

Frith, Simon 1983: *Sound Effects. Youth, Leisure, and the Politics of Rock'n'roll.* London: Constable.

Frith, Simon 1996a: Music and Identity. In Stuart Hall and Paul du Gay ed.: *Questions of Cultural Identity.* London: Sage.

Frith, Simon 1996b: *Performing Rites. On the Value of Popular Music.* Oxford: Oxford University Press.

Gronow, Pekka (s.a.) 1980: Suomalaiskulttuuri Ruotsissa: teatteria, kirjallisuutta, kuvataidetta, musiikkia. [Finnish culture in Sweden: theatre, literature, visual arts, music.] In *Ruotsinsuomalaisuus.* [Finnishness in Sweden.] Stockholm: Utbildningsradion.

Gronow, Pekka & Tingander, Riitta 1983: Siirtolaismusiikkia levyillä. [Immigrant music on records.] *Musiikin suunta* [Direction of Music, published by the Finnish Society for Ethnomusicology]. 2-3. 76-77.

Grossberg, Lawrence 1995: *Mielihyvän kytkennät. Risteilyjä populaarikulttuurissa.* [Connections of pleasure. Cruises in popular culture.] Tampere: Vastapaino.

Hall, Stuart 1992: *Kulttuurin ja politiikan murroksia.* [Breaks in culture and politics.] Tampere: Vastapaino.

Hall, Stuart 1996a: Introduction: Who Needs 'Identity'? In Stuart Hall and Paul Du Gay ed.: *Questions of Cultural Identity.* London: Sage.

Hall, Stuart 1996b (1988): Minimal Selves. In Houston A. Baker Jr., Manthia Biawara and Ruth H. Lindeborged ed.: *Black British Cultural Studies. A Reader.* Chicago and London: University of Chicago Press.

Hanna, Judith Lynne 1992: Dance. In Fred Myers ed.: *Ethnomusicology. An Introduction.* London: Macmillan.

Hoppu, Petri 1998: Hallitut ja vallattomat ruumiit: tanssi, yhteiskunta ja historia. [Controlled and unruled bodies: dance, society and history.] *Etnomusikologian vuosikirja* [Yearbook of Ethnomusicology.]. 10. 162-187.

Jaakkola, Magdaleena 1983: *Sverigefinländarnas etniska organisationer.* [Finnish ethnic organisations in Sweden.] Rapport 22. Expertgruppen för invandringsforskning. Stockholm: Liber.

Jokinen, Maijaliisa 1996: Sverigefinska kultursträvanden. [Finnish cultural efforts in Sweden] In Jarmo Lainio red.: *Finnarnas historia i Sverige, del 3. Tiden efter 1945.* [History of the Finns in Sweden, part 3, the time after 1945.] Helsingfors and Stockholm: SHS/NM.

Keil, Charles and Angeliki Keil 1992: *Polka Happiness*. Philadelphia: Temple University Press.

Kurkela, Vesa 1983: Siirtolaisuus musiikin näkökulmasta. [Immigration from the perspective of music.] *Musiikin suunta*. 2-3. 3-4.

Kurkela, Vesa 1989: *Musiikkifolklorismi ja järjestökulttuuri. Kansanmusiikin ideologinen ja taiteellinen hyödyntäminen suomalaisissa musiikki-ja nuorisojärjestöissä* . [Musical folklorism and the organisation culture. Ideological and artistic utilisation of folk music in Finnish musical and youth organisations.] Helsinki: Suomen Etnomusikologinen Seura.

Laakkonen, Risto 1982: Ruotsinsuomalainen kulttuurikehys. [Frames of Finnish culture in Sweden.] *Suomalainen vuosikirja 1983*. [Finnish Yearbook 1983.] Helsinki: Suomalaisen Kirjallisuuden Seura & Kansanvalistusseura. 140-145.

Lainio, Jarmo 1996: Finskans ställning i Sverige och dess betydelse för sverigefinnarna. [Status of the Finnish language in Sweden, and its meaning for the Finnish-Swedes] In Jarmo Lainio ed.: *Finnarnas Historia i Sverige, del 3. Tiden efter 1945*. [History of the Finns in Sweden, part 3, the period after 1945.] Helsingfors & Stockholm: SHS/NM.

Larsson, Tor & Svensson, Gustav 1992: *Twilight Time. Studier i svenskt dansmusikliv*. [Studies in Swedish dance music life.] SAMU 3. Uppsala: Samhällsvetenskapliga forksningsinstitutet.

Lilliestam, Lars 1996: The Sounds of Swedish Rock. In Tarja Hautamäki and Tarja Rautiainen ed.: *Popular Music in Seven Acts*. Tampere: The University of Tampere. Department of Folk Tradition.

McRobbie, Angela 1994: *Postmodernism and Popular Culture*. London and New York: Routledge.

Merriam, Alan P. 1964: *The Anthropology of Music*. Evanston, Illinois: Northwestern University Press.

Municio, Ingegerd 1993: Vallan varjossa: ruotsinsuomalaiset vanhemmat ja Ruotsin koulupolitiikka. [In the shadow of authority: the Finnish-Swedish parents and the school politics of Sweden.] In Vuonokari & Pelkonen ed.: *Luokan kynnyksen yli. Ruotsinsuomalaiset kirjoittavat kouluhistoriaa*. [Over the threshold of a classroom. The Finns in Sweden write a history of education.] Tukholma: Ruotsinsuomalaisten arkisto.

Muukkonen, Erkki 1980: *Ruotsinsuomalaiset ja musiikki*. [The Finns in Sweden and music.] Tukholma: Norden-yhdistys, Suomalais-ruotsalainen kulttuurirahasto & Finn-kirja.

Nettl, Bruno 1983: *The Study of Ethnomusicology. Twenty-nine Issues and Concepts*. Urbana and Chicago: University of Illinois Press.

Pynnönen, Marja-Liisa 1991: *Siirtolaisuuden vanavedessä. Tutkimus ruotsinsuomalaisen kirjallisuuden kentästä vuosina 1956-1988*. [In the wake of immigration. Research in the field of Finnish literacy in Sweden, 1956-1988.] Helsinki: Suomalaisen Kirjallisuuden Seura.

Reinans, Sven Alur 1996: Den finländska befolkningen i Sverige; en statistisk-demografisk beskrivning. [Finnish population in Sweden: a statistical-demographic description.] In Jarmo Lainio ed.: *Finnarnas historia i Sverige, del 3. Tiden efter 1945.* [History of the Finns in Sweden, part 3, the period after 1945.] Helsingfors & Stockholm: SHS/NM.

Salmela, Pasi 1999: Ruotsalainen koulu: suomen kieli harvojen etuoikeutena. [The Swedish school: The Finnish language as the privilege of the few.] *Viikkoviesti.* 40. 7.10.1999.

Shield, Renee Rose 1980: Country Corn: Performance in Context. In Norman McLeod and Marcia Herndon ed.: *The Ethnography of Musical Performance.* Norwood: Norwood Editions.

Sintonen, Teppo 1999: *Etninen identiteetti ja narratiivisuus. Kanadan suomalaiset miehet elämänsä kertojina.* [Ethnic identity and narration. Finnish men in Canada as the narrators of their lives.] Jyväskylä: SoPhi, Jyväskylän yliopisto.

Skutnabb-Kangas, Tove 1994: Sverigefinnar förhandlar om etnisk identitet. [Finns in Sweden discuss ethnic identity.] In Markku Peura & Tove Skutnabb-Kangas ed.: *Man kan vara tvåländare också.... Sverigefinnarnas väg från tystnad till kamp.* [You can be bi-national too.... The way of the Finnish minority in Sweden from silence to struggle.] Stockholm: Sverigefinländarnas arkiv.

SOU 1997: Steg mot en minoritetspolitik. Europarådets konvention för skydd av nationella minoriteter. Betänkande av minoritetsspråkskommittén. [Steps towards a minority policy. Council of Europe Framework Convention for the Protection of National Minorities. Report of the minority language committee.] *Statens offentliga utredningar* 1997: 193. [Official accounts of the state.] Stockholm.

Suutari, Pekka 2000: *Götajoen jenkka. Tanssimusiikki ruotsinsuomalaisen identiteetin rakentajana.* [Dance Music in the Construction of Finnish-Swedish Identity]. Helsinki & Tukholma: Suomen Etnomusikologinen Seura & Ruotsinsuomalaisten Arkisto.

Tarkiainen 1996: Sverigefinska infrastrukturer. [Finnish infrastructures in Sweden.] In Jarmo Lainio ed.: *Finnarnas historia i Sverige 3. Tiden efter 1945.* [History of the Finns in Sweden, part 3, the period after 1945.] Helsingfors & Stockholm: SHS/NM.

Thornton, Sarah 1995: *Club Cultures. Music, Media and Subcultural Capital.* Cambridge: Polity Press.

Wande, Erling 1988: Språkkunskaperna hos andra och tredje generationens finska invandrare. [Knowledge of a language among the second and third generation of the Finnish immigrants.] *Sverigefinländarna år 2000. En seminarierapport.* [The Finns in Sweden in 2000. A report of a seminar.] Delegationen för migrationsforskning, Helsingfors, och Delegationen för invandrarforskning, Stockholm.

Will, Udo 1998: An Ethnomusicologist's Dilemma: Technology and the Analysis of Music. *Etnomusikologian vuosikirja.* [Yearbook of Ethnomusicology.] 10. 5-12.

9

German Home and Hybridity: Reclaiming New Cultural Identities in Selected German Migrant Narratives from the 1990s

MARJA-LEENA HAKKARAINEN

Introduction

Since the fall of the Berlin wall in 1989 and German unification in the following year, such questions as "Who is German?" have re-emerged, this time combined with the problems of immigration and citizenship. Despite the increased emphasis on globalisation in Europe, a discernible return to earlier forms of national identification can also be traced, a return rendered overt in aggressive attacks on ethnic minorities. The purpose of this paper is to explore the constructions of Germanness and minority identities in the migrant narratives written in German by authors of different ethnic and national identities. I will draw on the concepts of cultural identity and cultural hybridity developed by Stuart Hall, Homi K. Bhabha and Lisa Lowe to demonstrate how the struggle for new identities in a few fictional narratives takes place within the domain of language.

People tend to think that cultural identity is something stable, and the homeland a place which must never change (Räthzel 1994: 81). The migrations caused by colonialism, the two world wars, development and the new global economy have, however, made homelessness the cultural characteristic of the late twentieth century. In fact, as Vandana Shiva (1993: 98) points out, there are two very different classes of homelessness: one group is mobile on a world scale ("no country as home, but the whole world as its property"), the other lives in refugee camps, resettlement colonies and other reserves. Paradoxically it also seems that when external borders disappear, internal borders and boundaries are recreated. The global integration is closely related to national disintegration. According to Stuart Hall (1991: 26-27), today's globalism is closely involved in the erosion of the nation-state:

> One of the things which happens when the nation-state begins to weaken, becoming less convincing and less powerful, is that the response seems to go in two ways simultaneously. It goes above the nation-state and it goes below it. It goes global and local in the same moment. Global and local are the two faces of the same movement from one epoch of globalization, the one which has been dominated by the nation-state, the national economies, the national cultural identities, to something new.

In Germany there has been a very intimate linkage between languages and nations. In 1795 Immanuel Kant argued that differences of language and religion were the most important means of separating peoples and preventing them from mixing and Fichte stressed the role of language as an invisible border of the nation (Fichte 1971: 460; Crowley 1996: 48). As Crowley points out, it was the nineteenth century that brought with it a rise in cultural nationalism, meaning the identification of language and nationality. The nation was, of course, considered a mono-linguistic and mono-cultural unit, though in Germany this never was the case.

In recent postcolonial studies the idea of cultural hybridity is regarded as a positive chance for new international communication. The post-colonial critic and theorist Homi K. Bhabha (1994: 37) maintains that any cultural identity in the contact zone of intercultural relations is constructed in a hybrid-transcultural space, which he calls the "third space of enunciation". The position of in-betweenness provides a new way of conceptualising an international culture, this time "based not on the exoticism of multiculturalism or the *diversity* of cultures, but on the inscription and articulation of culture's hybridity" (Bhabha 1994: 38). With reference to Bhabha's thesis that the modern nations are today being rewritten by those living on their margins — e.g. by the colonised, the women, the migrants and the immigrants — Gabriele Brinker-Gabler (1997: 264) claims that the new German society is also being rewritten by migrant authors coming from its margins. I will also argue that German migrant narratives are not only representations of reality but also performances that take part in changing reality.

The Marriage of East and West

In 1989 people in Leipzig shouted the slogan "Deutschland, einig Vaterland" and "Wir sind das Volk". The press represented the German unification as a "family reunion" which brought the "brothers and sisters" happily together. It soon came out, however, that the re-marriage of the parent states was not an easy one. Maria Mies (1993: 119) even goes so far as to say that East Germany is now again part of the political German nation-state but its actual status is that of a colony. The external border disappeared but the wall still exists in the minds of the people. On one side there are the Besserwessis — people from West Germany who know everything better and the Ossis who feel like near-foreigners in their own country. As Brinker-Gabler (1997: 265) points out, the East Germans were at the same time "insider(s) and outsider(s), familiar and foreign, central and marginal — participating in *one* (West) German nation-state but deprived of the history and traditions of their former nation-state".

The specific form of displacement and re-placement is in various ways represented in the so-called unification novel (Wenderoman). According to Christa Wolf (1999: 21), who spent 40 years of her life in the GDR, it is the task of literature to investigate the blind spots in the past and help people on their way to the future. In order to recover from their loss people must tell the past, construct it by means of memory, fantasy and narrative. Even the titles of the new novels show a mixture of Eastern and Western images and allusions. The title of Daniela Dahn's new book "Westwärts und nicht vergessen", for example, combines the advertising slogan "Go West" with a reference to the solidarity song "Vorwärts und nicht vergessen".

In *Auf dem Weg nach Tabou* Christa Wolf (1999: 271)

claims not to know any more who "we" are and who then are the "others". She expresses a wish to travel to a utopian place, Tabou, which is neither in the East nor in the West. This place would mean a home for the homeless. The symbol of belonging peculiar to Tabou is "bread":

> Bread as an archaic symbol ... that, together with wine, invites conversation, intimacy, friendship, hospitality. I would like that, and it does happen: Germans from different directions, who work together and develop projects, who then sit at the table, talk to one another, and also argue, eat, and together consume the soup into which they have broken their bread. To put bread on the table that they have brought from their different regions, to give it to one another to taste, and to share it gladly and generously with one another (Wolf 1999: 339; English translation by Brinker-Gabler 1997: 277).

Brinker-Gabler (1997: 275) points out that Wolf makes no call for national integration ("gesamtdeutsche Identität") but, instead, she creates an alternative community (Gemeinschaft). It is also remarkable, that a considerable number of the inhabitants of Tabou are dead German artists. So it seems to be more a nostalgic look backwards than a vision for the future.

Günter Grass, the most influential West German writer, who was awarded the Nobel Prize in 1999, mixes tragic and comic tones in both of his post-unification novels, *Unkenrufe* (1992) and *Ein Weites Feld* (1995). In *Unkenrufe* Grass tells the love-story of two elderly exiles, Alexander (Germany) and Alexandra (Poland). The events are set mainly in Danzig, Poland, and many characters are non-German or bi-national, like Grass himself. There are Poles, various refugees and Mister Chatterjee, a Bengali with a British passport. Grass lets the German language be hybridised while showing how it sounds when spoken by emigrants and immigrants.

Erna Brakup, an old German lady, who has managed to stay in Danzig after the world war, provides another example of hybrid German language when she says: "Ech mecht hiä nech räden vonne Jerechtigkait, wo nech jiebt, abä was haimat is, muss blaiben och Heimat" (Grass 1992: 151). The senior lovers work together to establish reconciliation cemeteries for the many homeless people so that they may finally rest in native soil ("Heimaterde"). The reconciliation cemetery turns out to be big business generating a totally new brand of tourism industry designed for elderly people looking forward to resting in peace. At the end of the novel the lovers die in a car accident in Italy and are buried there, far from home.

Christa Wolf, perhaps the best-known East German author, explores the particular dilemmas of female exiles and immigrants in her recent novels. In *Medea* (1996), for example, she rewrites the ancient myth as a polyphonic narrative consisting of six voices. Her story is a counter-myth presenting Medea as a victim, unlike in the ancient story of a woman who kills her own children. After fleeing from her homeland (Eastern Colchis) she takes refuge in Corinth. She remains a stranger who is attacked and banned, and her children are stoned to death. In fact, both Corinth and Kolchis are ruined by patriarchal power. Medea's father has his son murdered and also Creon, king of Corinth, has secretly killed his own daughter. Both countries want to prevent change, but by killing their children they destroy their own future. Though I do not think it advisable to read the novel as an allegory of the Wessis and the Ossis, as some German critics have done, it seems obvious that Medea's fate refers to the xenophobic attacks that have occurred in the unified Germany.

In recent unification novels there is a notable trend towards polyphonic settings. The unification novel *Simple Storys* (1998) of Ingo Schulze comprises of about 40 narrations spoken by different characters. Schulze's stories are brief extracts from the lives of people in a small eastern town of Altenburg. The first speaker, Renate Maurer, tells about her trip to Italy in 1990, soon after the wall had fallen but when there were still two Germanies. In the second chapter the German unification is metaphorically represented as the rape and surrender of a young East German girl by a West German real estate speculator.

> Weder er noch seine Hand hörten auf mich. Dann folgte ein Schmerz, der von dem Schulter den Rücken hinablief. "Die Arme hoch", rief jemand, "Arme hoch!" Für einen

> Moment wusste ich nicht, wo ich war und was auf mich geschoben hatte. Meine Bluse wurde hochgezerrt. Und immer wieder, jede Silbe betondend: "Die Arme hoch!" (Schulze 1998: 28).

In the following stories the same names and characters appear and the seemingly separate narratives reveal a network of social relationships. The people delve into their private affairs, losing and getting jobs and partners, moving in and out. The polyphony of various voices shows how the identities are constructed through speech. They also convey the concept that such a thing as a given and stable identity does not exist but, instead, there is a continuous process of constructing and deconstructing identities. The subtitle of *Simple Storys* ("ein Roman aus der ostdeutschen Provinz") reveals that it is also part of the project to rewrite German history from the margins.

Nowadays there is evidence of the relationship between the Wessis and the Ossis, namely a hybrid creature *Der Wossi,* who is able to establish him/herself in the West as well as in the East. Abdullah JanMohamed would call this character a syncretic intellectual. In his new novel called *Der Wossi* Eberhard Halbauer compares him to Goethe's Faust, who also has two souls. Der Wossi, the traveller between East and West, is a living example of cultural hybridity in present-day Germany.

Talking Back to Germany

While representatives of German minorities in Eastern Europe as well as the citizens of the former German Democratic Republic have received German citizenship without difficulty, the *Gastarbeiter* and refugees from southern Europe or from non-European countries still experience the German mode of immigration policy: *ius sanguis* instead of *ius soli,* meaning that citizenship is received by right of blood ties, not of birthplace. Germany's largest ethnic minority consists of more than two million Turkish-Germans. Bhabha (1990: 316-317) has compared the Turkish *Gastarbeiter* in Germany to the immigrants from former colonies. Germany, which was late in constructing overseas colonies, did, however, succeed in building foreign labour colonies inside its own borders, as

Emine Segi Özdamar (1996: 58) aptly points out. Especially after the wall was built in 1961 there was a great need for cheap labour from southern and eastern Europe. While the first generation of guest workers lived in relative isolation, the second generation is often more closely attached to German culture and society than it is to Turkey. Today one might speak of hyphenated identities, people who live in-between the cultures. They are at home in both cultures or, more probably, foreigners everywhere.

The literature written now in Germany by the non-German migrant authors is in many respects different from the *Gastarbeiterliteratur* of the 1960s and 1970s, also called "affected literature" (Literatur der Betroffenheit; on Gastarbeiterliteratur, see Adelson 1991: 67-68; Fischer and McGowan 1995: 42-44; Teraoka 1990: 294). The voice of the victim has been replaced by a variety of voices and styles. Some Turks living in Germany write in Turkish, for example Aras Ören and Güney Dal. Yet others, including Zafer Senoçak, Feridun Zaimoglu, Emine Sevgi Özdamar, Renan Demirkan and Kemal Kurt, to name only a few, write in German.

Emine Sevgi Özdamar, born in 1946 in Malatya, actually belongs to the first generation but has started writing novels in the 1990s. She is one of the most famous German Turkish writers and won the Ingeborg Bachmann price in 1991 for her first novel *Das Leben ist ein Karawanserai,* a novel memorising a childhood in Turkey in the 1950s. Its sequel, *Die Brücke vom goldenen Horn* (1998), is set in West Berlin and in Istanbul in the late 1960s. Kadriye Öztürk (1998: 159) demonstrates how in both novels Özdamar combines German words with Turkish metaphors and symbols, thus creating a hybrid language. In *Mutter Zunge* Özdamar focuses on the relevance of language in the construction of identity. In fact, the metaphor of *mother tongue* combines three important aspects of migrant writing: language, body and memory. It refers to the physical tongue of the mother, not to the general mother tongue. The protagonist thinks that she has lost her mother tongue in the Intercity train restaurant near Cologne:

> At first, I could not look at Cologne cathedral. Whenever the train arrived in Cologne, I always shut my eyes.

> Once, however, I opened an eye, and then I saw it: the cathedral was watching me. At that moment a razor-blade entered my body, ran through me, and there was no more pain. I opened my other eye. Perhaps I lost my mother tongue there, then, that time (Özdamar 1998b: 254).

In the first two stories the narrator searches for her lost mother and grandmother tongues, Turkish and Arabic, gradually learning to construct her identity in the space in-between, somewhere between the German, Turkish and Arabic cultures and languages.

Most of Özdamar's narratives are more or less autobiographical in nature. The only story not written in the first person is "Karagöz in Alamania", a parable which satirically reveals the German version of multiculturalism (Horrocks and Kolinsky 1996: xxiii). The story of Karagöz, Black-Eye and his Donkey refers intertextually to the popular hero from the Turkish shadow theatre, Karagöz. The sketches go back to the fourteenth century when Turkey was a multicultural country and Karagöz took part in an international brigade including, for example, the Jew, the Arab and the Greek (And 1975: 32-33; Seyhan 1997: 246-248). In Özdamar's story the character is sent as a guest worker to Alemania. The result is an international mixture of voices and narrations, jokes and curses. Özdamar (1996: 55) has pointed out that the broken German spoken by *Gastarbeiter* (Gastarbeiterdeutsch) plays an important role as the common language of the guest workers from different countries. The German of the Turks may sound like that:

> Krankenhaus da doktorla gavga ettim. Nirde Krankenscheinin dedi. Yahu, doktor, ben krankim. Yahu krank görmüyorum. Yok Krankenschein yok — para yok. Yahu, doktor, dedim. Doktor Nikis krank. Gesundschreiben yapti. Ver Gutpapier, ulan, nikis schlecht Papier dedim. Ben Urlauba gidiyorum dedim (Özdamar 1998a: 77).

One can notice a deep polarisation between the German vocabulary of bureaucracy and the feelings and emotions expressed in Turkish. The Islamic culture reveals itself in proverbs, curses and sayings from the *Quaran* (Koran). The repetition of the word *Inschallah,* Allah willing, is often heard in the German car plant where Karagöz is working. The pidgin German also proves to be a medium of subversive laughter. Some mistakes are apparently harmless, such as calling overwork "oversin" (Überstunden-Übersünden). The name *Bunepislik* for Bundesrepublik is already mischievous, in Turkish Bunepislik means "nonsense".

The play with the language is also at the centre of Kemal Kurt's novel *Ja, sagt Molly* (1998). Its title refers to the last lines of James Joyce's *Ulysses* and Kurt obviously follows the intertextual mode of Joyce when he says that the man who makes Molly Bloom happy is no one but Gregor Samsa. In the novel the European librarians decide to keep only one book as a token of the literature of the twentieth century. The protagonists of various well-known books struggle bitterly for survival. Most of them are known from twentieth century novels: Adrian Leverkühn, for example, and Bernard Marx, Franz Biberkopf, Leni Pfeiffer, Pelageja Vlasova, Philip Marlowe, Mersault and Shen Te. Mersault, symbolising the existentialist Other, finds the German word *Heimat* very strange. He claims that the first people were nomads. It was only later, when they settled down that they called the place "Heimat", and in so doing they mystified it to such an extent that people became prepared to die for the imagined community:

> In vielen Sprachen der Erde kennt man das Wort 'Heimat' nicht. *Hometown* or *homeland* hat nicht das Pathos von Heimat. *Memleket* bezeichnet lediglich den Herkunftsort. Das Wort *yurt* kommt der Sache schon näher, aber es ist von der Jurte, dem Nomadenzelt, abgeleitet. Die Heimat des Nomaden ist somit sein Zelt. *La patrie* ist das Vaterland und *le terroir* bezieht sich auf die Erde als Ackerland, als Scholle. *Il pais, la patria....* Aber wo bleibt die Heimat? (Kurt 1998: 43).

On the threshold of the millennium the concept of the national state seems old-fashioned. Along with the nation-state the canon of the world literature is shattered. In Kurt's narrative there are also many characters created by postcolonial authors holding meetings in Mr. Biswas's house. At a tea party Antoinette

Cosway, Saleem Sinai, Jing Mei Woo, Lord Jim and many others plan to publish a book together and draw in the readers of the whole world with the thesis "Die Zukunft der Literatur ist entweder multikulturell oder gar nicht" (Kurt 1998: 73). The meeting ends with an arson attack and the characters of the so-called "fifth literature" die in the flames. The racist characters also die soon, leaving Molly Bloom and Gregor Samsa as the winners of the battle.

Like Kemal Kurt, Feridun Zaimoglu also represents the third generation of German Turks. He has launched the term *Kanak Attack* for talking back to Germany as a form of cultural resistance. "Kanake" is an insulting German term for foreigners, especially for Turks. In his book *Kanak Sprak* (1995) Zaimoglu lets the Kanaks speak openly about their situation as "Gastarbeiterkinder" who are at home nowhere. In Germany they are Turks and in Turkey they are called "Deutschlanders". The short passages narrated by some two dozen young Turks living on the margins of society criticise the German stereotype of the Turk, claiming that only two alternatives exist: to be "lieb-alilein" or a "desperado" (Zaimoglu 1999: 31-32). Zaimoglu (1999: 13) explains that Kanak(a) Sprak is a jargon not unlike Creole or Rotwelsch. The rapid, aggressive speech is constructed on the basis of German and Turkish, a literary language and a dialect. It is to be understood as an oral performance, where mimicry and gestures play significant roles. The passages offer a new literary German combining German-Turkish slang with rap rhythms. The combination of rap music with German, Turkish and English also proves to be an example of the "aesthetics of the hybrid", as termed by Stuart Hall (1991: 39).

The sequel to *Kanak Sprak* is *Kopfstoff* (1998), where female Turks tell their own stories. The subtitle "Kanaka Sprak vom Rande der Gesellschaft" openly refers to the position on the margin of German society. Some of them criticise the increasing racism, especially the discrimination practised against the Muslims. One of them connects it with the German unification, which gave the "Aleman" a feeling of superiority:

> Jetzt sollen wir klatschen, der Aleman hat was Riesentolles zusammengelitten, er ist ja wieder ganz, er ist ja wieder einig deutsch, wenn der Aleman zur Ganzheit kommt,

> wird er zum Insgesichtspucker, da ist nicht mal ihr genagelter Herrgott davor, der ist nun mal n Judendreck und lange n Radieschenvonuntenriecher (Zaimoglu 1988: 32-33).

The xenophobia seems to include Jews as well, even Christ with his notorious Jewish origin.

As Nora M. Alter (1997: 131) points out, the German variant of the "dialectic between nationalism and racism" is overshadowed by the National Socialist anti-Semitism. Many speakers in *Kopfstoff* call for cultural resistance, even for battle. A female student points out that the Turks no longer need to attack Germany because they are already there as bastards, who combine Turkish temperament with Prussian discipline, and their original sentimentality with their acquired resistance:

> Ja, die Bastarde kommen, aber nicht mit Döner, Exportladenkitsch, Multikultigetrampel tränenreicher "In der Fremde" — Literatur und schlechtem Rap, goldbehangen im Sultanschick und anatolische Lieder lallend, wie's der Deutsche gern hätt, wenn überhaupt, sondern mit Qualität, erlernter preussischer Disziplin, angeborenem Feuer unterm Arsch, mitgebrachtem Kulturkoffer, nicht loszuwerdender Sentimentalität und erworbener Widerstandsfähigkeit, denn was nicht tötet, härtet angeblich ab, und es hat uns nicht umgebracht (Zaimoglu 1998: 61).

Conclusion

I should like to return to Christa Wolf's vision of a community where Germans coming from different regions gather together round a table and share their bread. I think Brinker-Gabler (1997: 277) is right in asking what happens when the newcomers do not bring German bread but their own pita bread, challah or lahvash, instead. Today the German home is far from the romantic ideas of groups of like-minded equals. However, the position of in-between cultures and languages seems to offer new possibilities for rewriting the past and thus also altering the present and the future.

There is, of course, no reason to overestimate the revolutionary capacity of the margins and of hybridity. In my view they offer at least a possibility of finding a Third Way between universalism and particularism, between a dominating globality and a narrow-minded locality. As Lisa Lowe (1996: 82) points out, the role of hybridity in society may oscillate between assimilation and resistance:

> The materialist concept of hybridity conveys that the histories of forced labor migrations, racial segregation, economic displacement and internment are left in the material traces of "hybrid" cultural identities; these hybridities are always in the process of, on the one hand, being appropriated and commodified by commercial culture and, on the other, of being rearticulated for the creation of oppositional 'resistance cultures'.

My analysis of contemporary texts written in German also reveals that parallel with the multiple identities, the authors display complex language usage. What is especially interesting are the various forms of hybrid language, in the emigrant speech in Günter Grass's writing or the "twisted tongue" of Emine Sevgi Özdamar and the Kanak Sprak of Feridun Zaimoglu. Although Zaimoglu's imaginary country "Kanakstan", referring to the new Germany, is called a graveyard for the Kanaks, it is also a space where new identities and issues of home and nationhood may be negotiated. The meeting of east and west in German literature has brought about a new literary German that is not rooted in German culture alone.

It seems that the erosion of the nation-state means a worldwide erosion of the national literatures. It also seems evident that the realm of today's world literature can no longer be the national tradition and its interpretation but its major theme seems to be that of transnational histories and the narratives of migrants. For Stuart Hall (1991: 38-39), hybrid ethnicity is a strategy of the local in the epoch of globalisation. The analysis of contemporary German novels confirms the idea that for migrant authors the German Heimat is not only an object to describe, but also a project to be created.

REFERENCES

Adelson, L.A. 1991: Migrantenliteratur oder deutsche Literatur? TORKANs Tufan: Brief an einen islamischen Bruder. In P.M. Lützeler Hrsg.: *Spätmoderne und Postmoderne.* Frankfurt am Main: Fischer Taschenbuch Verlag.

And, M. 1975: *Karagöz. Turkish Shadow Theatre with appendix on the history of Turkish puppet theatre.* Istanbul.

Alter, N.M. 1997: Re/Fusing Past and Present. Cinematic Reunification under the Sign of Nationalism and Racism. In K. Bullivant ed.: *Beyond 1989. Re-reading German Literature since 1945.* Providence, Oxford: Berghahn Books.

Bhabha, H.K. 1990: DissemiNation: Time, Narrative and the Margins of the Modern Nation. In H.K. Bhabha ed.: *Nation and Narration.* London and New York: Routledge.

Bhabha, H.K. 1994: *The Location of Culture.* London and New York: Routledge.

Brinker-Gabler, G. 1997: Exile, Immigrant, Re/Unified. Writing (East) Postunification Identity in Germany. In G. Brinker-Gabler, S. Smith ed.: *Writing New Identities. Gender, Nation and Immigration in Contemporary Europe.* Minneapolis, London.

Crowley, T. 1996: Signs of Belonging: Languages, Nations and Culture in the Old and New Europe. In C. Hoffmann ed.: *Language, Culture and Communication in Contemporary Europe.* Clevedon Philadelphia Adelaide: Multilingual Matters Ltd.

Fichte, J.G. 1971: Reden an die deutsche Nation (1809). In I.H. Fichte Hrsg.: *Fichtes Werke.* Band VII. Berlin: Walter de Gruyter. 259-499.

Fischer, S., McGowan M. 1995: From Pappkoffer to Pluralism. Migrant Writing in the German Federal Republic. In R. King, J. Connell, P. White ed.: *Writing Across Worlds. Literature and Migration.* London and New York: Routledge.

Grass, G. 1992: *Unkenrufe.* Göttingen: Steidl Verlag.

Hall, S. 1991: The Local and the Global: Globalization and Ethnicity. In A. King ed.: *Culture, Globalization and the World-System.* London, New York: Macmillan.

Horrocks, D., Kolinsky, E. 1996: Migrants or citizens? Turks in Germany between Exclusion and Acceptance. In Horocks D., Kolinsky E. ed.: *Turkish Culture in German Society Today.* Providence.

Kemal, K. 1998.: *Ja, sagt Molly.* Berlin: Hitit Verlag.

Lowe, L. 1996: *Immigrant Acts on Asian American Cultural Politics.* Durham: Duke University Press.

Mies, M. 1993: Women have no Fatherland. In M. Mies and V. Shiva ed.: *Ecofeminism.* London and New Jersey: Zed Books.

Räthzel, N. 1994: Harmonious 'Heimat' and Disturbing 'Ausländer'. In K. Bhavnani and A. Phoenix ed.: *Writing New Identities. Shifting Racisms. A Feminism Psychology Reader.* London: Sage.

Schulze, I. 1998: *Simple Storys. Ein Roman aus der ostdeutschen Provinz.* 5. Auflage. Berlin: Berlin Verlag.

Seyhan, A. 1997: Scherazade's Daughters. The Thousand and One Tales of Turkish-German Women Writers. In G. Brinker-Gabler and Smith S. ed.: *Writing New Identities. Gender, Nation and Immigration in Contemporary Europe.* Minneapolis, London.

Shiva, V. 1993: Homeless in the 'Global Village'. In M. Mies and V. Shiva ed.: *Ecofeminism.* London & New Jersey: Zed Books.

Teraoka, A.A. 1990: Gastarbeiterliteratur: The Other Speaks Back. In A.R. JanMohamed and D. Lloyd ed.: *The Nature and Context of Minority Discourse.* Oxford University Press.

Wolf, C. 1999: *Auf dem Weg nach Tabou. Texte 1990-1994.* 2. Auflage. München: Deutscher Taschenbuchverlag.

Zaimoglu, F. 1998: *Koppstoff. Kanaka Sprak vom Rande der Gesellschaft.* Hamburg: Rotbuch Verlag.

Zaimoglu, F. 1999: *Kanak Sprak. 24 Misstöne vom Rande der Gesellschaft.* 4. Auflage. Hamburg: Rotbuch Verlag.

Özdamar, E.S. 1996: Schwarzauge und sein Esel. 'Blackeye and his Donkey': A Multicultural Experience. In Horrocks D. and Kolinsky E. ed.: *Turkish Culture in German Society Today.* Providence.

Özdamar, E.S. 1998a: *Mutterzunge. Erzählungen.* Berlin: Kiepenheuer & Witsch.

Özdamar, E.S. 1998: Mother Tongue. In Harnisch A., Stokes A.M. and Weidauer F. ed.: *Fringe voices. An Anthology of Minority Writing in the Federal Republic of Germany.* Oxford, New York: Berg.

Öztürk, Kadriye 1998: Der Beitrag der Literatur zum Kulturwandel. Türkische Migrantenliteratur in Deutschland. In N. Kuryazici, Jahn S., Müller U., Zeger P, Zelewitz K. Hrsg.: *Schnittpunkt der Kulturen.* Stuttgarter Arbeiten zur Germanistik. Stuttgart: Verlag Hans Dieter Heinz.

PART FOUR
Repositioning Locality

10

Local Identity and Historical Memory of Community: The Case of "Communal Apartments" in St. Petersburg[1]

ILYA UTEKHIN

Introduction

This paper is the outcome of anthropological research project on the stereotypes of everyday behaviour. The topic of research, so-called "communal apartments" (CA), is a special type of dwelling characteristic to Leningrad (St. Petersburg) and other large Soviet cities. The "communality" of the apartment means that several families are living together in the same apartment and share all the facilities. Today, up to 20 per cent of the population of St. Petersburg live in this way, the number of inhabitants of apartments ranging from 2 non-kin single occupants to 30 persons or even more. Big CAs are mostly located in old residential buildings in the central part of the city, while small-size CAs are often found in three or four-room flats in modern block buildings in peripheral areas. The present study is dedicated to large size apartments in the historical centre of St. Petersburg.

For most of the Soviet period the CA was the predominant type of dwelling in Leningrad. Until now, however, CAs have never been studied by ethnographers or anthropologists. This is no surprise, for such a study in the USSR would definitely be impossible for ideological reasons: housing was one of the acute social and economic problems in that country, and the very fact of the existence of CAs demonstrated that the problem was not successfully resolved. Another circumstance of a rather methodological sort also prevented scholars from any inquiry in this field: until relatively recently, everyday life in a modern city could not be taken as a legitimate object of ethnographic study, the more so if done by a researcher who himself or herself belonged to the object community. Although the CA way of living was an important part of Soviet culture, it was nevertheless taken as a matter of fact and regarded as a background that did not deserve special attention.

The idea of studying typical patterns of local history narratives supposedly related to self-identity was not initially part of the project that was carried out in 1997-98. The focus of the research interest was on contemporary ways of living, on neighbours' relations, their means of coping with deviant behaviour, and other similar issues. However, as the fieldwork began with deep interviewing, observation (including participant observation) and photography, very soon I came to the conclusion that the only reason for a research activity that could be easily understood by the people interviewed was precisely the interest in the history of the place. Questions concerning the history of the building and the apartment were a natural part of conversations, the more so since all CAs within our scope were located in houses built before the 1917 revolution. Most of them had particular architectural features, and some the official status of a "monument of architecture" (which did not, however, prevent the premises from having poor technical conditions). It was logical on my part to ask about the building and the previous occupants before passing to personal histories and the contemporary situation.

Another reason for turning to the history of the CAs has been the fact that, in order to say anything about the current state of affairs, people usually needed to check it against something similar but nevertheless different. The past state, the way they lived some (or many) years ago, was often the most convenient object of comparison.

So it has been inevitable that their ideas about local history should be recognised as an important dimension. Local history viewed by anthropologists concerned with contemporary folkways may be approached from two different angles. Either researchers collect some established facts about the community history that motivate certain phenomena, which otherwise would be left unexplained to them, or they attempt to reconstruct the way in which the community represents to itself its local memory. Such representations are used to motivate certain actual practices, the current state of affairs. Often it is not possible to check what people say against a document other than other people's narratives, and thus the facts simply do not exist apart from particular interpretations.

Setting the Scene

In the classic late-1930s Ernst Lubitch's film *Ninochka*, Greta Garbo, in the role of a Soviet foreign trade employee, after a series of comic episodes returns from Paris to her humble room which she shares with two neighbours in a densely populated Moscow communal apartment. It is not easy to realise to what extent the Western public at that time was able to appreciate the inventiveness of the screenplay writer. He succeeded in presenting on the screen, in an episode of a few minutes, that surrealistically absurd deprivation of privacy inside the apartment (or even inside the room, as in cases like Ninochka's). Comic as it may have seemed to the film audience, the CA way of life surely appeared shocking and unnatural to those CA occupants who had known a more private domestic environment before. Along with them, those whose housing conditions had been relatively worse before they got to a CA also suffered from the necessity to cohabit with representatives of other social groups.

Living together has brought about cultural devices to cope with the daily problems of living: lines, schedules, a whole system intended for the distribution of responsibilities and authority. Even if this system functioned properly, it could not provide for anything more than survival in overcrowded premises. In his classic book on housing policy in the USSR, the emigrant author Timothy Sosnovy has described the ambience of a classical CA of the 1930s with the following words:

> It is not difficult to imagine the innumerable problems that arise from many families living together in such close proximity and using in common inadequate kitchen, bath and toilet facilities, particularly when this utility space is itself occupied by a family and encumbered

> with household items. Ventilation is, of course, poor, the air is stuffy, contagious diseases spread rapidly. The frequent absence of running water, plumbing, gas, and even kitchens, the lack of storage space for food and other things make the accumulation of dirt a foregone conclusion. The most insanitary conditions prevail and the apartments are infested with vermin. The din is constant; it is impossible to have a normal night's rest and studying is out of the question. The air is permeated with the smell of kerosene and with fumes from primus stoves, used for cooking and heating water in rooms.
>
> The physical hardship of everyday living has a telling effect on the nerves of the tenants who, more often than not, are stumbling over one another or waiting impatiently in a long line for toilet or other facilities. There is constant bickering and quarrelling within and among families, vociferous arguments often flare up and even fighting is not unknown (Sosnovy 1954: 212-213).

Many things have changed since then. What can be seen today and what I could see during fieldwork differs significantly from the picture presented by Sosnovy and repeatedly ridiculed in satirical literature (by Mikhail Zoshenko, Mikhail Bulgakov and others). Today's CAs are much less crowded, queues to the toilet are never as long as they used to be, but rivalry and quarrels remain as active as ever. It is worth noting that precisely the times described by Sosnovy are an object of nostalgia on the part of some of the old occupants.

Some basic data are necessary concerning the history of the CAs as a phenomenon of Soviet housing. It was due to several circumstances of both a practical and an ideological nature that CAs appeared in the USSR. The Bolshevik government tried to resolve its housing problems by means of the redistribution of living space. This corresponded to the slogan "Palaces to working people!" Since the private ownership of real estate was abolished in August 1918, it became possible to use the space confiscated from former owners for this purpose. The distribution of space was regulated by "a sanitary norm", according to which citizens had the right to get definite amount of "living space". This amount varied from city to city and along the period of the Soviet power, but for some thirty years it remained as 4.5 square metres per person in Leningrad. The right to get this living space was rather theoretical, because in practice it was more complicated, as is always the case with legislative norms lacking an efficient mechanism and resources for their implementation. As a result, in many apartments in downtown areas several tenants, despite belonging to different social strata, started to live together, often including the former property-owners (Boym 1994; Guerasimova 1999; 2000; Sosnovy 1954; Utekhin 2001).

Before a separate flat for each family became the goal of Soviet housing policy in the 1930s, an illusion existed as a part of the official ideology that living together would bring about a new type of comradeliness between people, leading to the formation of a true collectivist personality, the liberation of women from the "domestic slavery" typical of the old way of everyday life. It presupposed the collectivisation of all the aspects of everyday life, such as eating, sleep, child-rearing practices, all of which were to be separated from family life (which had to be utterly transformed, if not abolished altogether). The community of those who lived together was regarded as a potential source of order and educational moral influence. This trend propelled not only the creation of house-communes in buildings already constructed, but also a lot of utopian social and architectural projects of the new communist cities and buildings. Not all of the projects had such a leftist touch; many of them also provided for individual family dwelling (Bliznakov 1993). In 1930, some trends reflected in those projects were officially condemned as "highly groundless, semi-fantastic, and therefore extremely harmful" by the Central Committee of the All-Union Communist Party. However, it became quite clear in the 1930s that not the communes aimed at rebuilding of people's everyday routines, but rather the CAs represented the reality of Soviet urban housing. This "temporary difficulty" in the construction of Socialist society turned out to be permanent.

In spite of the fact that a separate apartment for each worker's family was proclaimed as the Soviet housing policy, for the vast majority of residents in the big cities the CA remained the only possible housing solution. The term "CA" meant initially "an apartment without a householder" where the order was maintained by the tenants themselves. Self-organisation in tenants' communities revealed the worse moral qualities of people involved in a struggle for survival in the difficult circumstances of over-population, and the order usually came from an external authority, be it a housing administration, the militia or the People's Court. Numerous instructions and rules intended for regulating internal order in the apartments were elaborated, with detailed prescriptions concerning potentially controversial issues in CA everyday life. Such instructions themselves seem to be canonisations of spontaneously established practices that had proved to be the most efficient.

Living together in CAs gave rise to special characteristic features of what may be referred to as a traditional "communal" mentality, the most important of which will be briefly outlined. In the first place, there was a particular organisation of privacy: the lack of space usually led to a situation where several people — usually belonging to the same family — lived in the same room. Alongside such intra-familiar and almost completely transparent life, the CA was quite transparent regarding neighbours' concerns, since all everyday practices, concerns and events were perceived by the other tenants, who could see, hear and smell everything which the other tenants did or had. Neglected privacy led to over-sensitivity to violations of privacy and its substitutes. Continuously being on a stage through sharing the same space was combined in the CAs with specific practices of hygiene and privacy, since the residents shared the same toilet, bathroom and kitchen facilities. The maintenance of a proper state of environment in spaces for public use followed the principle of minimal effort.

Owing to the lack of resources on the one hand, and to the existence of a definite amount of necessary costs and effort on the other, the fair sharing of goods and costs was implied in most activities. Queuing was an important dimension of everyday relations; it was often institutionalised through written schedules of activities intended to control the use of the bathroom as well as the order for cleaning the apartment. Sharing was heavily charged emotionally with envy, and people were extremely sensitive to the fairness of the distribution. At the same time, such close interaction often brought about quasi-familial relationship between neighbours that transcended the boundaries of social groups. However, endless conflicts were typical of CAs, originating from its very social structure. The most powerful tool used in conflicts was an outside authority, and so the drive to denounce found fertile soil in the CAs.

The impact of the CA way of living on other spheres of social life is clearly distinguishable: the same mentality is still found everywhere in Russia in the attitude to public space, in relations within a collective, in people's behaviour in groups. CA living is an important component part of the Soviet way of thinking, and we meet the same behaviour patterns in, for example, queuing outside the CAs, even if people standing in line (for example, outside a doctor's office at a polyclinic) actually live in separate apartments.

Form and Function of Communal Folklore

Local history in CA communities exists in the form of oral narratives and so belongs to folklore. CA folklore comprises a whole range of genres, from gossip to aetiological statements, and this is what a specific CA occupants' competence consists of.

Let us take a novice in a CA as an example. Even if the CA newcomer speaks the same language and belongs to the same culture as his new neighbours, to begin with, he does not share the local occupants' competence, he is not yet "one of us". This means, in particular, that many things that are an everyday matter of fact to those who have lived there for a long time are not evident to the newcomer, especially those things which concern relations inside the community. At the same time, each action in the public space of the CA concerns the neighbours' relations. Being perceived by the surrounding people, each step is being evaluated as either meeting or not meeting local expectation of the ordinary way of things. That is, the novice needs to acquire the local standards of action and interpretation. To be incorporated into the community means to gain one's own status — and the right to modify the existing order by one's very participation.

What does this local competence consist of? First of all, there exists data about the actual structure of community and its space. Imagine a guest who has come to a CA for the first time. He is not acquainted with the neighbours, so he enters the kitchen and his greeting is general, not personal. He has to ask where the toilet is located. He does not know where should he take his soap and towel, on which cooker he can put his teapot, where can he get some matches, etc. He knows perfectly that he can use only the property — and the places — of the person whose guest he is. A mistake would lead to a conflict between the neighbours and the occupant who has invited the guest but who has failed to explain to him the minimal necessary amount of information. The paragraph 6 from the "Rules for using the toilet" states that the use of the toilet by non-residents of the apartment (relatives and guests) must be carefully monitored and violations of hygiene by them must be strictly taken care of in the common toilet (Kabakov 1993: 177).

It would scarcely be possible to formulate the complete amount of this information through a set of rules and norms. They are too many, they include many exceptions, and they are modified in the course of their application. Their use implies entering the system of intra-apartment human relations. For these reasons, the resident cannot instruct his guest exhaustively, nor can the researcher give an exhaustive account of the practices.

Any guest knows, in principle, that to put his bag on a neighbour's table is risky, for he is liable to later find his bag lying on the floor. But no rule is without its exception: if the owner of the table is absent and there are no witnesses, or the table belongs to a "friendly" neighbour, one is allowed to violate the rule. The competence of a participant in the community enables him to use these special terms of the rules' application, whereas a stranger possesses only a very general idea of the relevant behaviour. However, the application of the rules remains unknown, for he is not aware of the status of things and places.

The motivations of the norms of the "normal way" exist in a more or less stereotypical verbal form and ascend to the local rationality or to a precedent. The first case can be illustrated with the following example. Laundering clothes are usually done in the bathroom or in the kitchen. Although both ways are possible, they are never combined in a single apartment. The motivation of the choice may be purely functional, but often it is not. In reality this choice is more often determined by custom alone, and forms part of the unconscious stereotypes, that is, of the habits that are neither ever thought about nor expressed openly, except in the case of a violation of the custom by a newcomer. "Are you nuts? Don't you know that the bathroom is to be used for taking a bath? No one will wait until you finish your laundry to wash his hands. So go and do your laundry in the kitchen like everybody else!" This explanation given to the newcomer is as valid as another one: "You should take into account that people cook here. What a silly idea to do your laundry in the kitchen when the bathroom is made for it!" Both explanations have the appearance of being rational.

Often an appeal to a precedent is used. People say something like "We've always done it this way" or "it is my grandfather who put the hook here, so now it is mine".

Along with mastering the "normal way", knowledge of one's neighbours' personal histories, characters and inclinations is also needed for full-scale incorporation into the everyday life of a community. One can have more or less reliable information about a neighbour from one's own observations and from personal communication with the neighbour. At the same time, some information comes from what other people say about this neighbour — and that is what usually is considered to be gossip. Gossip information is not evident and not available other than through gossip. The protagonist of an item of gossip does not intend for publication the particular aspect of his life that is reflected in the gossip. For this reason there is plenty of space for neighbours' fantasy and speakers try to avoid the protagonist's ears while engaged in activity of gossip.

The curious nature of gossip consists in the fact that the attempt to retell the gossip to a stranger in a comprehensible form would be meaningless. The whole meaning of an item of gossip can be understood only by those belong to the same community and share the same interests. So, if we cite here a certain text and call it gossip, we also have to describe all the details of the context and explain why it is gossip and not a true story. That is, we have to re-write the text we call gossip in other more explicit and more general terms. As result, at best we will show what the members of community say about the given person. To understand and evaluate an item of gossip, one should master the context. We can, at best, trace the main grounds that have given rise to various items of gossip. Everything that differs from the normal way of things — and so deserves special attention and a special explanation and commentary — becomes a topic. Everything that seems to have non-evident aspects and motives is liable to excite envy or interest aimed at the individual's privacy.

In CAs, such aspects include neighbours' expensive purchases and novelties in their private life. Persons whose habits and occupations notably differ from the average attract community interest. In spite of the transparency of space and the high degree of neighbours' awareness of each other's lives, this awareness is never complete. It can be intentionally reduced by those people who keep secret their occupations and their private lives as much as possible. Neighbours try to solve the riddle, to find "rational" explanations for strange habits: any particular circumstances need to be explained within the framework of local rationality. Spying, peeping and eavesdropping are the sources of information for those who are inclined to such activities. Consequently, the use of tendentious gossip (where interpretation prevails over observation) in a conflict game in order to influence public opinion is an art typical of quarrelsome individuals with a traditional CA mentality. Gossip is always biased. However, we should distinguish the kind of gossip where the share of observation is high from gossip in which the speaker's fantasy is the predominant source.

Gossip forms part of the background knowledge underlying everyday behaviour; this is a kind of "Present Perfect" of social reality. That is why it can be regarded as a provider of background knowledge. People, things, and places also have their own Present Perfect. Even if this information *per se* is private, in some circumstances it is being actualised: for example, the fact that you bought a cup in Nizhny Taguil in 1976 is a part of your personal story that is not relevant to your relations with other people until a neighbour of yours has broken or stolen this cup.

Of seemingly less importance for everyday behaviour is another type of data, information about the former occupants and their relations with those who actually live in the apartment, and also information about the circumstances that motivate this or that feature of the environment. To some extent this has to do with the motivation for why the space is organised and distributed in this particular way, and where "the survivals" come from (e.g., old geyser, or someone's skis on a shelf in a public place). This kind of information should not be underestimated as it forms a substantial part of the conceptual mapping of the apartment's territory. A newcomer lacking this knowledge needs explanations about what territory and artefacts belong to this or that neighbour, and to what extent it is recognised as legal by the community (e.g., whether you can move this particular chair or put your bag on it, or whether it would lead to conflict). Those data which have no direct practical importance to everyday interaction are the "Past Indefinite" of CA life, that is, properly local history (partly made up of old gossips).

Separate categories of gossip are the stories about deviant behaviour (mainly about the drunken individuals). In such stories the share of observation is much bigger than that of interpretation, and so such gossip may be regarded as consisting of true stories. With time, the stories are retold many times and acquire a legendary dimension, the tendentious ingredient being completely deleted. The stories are remembered and told long after the protagonists have moved away from the apartment. That is, from the Present Perfect these stories move to the Past Indefinite.

Telling such stories to guests, newcomers or simply young people ("You certainly cannot remember this, but I do, so listen to what it was like...") may be provoked by an event, but also may have no special motive. You can often hear the memories told in the kitchen by older women to their younger neighbours during the preparation of holiday meals, or when somebody joins his neighbour friends at the table for a celebration.

Patterns of Local Memory

The memory of the past of the apartment contains definite stereotypes for each of the periods into which the CA history can be subdivided. These provisionally set subdivisions correspond to the main periods of twentieth-century Russian history and are as follows: Perestroika; the years from after Stalin up to Perestroika; the years following the World War II period; the blockade of the city; the years between the Revolution and the War; before the Revolution. We will not consider here the particular historical data connected with each period; we are interested, rather, in the most frequent ways of constructing and presenting these data in oral narratives.

A part of the body of local history knowledge that may be considered separately is what the actual occupants know about the origin and past of their building and their apartment. Being located downtown and mainly constructed before the 1917 revolution, practically each building has its own face, sometimes its name (after the name of the former owner or the architect) — and often also an historical and architectural value. The buildings are all different, and a building's speciality has a meaning in the eyes of its occupants. Few of the living remember the far past from their own experience. What people know about the history of the building, its original owners and occupants, etc. is taken for the most part from what the old people once told, that is, from oral narratives. This information being a sort of "Past Perfect", it is not relevant to everyday behaviour, but is important for people's self-identification. It is unfolded before strangers and newcomers in order to show what is special about this place (and thus about its actual occupants), and so this knowledge is appreciated by the community as prestigious. Younger members have no other way of obtaining this kind of information than by questioning and listening to the old occupants, and these data acquire the elaborated form of a story told more than once. In some cases, however, even Past Perfect information is used to explain actual features of the environment. Thus, one of our informers explained why there were yearly problems with leakage in the apartment where she lived. She said that a military hospital was located in the building during World War I, and a special open gallery for walking was constructed along the facade of the building. Its floor was, at the same time, the roof of a part of the apartment, and it was made of copper leafing. The leafing was removed in the 1920s during one of the Bolshevik campaigns to collect scrap metal.

After the revolution, large apartments were handed over to more or less significant communist functionaries and high-ranking military officers. This fact is remembered, even though there can be no one left in the apartment who is one of those initial occupants' descendants. In our material concerning different apartments in the same building, a strikingly similar story was told by various speakers about how the apartment became communal. More than once our informers explained the initial sharing of the apartment by the wish of the occupants to find good company: "he [an army general] was bored living alone with his family and so he invited some people, all of them well-educated intelligentsia, to live together". Another version: "He [a party functionary] invited some people to live from the first floor for some time in the apartment who had suffered during the 1924 flood. They left here, and then took their relatives with them."

Practically the same explanation is given in another apartment where the engineer lived who had directed the last decoration works in the building (this fact is confirmed by his daughter still living in the apartment). The presumably voluntary character of this initial decision is remarkable: people believe that it is uncomfortable for a family to live alone in the apartment. That is why it seems logical that the initial occupants themselves looked for suitable company. This idea may have some real basis, since the new elite was not accustomed to live in luxurious conditions with the number of rooms greater than the number of inhabitants. However, a much more plausible source of this idea is another real, though very far from voluntary, circumstance: the so-called "right to *samouplotnenie* (= self-compression)", that is, the right to choose people to live together with in order to reduce the per capita living space in the apartment. This existed in the 1920s and meant that if some tenants had more space than prescribed by the sanitary norm (eight square metres per person), they were obliged to share their living space. After the official notice, they had a definite period during which they were allowed to choose those with whom they would share the dwelling. After this period had expired, the housing administration did not take into account the wishes of the "compressed" tenants while handing the living space over to other people.

To avoid the company of strangers and of representatives of socially alien strata of the population, the tenants formalised their cohabitation with their household servants, or invited their relatives from the country. Traces of this situation can still be found in some apartments where former masters and servants or their descendants live. In other cases, the masters (who could be the original owners of the apartment) left the apartment, while the servants remained. Compare the following passage from an interview where the former owner of the apartment is mentioned: "He was a banker...I don't remember the name.... We have a neighbour woman who should be able to remember — not the banker himself, of course, but.... This neighbour's mother worked as a chambermaid for the banker's family. She doesn't like mentioning this fact, that the mother was a chambermaid. Perhaps, it seems humiliating to her...."

Samouplotnenie (self-compression) and simply *uplotnenie* (compulsory compression) may have affected both the occupants who lived in the apartment from pre-Revolutionary times and the post-revolutionary occupants who had fallen into disgrace. The legendary individuals who had occupied the whole apartment, before or right after the revolution, are usually conceived of as outstanding personalities. The few data that remain about their habits and way of life are linked with the historical topography of the place. In practically every big CA there are tenants — not necessarily elderly people — who act as your guides and explain the initial purpose of each room. Living for a long time in the former dining-room or in a small room intended for a domestic, one can nevertheless keep in mind the whole of apartment and be able to restore mentally the initial plan, regardless of the fact that the speaker never saw it with his own eyes. The remaining original decoration is the main guideline. Thus, the story of the apartment is the story of rebuilding and partitioning, the story of the fight of Living Together against the original living environment with its decoration and planning. Leaving no traces of a past state, some rebuilding deletes the supports to memory; however, the rebuilding and partitions were usually done in the cheapest way, and so traces remained.

Consider an extract from an interview with an elderly woman remarkable for her references to the initial occupant. The informant attempts to see the apartment through the eyes of the first occupant, though she never saw him personally and has only heard about him from other people. It is after she mentions the origin of the pieces of furniture from her room that she starts to comment on the original plan of the apartment. Note that she was proud of the pieces of furniture:

> The bookstand and the small table are pre-revolutionary things, they belonged to the engineer who lived here before the revolution and occupied the whole apartment. I was born in 1932 and never saw him. The first room, while once had crystal doors, that was the servants room, 15 [square] metres. The second room...40 metres ...that was a big one...that was the dancing room. The following place, now there are two rooms there, with plywood walls, there were no rooms there originally, it was a small corridor. And they made the rooms before the war. The next room, just in front, 24 metres. That was his bedroom. Then comes a small narrow room, in the corner, he had a smoking room there. Another room, it was his study with a door that led to the smoking room. Before the war what is now the toilet and bathroom did not exist. The toilets, and he had two toilets, were located where the lumber-room is now. And his lumber-rooms were where we now have the toilet and bathroom. In the kitchen, he had floors made of rose tufa. Now it is covered with plastic, and before that it was difficult to wash it. This room where we are was the children's room. This door was made before the war, but he had no door here. The next room was his dining room. And

> the next one, another children's room. There was a white fireplace there.

The attic and other peripheral places are thought to shelter the secrets of the founders. People supposed that when the former occupants fled after the revolution, they left their treasures in a secret place in the building. Looking for hidden treasure, the occupants checked the walls and the floors, the attic and the cellar. It was more than a children's play (though children, of course, took the most active part in it), for adult people did it even after World War II.

Interior rebuilding involving divisions of big apartments added mysteries and riddles to the place in the form of doors which are always closed — they can often be seen in the staircases and inside the apartments: it was too expensive to make walls instead. Few inhabitants have an exact idea of the complicated planning of the building, and sometimes the most curious things are said about where these doors lead. Sometimes the curiosity is sparked by the sounds coming from behind those doors.

CA people feel that they live in a special place — this feeling is totally alien to people living in the new standard blocks built in the new residential areas, with standard apartment planning. There can scarcely be a memorial plate on a block building — this construction is not intended to be a tool of memory but is just a sleeping place of doubtful individuality. It is not a memorial; rather it has something of a temporary living place. In contrast, since the centre of the city is rich in literary and historical connotations, the memory affects even those people who are not interested in history or literature, though only through the names of the streets and buildings. Living in a CA from birth, people feel themselves deeply rooted in the history of the place.

CA occupants even claim a greater degree of specialty for their living place. Thus, for instance, in several apartments of one building people claimed that it was there that the architect of the building had lived. One old woman insisted that the architect kept on living secretly in the attic for many years after the revolution, together with his housekeeper, who sold jewels to survive, until the NKVD (the predecessor of the

KGB) arrested him in 1937. As we found from other sources, the architect had in fact never lived in this building and had left the country in 1923.

A similar belief is sometimes found about the apartment of the former owner of the whole building. Since many buildings in the centre of the city are known to have belonged to a man whose name is remembered (usually nothing more than his name), the actual occupants often claim that, say, his cabinet or his drawing room was located somewhere in their apartment. In most cases these claims, when checked against the available documentary sources, turn out to be groundless.

The period after the revolution is usually remembered as the time of well-organised CA life, in spite of the high density of CA population. The most remarkable object of nostalgia is the clean state of the staircases and the care taken of the public areas outside the apartment.

The war and blockade of the city, as well as the first years after 1945, were a period when occupants changed in CAs more actively then ever: many old residents died during the war, and the newcomers of that period are considered the cause of the first serious deterioration of order in the apartment (the second cause is thought to be related to the Perestroika years). Consider this extract from an interview:

> "When did they stop polishing the floors?"
> "Right after the war. Village people moved in, from various provinces, and they started to wash the parquet, which was strictly forbidden before."
> "Wh[illegible] f[illegible]rbidden?"
> "[illegible] ary to apply polish to oak floors, or parquet....
> [illegible] war people lived well, in friendship. They
> [illegible] ther, never got any quarrels. No one
> [illegible] ey, and once they got their wages,
> [illegible] npletely. It was a good life. And
> [illegible] one started to save up money, there
> [illegible] each other's room, nothing.... Every
> [illegible] s discussed in the kitchen...."
> "[illegible] ow where your neighbours came from?"
> "C[illegible]inly. The first room, from Belorussia, the second, from Novgorod, those next, I don't know, they never

> said. These to this side, from Pskov, those, from Yaroslavl, and those, from Kalinin. Different provinces. I am the only one who has remained here since the war."

The informant estimated the number of occupants by counting them room by room, as follows: before the war, 21, right after the war, 40, today, 17 persons. Thus, old residents, on the one hand, and the intelligentsia, on the other, usually regard the country origins of those newcomers — and their correspondent "lack of culture" — as the main reason for the conflicting ambience in the apartment that is believed to have emerged in those times. The times before the war are obviously idealised in this way.

The last two of the historical periods (the years after Stalin and before Perestroika, and Perestroika itself) are manifest in the current structure of the community: the participants in events to some extent are still living in the same place, while others have moved elsewhere recently. Their conflicts, thefts, births, deaths and marriages are parts of the actual landscape. Although changes dating back to the late 1980s have led to a far less overcrowded situation, the deterioration in general order in housing generally, and inside the apartment in particular is the usual subject of comments. A significant event in the chain of the signs of decay is, as far as people are aware, the abolition in the late 1950s of the night-watch duties of the *dvorniks*. Dvornik is the usual term denoting workers responsible for cleanliness and order in a specific area of the yard and on the street. The significance of dvorniks for everyday CA life was greatly reduced after the introduction, mainly in the early 1950s, of central heating (before that, dvorniks were responsible for the wood supply). With the night guard of the dvorniks suspended, the first graffiti appeared on the walls of the staircases. This is how Blair Ruble (1998: 16) characterises the role of the *dvornik* (from the Russian *dvor*, that is, courtyard: "Authoritarian control began in the dvor, which was often presided over by the dvornik — a Russian style concierge who reported more frequently to the police than to the landlord". This characteristic applied to pre-revolutionary *dvorniks* remained relevant for their successors during the Soviet period.

As for the Perestroika years, our informers unanimously remarked that this period brought more widespread deviant behaviour and a complete abandonment of care about the technical state of the premises. Here the most remarkable event is the change in the system of garbage disposal. Until the mid-1980s, there were special buckets for scraps on the staircase landings of back staircases. The removal of the scraps was the obligation of the dvornik, whereas other garbage in buckets for common use was taken to the dump by CA community members, taking turns. Today, each family has its own plastic bag or bucket for garbage and takes it to the dump. The bags are placed in the kitchen or in the corridor by the door of the room, and no separation of scraps and other garbage is made at the dumps.

The common motives of people's opinions about the past reveal their reflections on the general changes that occurred in the living environment and in society in general. In the past, life in the CAs was more intense and the tenants more numerous, but there was much more order, people say. There were no deviant drunkards and drug-addicts, the apartment was cleaned more often, people were more honest and theft from inside the apartment was impossible. This "Golden Age" approach and certain nostalgia are typical at the classic CA mentality; the new generation first of all appreciates the increasing privatisation of life and tolerance of various marginal lifestyles.

Let us take a closer look at some cases and circumstances that testify to the importance of the more or less recent past and the ideas about the past for the actual behaviour and attitudes of CA tenants. In the CA the most evident expression of a conflict is a refusal to greet each other, that is, the withdrawal from communication. This was the case of our informant, an elderly woman born in 1934:

> My son bought a new cable for the telephone, for 21 thousand rubles. The old one was broken, the contact kept on disappearing, and it was impossible to speak. We installed it [and posted a list of the neighbours for the collection money, as is the custom in CAs], and she refused to pay. I said her: "Mara, now think that you've

> put your hand in my pocket". It wasn't a big sum of money, two thousand six hundred, but it wasn't good. In my opinion, she no longer existed for me. For some time we didn't say a word to each other. But time passed. Christ had risen [Easter had come], I was going along the corridor and happened to see her. So I said to her: "Christ has risen! Hristos voskres! [An Easter greeting] Let us live in peace." As soon as I called her "Marochka" [diminutive of Mara] — when we were children, I used to call her that — I felt she was pleased.... But she never paid back the money.

Note that the refuse to pay a share of the community expenses is something quite symptomatic of the decay in the traditional CA mentality: today, neighbours usually have no way to enforce payment. And an even more serious symptom is that such a transgression remains only an interpersonal problem: the victim has stopped speaking to Mara, while the rest of the neighbours have not. Nowadays, the community as a whole is not affected by such incidents, because the money used for buying a thing for common use is a kind of credit given to the community by a tenant; the collection of money does not precede the purchase.

Note, too, how the women who are neighbours have returned to the "normal" type of communication. The diminutive name, used by the woman informant, is the way she called her offending neighbour when they both were children. Having grown up together, CA people retain a part of their childhood attitude to each other. Russian baby-talk contains the words "d'ad'a" and "t'ot'a" for addressing men and women respectively. These words, used even when addressing (or referring to) strangers, also have the meaning of "uncle" and "aunt". Thus, not only children call their neighbours "uncle X" or "aunt Y". They continue addressing them in this way even when the child has become an adult, and the "uncle" or "aunt" is old. It would be erroneous to look for hidden trends in the communal soul in this way of addressing people. Basically, there is no connotation of belonging to the same family. In the CA, children gradually learn to add name of the "uncle" or "aunt" to this word of address, and it becomes, say, "d'ad'a Pet'a" or "t'ot'a Kat'a". This quasi-familial way of addressing people is not usually regarded as suitable for addressing deviant personages and intra-apartment enemies (who will be referred to by their family names or by demeaning nicknames).

As I have already remarked, "CA" would mean an apartment where there is no owner to take responsibility for collecting the rent and ensuring order. Throughout the Soviet period regulations concerning the maintenance and order of apartments provided an interesting formula that is still repeated: this or that thing "shall be done according to the lessees' agreement." In the case of the absence of such an agreement the order comes from outside in the person of the housing administration, the *uchaskovyi militsioner* (police officer responsible for the district), or the *domovoi komitet* (house committee). At the start of the classic CA times, before World War II, every apartment community had to elect a leader (*kvartupolnomochennyi*). It is characteristic that in the post-Stalinist period people in many apartments refused to become leaders — and thus they remained without formal leadership. One could, of course, be a non-formal authority, but that was different: "Here people do not like to voice their claims. But they always make millions of claims, they are always discontent. So the *kvartupolnomochennyi* is the person who is entitled to address accusations to a transgressor. When he does so officially, he speaks not as a private person but on behalf of the collective. And this is a quite different role, it is easier [than to do it privately]." Nevertheless, no one wanted to become a *kvartupolnomochennyi* and to undertake the formal responsibilities of the position.

Instead, some energetic people actually did the same as a *kvartupolnomochennyi* would do. Their active position originated from the wish to live in better conditions, not from any desire to enjoy the power. Consider the following comment about one such man: "His opinion was always taken into consideration. He even put up the rules on a piece of cardboard posted in the corridor. Somebody must have thrown those rules away now. I remember seeing them in the lumber-room; maybe, someone took the card to cover something."

The rules written by that man consisted of more detailed regulations than in the official Rules governing everyday practices. With maximum pedantry possible, he wrote that while sweeping the corridor one should have the dustpan close by, so that dust could be swept up, heap by heap, and made into piles along the corridor; that telephone conversations should last a specific time, in minutes; that smoking was not allowed in public areas, because it damaged people's health; that the doors of rooms should be properly closed; that no noise could be allowed after 11 o'clock, etc. In the bathroom he posted up notices like "Please do not turn on the tap too strongly."

Written regulations or official rules posted on the wall are often remembered by the old occupants. The spirit of such rules and the degree of detail is truthfully reflected in the materials collected by Ilya Kabakov, as we can observe from the "Rules for Using the Toilet" already mentioned:

> 3. It is forbidden to occupy the toilet for more than a certain time; it is necessary to respect other people and neighbours.
> 7. Do not clutter up the toilet with extraneous objects (except for those allowed by a joint meeting); do not litter and do not burn paper.
> 8. To avoid falling and breaking the toilet, do not stand up on it. (Kabakov 1993: 177.)

To understand this rather cryptic text one should know that a habit existed of freshening the air in the toilet by burning a piece of paper in the toilet-pan in order to remove the odour, that standing with the feet on the pan, especially by strangers, was a way of avoiding contact with a toilet seat regarded as dirty, and that this posture would lead to dangerous consequences because the pan was not usually very strong and could easily be broken, etc. The private initiative to publish rules like these was an attempt to give an official-looking basis to the position of informal leaders in quarrels while they were arguing with transgressors of the communal order.

Individual initiatives led some people to modify their environment (by installing a geyser or a bathtub) with their own effort and money, and not counting on the help of the community. Nowadays it would be impossible to find an apartment with this kind of leadership. In addition, women are mainly sceptical about men's ability to be leaders:

> As for me, I don't believe in men. Men become petty. When there's a problem, women always have to kick the men, to get them going. Go and arrange this or that, be it a broken tap or the electricity...you have to make a scene...I've got enough fingers on my hands to count the number of men I've known who were not idle. I mean not their professional activity, but everyday life. When I say "not idle", I mean globally active people. Those who are inherently active. Any imperfection irritates them. Such a man will not think about who should arrange something, or who can arrange it, or why he must arrange it and not you. He is simply itching to do it himself. There are people like this, but they are very few. None of them in this apartment.

The ideal man described above cannot live in a CA. Not because men really have become petty, as our informer believes, but because the public environment cannot be privatised to such an extent that the attitude described would become possible. In earlier years, the tough circumstances demanded more of people than today's relatively relaxed way of life.

Memory and Identity

The mastering of community memory by an individual is one of the most important factors in his self-identity as community member. Here we can touch on the uses of local history. Old occupants' status and their claims to special rights in Soviet times were supported not only by customary law but also by the active legislation. Thus, they had privileged rights to obtain additional living space. Even today some old people are sure that one day "the state" will provide them with separate apartments just because they are old occupants, living here "since blockade times". This status and implied references to the historical motivation of this or that claim are tools that are used in conflicts and controversies inside an apartment. Reference can be made not to one's personal involvement in the history of a particular community but rather to the history of the place (building, district, or city).

Thus, the special feeling of identity may to some extent be related to the place with all its historical connotations, not only to the given community. In recent years, realtors have done a lot of profitable business with the so-called *rasselenie,* that is, by moving a CA's occupants to separate flats away from the city centre and selling the former CA to wealthy private owners. However attractive may seem the perspective of receiving a separate and private flat instead of a CA room, many CA occupants are vehemently opposed to such a change in their lives. Sometimes neighbours from the same apartment are so used to living together that they will not agree to move to newly constructed buildings unless they get flats in the same building, together with their former CA neighbours. Sometimes, they refuse to change their lives, though such a change is called "to better one's living conditions". Of course, to some extent it is not only due to warm feelings for a particular place, but rather because the workplace, the college and favourite shops are nearby, while the municipal transport is quite convenient to go downtown. People are deeply involved in the social nets that are partly related to the dwelling place.

CA occupants of this kind ask the realtors to provide them with a separate apartment in the same district instead of their CA room, which turns out to be impossible on account of the high prices of real estate in the centre of the city. Moreover, low-income CA occupants are generally reluctant to make any changes in their living condition, and they justify this attitude by referring to their lack of the money needed to set up of a new apartment, items such as moving, repairing and buying new furniture. The same reasons are evident when the project of eventual modifications to be made to existing rooms is discussed in interviews: the possibility of rebuilding the existing rooms in order to get a separate entrance door or private toilet are refused. People have never thought of this and have no real idea of the amount of work and money required for such an affair.

Along with this kind of people who are so linked to their place or their CA community we find another sort of inhabitant in today's CA. These are "temporary" residents whose attitude to the place is sharply different. For them, the CA where they live for the moment is a temporary residence and so has no special value. Everything said about local identity and related to local history is much less relevant to such people, whose attitude to the place is evident even in their lack of responsibility for order and cleanness in the apartment. Consider this extract from one interview:

> "If someone moves into a room in the apartment, is he aware about the past of this room?"
> "Well, if the former occupant of this room was interested in such things and told them to the new resident, yes. But the question is that those who come here to live these days, they are probably too young in their minds. They take it as a residence, and they don't give a damn about who built this house and who has lived here. They are temporary themselves."
> "How many such occupants are there compared to those who live here permanently?"
> "Half. As for me, I regard myself as a permanent one, because it matters a lot to me...not the square metres of *zhilploshchad* (living space), but the notion of home. And they, if they have a 25-metre room and hear that 26 metres are proposed somewhere else, they will move immediately. But as for me, if somebody suggested an apartment three times bigger somewhere else, I would stay here anyway."
> "Have you have had real offers like this?"
> "Yes, some private companies dealing with *resselenie* have come here more than once and made offers. They wanted to make offices here. They offered a three-room apartment for this one room where we live, because we have a high ceiling, a fireplace, and a view from the windows. Naturally, we refused. ...Some neighbours were indignant, but they will live here until they save up enough money to move somewhere else."

The notion of home as something more than a temporary place for rest and sleep, and where one's things are kept, should also include, as our informant believes, an element of relation to the given district and building. Especially when one has grown up here and his personal story is intimately related to the history of the apartment and, more broadly, of the place. Such people cannot accept the idea that all of these factors can be changed along with the usual way of things, while your home can be evaluated in dollars according to the current state of the real estate market. And so they tell the realtors: "I won't go anywhere away from here", to the distress of the realtors — and also to that of some of their neighbours. Probably the realtors simply cannot offer a good price for their homes.

The new occupants who rent rooms in CAs from the regular tenants (which became possible when the CA population density fell) represent a continuously increasing category of CA inhabitants. CAs as a social institution will scarcely disappear in the near future, but their types and their population will change. They will become a form of cheap housing for students and temporary workers from the provinces on the one hand, and for marginal people of all sorts on the other. Such people are much more mobile than traditional CA occupants; their childhood has been spent elsewhere, their folklore is less related to the place of residence. In a sense, they are more "global" than "local".

NOTE

1. The fieldwork in the communal apartments in St. Petersburg was supported by the Open Society Institute grant, RSS No.: 1460/1997. The illustrative materials collected during the work on this project have been used to create the virtual museum of communal apartment: http://www.kommunalka.spb.ru.

REFERENCES

Bliznakov, M. 1993: Soviet Housing During the Experimental Years, 1918 to 1933. In Brumfield, W.C. and Ruble, B.A. ed.: *Russian Housing in the Modern Age*. Cambridge: Woodrow Wilson Center. 85-148.

Boym, S. 1994: *Common Places*. Cambridge: Harvard University Press.

Guerasimova, K. 1999: The Soviet Communal Apartment. In Jeremy Smith ed.: *Beyond the Limits. The Concept of Space in Russian History and Culture*. Studia Historica 62. Helsinki.

Guerasimova, K. 2000: *Sovetskaia Kommunal'naia Kvartira Kak Sotsial'nyi Institut*. Unpublished Candidate (PhD) dissertation. St. Petersburg.

Kabakov, I. 1993: *In the Communal Kitchen. New Documents and Materials*. Paris: Galerie Dina Vierny.

Ruble, B. 1998: St. Petersburg's Courtyards and Washington's Alleys: Officialdom's Neglected Neighbors. In Pep Subiros ed.: *Ciutat real, ciutat ideal. Significat i funcio a l'espai urba modern*. Barcelona: Centre de Cultura Contemporáania de Barcelona. 12-27.

Sosnovy, T. 1954: *The Housing Problem in the Soviet Union*. New York: Research Program on the USSR.

Utekhin, I. 2001: *Ocherki Kommunal' nogo Byta* (Essays on everyday communal life). Moscow: O.G.I.

11

The Erosion of the Local Identity of Cities in Postmodernity: A Study of Two Novels

MIKKO LAAKSONEN

In urban contemporary society the identities of people are closely intertwined with the local identity of the cities they live in. The local identity of a city is shaped by its citizens, and their identities are formed by the local identity of their city, which is the framework for their everyday life. In contemporary society the processes of modernization, such as technical development and the expansion of the capitalist economy and growth in the state structure have turned against each other and demolished the structures of modern societies. The quintessential environment of modernity, the modern cities, is changing rapidly under intense economic, technological and cultural pressures. The social fabric of a city and the built environment itself may dissolve or mutate entirely. The identities of cities change, changing conditions in which people have to shape their own cultural identity.

How do people experience the erosion of the modern local identity of cities in postmodernity? In this article I will study the meanings attached by individuals to the city in two contemporary novels, Kerstin Ekman's *Gör mig levande igen* (1996, [Resurrect Me]; Ekman 1997), which is set in Stockholm, the capital city of Sweden, and Don DeLillo's *Underworld* (1997; DeLillo 1999), which contrasts the present-day Bronx in New York with its history and with the anti-city of Phoenix.

The modernisation processes that create present-day Western cities around the globe can be described as three major processes of city development. They emerge in the following sequence but continue to coexist simultaneously up to the present-day.

The first process is the development of the modern city street that permitted the dramatic expansion of cities in the nineteenth century. The modern city street is simultaneously a traffic instrument, a business booster and a social space. It allows for a cohesive identity both for the entire city and for its different neighbourhoods. The street forms the local society of cities that gives a meaning to human life and creates safety in the city. The city street is the scene for the urban spectacles of shopping, promenading, nightlife, sidewalk cafes and street demonstrations. It is distinctly egalitarian; on the city street all walks of life meet. Life on the city street has been the central inspiration for Dostoevsky and for Baudelaire, as Marshall Berman has demonstrated (Berman 1993; see also Jacobs 1977).

The second major process is rationalised city planning based on the aesthetics of modernist architecture. Modernist city planning aims at creating a rational environment for a democratic and egalitarian modern society and for the modern person living in it. In effect, the modernist architecture provided a built form for the utopian processes of modernisation. Modernist city planning is the direct antithesis of the modern city street; it differentiates the functions of the city into residential, industrial and business zones, preferably set in a park according to the ideal of "the city in the park", and replaces the city street with highways. As its instruments it employs various techniques such as various kinds of suburban and urban housing projects and opening freeways (see also Berman 1993: 164-171).

The third major process is the suburban anti-city, which replaces the urban spaces of streets with freeways and shopping malls and the planned city with unplanned suburban sprawl. It adapts the products of the two previous processes to its own uses. This process may be the truest form of capitalist city development. Simultaneously with suburbanisation, fast flight, trains, freeways and the electronic media connect different cities to neighbourhoods of a single global metropolis.

These three processes all exist both in North America and in the Nordic countries of Europe. However, they create different local identities of cities which erode in different ways when subjected to the progress of the global metropolis. The local identity of these cities created in modernity still haunts the cities beneath their global uniformity. Particularly in the Nordic countries, the city structure of modernity still retains in itself the utopian ideals of modernist architecture, and even in the United States contemporary society has to adapt to the remains of the old city structures of modernity in historic cities like New York.

In modernity the utopian perspectives of an improved future or freedom from oppression for the individual were invested in collective political utopias. In *The New Conservatism* (1989) Jürgen Habermas has considered the connection of the utopian perspective with a politically active consciousness of history as a central feature of modern thinking. Habermas sees that in the present condition these utopian energies of the modern have largely ebbed, and their destructive potential has become apparent (Habermas 1989: 48-71). This provides opportunities for a neoconservative critique of the welfare state and its architecture, which blames the utopian aims given to modernisation processes for the problems of modernity and demands their abolition. The utopian promise of modernist architecture to create an ideal living environment for modern man is blamed for the bleak housing projects, not the economical interests that made the projects so inhuman (Habermas 1989: 9, 12, 15, 25-26, 36-37, 49-609; 1996: 3, 74). Habermas considers that the modernist architecture promised too much, as no sufficient analysis of modern life existed to provide a basis for the planning of the ideal human environment. Proponents of postmodernist architecture such as Charles Jencks (1984: 6, 87-88, 127-129) suggest that the solution to an inhuman environment would be to strip architecture of its elitist aims of a universal aesthetic and societal renewal, and to replace them with conservative form-languages that could communicate better with local society. Habermas criticises this argument for its poor analysis and false solutions in which form is separated from function. He considers the self-critique of modernist architecture a better solution, true to his idea of modernization as an incomplete project which should be continued (Habermas 1989: 3-20).

In postmodernity an individual cannot invest his utopian perspective of a better future in the progress of the utopian processes of modernisation of the whole of society — such as the utopian city created by modernist architecture. The connection between the utopian ideal of a better living environment and the universal form-language of architecture dissolves. In postmodern architecture the utopian aims of modernization are dismissed and architecture is no longer based on the universal principles of a uniform form-language. The cultural context and local historical or classicist architecture are the basis of architectural form. (See Sarfatti Larson 1995: 148, 154-155, 173, 175.) The possibilities of the modern city can no longer serve as a major promise made to individuals.

Under these conditions individuals have to orient differently to their urban environment and provide their lives with new meanings in an urban context. The conflict between the different stages of urban development in contemporary cities supplies an interesting basis for the individual identity. Beyond the physical structure of the city, the social structure of the cities also changes under new pressures such as new patterns of immigration, new economic developments and new technologies.

I will now compare the meanings given in literature to the urban environment in two complex contemporary cities, Stockholm and New York. Both cities have been powerful symbols of modern life in their respective cultural contexts.

The new meanings of the utopian city supplied by modernist architecture in Kerstin Ekman's *Gör mig levande igen.*

In contemporary Nordic cities the cityscape produced through modernist city planning clashes with the changing forms of urban life. Kerstin Ekman's novel *Gör mig levande igen* is set in the predominantly modernist environment of Stockholm, which still carries the utopian message of planned life in the capital of the Swedish welfare state, however much Swedish society has changed as a result of immigration and growing economical inequality.

The utopian character of modernist architecture in the Nordic countries is well-known, but it has actually had a long prehistory. On the basis of an authoritative study of the development of Stockholm, Ingemar Johansson's *Storstockholms bebyggelsehistoria* (1987) [The Construction History of Greater Stockholm], we may consider that in the Nordic context the idea of building a better society through rational city planning predated functionalism considerably and was already well established by the early twentieth century. At the time, the city of Stockholm dealt with the social problems of industrial society by planning, financing and encouraging well-planned Garden City suburbs for the working class such as Enskede.

In effect, the early modernist architecture emerged as a suitable form for an existing process of social housing production. In the 1930s the Social Democrats, then in power both in the Swedish government and in Stockholm City Council, appropriated the aesthetic ideals of the visionary architect Le Corbusier and the *Siedlung* housing projects of the 1920s German modernist architecture as the form for their ambitious housing programme (see also Sarfatti Larsson 1995). This programme directly implemented the *Existenzminimum* (minimum necessities) ideals of modernism for small, high-quality apartments in the low housing units *smalhus* set in a park-like environment in the new suburbs of Stockholm. The crisis measures taken during the Second World War, such as rent control, permanently solidified the structure of the Swedish public housing programme. The utopian ideal of a planned environment for human life in the city was directly connected with the Swedish Social Democratic visions of the *Folkhem* (people's home) and the *välfärdssamhället* (welfare state), and the Stockholm models were quickly adopted in other Nordic countries as well during the late 1940s and the following decade (Johansson 1991: 428-444, 447-448, 450, 479-480, 482).

Gör mig levande igen is centred around a women's discussion club led by an elderly woman, Oda Arpman. An underlying thread of the whole novel is the murder of a young girl, Rosemarie, for racist motives. A central theme in the novel is the functionalist villa area of Fredens Dal in Gamla Enskede, a southern suburb of Stockholm, which is the place in which Oda Arpman's discussion club meets. Gamla Enskede itself is the major prototype of Stockholm's city-subsidised Garden City suburbs. The construction of villas, double and row houses was started in 1907 (Johansson 1991: 121, 398-403). The Fredens Dal area has been created in the 1930s by idealistic entrepreneurs such as the building master Fredh, with the best Swedish functionalist architects of the time as the designers.

The wholesale merchant Johan Krylund, the now long-dead lover of Oda Arpman, is the central visionary behind the Fredens Dal. He falls in love with functionalist architecture when from his boat he sees the Stockholm Exhibition (*Stockholmsutställningen*) of 1930. The Stockholm Exhibition presented the new architecture and industries and it became the major manifesto of functionalist architecture in Nordic countries, co-ordinated by the architect Gunnar Asplund:

> It was the year 1930. It was summer. By Djurgårdsbrunnvik Bay a city had floated down from the future. Summoned by Asplund into the greenery and mirrored by the water. He remembered it as white. But with coloured touches. Spots, surfaces, shocks. The inevitable victory of functionality over the directions of greed and power, their self-beautifying garlands and frills. Over staleness and filth and darkness. Over the poverty itself. Oh, this sunlit power! The narrow boat rocked with the discussions. Only Johan was fully carried away. In one moment. He fell in love at lightning speed. The light, the water, the spirituality and the matter-of-factness. He found his time there. It lay there in the sun (Ekman 1997: 61; translation M.L.).
>
> Året var 1930. Det var sommar. Vid Djurgårdsbrunnsvikens strand hade staden svävat ner ur framtiden. Frammanad av Asplund i grönskan och vattenspeglingarna. Vit mindes han den. Men med kolorit. Fläckar, ytor, chocker. Ändamålsenlighetens obevekliga seger över girighetens och maktens omskrivingar, dess självförhärligande girlander och krusiduller. Över unkenhet och lort och mörker. Över själva fattigdomen.
>
> Denna soliga styrka! Den smala båten vacklade i diskussionerna. Det var bara Johan som var hänförd. På en gång. En blixtlik förälskelse. Ljuset, vattnet, spiritualiteten och sakligheten. Han fann sin tid där. Den låg där i solen (Ekman 1997: 61).

Functionalism represented the cleanliness and prosperity has created by new industries, trade and politics as compared with the old power. Thus it is the natural aesthetic for the projects of Krylund and his companions. It represents the dynamic of the modern society through its radical, futuristic forms and gives a visual form to the dream of a better, more equal and prosperous society. The functionalism of Fredens Dal is directly connected with utopian visions of the modern society:

> - The Fredens Dal represents our cultural heritage.
> On this point Ulla truly agrees.
> - And the Villa Krylund is its pearl. Pure functionalism. Belief in the future. Bright dreams. But not only dreams but social and political visions!
> Oh really. How many times has Ulla heard Oda lay out the Krylundian dream there in the villa. How he saw the world: the telephone wires sang, the railway tracks clanked. On newly asphalted and straightened roads stretching to the horizon, cars shot forward like shuttles and weaved the fabric of civilisation. The chaotic, jagged, thunderous. A world for everyone. The sweat on the brow and the explosive power of the muscles; they all brought forth the riches of the earth to satisfy the hunger in the world. They met in the blue light of the arc lamps on the quays, on the airfields, in the great clamouring railway stations. A humanity that moved across the globe, blending languages and binding ties of friendship. No melancholic villagers enclosed in a country of pine trees. No wretches living in filth and darkness listening to whining accordions. But world citizens. And he thought that the Norrlandie defiance roared in the rapids! (Ekman 1997: 166-167; translation M.L.).
>
> - Dalen representerar ett kulturarv.
> Det håller Ulla verkligen med om.
> - Och Krylundska villan är dess pärla. Ren funktionalism. Framtidstro. Ljusa drömmar. Men inte bara drömmar utan sociala och politiska visioner!
> Oja. Hur många gånger har inte Ulla hört Oda lägga ut den krylundska drömmen därinne i villan. Hur han såg världen: det sjöng i telefontrådarna, järnvägsräls dunkade.

> På nyasfalterade, uträtade vägbanor som sträckte sig mot horisonten sköt bilarna fram som skyttlar och vävde civilsationens väv. Den kaotiska, brokiga, blixtrande. Alla människors värld. Pannors svett och musklers explosiva kraft: alla bar de fram jordens rikedomar för att mätta hungern i världen. Alla möttes de i båglampors blåvioletta sken på kajer, på flygplatser, på stora slamrande järnvägsstationer. En mänsklighet som rörde sig över klotet, som blandade språk och knöt vänskapsband. Inte melankoliska byinvånare instängda i ett granskogsland. Inga särlingar som levde i lort och mörker och lyssnade till gnälliga dragspel. Utan världsmedborgare. Och han tyckte att norrlandstrotset röt i forsarna! (Ekman 1997: 166-167).

When the Second World War threatens this vision of global progress, the functionalist environment of Fredens Dal become an important environment of resistance. Krylund and his friends form a discussion club, which aims through rational discussion to repel the shadows of fascism from Sweden (Ekman 1997: 99). This is a direct reference to a similar discussion club led by the real estate agent Johannes Krilon in Eyvind Johnson's *Krilon*-trilogy, written during the Second World War. The villa Krylund becomes, however, an object of entirely different projects after Johan Krylund has died and his widow Aina has moved out. In the 1970s it becomes the home of a hippie collective, and after that the local authorities use it as a kindergarten. In the 1980s it is used as the object of building speculators like Ove Fehzén and Adam Oxehufvud. As the pilot project of gentrification of the Fredens Dal it fails because the businessmen overdo the renovation. Gentrification is the process in which former slums, working-class areas or industrial sites become fashionable and are populated with higher-income people (e.g. Johansson 1991: 403, 412):

> She misses the villa already. It may be actually ugly inside. Its Nordic character has been broken down long ago. When Fehzén bought it in the eighties, kindergarten kids had fingerpainted the walls. He let his Italians decorate it with a stucco paintjob similar to those in his pizza restaurants. It became unsaleable. But Fehzén is not stupid. He learnt quickly. The villas he later

> bought in the area were decorated by interior design women who were so aesthetic they spoke in nasal tones (Ekman 1997: 23; translation M.L.).
>
> Hon saknar redan villan. Den är kanske egentligen ful inuti. Dess nordiska säregenhet har för länge sen brutits ner. När Fehzén köpte den på åttiotalet hade daghemsbarn fingermålat väggarna. Han låt sina italienare dekorera den med samma stuckarbeten som i hans pizzarestauranter. Den blev osäljbar. Men Fehzén är inte dum. Han lärde sig snabbt. De villor han senare köpte upp i området dekorerades av inredningsdamer som var så estetiska att de talade i näsan (Ekman 1997: 23).

As the villa cannot be sold, it is first used by the businessmen as a studio for their music business, and then they sell it to the municipality in the hope that the villa will be converted into an art gallery or something similar that could improve the upper-class image of the Fredens Dal area. Instead, the municipality decides to convert it into a refugee centre. Even during the sparse renovations in preparation of this, it retains the skeleton of the functionalist utopian aesthetic of its architect, Sven Markelius:

> Inside the new paint smells already. The villa is empty and full of light. The beauty is no longer visible. But she gets a strong feeling of its presence. The light that shines through it, a hint of it through the degradation. Like a trace of a beautiful, polished skeleton through water. It is silent inside. It is one of those rare moments when the mass of noise is far away and dull, and closest to oneself is a silence that would be healing if it were allowed to last. She wonders if Markelius designed the villa in winter, if he thought about snowlight and silence (Ekman 1997: 474; translation M.L.).
>
> Inne luktar det målarfärg redan. Villan är tom och ljus. Här syns ju inte längre skönheten, Men hon får en stark känsla av dess närvaro. Den ljusgenomdragna, den genom förnedringen anade. Som skymten av ett vackert, renspolad skelett under vatten. Det är tyst inne. Det är ett av de sällsynta ögonblick då ljudmassan är

> avlägsen och dov och det allra närmaste är en tystnad som skulle läka om den finge vara länge. Hon undrar om Markelius ritade villan om vintern, om han tänkte på snöljus och tystnad (Ekman 1997: 474).

The Fredens Dal has a different kind of meaning for the local youth gang, *Gudabarn* (God's children). In a curious inversion of typical youth subcultures, they aim to keep Fredens Dal free of graffiti and skinhead gangs. Mariella, a girl who is trying to find her sister Rosemarie, who disappeared when she went around the villas as Virgin Lucia in the Swedish tradition, meets a gang member, who explains the gang's ideology to her. Lucia's day (13 December) is one of the most important pre-Christmas traditions of Swedish-speaking people. The cutest young girl in the community is selected to be the Virgin Lucia, clothed in white and crowned with candles, and goes around singing Christmas carols. In this context, it must be pointed out that blonde girls are traditionally selected as Lucia, and that Rosemarie has had a black father and a white mother:

> As they walk towards Tallkrogen he says:
>
> - The God's Children keep Fredens Dal free from graffiti. If somebody fails to keep watch and a tag appears on an electricity box or something, then he tries to scrub it away himself.
> He snorts.
> - The Tiger hates tags. The Children of God will keep the Fredens Dal clean.
> - The Tiger is the guy in the ninth grade? The one with the light hair and boots.
> - Yes, says Rickie. Now he has those. Before, he thought that boots were wrong because he hated skinheads. He hates all the crazy types. But now he has boots. They are available in the COPY CAT range now. But they are expensive. Perhaps all of us will get them, too (Ekman 1997: 173; translation M.L.).
>
> Medan de går mot Tallkrogen säger han:
> - Gudabarn håller Dalen fri från klotter. Om nån misslyckas med att vakta och det blir en tag på nåt elskåp eller så, då försöker han ta bort det själv.

> Han fnissar till.
> - Tigern hatar tags. Gudabarnen ska hålla Dalen ren.
> - Tigern är han som går i nian va? Han med ljust hår och känger.
> - Ja, säger Rickie. Nu har han det. Förut tyckte han känger var fel för han hatar skins. Alla urballade typer hatar han. Men nu har han känger. Dom finns i COPY CAT nu. Fast dom är dyra. Vi kanske ska ha såna också (Ekman 1997: 173).

We may notice how the gang's ideology is based on a fear of different people similar to that of the racist skinhead ideology, but it is directed instead at the other youth gangs. It is organised to protect the villa area from "different" people and everything that deviates from the gang's model of normality — which is based on the most commercial forms of culture and fashion industry, such as the Swedish clothing company COPY CAT. The gang has also found a truly emblematic object for their worship. In the cellar of the Villa Krylund they worship the body of Rosemarie, who has been hidden there in a freezer by her murderer Lotar, a henchman of the businessmen Ove Fehzén and Adam Oxehufvud. Mariella witnesses an act of worship, not knowing that it is her sister who is being worshipped:

> There are two small cellar windows on both sides of a door. She peeks in very carefully. Full of people.
> They sit in two rows and have candles between them and in front of them. In small cans. The candles flicker and there are shadows on the faces. But she recognises several of them. Rickie sits there. And many kids who belong to the Tiger's gang. But she doesn't see the Tiger.
> All the kids are stiff and look odd. They don't move. It is weird that they can sit still so long and don't speak. They stare straight at the wall or into the darkness or somewhere (Ekman 1997: 220; translation M.L.).

> Det finns två smala källarfönster på var sin sida om en dörr. Hon kikar in väldigt försiktigt. Fullt med folk.
> De sitter på två rader och har ljus mellan sig och framför sig. I små burkar. Ljusen fladdrar och det blir skuggor i

> ansiktena. Men hon känner igen flera stycken. Rickie sitter där. Och en massa folk som är med i Tigerns gäng. Fast Tigern ser hon inte.
> Allihop är stela och konstiga. De rör sig inte. Det är underligt att de kan sitta stilla så länge och att de inte pratar. De stirrar rakt ut i väggen eller i mörkret eller nånstans (Ekman 1997: 220).

We may notice in these scenes how the functionalist architecture gains completely different meanings when compared to its original meaning as the embodiment of the utopian ideals of modernisation. It becomes a capitalised object of speculation in the gentrification projects of the Fredens Dal. On the other hand, it also becomes the object of religious worship by the Gudabarn gang. In these new contexts, only the aesthetic quality is still left intact when it is worshipped or capitalised. The functionalist architecture is still able to carry the historical memory of the utopian modernist city created by the 1930s visionaries.

However, the utopian modernist architecture has also created living environments in Stockholm that have gained entirely different meanings than those originally intended. The Swedish public housing programme expanded in scale and in the mid-1960s the Swedish government announced that it would build one million apartments during the following decade, the so-called million units programme of housing, *millionprogrammet*. In Stockholm increasingly larger housing projects were built along the new subway *tunnelbana* lines, firstly inside the city limits in the 1950s, then also beyond the city limits in the 1960s *(Lex Bollmora-städer)*, and then in the late 1960s as far as the old military training field of Järvafältet. The housing projects were built as self-contained units with commercial and public services centred around the subway station, and the Vällingby project, in particular, gained international fame as a model suburb. However, the increasingly inhuman scale of the new housing projects started to arouse criticism in the late 1960s. Many of these suburbs, such as Tensta and Rinkeby on the Järvafältet, gained a negative image through mistakes in city planning and the timing of the construction of services. Finally, the impetus behind the projects stalled completely in the early 1970s as the growth of Swedish cities slowed down, and the housing projects of the Million Units programme could not be rented — except to the immigrants moving to Sweden (Johansson 1991). Instead of acting as the utopian environment for the Swedish *Folkhem*, "people's home", they have been occupied by immigrants from all around the world like many areas in other large cities of Europe:

> It was not to the high-rises of Tallkrogen where Assia drove her in her white Audi. There lived the girls in the mink furs and the others from the weaving class. There lived Kryddan in a tight one-roomer, he who would move to Villa Krylund now that the municipality had bought it. Or perhaps he wouldn't move in. There were anyway many dark people, women with scarves, old men in slippers. And as Blenda had worked in the weaving cellar, she had thought she knew something about these people. But Rinkeby! God. A world of its own.
>
> Blenda tries to describe it. The smell of masala and mint and garlic and raw meat in the convenience store. Old brown-eyed men in Persian hats, on park benches. Like they rested in some other time that never ends. Sylvia sat and thought of her first trip to Paris, her very first trip abroad and she had never seen a Negro. As they said then. Later, on another trip there, in the eighties, she found out what had happened to the quartiers behind Pigalle.
>
> Dark waves across the world.
>
> Most of the people are very dark and very poor. Now they move over the continents in huge waves. Build worlds inside the known world. Kreuzberg, Rue des Abesses, Rinkeby. Fill it from the inside with growth that explodes, inevitably (Ekman 1997: 95; translation M.L.).
>
> Det var inte till höghusen i Tallkrogen som Assia förde henne i sin vita Audi. Där bodde minkflickorna och de andra som gick på vävningen. Där fanns Kryddan i en trång etta, han som skulle flytta in i Krylundska villan nu när kommunen köpt den. Eller om han inte skulle flytta in. Där fanns överhuvudtaget en hel del mörkt folk, kvinnor med sjaletter, gamla män i tofflor. Och

> eftersom Blenda hade jobbat i vävkällaren så hade hon trott att hon visste lite om det där. Men Rinkeby! Gud. En värld.
> Blenda försöker beskriva den. Lukten av masala och mynts och vitlök och rått kött i snabbköpet. Gamla brunögda män i persianmössor, på parkbänkar. Liksom vilande i nån tid som aldrig tar slut. Sylvia satt och tänkte på sin första Parisresa, det var första resan utomlands överhuvudtaget och hon hade aldrig sett en neger. Som man sa. Sen var det en annan resa dit, på åttiotalet, då hon upptäckte vad som hade hänt med kvarteren bortom Pigalle.
> Mörka vågor över världen.
> De flasta människor är mycket mörka och mycket fattiga. Nu rör de sig i väldiga vågor över kontinenterna. Bildar världar inuti den kända världen: Kreuzberg, Rue des Abesses, Rinkeby. Fyller den ininfrån med växtkraft som spränger, obevekligen (Ekman 1997: 95).

This new content threatens to give an entirely different meaning to the modern city. The poor immigrants create a different social environment inside the city intended for the use of the ideal modern man — inevitably, a Northern European taking part in the system of paid labour. However, in comparing Nordic cities with American cities, we need to recognise certain crucial differences. In the Nordic countries modernist housing projects and suburbs were often the first generation of urbanisation of a previously rural landscape. Few of the projects involved large-scale clearance, except for the city centres. In addition, the scale of new development and the aesthetic ideals of architects were often more humane than in American projects. Thus, even though it was criticised, the modernist city planning had — and still has — a far more positive image in the Nordic countries than in America.

In *Gör mig levande igen* the modernist environment of Stockholm is given new meanings by its citizens as the life of the city changes. In the novel, the Fredens Dal area carries several different meanings at once. While to the Oda Arpman discussion group the beauty of functionalist buildings serves as a memento of the utopian ideals of the 1930s and 1940s, the businessmen try to employ the same qualities to building speculation, directly contrary to the original meaning. The Gudabarn gang employs the area to differentiate itself from other youth groups. For all these people, the urban environment is a major instrument of differentiation from other people. Fredens Dal is a booster to the élitist self-image of both the commercial and cultural élite, while Rinkeby becomes a symbol of major difference, between the "ordinary" Swedish life of the old 1950s housing projects like Tallkrogen and the completely alien society of immigrants at Rinkeby. Indeed, we may note that while the modernist environment of Stockholm still carries the message of achieving the utopian *Folkhem* through city planning, it serves totally different meanings and differentations than those originally intended. Contemporary society uses the old modernist city for its own ends, even though this society is itself shaped by the modernist city.

The decay of the modern city and the emergence of the postmodern anti-city in *Underworld* (1997) by Don DeLillo

Even though modernist city planning is an important factor in modern cities, it is not the only factor that shapes the local identity of cities. The modernisation processes themselves create the local society of cities that creates meaning for human life in modernity. When the processes of modernisation turn against each other in contemporary society, they inevitably create a new kind of local identity. In Don DeLillo's novel *Underworld* (1997) we may see three different kinds of local identity in modernity and postmodernity. In this novel the 1950s Bronx still retains the idea of an organic community created by modernisation. This is then contrasted with two different possibilities of development: the postmodern anti-city of Phoenix and the destroyed landscape of the 1970s and 1990s Bronx created by slum clearance and urban decay.

The modern cities in the United States were built, like all new city structures, along "gridiron" street plans, the most outstanding examples of which were the Chicago and Manhattan plans. The typical American cityscape prior to the Second World War was a mixed-use city street with both residential, commercial and industrial uses and served by a streetcar or subway line, however much it might be blocked in by skyscrapers and stretches of single uses. These streets created a lively social background for city life, whose benefits are presented almost pastorally in Jane Jacobs' *The Death and Life of Great American Cities* (1961).

Modernisation of cities in the United States after the Second World War was mostly based on Garden City and International Modernism models imported from Europe and inadequately adapted to local conditions. Jane Jacobs points out that modernist city planning in the United States was based on many wrong assumptions about cities, such as that city density itself causes problems that are actually caused by overcrowding, that the multiple uses of districts cause problems, and that people would prefer a modernist "city in the park" to the social life of the city street. A major reason for this was that the planners lacked analyses of the social life of the city streets and the social processes that unslummed or slummed city districts. The focus in city planning was laid on factors which conformed with conventional mathematical methods of analysis, such as traffic or building density. This led to false principles for both public and private financing, which cut the funding for old areas designated as "slums" in these analyses and tried to solve the problems with completely new construction. It was virtually impossible to gain funding for improvements in old, dense inner city districts and it was very easy to finance total demolition, "slum clearance", of the old city structure to be replaced with new housing projects and highways. The public transit system collapsed through lack of funding. The new projects often succumbed to social and economical problems caused by their design faults. The policies which were intended to solve traffic problems and social problems actually intensified them through positive feedback — more traffic to jam, more social problems concentrated on the housing project hill, more derelict buildings in old areas (Jacobs 1977). As Marshall Berman notes, the "urban renewal" projects literally destroyed "the only environment in which modern values can be realized" — the city street (Berman 1993: 309, 317).

In *All That Is Solid Melts Into Air. The Experience of Modernity* (1982) Marshall Berman considers that the urban structure of New York has become a major symbol of modernity itself, and its monuments, buildings and neighbourhoods symbolise different aspects of modernity. The Bronx, in particular, has become "an international code word for our epoch's accumulated urban nightmares: drugs, gangs, arson, murder, terror, thousands of buildings abandoned, neighbourhoods transformed into garbage — and brick-strewn wilderness" — the internationally known example of late-twentieth century urban slum, of modernisation gone wrong. Initially, the Bronx was considered to be a particularly "modern" borough of New York City, and the Grand Concourse with its Art Deco apartment buildings was its symbolic centre. According to Berman, the destruction of the modern Bronx was caused by the Cross-Bronx Expressway, built in the 1950s by the road magnate Robert Moses. The expressway ruptured the urban fabric of the Bronx, requiring the demolition and division of residential areas, commercial centres and city streets so that the borough could no longer withstand the pressure of slumming and affluent people moving out (Berman 1993: 288-309, 325-329, 344; see also Jacobs 1977: 272-274, 278).

The economic expansion that facilitated "urban renewal" stalled in the 1970s, and old structures could no longer be annihilated and replaced (Berman 1993: 329-330, 332, 337-338). In *Behind the Postmodern Facade. Architectural Change in Late Twentieth-Century America* (1993) Magali Sarfatti Larson presents the way in which the postmodernist architecture and new kinds of inner city development, such as congress centres, gentrified historical districts and covered malls, emerged in connection with the economic crisis and downtrend in population experienced by the large American cities in the 1960s and the 1970s. These factors forced cities to quit slum clearing and projects funded only by public money. With the economic upswing of the next decade, postmodernist architecture became the dominant style (Sarfatti Larson 1995: 68, 83-86, 91,125, 197-198; Berman 1993: 329-330, 332).

The anti-cities of suburban housing, industrial parks and highways were also created by extensive government programmes which allowed government-guaranteed loans for suburban development on a nationwide market, in which a Brooklyn bank could be financing a suburb in the Midwest. The suburban developments were fuelled with a different ideology than city renewal; it involved an ideology of "return to nature". Nature was replaced by low-density, dull suburban development, which would rapidly decay, as Jacobs already predicted in 1961 (Berman 1993: 307, 317; Jacobs 1977: 322-323, 458-459). However, the suburban expansion would continue unchecked. The prototype model of the suburban postmodern anti-city may be Las Vegas, the casino city of Nevada. According to *Learning from Las Vegas* (1972), by the research group led by Robert Venturi, Las Vegas is not a space, it is a street with signs along it. The main street, "The Strip", organises Las Vegas and permits the spread of functions along the street since all trips are travelled by car and distance no longer matters. The main principle in situating the buildings is to present a token parking lot and an attractive facade to cars that approach along the Strip. The whole space can be experienced only in motion. Visual shock is increased by signs up to 60 metres high, neon lights, sound effects and moving parts (Venturi 1988: 3-6, 8-35, 51-54, pictures 1-16, 18-20, 42-43).

Both the slum clearance projects, urban decay and the postmodern anti-city break the connection between the present-day city and the modern city through destruction of the old city and by creating a new structure. All these factors appear in Don DeLillo's *Underworld.* The basic nature of modern society in the Bronx in 1951 can be briefly sketched through the impressions of Albert Bronzini, a high school teacher in Bronx, during his walk home from work:

> Even in this compact neighborhood there were streets to revisit and men doing interesting jobs, day labor, painters in drip coveralls or men with sledgehammers he might pass time with, Sicilians busting up a sidewalk, faces grained with stone dust. The less a job pays, Bronzini thought, the harder the work, the more impressive the spectacle. Or a waiter having a smoke during a lull, one of those fast-aging men who are tired all the time (DeLillo 1999: 661).

In this impression we may notice that even though the workers, the painters and pavement repairmen or waiters are tired by their integration into paid labour, they are still active members of an active society. The streets of Bronx are filled with work and day-to-day ordinary life, which create a tangible sense of community. In the next scene, Bronzini encounters children on a play street:

> He heard voices and looked down a side street filled with children playing. A traffic stanchion carried a sign marking the area a play street and blocking the way to cars and delivery trucks. With cars, more cars, with the status hunger, the hot horsepower, the silver smash of chrome, Bronzini saw that the pressure to free the streets of children would make even these designated areas extinct.
>
> He imagined a fragment of chalked pavement cut clean and lifted out and elaborately packed — shipped to some museum in California where it would share the hushed sunlight with marble carvings from antiquity. *Street drawing, hopscotch, chalk on paved asphalt, Bronx, 1951* (DeLillo 1999: 662).

The modern city carries a sense of meaningful society, which can reserve streets as play areas for children. However, these social spaces are already under threat; they will soon be swamped with cars, and the children will no longer have a place to play in. This is obviously a reference to the Cross-Bronx Expressway, an interesting device, since the construction of the road was declared only in the autumn of 1953 (Berman 1993: 292).

In short, even though the urban society of the 1950s Bronx is presented in *Underworld* as problematic in many ways, with crime, drugs and labour exploitation running rampant, it still remains a meaningful society, in which a walking man can strike up a conversation with the workers on the street. Don DeLillo's presentation of the Bronx has close affinities with the vision of the modern city street of Jacobs or Berman.

This society changes radically towards the 1990s through urban decay, slum clearance projects and social differentiation that radically change society. We may consider this through a scene in which two brothers, Nick and Matt Shay discuss whether their elderly mother should remain at her home in Bronx or move with Nick to live in Phoenix:

> They drank seltzer and took turns looking out the window. There was a picture window with a broad view west. El Bronx. People sat on lawn chairs on the roof of a motel nearby. Nick could tell these were local men and women who'd gained entry to the roof from an adjacent building, carrying their chairs and newspapers. He knew it was evidence of brisk improvisation, people extracting pleasure from the grudging streets, but it made him nervous, it was a breach, another opening, another local sign of instability and risk (DeLillo 1999: 196).

Nick boosts himself by looking out the window. What he sees is not a community in which people improvise to get the best out of the little that they are given; rather, he sees a breach of the controlled society. Matt, on the other hand, considers that it would be more rational to still have their mother live at her old neighbourhood with her friends:

> "I'm getting her out of here," Nick said.
> "Is that right?"
> "To Phoenix. That's right. There's no reason anymore for her to be here."
> "She has friends here. You know this."
> "I know this? How many friends? What friends?"
> "To Phoenix," Matt said.
> "How many friends?"
> "We haven't done a head count lately. But if she wanted to go, we'd take her gladly" (DeLillo 1999: 196).

Nick needs to discredit the Bronx, so he presents the neighbouring motel as a den of depravity, a convenient place to hide drug dealing and prostitution. Nick sees the old city, its excesses, diversity and improvisation as a slum that produces criminal behaviour — borrowing the imagery of the modernist city planners:

> Nick was in the window again.
> "Why would they put a motel in a place like this?"
> "I don't know."
> "It's a convenience, this motel, for sex and drugs. Because

> what else is it here for? Or homeless. A shelter for homeless people. They put them in motels now."
> "She likes it here, Nick. It's her life, it's what she's used to. She has her church, her stores, all the familiar things. And the friends that are still alive. Ask her for a list" (DeLillo 1999: 196-197).

We may see here that Nick and Matt see the Bronx of the 1990s as two entirely different things. Nick sees only the crime, the decay and the threats of dense urban life. Matt, on the other hand, sees that the Bronx is still a living community, where people can trust each other and organise their lives by participating in familiar activities such as attending church and going to the familiar stores. It is rather obvious that Nick sees the Bronx in the way that he wants to see it, without any positive aspects, when, for example, he sees the hallways of the huge housing block his mother lives in. The tower block is obviously a very typical New York Le Corbuserian red-or-brown-brick housing project built to replace the slums in the 1950s and the 1960s:

> "Listen to me. Stand at the elevator. Look to your left. Then look to your right. What do you see?"
> "I don't know. What do I see?"
> "You see the longest, saddest, scariest, most depressing — that feeling, you know?"
> "It's a hallway," Matt said.
> "It's that feeling. A nightmare out of some Stalinist — all right, I'm overreacting."
> "It's a hallway. Filled as a matter of fact with little kids most of the time" (DeLillo 1999: 202).

Here we can see how the tower block is connected in Nick's view with the dark side of modernisation .and modernist architecture, with Stalinism, with a utopia gone wrong. He does not see the little kids that play in the hallways — now that the play streets in Bronx have gone. In Nick's thinking the tower block becomes a symbol of modernisation gone wrong, which his mother should leave behind. We can note here how Nick's thinking is immediately connected with the conservative anti-utopian views of modernity and modern architecture. In the end Nick succeeds in taking his mother from Bronx to live with him in Phoenix, to watch television from the East coast, "out of the daily drama of violence":

> Marian wanted me to tell her about the old streets, the street gangs, the street fights, the alley sex, the petty theft. I told her about the car, not so petty, but she wanted to hear more. She wanted to hear about the execution now and then of some wayward member of whatever organized group she imagined might be operating thereabouts, the projectile entering the back of the head and making a pathway to the brain. She thought my mother's arrival might yield the basic savor she could not get from laconic Nick. But my mother only talked about the lazy grades I got in school and how I fell out of a tree when I was eight.
>
> And I liked the way history did not run loose here. They segregated the visible history. They caged it, funded and bronzed it, they enshrined it carefully in museums and plazas and memorial parks. The rest was geography, all space and light and shadow and unspeakable hanging heat (DeLillo 1999: 86).

Here we can see how the postmodern city of Phoenix replaces the history of the modern city with new meanings. In Phoenix, the only remembered version of Bronx is the violent city with its organised crime, not the peaceful city of Nick's mother's history with memories of the kid falling from a tree and getting bad grades in school. In Phoenix, history is no longer present except as simulacra, as objects in the postmodern museum like the play street in Bronzini's vision. It is easy to understand this when one considers the way in which Phoenix is created:

> "And the place is strategically located, out at the new frontier," he said. "I can see a satellite city growing out from this one shop, a thousand buildings, this is my vision, sort of spoked around the condom outlet. Like some medieval town with the castle smack at the center" (DeLillo 1999: 109).

Phoenix is a city that continuously grows new suburbs along the patterns set by capitalism. Like Las Vegas, it is organized along the needs of retail and suburban housing for large, cheap lots along motorways and other traffic arteries. The suburban city leaves the old downtowns, long forgotten, behind them. It can create a properly postmodern pattern of life for its residents without the restraints set by the historical memory inherent in the modern city. This emptiness serves Nick's need for an environment free of his own tragic historical memory. In the novel he constantly tries both to escape his own memory — the accidental manslaughter he has committed as a teenager — and to recapture the collective historical memory — the baseball, which is a central motif in the novel. Phoenix serves these needs directly, and it only contains the sanitised version of the collective memory.

What happens, on the other hand, to the inner city, such as the Bronx? We may return to the same landscape Bronzini strolled through in 1951. In the early 1990s, the southern Bronx is a deserted landscape, a no-man's-land inhabited only by the very poor or the most eccentric of people. It is a landscape where child abuse, organised crime, and illnesses which could be countered with simple medical aid, kill children:

> The nuns looked across all this. There were networks of vermin, craters chocked with plumbing fixtures and sheetrock. There were hillocks of slashed tires laced with thriving vine. Gunfire sang at sunset off the low walls of demolished buildings. The nuns sat in the van and looked. At the far end was a lone standing structure, a derelict tenement with an exposed wall where another building had once abutted. This wall was where Ismael Muñoz and his crew of graffiti writers spray-painted a memorial angel every time a child died in the neighborhood. Angels in blue and pink covered roughly half the high slab. The child's name and age were printed under each angel, sometimes with cause of death or personal comments by the family, and as the van drew closer Edgar could see entries for TB, AIDS, beatings, drive-by shootings, measles, asthma, abandonment at birth — left in dumpster, forgot in car, left in Glad Bag stormy night. This area was called the Wall, partly for the graffiti facade and partly the general sense of exclusion — it was a tuck of land adrift from the social order (DeLillo 1999: 239).

What has happened to the modern city in postmodernity? As we see in *Underworld*, the modern city can be deeply eroded by the continuing technological and economical modernisation; the modern Bronx is wiped off the map. Postmodernity can replace the modern city with the postmodern fringe city. In addition, the meanings of the modern city can be forced to change to postmodern ones through processes such as gentrification or by the new social formations such as youth gangs, as we see in *Gör mig levande igen*. These processes are based on the changing meanings the citizens give to their cities, meanings formed by the city itself, as we see both in Nick Shay's perceptions of New York and Phoenix, and in the different meanings given to Fredens Dal by its inhabitants. It can be pointed out that certain differences exist between the Swedish and American cities. In the USA, the modern city structures have decayed and even disappeared to a considerable degree, which is not the case in Sweden.

The cities planned along the principles of modernist architecture may at first sight appear to be the ideal environments that pattern the life of their residents according to the models of modernity. They should also act as the refuge of modern forms of life in postmodernity, as the last bastion of utopian modernity. However, to contradict this we may also make two important observations. Firstly, the ideal cities of modernist architecture, the modernist housing projects and suburbs built all over the world, did not in fact pattern the lives of their residents according to the ideal model of modernity. Rather, they became places in which the postmodern forms of life first flourished — in them people watched television and accepted the vision offered by the culture industry, the subcultures of punk or graffiti were created in them, in them flourished the truly commercialised life filled with cheap products from the local convenience store or supermarket. They can readily be employed for the patterns of postmodern life and they may even be given completely new meanings, as we see in the meanings given to Fredens Dal by the businessmen or the Gudabarn youth gang. Though the different modernist projects share the same ideological basis, they have gained totally different meanings — as we can see of the model projects, such as Vällingby in Stockholm, or Tapiola in Helsinki, that still have a positive image in the Nordic countries, and the housing project ghettos like Rinkeby or the projects of the Bronx.

Secondly, the housing projects became a key target for anti-modernist politics. In states with neoconservative governments the demolition of housing projects became a fashion after the demolition with explosives of the Pruitt-Igoe housing project in St. Louis in 1970. The demolition of the Pruitt-Igoe project is the favourite example of antimodernist critics such as Charles Jencks or Tom Wolfe. The social problems were pushed off the housing project hill to the streets. The idea behind this was not the freeing of people from inhuman conditions as it was presented then — it was the cleansing of the cities of modernist, utopian influence. Even though the housing projects still stand in Sweden, many of them have become ghettos for immigrants and they are excluded from the world of well-off people. The role of the scapegoat is carried not only by modernist housing projects, as we see in *Underworld*. Rather, the scapegoat for the problems of modernity is the entire modern urban structure of Bronx with its conflicting elements. The apparent escape from this scarecrow is offered by a suburban anti-city like Phoenix.

Conclusion

The changing identity of cities provides new potentials for the identities of their inhabitants. In the examined novels examined here, people use the old city in new ways. The functionalist environment of Fredens Dal is employed to boost the intellectual superiority of Oda Arpman's discussion group, the businesses of Fehzén and Oxehufvud, and also the ideology of the Gudabarn gang. The modernist housing projects serve as a frame for the new society of the immigrants of Rinkeby or to give a boost to Nick Shay's view of the Bronx as the ultimate hell of modernisation gone wrong. The fading and eroding modern city can be seen nostalgically, as by Bronzini on his stroll, or best forgotten, as by Nick Shay in Phoenix. The local identity of cities performs a major role in the formation of the cultural identity of the characters of the novels, and the meanings given to the city can be changed and transformed into new ones to serve new ends in the changing contemporary world.

SOURCES

Ekman, Kerstin 1997 (1996): *Gör mig levande igen* [Resurrect Me]. Stockholm: Albert Bonniers förlag.

Berman, Marshall 1993 (1982): *All That is Solid Melts into Air. The Experience of Modernity.* London: Verso.

DeLillo, Don 1999 (1997): *Underworld.* London: Picador.

Habermas, Jürgen 1989: *The New Conservatism. Cultural Criticism and the Historians' Debate.* Edited and English translation by Shierry Weber Nicholsen. Cambridge, Massachusetts: MIT Press.

Habermas, Jürgen 1996 (1987): *The Philosophical Discourse of Modernity. Twelve Lectures.* Originally published in 1985 as *Der philosophische Diskurs der Moderne. Zwölf Vorlesungen.* English translation Frederick G. Lawrence. Cambridge, Massachusetts: MIT Press.

Jacobs, Jane 1977 (1961): *The Death and Life of Great American Cities.* Harmondsworth: Penguin.

Jencks, Charles 1984 (1977): *The Language of Post-Modern Architecture.* London: Academy Editions.

Johansson, Ingemar 1991 (1987): *Storstockholms bebyggelsehistoria. Markpolitik, planering och byggande under sju sekler* [The Construction History of Greater Stockholm. Land Use Politics, Planning and Building during Seven Centuries]. Värnamo: Gidlunds.

Sarfatti Larson, Magali 1995 (1993): *Behind the Postmodern Facade. Architectural Change in Late Twentieth-Century America.* Berkeley and Los Angeles: University of California Press.

Venturi, Robert, Denise Scott Brown and Steven Izenour 1988 (1977, 1972): *Learning from Las Vegas.* Cambridge and Massachusetts: MIT Press.

12

The Glocal New Age

TUOMAS MARTIKAINEN

Introduction

Sociologists of religion are a happy bunch of people. Being somewhat turned off by the all-embracing secularisation tendencies in post-war Europe and apparently becoming an extinct academic breed, they once again have a multiplicity of new, exciting phenomena to study. It is not that the mainstream churches starting to grow again or that secularisation has disappeared, but rather that there are several new, important developments to study, including new religious movements, immigrant religions and New Age (Davie 2000). And all this in a globalising world, where old boundaries are being challenged and new agendas set.

The globalisation debate has opened up fresh horizons for interpreting religion both historically and in relation to the present-day (e.g. Beckford 2001; Beyer 1994; Robertson 1992: 42-43). Religions have always created important transnational connections and played a key-role in spreading new ideas and practices. Just a brief look at the world's religious geography reveals the elementary importance of Christianity and Islam in creating both large-scale transcultural religious families and cultural boundaries, not to mention the age-old Jewish diaspora that has inspired the study of transnational, diasporic communities (Wahlbeck 1999: 29). These are seen to be among the central features of the global condition (Appadurai 1996: 49; Hannerz 1996: 19-22).

The ideal type of a world religion is a faith that has a wide following, has spread over a large area and shares a number of characteristics which can be reduced to certain key-features. Christianity, Buddhism and Islam are the most typical world religions, and their spread highlights an elementary feature of the globalisation process. Even though the religions in question can be abstracted back to certain key ideas and features, they do not really constitute any uniform whole. In reality, the so-called world religions consist of a huge variety of local interpretations and traditions that only to varying degrees resemble each other (Smart 1989: 11-12). This dual nature of globalisation has attracted critical attention to the study of *glocality*, which implies that the globalisation process does not produce similar responses in different parts of the world, but rather that the accommodation of globalisation incorporates a local aspect — otherwise it could not exist in a new environment. Hence, globalisation is in a sense always glocal (Eade 1997: 3-5; Robertson 1995).

The purpose of this article is to explore some of the dimensions of the global spread of New Age through a specific case, which is the localised New Age in a single Finnish city, Turku. Initially, I will locate the New Age phenomenon on the map of religion in late modernity and Finland while reflecting on some of its main characteristics. Secondly, my discussion will focus on New Age in the religious field of Turku: the forms it takes and the ways in which local bookstores tell us about New Age. Finally, in connection with a discussion of glocality I will explore ways in which the concept may help us to understand contemporary local-global relations. My general aim is to show that we can find a combination of both global and local features that can best be described as glocal.

Religion in Late Modernity

Religion in late modernity refers to the forms of religious life practised in the West from roughly the late 1960s onwards. Generally speaking, we can say that the role of the established Christian churches in Europe has become less important and that the churches play a less significant role in almost all aspects of social life than they did before. This process has usually been called secularisation. Theorists understand the development in different ways. For the hard-line secularisation theorists it is proof of the inevitable decline of religion (Bruce 1997), for others it is a similar but multidimensional development (Davie 2000), and for some it is just a change in the form of religion (Luckmann 1967; 1999).

Thomas Luckmann (1967; 1999) argues that since the immediate post-war period the traditional, institutionally specialised forms of religion (state churches and other denominations) have given way to a new social form of religion: the structurally privatised social form. The traditional religious institutions are still there, but their clientele is smaller than before and their meaning has retreated into the private realm. Privatised religion takes many forms, of which New Age is one example. New Age religion or spirituality exists in a pluralistic, market-like environment, where the religious or spiritual consumer chooses between different options of her own choice (Martikainen 2001). Religion is mostly meaningful on the individual level; it emphasises experimentation and emotions, and incorporates a holistic view of humankind. We are living in an *Erlebnisgesellschaft* that is characterised by consumption and by a search for deep, original experiences (Featherstone 1991; Schulze 1992).

The concept of New Age has been used in at least two ways: (1) as a social movement, and (2) as a type of contemporary religiosity. The understanding of New Age as a social movement positions it in a historical frame of predecessors (Theosophy, New Thought), key-moments (the Hippie era), 'prophets' (Marilyn Ferguson) and ideas (karma, self-sacralisation), many of which stem from Eastern philosophies and Western occult-esoteric traditions (cf. Ketola 1999: 193-196). New Age incorporates a strong emphasis on healing and alternative medicine, and it is often critical of mainstream institutions, offering alternative visions of personal development. The recent roots of New Age are in the "cultic milieu" of the 1960s United States. As a distinct movement it emerged in the 1970s and, since then, has rapidly spread in the Western world (Melton et al. 1990: xiii-xxxi; York 1995: 1-2, 33-35).

New Age can be distinguished from other contemporary religious movements, such as neo-Paganism and new religious movements. According to Gordon Melton et al. (1990: viii):

> unlike some newer religions, the New Age Movement has no single leader, no central organization, no firm agenda, and no group of official spokespersons. It is, in other words, a genuine social movement — dispersed into hundreds of individual efforts and organizations, fast paced, complex, and extremely malleable.

This quotation makes it clear why the study of New Age has sometimes been a difficult undertaking, since the closer one gets to it, the farther it seems to disappear as a conceptual whole (see Sundback 1996: 216). This trait in New Age has led scholars to search for the common, underlying themes or "doctrines" of New Age thought. Paul Heelas' (1996) view of New Age as a kind of holistic self-sacralisation and the wait for an emerging new consciousness has been an influential attempt to find a common denominator for the disturbing variety of phenomena labelled New Age. Nevertheless, quite often the term is used as a broad umbrella term covering even some other religious movements or certain aspects of them (e.g. Bruce 1997: 198-229; Junnonaho 1999), which simply confirms the fluidity of the movement.

The second common usage of the term New Age understands it as a kind of contemporary religiosity or spirituality. Wouter Hanegraaff (1999: 147) defines spirituality in the following way:

> *A spirituality* = any human practice which maintains contact between the everyday world and a more general meta-empirical framework of meaning by way of the individual manipulation of symbolic systems.

This new spirituality is caused by secularisation and is by nature deeply individualistic. Its emergence is explained by structural changes in society. The new spirituality draws its material from already existing religious and spiritual sources, but combines it in unorthodox and novel ways. It always needs to be constructed on the individual plane, because, by its very nature, it does not accept the idea of simply emulating previous, ready-made spiritualities. These ideas become New Age spiritualities when they incorporate New Age ideas (Hanegraaff 1999). This connects the view to the first understanding of New Age as a social movement, but, in practice, it identifies New Age manifestations far beyond the obvious New Age organisations and other such structures.

Both approaches talk about the same phenomenon but on different planes. The social movement approach is useful for distinguishing the actual manifestations of New Age, whereas the spirituality approach is helpful in identifying changes in a more general religiousness that extends wider than the direct influence of the movement itself. There is one characteristic of the New Age Movement that makes this 'duality' quite predictable: New Age is an extremely literary movement (Bruce 1997: 197-200; Heelas 1996: 6-9). All of its central "prophets" are authors, including Marilyn Ferguson, Shirley MacLaine and David Spangler (Melton et al. 1990: xxviii). This means that New Age ideas are to a large extent spread through a variety of media (books, magazines, newspapers, videos, the Internet etc.) and not through direct human contact. It also implies that people are freer to draw their own interpretations from the material. Whereas the New Age message seems to have credibility and to experience demand from outside the movement's milieu (Ketola 1999: 208-212), it is only natural that some of its key ideas can be found among people who have no direct contact with the movement.

Various New Age phenomena have often been described as *audience* or *clients cults* (Bruce 1997: 198). Rodney Stark and William Sims Bainbridge (1985) originally coined the concepts within the religious economies or rational choice theory of religion, but they have also been used outside the original theoretical approach (e.g. Bruce 1997). The audience cult is a diffuse and loosely, if at all, organised group of people that might occasionally gather for a lecture but is mainly active through the consumption of books, magazines and other publications. The shared interest can be quite diverse and incorporate many diffuse elements. The client cult is an equally loosely organised group that is united by its interest in therapy, service, product, etc. The central relationship is the one between consultant and client (York 1995: 259-260). Whether such cults can be called groups in any conventional meaning is debatable; in fact, they are more reminiscent of the temporary neo-tribes that, according to Michel Maffesoli (1996), are characteristic of contemporary times. In any case, the audience and client cults are typical of the New Age milieu.

New Age in Finland

There is sometimes a tendency in Finnish research (e.g., Junnonaho 1996: 37-39) to see various "alternative religions" — that is non-Christian and non-immigrant religions and spiritualities — without seeing the actual differences between them. This means that such diverse phenomena as new religious movements, New Age, neo-Paganism and pseudo-science are regarded as manifestations of the same thing: presenting an alternative to mainstream Christianity. One explanation for this is that we are dealing with relatively marginal groups, many of which do not require strict membership identity. For example, in Turku, while on the one hand there are distinct movements (for example, New Age, Theosophy and yoga), on the other hand they seem to form an "alternative religious field" in contrast to the "traditional religious field" that is made up of traditional religious communities. To speak of alternative religions is especially problematic on an organisational level and among people with strong convictions, but on a more general plane, it seems to be acceptable. For example, books on these topics are usually sold on the same counter in bookstores. While more research is needed on the topic, we can still assume that among those who are not so deeply involved in certain movements there may exist a mix of beliefs that belong to different movement categories.

Given this approximate idea of religion in the contemporary West and what New Age is about, the next question is about how this relates to Finland, which is a part of the late modern West. In large comparative studies Finland is seen as an example of the Nordic, strong "state church" societies with low religious plurality and high secularisation. These countries have been called "belonging but not believing" societies (Davie 2000). The notion of "belonging but not believing" is easily illustrated by a high church membership (85.2% of total population) but a low church attendance (3.2% of church members weekly). Furthermore, less than half of the church members believe as they "should" according to the official doctrine, which is understood as an indication of the privatisation of religion (Salonen et al. 2000: 22, 25-31, 54; Sundback 1996).

Alongside the numerically dominant Lutheran Church there exists a multiplicity of small religious communities: Protestant denominations, immigrant religions and new religious movements as well as various New Age communities and phenomena (Heino 1997: 24-41; Junnonaho 1999; Kaplan 2000). New Agers seem to be mostly urban, highly educated, middle-class and middle-aged women, even though there is interest among the younger generation and males as well (Sundback 1996: 222-224; Takanen 2001: 39). With regard to gender differences, the international observation that interest in the paranormal and esoteric knowledge is male dominated and that the healing, channelling and spirituality side is female dominated seems to be correct (Bruce 1997: 220). Certain beliefs related to New Age are commonly spread among the population — for example, belief in reincarnation (22%), UFOs (19%) and Astrology (12%) (Heino 1997: 358-366, 384; Salonen et al. 2000: 30-31) — which confirms that the movement has significant influence outside its own milieu.

While relatively few studies have been written on New Age in Finland (these include Mattsson 2000; Mikkola 1999; Mikkonen 2000; Sundback 1996; Takanen 2001), it still has become a recognised part of the national religious field (Junnonaho 1996: 37-39; 1999; Heino 1997: 33-41). There are, for example, specific organisations, communities, fairs, magazines, methods of alternative healing and commercial enterprises that can be directly related to New Age (Heino 1997). The Finnish New Age landscape is as diverse and heterogeneous as anywhere in Europe. One national characteristic seems to be a larger than average interest in Anthroposophy and Theosophy (Mikkonen 2000: 262).

The current number of Finnish New Age practitioners can be estimated only indirectly. I am not aware of any detailed estimates, and therefore the following should be understood as a rough and preliminary estimate based on personal reflections, discussions with New Age practitioners and literature on the subject, on copies sold of Finnish New Age magazines, and on visitors in *Hengen ja Tiedon messut* — A Finnish New Age fair (e.g. Mikkonen 2000: 258-261; Takanen 2001: 54).

People influenced by New Age can be divided into three groups: (1) activists, (2) seekers and (3) observers. The first group is quite small, most likely ranging from several hundred to a few thousand individuals. They are members of various associations, active participants and organisers of events, and subscribers to distinct New Age magazines such as *Minä Olen* ("I Am"), *Polku* ("Path") and *Ultra*. New Age ideology is a central part of their worldview. The second group is like the first one, but involvement is much more sporadic and less binding. This includes taking part occasionally in lectures and courses, reading the more generally appealing New Age magazines such as *Voi Hyvin* ("Wellness"), and visiting New Age fairs. Their number is probably around ten thousand. They can be called seekers, who have found the New Age environment attractive for their own personal growth. The third group does not usually take part in activities (with the exception of mainstream fairs), but has a slight interest in New Age literature and follows the theme mainly through popular magazines, such as women's magazines. Their number can be estimated as several tens of thousands. This group uses New Age ideas and services for recreation and personal reflections on life. All three groups have a larger than average interest in alternative therapies. With this sketchy picture of New Age in Finland in mind, let us now see how the movement manifests itself in Turku.

New Age in Turku

Turku is the regional centre of South-Western Finland which caters services for some 250,000 people in the area. It is the fifth largest city in Finland with 172,000 inhabitants. The local religious field is dominated by the Lutheran Church, but there is a remarkable variety of other communities as well; including Protestant, Catholic and Orthodox Christians alongside a growing immigrant Muslim presence. Turku has the second largest immigrant population in the country after the capital region. Altogether, over thirty different religious congregations and a large number of various, specialised religious associations conduct religious activities in the city (Martikainen 1996; 2000).

Field

Before presenting the local field it must be pointed out that, in practice, it is quite difficult to draw clear distinctions between New Age and certain other religious or quasi-religious phenomena in the local field. For example, a local New Age group arranged a two-day festival called *Sateenkaaripäivät* ("Rainbow Days") in Autumn 2000, which catered for people interested in spiritual growth. Present in the programme were such diverse phenomena as biodynamical cultivation, Bible singing, Chi Kong, Hare Krishna, meditation, parapsychology, Spiritualism, Theosophy and the UFOs. While it was stated in the programme that the festival was an attempt to unite diverse groups and to fight against internal prejudices (*Sateenkaarisanomat,* August 2000), it is, however, a clear indication that the wish to incorporate such diverse viewpoints into a New Age festival means that there are no clear boundaries to what is or is not New Age.

Three studies exist that examine aspects of the local scene on a broader basis: Martikainen (1996) on organisations, Kurkinen (1997) on alternative medicine, and Mattsson (2000) on profiles of participants in local New Age activities. Furthermore, there is one special issue of the *Ultra* magazine (5-6/1998) with several articles on Turku. The local New Age scene is as many-sided as can be expected: associations, fairs, alternative therapists, commercial enterprises, and similar activities. However, on the local level not all groups, services and activities that are presented here label themselves as New Age. Rather, this is the borderland of various movements which in reality co-exist and sometimes co-operate. A further reason for not identifying with New Age is that the word is understood as too limiting, commercially exploitative and, to some extent, also negative (Hirvonen 8. September 2000). The common feature in these groups is that they see themselves as presenting a new, alternative consciousness unlike traditional religions that have stagnated in old forms (*Sateenkaarisanomat* August 2000: 2; Teide 1998). Also, I have found it uncomfortable to use the term New Age when I tell my informants what I am studying. I prefer to tell them that I am studying "alternative spirituality", which is accepted by them as a good description of their activities. However, I use New Age to describe their activities in this article, because that is the term used in academic literature for the 'alternative spirituality' in question.

The historical roots of the local New Age scene go back to the beginning of the twentieth century, when the Theosophical Society started in the city (Martikainen 1996: 85). The actual New Age scene emerged in the 1970s and expanded tremendously during the 1990s, especially in the latter part of the decade (Kurkinen 1997: 14-15; Teide 1998). Associations are amongst the major players and there are several of them (see Table 1). They have been founded mainly in the past two decades and represent different aspects of New Age. They are typically centred on several key-individuals, whose withdrawal could end the activity altogether. People can also be members of several associations at the same time. The associations arrange activities such as lectures, seminars and courses. Some are specialised in specific topics, while others offer a broad range of titles that resemble the variety in *Sateenkaaripäivät*. Alongside the more obvious New Age associations there exist groups close to them: yoga groups, Tibetan Buddhists, Theosophical lodges, UFO associations and non-orthodox Masonic groups (Martikainen 1996: 85-93; Teide 1998). Together these groups form the alternative religious scene in Turku.

Association	*Founded (Registered)*	Members
Turun Parapsykologinen Seura ry "The Parapsychological Society of Turku"	1963 (1963)	140
Turun Henkisen Kehityksen Yhdistys ry "The Spiritual Growth Association of Turku"	1980 (1982)	?
Turun Seudun Spiritualistit ry "Spiritualists of the Turku Region"	(1989)	140
Pikkumettäläiset ry "People of the Little Forest"	(1991)	20-30
Galacticus ry	1995 (1997)	not active
Turun Henkinen Keskus ry "The Spiritual Centre of Turku"	1997 (1998)	20-30
Turun Viriditas ry	1999 (1999)	not active

Table 1: New Age related associations in Turku (Hirvonen 25-4-2001; Jaakkola-Puhakainen 1998; Koskinen 25-4-2001; Makkonen 23-2-2000; Martikainen 1996: 92; Mäntylä 25-4-2001; Oksanen 25-4-2001; Teide 1998; 25-4-2001).

The associations often hold their meetings in particular centres, such as *Turun Luontaishoitola* ("The Natural Health Home of Turku"), *Ruusuportti* ("The Rose Gate") and the *Sophia* lecture hall. The centres house many diverse activities, including lectures, courses, alternative therapies and other commercial enterprises. The number of participants in the lectures and courses is usually between ten and thirty, and seldom significantly more. According to Cecilia Mattsson (2000: 50-51), the most popular courses have been on meditation, yoga, Reiki and healing.

Many forms of commercial enterprise attract New Agers and also offer them inspiration. Alternative medicine and therapies are by far the most popular New Age related activities to be found. Alternative therapy refers to a therapy that does not receive state compensation as officially recognised therapies do (Kurkinen 1997: 4-5). In Turku alone there are over 200 alternative therapists who provide such methods as Acupuncture, Aromatherapy, Homeopathy, Pranic Healing, Reiki and Shiatsu. Many therapists offer several different therapies. Not the whole of the alternative medicine scene can be related to New Age, but a significant portion of it is close to that (Kurkinen 1997). In addition, there are many health food stores that sell products related to New Age (Teide 1998: 7). There is also one specialist New Age bookstore (Martikainen 1996: 93).

Several local fairs are connected with New Age (see Table 2). These include two specialist fairs and three fairs for the general public. The first specialist fair was the biannual *Henkisen kasvun päivät,* which functioned from 1997 to 1999, and the second one is the annual *Sateenkaaripäivät,* which started in 2000. The attendance at them has been some 200-400 persons. The three other fairs all include various New Age retailers — often related to alternative medicine — but their main emphasis is elsewhere. These are the *Uskonto ja elämänkatsomus* ("Religion and worldview"; a 1998 addition to the Book and Science Fairs), the *NaisDay* ("Women's day") and the *Osaava Nainen* ("Able woman") fairs (Teide 1998). These fairs attracted, respectively, 16,000, 10,000 and 36,000 visitors in 2000. These latter fairs seem to indicate that New Age has become more mainstream and that some of its manifestations attract a substantial demand. The majority of visitors at all the fairs have been women.

Information about activities is spread by means of certain notice boards, internal newsletters and local media. The two most important notice boards seem to be those in the *Humanova* ("The New Human") bookstore and the *Verso* ("Sprout") vegetarian restaurant (Teide 1998 also notes this). Both are places that people interested in New Age visit. However, among those people who come to eat in *Verso* there are more potential new candidates, whereas *Humanova* is mostly visited by people already interested in the matter. A local newsletter titled *Sateenkaarisanomat* ("Rainbow News"), published since 1999, provides information about the various associations' activities. With some 200 subscribers and an average edition of several thousands it serves readers in the area (Oksanen 25-4-2001).

Fair	*Arranged*	*Takes place*	*Exhibitors in 2000*	*Attendance in 2000*
Osaava Nainen "The Able Woman"	since 1995	annually	610	35.000
NaisDay "Women's Day"	since 1996	annually	c. 100	10.000
Henkisen kasvun päivät "Spiritual Growth Days" (1)	1997-1999	biannually	—	—
Uskonto ja Elämänkatsomus - messut "Religion and Worldview Fairs" (2)	since 1998	every second year	c. 50	16.000
Sateenkaaripäivät "Rainbow Days"	since 2000	annually	c. 30	300

Table 2: Fairs that have a relation to New Age in Turku (Hirvonen 25-4-2001; Hongisto 25-4-2001; Mäntylä 25-4-2001; Nieminen 25-4-2001; Oksanen 25-4-2001; Promonova 10-4-2001; *Sateenkaarisanomat* August 2000; Teide 1998).

(1) On average, The Spiritual Growth Days had 25 exhibitors and 300 visitors per fair.

(2) The attendance figure for the Religion and Worldview fairs is the total for the Book, Science, Religion and Worldview fairs, which were held simultaneously and with the same entrance fee.

New Age is visible in the local media mainly through advertisements and occasional articles. A local, biweekly free distribution paper, *Turkulainen,* is the main channel for advertisements, mainly because it is significantly cheaper than the main local newspaper *Turun Sanomat.* My general impression after reading both of these papers for many years is that after the news coverage of local Lutheran parishes and some immigrant religions (mainly Islam), the most common are those themes related to New Age. News coverage of other religious phenomena is almost negligible, and sporadic at best.

To estimate the number of local New Age practitioners we are faced with difficulties similar to these connected with national estimates, as discussed earlier. Membership in associations, participation in fairs and the distribution of *Sateenkaarisanomat* can be of some help in the matter. The activists seem to form a group of approximately 200-300 people and the number of seekers is several hundred individuals. The attendance at the *NaisDay* fair — the most New Age of all of the mainstream fairs — indicates that the number of observers may be as many as ten thousand people.

Bookstores

Books are one of the main channels through which New Age ideas spread. Let us now examine the supply of New Age literature in local bookstores to see what they tell us about the nature of New Age in Turku. We need to remember that books can also be borrowed from friends and from libraries, bought from other cities or countries, and ordered through the Internet. Furthermore, there are many specialist booksellers in Finland, not least several minor publishers that sell their products via mail order and local associations. At this stage I will assume that these channels cater mainly for those who already are deeply involved, whereas the local bookstores are the main channel for the general public.

All of the major bookstores in Turku (*Akateeminen, Kansallinen* and *Suomalainen Kirjakauppa*) sell literature that can be defined as New Age. In early September 2000 I made some preliminary comparisons between the bookstores. First, traditional religious and New Age literature were always situated close to each other and if one of them was somewhat out of sight it was in fact traditional religious literature. Second, New Age literature was never found under the title of Religion or New Age. In *Kansallinen* (National Bookstore) and *Suomalainen Kirjakauppa* (Finnish Bookstore) the books were found in sections reserved for Philosophy and Psychology. In *Kansallinen Kirjakauppa* there was also a third section titled Reflections (*mietelmiä* in Finnish). Additionally, one could find New Age books in sections on health and human relations. *Akateeminen Kirjakauppa* (Academic Bookstore) was rather different from these two bookstores, however. In its psychology and philosophy sections there were mainly academic studies, and New Age books were found at a counter titled Esoteric Knowledge and Para-knowledge (*esoteriikka* and *rajatieto* in Finnish). It seemed to me that *Akateeminen Kirjakauppa* was the only bookstore in which some sort of deeper expertise had been used to sort the books into proper categories (also Hirvonen 8. September 2000 and Teide 1998 note this). Turku has also one specialist bookstore devoted to New Age, *Humanova*, which was established in 1991 and carries a large supply of New Age related books, music and other artefacts.

The selection of New Age books was relatively similar in all the four local bookstores that I visited. Most of the books were either Finnish translations of English texts or national contributions. In the three mainstream stores the visible books covered topics such as astrology, Feng Shui, meditation, tarot and UFOs. The same books were also available in *Humanova*, but many other topics were also present. As a specialist store, the naming of the sections was far more advanced: for instance, there were individual shelves for healing, numerology, theosophy and yoga. Table 3 illustrates the section titles in the four local bookstores. The sections containing books on New Age also had books on new religious movements, pseudo-science and quasi-religions. In my opinion this simply confirms the fact that for the general reading public New Age does not exist as a distinct movement. It also implies that people interested in one movement are often interested in other alternative phenomena. In this sense it seems to be justified to speak of an alternative religiousness.

Akateeminen Kirjakauppa (Academic Bookstore)	Kansallinen Kirjakauppa (National Bookstore)	Suomalainen Kirjakauppa (Finnish Bookstore)	Humanova	
Esoteric knowledge Para-knowledge *Religion* *Devotional literature*	Philosophy Psychology Reflections *Religion*	Philosophy Psychology *Religion*	Alchemy Alternative medicine Antroposophy Aromatherapy Astrology Creativity Death Dreams Egypt Energies Foretelling Healing Health Homeopathy Man and woman Meditation	Michael's teachings Numerology Nourishment Organisations Para-knowledge Personal resources Philosophy Psychology Qabbalah Spirit world Tarot Theosophy UFOs Yoga *Religions*

Table 3: Religious and New Age related book section titles in local bookstores in September 2000. Sections containing traditional religious literature are marked in italics.

Global, Local or Glocal New Age?

From this description of New Age in Turku it would appear that the local scene generally matches the general features of the global movement. The local field consists of client and audience cults, where New Age ideas are mediated through books, participation in courses, lectures, consumer goods and services, and the field is as heterogeneous as might be expected. At first glance it seems that New Age has localised surprisingly well and that there seem not to be any major differences from other countries. Does this indicate successful, one-way globalisation, where local differences have no influence or meaning? Before answering this question, let us turn back to the origins of the glocality debate.

The concepts of "glocality" and "glocalisation" entered academic debate through the writings of Roland Robertson, who is one of the main proponents of globalisation theory in sociology. He covered the topic in his influential study *Globalization: Social Theory and Global Culture* (1992: 97-114) by discussing the "universalism-particularism issue" and returned to introduce the term glocality in his article *Glocalization: Time-Space and Homogeneity-Heterogeneity* (1995). Since then, the term has spread to various academic disciplines to describe contemporary local-global relations. Among social theorists its core ideas have found their way mainly to the proponents of the so-called transformational globalisation theory (Held et al. 1999: 2-10), including such writers as Arjun Appadurai (1996), John Eade (1997) and Ulf Hannerz (1996).

Robertson understands globalisation both as the compression of the world in time and space and also as the increasing consciousness of the world as a meaningful category in thought (1992: 8). Furthermore, he suggests, "we are, in the twentieth century, witnesses to — and participants in — a massive, twofold process involving *the interpenetration of the universalization of particularism and the particularization of universalism*" (Robertson 1992: 100, italics original).

First, the universalisation of particularism means that there are practically no limits to particularity, difference and uniqueness. Second, the particularisation of universalism refers to the idea of "global-human concreteness", which means that human beings are essentially the same everywhere. This implies that people see themselves as *sharing* a universal human life in many — almost limitless — particular forms and they *expect* that realisation from others (1992: 100). Combined together with the shrinking meaning of nation-states as the main category through which local life should be understood this (1995: 34) leads Robertson to state that "the local is essentially included within the global" (1995: 35).

The glocalisation concept has also been used as a critique of traditional anthropological, ethnological and sociological community studies and as a stimulus to provide a fresh perspective for understanding local communities in a globalising world. The core argument has been that the earlier studies have been over-restricted to the perspective of the nation-state and sight has been lost of the significant extra-local dimensions also of and the changing nature of contemporary local communities (Albrow 1997; Albrow et al. 1997). The study of diasporic communities is one of the manifestations of this line of thought (Forsander 2001: 47-54). The new studies have concentrated attention on the nature of local relationships. For instance, Appadurai (1996: 178) understands "locality as primarily relational and contextual rather than as scalar or spatial", thus making local identifications independent of a common, shared place. Dürrschmidt (1997) adopts a similar stance developing the concept of *milieu* to describe local relations. With the help of these concepts we are able to contextualise localities in completely new ways: local identity is not strictly bound to a place (locality) that is occupied by certain people (community). Instead, local communities can be imagined and experienced differently by different groups of people sharing the same place, and their particular identities may be largely independent of and distinct from each other.

These and many other contributions clarify the point: to understand local change in the contemporary world requires a new perspective for looking at local communities that is not implicitly bound to the nation-state level. Let us return to New Age and see, how these viewpoints on glocality may help us to understand the local New Age scene. First, I shall start by investigating whether there is something inherently glocal in the nature of New Age. Second, I shall examine at whether we can indeed find some deeply local aspects of local New Age organisation. Third, I shall elaborate further on the extra-local dimensions of the local field.

First, let us start with Robertson's particularism-universalism thoughts and relate them to the diversity of selection in local bookstores. The local variety of New Age book titles provides an example of the *universalisation of particularism.* The diversity is seen as a natural component of New Age religion and customers expect it. New Age exemplifies a religious form that arises basically in the global circumstance of religious diversity. It is supposed that through a comprehensive study of these works one is able to go beyond the diversity and find the cure for one's religious quest. Hence a plurality of titles is needed because the truth lies in the heterogeneity of ideas that, in the end all speak about the same, deep human spiritual needs, while the works themselves are presentations and reinterpretations of an eclectic mix of the world's religious heritage (Bruce 1997: 196-222). Through plural reading one can reach beyond the diversity and find the unifying human nature, which refers to the *particularisation of universalism*, that we are essentially alike. Thus, New Age is a fine example of how these two processes are present simultaneously.

If New Age is then glocal by its very nature, what does the local context contribute to it? The local aspect lies in the addition of Finnish writings and interpretations. For instance, Theosophical interpretations of Finnish folklore are used in New Age circles. One of the prominent authors is Pekka Ervast (1875-1934), who has written numerous works on various religious traditions, including the Finnish, which are still read today. Furthermore, there exist a plethora of titles produced in Finnish for the national audience on New Age, which together with translations constitute the main corpus of the books on sale. Wherever New Age ideas find an interested audience, it leads to the emergence of locally inspired works by national authors, and sometimes these works may become important internationally as well. New Age is both based on and feeds on glocality. It is an example of the interpenetration of the universalisation of particularism and the particularisation of universalism, *par excellence*.

Second, New Age has entered the locality through organisations (associations) that already exist, and it has led to the founding of new organisations (associations, commercial enterprises, etc.) that are formed according to national organisational models. In other words, innovations adapt to the local structural environment. Does this have any major consequences? Let us take an example; *Galacticus ry* is a recently formed New Age association with the aim of promoting interest in extraterrestrial intelligence, "contactees" and the UFOs. *Galacticus* started in the aftermath of a lecture held by the UFO "contactee" Kalevi Riikonen in May 1995 (Teide 1998). The global link here is that the emergence of UFO "contactees" is a transnational phenomenon, starting in the USA in the 1940s and dramatically growing in the 1980s (Melton et al. 1990: 476-480). People interested in the UFO contactees are essentially New Age, whereas most of the other ufologists are more "scientifically" oriented and highly critical of the claims made by the contactees (ibid.: 477). At first *Galacticus* was an informal group, but as membership grew it was registered as an association (Teide 1998). The association form requires, for instance, a structure of meetings, democratic decision-making and open finances. We do not need to know how exactly the change in organisational form affected the group in question, because the main point is that the national organisational forms provided the model according to which they were formed. The form of the association affects some of the fundamental features of the group organisation. This implies that the form of organisation is important and confines within it numerous hidden assumptions. Hence the adaptation process of innovations includes structural accommodation by necessity. Thus, when a global movement enters a new locality it adapts a local form that makes it glocal, rather than global or local.

Third, while arguments related to globalisation/glocalisation forecast the breakdown of traditional centre-periphery relations (Appadurai 1996: 32), they still seem somewhat pervasive. For example, the Helsinki region is the main national innovation centre of New Age (Junnonaho 1999: 415), and Turku also seems to get most of its impulses from there (Hirvonen 8.9.2000). This is not surprising, because the capital region also leads the way in many other cultural developments. However, one distinctly new feature with regard to New Age consumer behaviour hints at an important change in traditional centre-periphery relations. According to Antero Hirvonen (8. September 2000), a change occurred in Humanova book sales in the late 1990s, indicating that people have started to use the Internet as a major channel for buying New Age books. Since its foundation in 1991, Humanova applied a large selection of English language, USA-imported titles, which constituted some 60-70 per cent of the whole selection. In the latter half of the 1990s, the sales of English titles fell dramatically over a short period of time, so that by 2000 there were only a few individual items available. While the number of Finnish titles grew at the same time, this alone cannot explain the change — nor can it be supposed that the books simply lost their appeal. The only explanation seems to be that people started to use international Internet bookstores to obtain books in English.

This observation of the change in book sales becomes more comprehensible when seen through the different natures of the globalisation of human and media mobility. According to Appadurai (1996), the global *ethnoscapes* (mobile people) and *mediascapes* constitute the main axis through which the globalisation of culture occurs. People are more mobile today than ever before in history, but they are still bound to the place where they happen to find themselves. Furthermore, there are limits to mobility, such as distance and cost. Mediascapes, however, are much more mobile, fluid, and less bound to place. With only a small effort it is easy to access even the most exotic media messages in the world. The Internet is perhaps the most accessible and mobile media resource in contemporary world. Thus it is much easier for people to gain access to media messages than to travel to their origins. While a large part of New Age is made up of audience cults, it makes sense that widespread use is made of a new, easy-access resource such as the Internet.

The use of the Internet may have interesting consequences. Whereas the local book selections were based on storekeepers' choices and customer demand, there are now no mediators for the books people can buy. For example, Hirvonen (8. September 2000) states that he refuses to sell certain kinds of literature, because he considers it harmful, even though there is a demand for it. This again is an opening for the universalisation of particularism. While it is difficult to estimate the consequences of this change, we can forecast that, to some extent at least, this will increase the local diversity of religious ideas, but it may also lessen the role of the local context with regard to the ideas that are available. This also implies a breakdown in traditional centre-periphery relations.

To sum up, my conclusion is that New Age in Turku is a localised version of the global New Age movement, which has adapted itself to local structures. Whereas the movement itself is glocal in nature, so too are its local manifestations. To describe New Age in Turku in a single word, we need the term glocal.

Conclusions

This article has revolved around globalisation, locality and New Age, a late modern form of religion. I have presented the forms that New Age takes and what this tells us about the nature of globalisation. Whereas institutionalised religion is often connected with the early modern world, the case of New Age is an example of how religion can take new forms and adapt to different times and eras. New Age religion is comfortable in a globalising world and consumer society. It is also an example of a global movement that both draws on the multiplicity of human religious heritage and contributes to it.

The Finnish New Age is not a one-way import, nor is it further evidence of the "Americanisation" of the Finnish society. Obviously it draws most of its originality from imported ideas, but it also shows signs of revitalisation of interest in the national religious heritage and produces original contributions. Both are signs of the interesting relationship between the global and the local, which was renamed the glocal by the sociologist Roland Robertson.

The local New Age in Turku is a combination of various voluntary organisations and commercial entrepreneurs at work that feed the spiritually hungry in the locality. Embedded in the city's religious history, New Age has become a distinct part of the local spiritual scene. It exists together with and parallel to other alternative religious groups. The glocal nature of New Age is obvious in the structural adaptation of New Age, local book selections and changing consumer behaviour. The local scene is simultaneously an illustration of globalisation and localisation.

The concept of glocality opens up a fresh perspective for understanding global religious manifestations in a particular locality. It breaks down the seemingly oppositional poles of the global and the local to become a mutually supportive and interrelated pair. The global is included in the local, and *vice versa*. This study has only scratched the surface of the potential interpretation of the glocal New Age in Turku, and I am more than convinced that a closer study, for example, of translocal networks would open up exciting perspectives for understanding religious change in the contemporary world.

REFERENCES

Albrow, M. 1997: Travelling beyond Local Cultures: Socioscapes in a Global City. In J. Eade ed.: *Living the Global City. Globalization as Local Process.* London: Routledge.

Albrow, M., J. Eade, J. Dürrschmidt and N. Washbourne 1997: The Impact of Globalization on Sociological Concepts: Community, Culture and Milieu. In John Eade ed.: *Living the Global City. Globalization as Local Process.* London: Routledge.

Appadurai, A. 1996: *Modernity at Large. Cultural Dimensions of Globalization.* Minneapolis: University of Minnesota Press.

Beckford, J. 2001: *Is Secularisation Good for the Sociology of Religion?* An unpublished paper presented at the Department of Sociology, University of Edinburgh, 7th March 2001.

Beyer, P. 1994: *Religion and Globalization.* London: Sage.

Bruce, S. 1997: *Religion in the Modern World. From Cathedrals to Cults.* Oxford: Oxford University Press.

Davie, G. 2000: *Religion in Modern Europe. A Memory Mutates.* Oxford: Oxford University Press.

Dürrschmidt, Jörg 1997: The Delinking of Locale and Milieu: On the Situatedness of Extended Milieux in a Global Environment. In J. Eade ed.: *Living the Global City. Globalization as Local Process.* London: Routledge.

Eade, J. 1997: Introduction. In J. Eade ed.: *Living the Global City. Globalization as Local Process.* London: Routledge.

Featherstone, M. 1991: *Consumer Culture & Postmodernism.* London: Sage.

Forsander, A. 2001: Etnisten ryhmien kohtaaminen [Encountering ethnic groups]. In A. Forsander, E. Ekholm, P. Hautaniemi, A. Ali, A. Alitolppa-Niitamo, E. Kyntäjä and N.Q. Cuong ed.: *Monietnisyys, yhteiskunta ja työ* [Multiethnicity, society and work]. Helsinki: Yliopistopaino.

Hanegraaff, W. 1999: New Age Spiritualities as Secular Religion. *Social Compass.* 46:2. 145-160.

Hannerz, U. 1996: *Transnational Connections.* London: Routledge.

Heelas, P. 1996: *The New Age Movement. The Celebration of the Self and the Sacralization of Modernity.* Oxford: Blackwell.

Heino, H. 1997: *Mihin Suomi tänään uskoo* [What the Finns believe today]. Porvoo: WSOY.

Held, D., A. McGrew, D. Goldblatt and J. Perraton 1999: *Global Transformations. Politics, Economy and Culture.* Cambridge: Polity.

Hirvonen, A. 8. September 2000: Storekeeper of the Humanova bookstore. Personal interview conducted by Tuomas Martikainen. Turku.

Hirvonen, A. 25. April 2001: Storekeeper of the Humanova bookstore. Telephone interview conducted by Tuomas Martikainen. Turku.

Hongisto, S. 25. April 2001: Employee of Turun Messukeskus Oy. Telephone interview conducted by Tuomas Martikainen. Turku.

Jaakkola-Puhakainen, I. 1998: Turun Henkisen Kehityksen yhdistys ry. [The spiritual development association of Turku]. *Ultra* 27:5-6. 9.

Junnonaho, M. 1996: *Uudet uskonnot — vastakulttuuria ja vaihtoehtoja. Tutkimus TM-, DLM- ja Hare Krishna-liikkeistä suomalaisessa uskonmaisemassa* [New religions — counter cultures and alternatives. A study of TM-, DLM- and Hare Krishna movements in the Finnish religiosity]. Helsinki: The Finnish Literature Society.

Junnonaho, M. 1999: Uususkonnollisuus ja länsimaat [New religiosity and the West]. In K. Hyry and J. Pentikäinen ed.: *Uskonnot maailmassa* [Religions in the World]. Fourth edition. Helsinki: WSOY.

Kaplan, J. ed. 2000: *Beyond the Mainstream: The Emergence of Religious Pluralism in Finland, Estonia, and Russia.* Helsinki: The Finnish Literary Society.

Ketola, K. 1999: Uusi aika — uusi luontosuhde? Jim Nollmanin spirituaaliekologia esimerkkinä New Age -liikkeen maailmankuvasta [New age — new nature relationship? The spiritual ecology of Jim Nollman as an example of the New Age worldview]. In H. Pesonen ed.: *Uskonnon luonto. Ihmisen ja luonnon suhde uskonnollisessa ajattelussa* [Religion's nature. The relationship between humans and nature in religious thinking]. Jyväskylä: Atena.

Koskinen, R. 25. April 2001: Chairman of Turun Parapsykologinen Seura ry. Telephone interview conducted by Tuomas Martikainen. Turku.

Kurkinen, U. 1997: Vaihtoehtolääkintä Turussa [Alternative medicine in Turku]. Unpublished Master's thesis. Turku: University of Turku, Comparative Religion.

Luckmann, T. 1967: *The Invisible Religion. The Transformation of Symbols in Industrial Society.* New York: Macmillan.

Luckmann, T. 1999: The Religious Situation in Europe. The Background to Contemporary Conversions. *Social Compass.* 46:3. 251-258.

Maffesoli, Michel 1996: *The Time of the Tribes. The Decline of Individualism in Mass Society.* London: Sage.

Makkonen, V. 23. February 2000: Secretary of Turun Seudun Spiritualistit ry. Personal interview conducted by Tuomas Martikainen. Turku.

Martikainen, T. 1996: *Moniarvoinen Turku. Käsikirja uskonnollisista, maailmankatsomuksellisista ja etnisistä yhteisöistä* [Multivalued Turku. A handbook of religious, 'Weltanschauung' and ethnic communities]. Åbo: Åbo Akademi.

Martikainen, T. 2000: Muslim Groups in Turku. *Journal of Muslim Minority Affairs.* 20:2. 329-345.

Martikainen T. 2001: Religion and Consumer Culture. *Tidskrift for kirke, religion og samfunn.* 14:2. 111-125.

Mattsson, C. 2000: Att utveckla sig själv. New Age-relaterade program och aktiviteter i Åbo [To develop oneself. New Age-related programmes and activities in Turku]. Unpublished Master's thesis. Åbo: Åbo Akademi University, Comparative Religion.

Melton, G.J., J. Clark and A.I. Kelly 1990: *New Age Encyclopedia*. First Edition. Detroit: Gale Research Inc.

Mikkola, T. 1999: Uusia tuulia maailmankuvamarkkinoilla: New Age -liikkeen, ympäristönsuojeluaatteen ja postmodernin yhtymäkohtia [New winds in the worldview market: Intersections between the New Age movement, enviromental ideology and postmodern]. In H. Pesonen ed.: *Uskonnon luonto. Ihmisen ja luonnon suhde uskonnollisessa ajattelussa* [Religion's nature. The relationship between humans and nature in religious thinking]. Jyväskylä: Atena. 151-189.

Mikkonen, P. 2000: New Age in Finland. A View Through Finnish New Age Magazines. In J. Kaplan ed.: *Beyond the Mainstream. The Emergence of Religious Pluralism in Finland, Estonia, and Russia.* Helsinki: The Finnish Literary Society.

Mäntylä, T. 25. April 2001: Chairman of Turun Henkisen Kehityksen Keskus ry. Telephone interview conducted by Tuomas Martikainen. Turku.

Nieminen, M. 25. April 2001: Employee of Interdialogi Markkinointipalvelut Oy. Telephone interview conducted by Tuomas Martikainen. Turku.

Oksanen, U. 5. April 2001: Telephone interview conducted by Tuomas Martikainen. Turku.

Promonova Oy 10. April 2001: Tervetuloa mukaan rakentamaan vuoden 2001 naistapahtumaa! [Welcome to the construction of the women's event of 2001!]. *http://www.osaavanainen.fi/tapahtuma/info_3lomake.html.*

Robertson, R. 1992: *Globalization. Social Theory and Global Culture.* London: Sage.

Robertson, R. 1995: Glocalization. Time-Space and Homogeneity-Heterogeneity. In M. Featherstone, S. Lash and R. Robertson ed.: *Global Modernities.* London: Sage. 25-44.

Salonen, K.; Kääriäinen, K. and Niemelä, K. 2000: *Kirkko uudelle vuosituhannelle. Suomen evankelis-luterilainen kirkko vuosina 1996-1999* [The church towards the new millennium. The Finnish evanchelic-lutheran church in the years 1996-1999]. Tampere: Kirkon tutkimuskeskus.

Sateenkaarisanomat. August 2000.

Schulze, G. 1992: *Die Erlebninsgesellschaft. Kultursoziologie der Gegenwart.* Frankfurt: Campus.

Smart, Ninian 1989: *The World's Religions.* Cambridge: Cambridge University Press.

Stark, R. and W.S. Bainbridge 1985: *The Future of Religion. Secularization, Revival and Cult Formation.* Berkeley: University of California Press.

Sundback, S. 1996: New Age och religiositetens förändring i Norden [New

Age and the change of religiosity in the Nordic countries]. *Sosiologia.* 33:3. 216-226.

Takanen, M. 2001: *Suomalainen uushenkisyys: Hengen ja Tiedon messut. Uskonnon sosiaalisen muodon muutos suomalaisessa yhteiskunnassa* [The Finnish new spirituality. The spirit and knowledge fair. The transformation of the social form of religion in the Finnish society]. An unpublished Master's thesis. Helsinki: University of Helsinki, Comparative Religion.

Teide, T. 1998: Turku, seitsemän kukkulan kaupunki [Turku, the city of seven hills]. *Ultra.* 27:5-6. 4-8.

Teide, T. 25. April 2001: Chairman of Galacticus ry. Telephone interview conducted by Tuomas Martikainen. Turku.

Wahlbeck, Ö. 1999: *Kurdish Diasporas. A Comparative Study of Kurdish Refugee Communities.* London: Macmillan.

York, M. 1995: *The Emerging Network. A Sociology of the New Age and Neo-pagan Movements.* London: Rowman & Littlefield.

13

Flying in the Liminality between Alienation and Identification: Interpreting the Border-crossing of Migrants

PIRKKOLIISA AHPONEN

Introduction

Borders have not disappeared from the globalising world. In addition to geopolitical borders, which mark nation-states and state coalitions, society is composed of numerous group-formations consisting of cultural qualifications and differences. The existence of social and cultural boundaries is not always clear. The signs of culturally constructed and socially significant boundaries are becoming increasingly invisible and fluid in their flexibility. Through personal experiences it is possible to see how the existence of boundaries is realised by people living under changing life-conditions. This article is motivated by an interest in dealing with how migrants become conscious of the existence of borderlines when they meet with difficulties in alienating situations. Discussed here is how different boundaries and barriers are crossed and overcome in the course of life and how an identity is changed as the result of this process. Subjective experiences are interpreted in relation to the social cultural contexts through which the personal identities of migrants become constructed and reconstructed under changing life-conditions. A theoretical context applied here is introduced in some earlier articles in which borders and boundaries, the marginal situations of wanderers and the construction of habitat as well as alienation have been discussed as cultural concepts (see especially Ahponen 1996: 171-180; 1998: 31-45; 2001a: 284-309).

The empirical material used here for illustrations and interpretations of the changing identity of migrants is based on narratives collected in a writing competition organised for immigrants entering Finland. Many of the authors of these autobiographies have crossed borders in their fateful way through the system-controlled barriers between their destination and departure points when they have existed as refugees or other kinds of involuntary migrants. Their experiences are contrasted with the stories of people who have left their original home districts voluntarily.

These narratives are taken into consideration by believing, as W.I. Thomas and Florian Znaniecki already expressed in their classical study (Thomas and Znaniecki 1918-20; see also Blumer 1949) that personal documents, especially in the form of autobiographies, letters and diaries, are valuable for meaningful cultural interpretation of social situations, and even for understanding how the social structures of societies are changing. Thomas and Znaniecki used personal documents effectively to analyse the changing cultural values and attitudes of Polish migrants who went to the USA in the 1910s. Their strategy is appreciated among social scientists even today as a basis for qualitative studies. However, debate abounds on the topic of how realistic a picture of society can be constructed through life-stories, since the subjects of life stories will tend to illustrate "heroism" in their own lives (see Ahponen 1999: 107-118). It is also debated whether authors are telling the truth about their lives and how this truth aspect should be considered in analysis (e.g. Roos 1987: 151-153; Denzin 1989: 61-62). At least it is the privilege of any author to select what to include and exclude and what to emphasise in the composition of his or her life-story. It is a fact that the narrative form gives a specific nature to this kind of data. It is remarkable that the episodes described are subjective in their character. This means that the intentions of the authors influence the way they describe their life-situations. The evaluation of experiences also depends on the life-phase and social conditions lived through by the author during the writing process.

The intention of this article is, then, to discuss how people live within an alienating diaspora and how they transfer from the liminalities of not yet feeling at home to closer to their own habitat. People in dramatically changing conditions interpret their experiences of border-crossing situations in narratives by emphasising the meaningful episodes included in their life-course. After losing a home in their country of origin it is not easy to become familiar with new life-conditions or to establish a new identity. This may be a question of alienation or it can be interpreted as a problem deeply embedded in the idea of becoming culturally rooted.

Interpreting Autobiographies

Border-crossings are discussed here by referring, on the one hand, to concrete descriptions of how geopolitical borders have been crossed during journeys from one country to another. This term is also used metaphorically to illustrate the social, cultural and mental boundaries encountered by migrants during their life-processes. Obstacles met in the place of departure, in the place of destination and during the migration process are meaningful for interpreting experiences of strangeness, discrimination and alienation. The autobiographical material consists of descriptions of loneliness, situations of being excluded, misunderstood or rejected as a foreigner. Through strategies of overcoming such experiences, strangers will discover ways in which they can make themselves at home and feel familiar in their new locations.

The autobiographies interpreted here were received from migrants who participated in a writing competition in 1997 organised for immigrants into Finland by the Department of Sociology and Social Psychology at the University of Tampere, together with the Advisory Committee for the Affairs of Refugees and Migrants and the Finnish Literature Society. Autobiographies of 73 immigrants were received in the given time-period and the length of written autobiographies varied from one to forty pages. The number of women and men participating was almost equal (37/36) and their ages varied from ten years to nearly seventy years. The languages used by the authors were various and, in the end, stories written in 16 languages were received and later translated into Finnish. A collection consisting of a selection of these autobiographies was edited by Laura Huttunen for the anthology *Sama taivas, eri maa* [The same sky, a different country] (Huttunen 1999). In order to interpret how boundary-crossings were experienced by migrants coming from distant places of departure, I selected twenty-five autobiographies from the original material written by immigrants who had left their homes somewhere outside Europe. These narratives were written either in English or in Finnish, or they were translated into Finnish from some other language. For the purposes of this article the author has translated all of the quotations into English.

The experiences of border-crossings made by refugees and other wanderers are brought into focus with the aim of finding out how the stages of voluntary activity and compulsory phases are dealt with in the move from one country to another. Episodes have been selected from the material and presented by following the principle of best argumentation. The clearer the experience of border-crossing between alienation and identification is described, the better the quotation is for the aims of analysis. These wanderers in liminal situations have had to realise how their personally alienating experiences can be turned toward being culturally rooted in their new home. The relevance of the concept of multiculturalism is inevitably taken into consideration as a part of this problem. The question is whether even alienation can be used as a source of creative energy for these autobiographers, who identify themselves in the process of their changing life-conditions. The travellers have had to ask about the relevance of the habitual behaviour when unconditional observance of local traditions can no longer occur and therefore they have, inevitably, as Zygmunt Bauman (e.g. Bauman 1992: 201-203) points out, become culturally more conscious than locals. The self-awareness of agents becomes a moral test marking a line between identity and alienation.

Cultural Identity and Alienation

Cultural identity is conventionally seen as attached to the location of a person in his or her environment. Specifically, by using ethnic terms, people are identified as integrated into their home communities in rooted conditions (Horowitz 1996: 17). Membership is based on qualities that are known and accepted in a certain community. The community in which somebody is rooted is understood to be stable or relatively unchangeable in the course of time. It is expected to be different from external entities, even from those with which the boundaries are shared. Everything meaningful inside the ideal home community is familiar and does not demand to be questioned. The personal identity — subjectivity — is defined by habitual properties that are characteristic of the ordinary people who represent the authentic members of this community.

Contrary to the concept of cultural identity, alienation means that one is separated from one's communal ties. Alienated people live outside a membership circle in isolation. Aliens are no more enemies than they are friends insofar as they are not identified by certain properties according to which they are known. They have no home in a familiar community and they lack culturally identifying common properties. The alienated existence means that one is flying loose in a situation in which everything is strange and without a meaningful context. But is this kind of life possible for any human being? Certainly a desire to feel at home is a basic condition of human existence. When wanderers such as refugees are situated on the margins of homelessness they start to construct a habitat as soon as possible in order to feel at home even in their diaspora (see Ahponen 2001b: 103-123).

In reality, most of us are situated somewhere between a fixed cultural location and changing social conditions. Experiences of rootless alienation are the fate of the modern subject in a quickly changing world. The more we move from one place to another, the more we meet different people; and the more we have contacts with different communities, the more we also are loosened from the ties of the one-dimensionality of a fixed cultural community. The basic idea of separating modernity from traditional social structure is the idea of the continuous change that concerns both our environment and us. In consequence, an elementary condition of our existence is to be on the move without being fixed to a specific community with a certain location with culturally identifying properties and strict boundaries.

Understood as a productive life-force, culture is made up of the creative capacity of its performers. When this aspect is emphasised above the stabilising characteristics of cultural properties in the concept of culture, it becomes necessary to think about alienation as an inevitable starting point for resisting unbearable pressure towards unquestioned communality in the continuous chain of identification by means of integrative terms that refer to acculturation and assimilation. I would argue, like Irving Louis Horowitz (1996: 18), that alienation is not only a state of a lack of communal ties but also an inalienable right for individuality. This point of view is sensible for analysing expressions of personal eccentricities but it can also help in understanding how individual experiences are used as a source of creative energy for interpreting difficulties during the life course, especially when living conditions have been changed. From this perspective I will discuss the border-crossings of migrants.

One aspect needs to be discussed before diving into the sea of experiences where boundaries become movable; in other words, into the empirical world of immigrants who lack a firm foundation in their country of origin. This concerns the concept of citizenship. Insofar as the concept of the nation-state was a self-evident starting point for defining the rights of citizenship — if it ever was — there were no problems involved in seeing who were included as members in a certain society. The rules for defining who would be foreigners excluded from this membership were seen as valid. As long as the nation-state was the only proper institution where citizenship could take place, the political equality of included citizens was guaranteed by the state of democracy in the nation-state in question. The principles of domination and colonisation by economic and cultural means were, however, inscribed in the democratic development of the industrial modernity, as Stephen Castles and Alasdair Davidson (2000: 1-7) point out. This was the price paid by the stigmatised and excluded others. Although the mobility of people has always been an inherent part of colonialism in the process of industrial modernisation, the scale, the speed and the ethnocultural character of the current migration is now different than it was earlier, as Castles and Davidson (2000: 8-9) continue. New groups demand citizenship rights in the new situation in which they find themselves, between inclusion and exclusion.

Both concrete and abstract borders are frequently crossed when migrants move from the place of departure to the place of destination — if the new home can even be found. The obstacles to becoming included as members of the new community can be both visible and invisible. The extent to which citizenship rights are allowed to newcomers can be questioned in terms of same principles of equality that have been followed inside the nation-state. Without this privilege, the condition of alienation, as far as relative exclusion is concerned, will always be the fate of wanderers. In this case, the principal question is about the extent to which the place of departure has ever been a reliable enough home nest to feel familiar and, further, the extent to which the place of destination can become a nest which will permit new social identification.

The concept of alienation opposes the concept of identity in the context of the membership community. If these concepts refer to fixed locations, we may ask how fruitful they may, then, be for defining the situation of the displaced. Politically active citizens are necessarily displaced from the total membership of a community in the sense that displacement is a precondition for becoming politically radical and conscious of minority rights. Ernesto Laclau and Chantal Mouffe (1985: 169) emphasise that the articulation of struggle provides the characteristics of the political subject rather than those of the place where the subject comes from. This is an effective manifesto for radical democracy. It is required in conditions where cultural identities are becoming unstable and the boundaries between social actors have been blurred. The demarcating lines between identity groups are constructed by following the requirements of the agents in the current situations.

Borders and Boundary-crossings along Migrants' Routes to Finland

The co-ordinates used by migrants for interpreting their social situation are multi-dimensional in the sense that the situation is either seen as improving or worsening after the moment of departure. One of the autobiographers uses a well-known slogan to describe his status by saying that in a foreign country a prince becomes a servant (Huttunen 1999: 34). Another author experiences richness because "I now have two home-countries". A talented young woman was born and studied in Ethiopia, became a mother at a young age, moved voluntarily to Finland and continued her studies here. She says:

> Currently I work as a teacher in Helsinki. I have not experienced any discrimination in the labour market either because of my sex or because of my foreign origin. ...One year after my marriage I was granted a permanent residence permit, and this made my life easier. I will probably not apply for Finnish citizenship although my husband is trying to persuade me to do so. I still have another homeland, Ethiopia, and I am proud of her thousand years of history and her people. Ethiopia is not a worse country than Finland although it is not better, either (Autobiography in Huttunen 1999: 46-47, translation P.A.).

She continues in the original manuscript: "I have done nothing against my own country or its legislation. Therefore I am free to return. ...My new family and the relatives of my husband accept me fully and this is important in my own culture. Therefore I feel that a part of me already belongs here. I long only for my child. Maybe we will have him here some day" (an unpublished autobiography).

•Migrants have to cross natural, geopolitical, cultural and social obstacles on their travels. People build different routes (bridges, channels) across mountains, rivers and lakes. They use fairways and airways to make intercontinental connections. On the other hand, in a common natural terrain border-constructions signal the political character of separated social communities. The methods of practising sociality, culture, economy and politics are different in different communities. The habitants are identified by means of cultural and social boundaries. Constructed obstacles and visible border-signals express the political character of borders in concrete ways but they are also symbolically significant, like differences in language, appearance and habits. People are identified by all of these means.

Borders are controlled because foreign people are not allowed to cross lines between nation-states without specific preconditions. International and global transfers are seen as important because of the progress of economic, social and cultural exchanges (money, goods, services, labour). Migrants are seen to carry risks with them. If they are, to adopt an expression used by Georg Simmel, strangers who come today and stay tomorrow, we — who are already here — have to be certain that they have something positive to give us. At least we wish to be as certain as possible that they do not bring too many problems, difficulties or sorrow into our life. They should be useful and make a profit rather than bring about costs and charges. They should adjust themselves to the community and not disturb the imagined peaceful coexistence of the members of the community. As newcomers they should be satisfied with the existing conditions, even grateful if they are tolerated sufficiently within this home-circle. At least their troubles must be tolerated without turning them down because of their different qualities, habits and appearance. As refugees the newcomers are expected to be humble, although it is known that before entering their destination they had to encounter many "high" borders in the course of their travel, filled with difficulties. They may also have experienced ideological pressure by means of political or religious indoctrination, or they may even have met with cruel physical torture before and during their escape.

A refugee from Iraq tells how he felt the influence of ideology in his studies:

> We did not inherit our problems from a "red home" because our problems were caused by the board of the university. The political life inside the university worsened so that academic conversations were replaced by fist-fights, the result being that the Security Police interfered in our affairs. ...In fact, the subjects in our faculty led to political disputes, so these fights were continuous. I have personally both witnessed such conditions and been assaulted. Because of this state of affairs I felt sick with my studies (Unpublished autobiography).

When asylum seekers or other kinds of refugees enter their destination they have, before being accepted, to testify that their earlier home-nest has been lost because of an unjust political system, which in turn would mean that asylum is justified. But they also have to remember that only when they have adopted enough national qualities will they, in the best case, considered worthy of having citizenship rights in their new home country. The process of integration presupposes conformist attitudes.

In general, people do not move from one country to another like driftwood. Migration is reasoned and it is often difficult to make the decision to leave one's home country. However, mobility across national boundaries is increasing in our globalising world, described now as a world of flows, global networks and virtual images of imagined landscapes (e.g. Featherstone 1990; Castells 1996). By means of mediascapes we can realise the appearance of strange places with their inhabitants on different sides of the globe. The more voluntary the mobility is, the easier it is to cross the borderlines and overcome obstacles to whatever extent is demanded. The voluntary move may be planned for family reasons, with the intention of studying abroad or of improving working conditions so that the individual can make profit from his or her professional capacities.

It is remarkable that descriptions of how borders are encountered and crossed are not emphasised in the autobiographies of voluntary migrants, or those processes are described as positive and sometimes surprisingly positive events. But when the departure from home has been compulsory, all kinds of boundaries between the original home country and the destination become politically, economically, socially and culturally meaningful, often like "sediments" from one level to another, containing all the dimensions already mentioned. This aspect makes the autobiographies of refugees significantly different from the life-stories of other kinds of migrants.

Border-crossings of Refugees

Many of the authors who came to Finland as refugees tell us in considerable detail about their movement from one country to another and how they entered Finland through some third country, sometimes through many transitional territories. In the case of Finland, almost the only valid way to obtain a residence permit with refugee status has been reserved for a national group situated in a refugee camp. People are selected for entry into Finland according to human reasons. The counted group criteria are used in this selection on the basis of agreed quota principles. In some cases people have been granted political asylum and residence permits after a too extensive, indeterminate period during which they did not know whether they would have to leave or to stay. Finnish legislation has been adjusted recently to account for the conditions of asylum seekers coming from states where national security is guaranteed.

The stories of refugees include descriptions of inhuman conditions, cruelty and torture, politically excused by the authorities of an ideologically controlled totalitarian system. Here is one story from Iran:

> In the prison there was no end to the mischief and persecution. I remember that all of us prisoners were kept together but everyone was very lonely. Nobody was allowed to be in contact with others. If we were caught we were punished in a cell which was placed under the staff office. Without food and sleep, one had to stand up there as long as one could. Nobody could stand this kind of punishment for more than four or five days. In prison I had to listen 12-16 hours daily to the government religious propaganda. It echoed from the large loudspeakers. I could not sleep or rest. I had to sit still and listen to their nonsense about how this religious government was God's will, an order given by heaven, and that every person had to pray and obey the government. This was how they attempted to wipe out our differing opinions (Autobiography in Huttunen 1999: 185).

It is interesting, however, that the political activity is expressed in these stories as having been produced by the system and the prevailing inhuman situation. Political resistance is interpreted as having begun, for instance, when one had refused to go to the military service under wartime conditions or under conditions of the threat of war. For example, a young Albanian refugee told, when interviewed in the newspaper *Helsingin Sanomat*, how her mother had sent him away from Kosovo when he was obliged to turn his gun against Croatian people in the Serbian army and the family could see no reason in this process. The autobiography includes a touching story about a small boy in Kurdistan, a clever and industrious pupil at the Koran school, who has been punished severely for the slightest neglect of his duties. He is compelled to obey; however, he is curious about life and willing to open his eyes to see the world beyond his narrow reality: "I knew that this is a world of helpless and oppressed people but I also realised that this is not the only world, that there is another kind of world somewhere. I learned to write in the Kurd and Persian languages quickly and then I went to find a book on the history of the Kurds" (unpublished autobiography).

The right to study is the keyword in these stories. To study means a risk for the dictatorial system; it is dangerous because by knowing more than single-dimensional obedience becomes increasingly suspect and is rejected in terms of equality. The critical point of resistance can be attained by studying the conditions of the political system and its alternatives. If the system does not allow any criticism, you may find yourself in an abnormal situation:

> My name was on the list of those "not permitted to travel"; in other words I could not apply for a passport and travel by normal means through harbours and airports. I tried to get a forged passport but this effort did not succeed. The only possibility was to secretly cross the border...[M]y friends found a smuggler who transported people once a month. I chose July because in July it is hot and smuggling decreases, so the activity of the frontier police also decreases (Unpublished autobiography).

The authors also describe why they found themselves in a boat on the open sea with no firm destination. A Vietnamese refugee explains his situation by rationalising his leaving in terms of family solidarity:

> My mother's business did not succeed because she could not offer enough bribes to the police and the officials declared that they would stop this enterprise.... Mother was put in prison for two months. She was set free after paying bribes. The second attempt to escape was successful and our boat set out for the open sea at midnight (Unpublished autobiography).

This kind of escaping is very dangerous, uncertain and frightening, especially because the destination is unknown. One of the authors, who also escaped from Vietnam, contemplates metaphorically the process of sailing as a refugee by comparing it with the crossing of "life's sea" without knowing where the home harbour might be found: "Those who have endangered their lives when crossing a sea and pursuing freedom easily believe that there are many people like them who are still floating after ten years on a sea of pains. They have not yet entered a safe harbour" (unpublished autobiography).

An involuntary migrant is floating ambivalently in his or her life with no clear destination or purposeful intentions for reaching safety. Unsettled nomads have to continue wandering around. Home is always missed in diaspora. Living in exile is an extreme example of the ambivalence that illustrates how important the "politics of location" are for a modern cultural identity (e.g. Bauman 1990; Braidotti 1994: 21-27). The right to belong, the right to enter, and the right to asylum must be taken seriously as far as human rights are concerned. The contents of these rights cannot perhaps be translated metaphorically into the language of the nomadic ideals of identification. Rosi Braidotti (1994: 21) deals with this problem in the context of post-feminist subjects. She contributes to our understanding of the ambivalent situation of migrants who have lost the innocent belief that one can live a real life only in one's original place of birth. After leaving their homes for obligatory reasons, the travellers cannot expect that the past has been their ideal existence, and conversely, one of them is obliged to confess: "Everything that I had thought and believed in throughout my whole youth has been a lie; everything that I have hoped and suffered for was only illusion and lies" (autobiography in Huttunen 1999: 190).

Nor did they imagine that the destination would be a paradise where everything would be prepared for them ready-made. Home — how nostalgically the past may be remembered in the future — becomes a place to be made by oneself to construct one's identity. As long as the new home is not constructed like a habitat of one's own, the existence of a conscious subject is liminal. The traveller tries to order her or his life meaningfully enough to stay alive by following alienating rules that are standardised by the reality external to the newcomer's familiar conditions.

Living in exile is an alienated life. One reason for this situation may be that one has rejected the classifications between them and us because it has become impossible to identify friends and enemies by means of given social groupings. The life of a stranger lacks safe boundaries but, nevertheless, the frontiers are always present in this liminality. In no-man's-land it is impossible to find a place to hide from fear, and to find out how to escape further. In a refugee camp all of the ordeals and hard experiences are concentrated:

> I walked for two nights, and during the daytime I did not dare to move. I was hiding in forests or staying in a village among people from Cambodia...[In the camp] we had a meal only once a day, a plateful of rice in a bowl with salted vegetables. When hungry the coldness is even harder to bear. Almost all of us ate rats and mice which — poor them! — came to seek for food in the camp. The winter was the worst season. Nobody had enough blankets, the hunger was harder and the coldness was unbearable. We could not sleep but we had to stay still, immovable. It was forbidden to be awake, to move or to talk during the night (Unpublished autobiography).

It is risky to escape unbearable conditions, especially under a totalitarian regime. Every border successfully crossed can have a symbolic meaning. Metaphorical boundaries are interpreted as connected to the borders concretely crossed, the symbolic marks of boundaries can have a special significance in these situations, and their ideological function is emphasised:

> The only possibility was to cross the border with the help of a smuggler.... Our leader, the smuggler, stood in front of us like a general giving a speech to his army after a victory. He said: "This concrete stone is the border point between two states". It was a conical concrete stone, a number on each side, and sand around as far as the eye could see. I was the last to cross this border and I wanted to say something before going further; to speak for myself like heroes do in novels, but I could not, the words were lacking (Unpublished autobiography).

After leaving the totalitarian order that prevailed in the place of departure, refugees have generally experienced many difficult phases before they have — often by accident, sometimes for some secondary reason or because of a decision made by the authorities — entered their destinations, in this case Finland. If they come, as is the normal case, in a group formed by following the quota principles, they effectively become monitored during their first period in their new country.

From a sultry hell to a cold paradise:

> We came to Finland and the reception was warm. The press, TV and other media were present. A late dinner was served. But right at the very first moment, when I stepped down from the bus taking us to the first place where we would live, my feet slipped on the Finnish ice and I broke my arm. Could this be a bad sign? (an unpublished autobiography).

There is no guaranteed warm reception awaiting the immigrant. According to most of the autobiographers, in this collection, the first moments after their arrival were confusing. Finland is described as having beautiful nature but the coldness in the wintertime is frightening, and the coldness is seen as reflecting the ways in which human relations are ordered. The migrants may even have a presentiment that they are entering a country settled by inhabitants who have been locals from immemorial times, people who have had few encounters with foreigners and who do not know too much about other cultures.

Perhaps this also illustrates the speed and level at which the principles of technological modernity have been adopted in Finland. Those principles can be seen as alienating from the kind of human perspective where proximity, immediate contacts and the open expression of emotions are appreciated. This can also signify how important it has been to separate familiar people from strangers. Perhaps it is also true that home-building is valued as a demanding project and those newcomers who have succeeded in making themselves at home are respected in this country for their own individual capacities. But these kinds of "cultural facts" are never self-evident.

In any case, the administration is based on bureaucracy, and those entering as refugees first encounter the official authorities such as the police, social administrators and immigration officers. A common opinion among migrants is that the attitudes of the authorities are unkind, and often even hostile toward immigrants. Civil servants are presupposed to behave precisely in their role by following the strict rules according to which things are ordered. But if the received person feels that only surplus or minimal standards of welfare are reserved for refugees in this society, this tends to feed suspicions and increase the difficulties involved in making oneself at home. A Kurdish refugee describes how he was received by the Finnish municipal authorities:

> We came to Finland in February 1994. We entered via the airport at Vaasa in the evening. We feared exactly what we met immediately: it was blowing with snow and minus 20-25 Centigrades. It was really cold when we were brought to this community. We were taken into a house — no elevator there: we had to walk up to the fourth floor, 53 steps. Our future home was completely empty. However, there was a broken sofa, even worse than those you can find in the second-hand market. The bedclothes for children were old and poor. It was supposedly the attitude in this community that nothing is too poor for Kurdish people. They claimed that even these things were extra for "such people".... For my wife and me they had reserved a bed — it is impossible to find such a bed in the whole world. In

> the whole world the standard size for a bed for two persons is 160 cm. This bed was 120 cm and the springs on one side were broken; the cover was dirty and the quilt even worse. One can say that nobody would have the decency to reserve such things for anybody except refugees and homeless people (Unpublished autobiography).

Difficulties accumulate when it comes to the question of a residence permit. The natural environment and everyday living conditions in Finland are characterised as clean and safe. But punctuality is also interpreted to mean, as one of the authors emphasises, that there is far too little love or human caring for immigrants in Finland. According to the author, the general rule to follow is: "Do not think about anything. The other people think, they think even for your part". It may be confusing for a Finnish person to read these comments because we are used to considering Finland to be an open welfare democracy where freedom of opinion is respected. The concept of political democracy is, however, mostly based on majority rights (Ahponen and Langer 2000: 151-152). Discussion of the citizen in terms of the rights of other minorities, apart from the Swedish-speaking language minority, has only recently started. According to the stories written by migrants coming from outside Europe, the expectations of being made welcome are nullified too frequently. For instance, when an immigrant who has dark skin receives a piece of paper in a café from a passer-by she thinks at first that it may be a ticket for a nice party. Instead, the note may state: "Foreign pigs, go away".

To have a Family, to Build a Home

The conditions for settling down as a migrant are different if the reason for coming is marriage between a Finn and a foreigner. In fact, at least as long ago as in the 1980s, 80 per cent of immigrants were married to Finnish citizens (Jaakkola 1994: 128). The living conditions are also described as having been mostly good in cases where an individual has started by studying and working in the country where she or he has arrived with the aim of fulfilling personal plans and dreams. This period is often felt to be temporary, with no plans to establish firm and stable intimate relations. But it seems that the easiest way for an immigrant to start to feel familiar is to set up a family with a Finnish citizen. The first author cited in this article also tells how she considers her relationship with her Finnish husband "very ordinary" when compared with other good couples: "We manage well together". She is quite sure that, in many cases, problems of multicultural marriages are exaggerated by the public. There are, however, many socio-cultural problems described in the autobiographies as far as family life is concerned. Family habits, or rules of normality, a common understanding of how a good husband or a good wife should behave and interact, are not always agreed. Even the role of a good boyfriend or a girlfriend is not culturally self-evident:

> After settling down in Finland with my girlfriend our relations started to worsen. I thought that she wanted to own me too much. I felt like war booty from Africa, a thing that she could proudly present to her friends and to other women.... I was offended because she spoke about me as if I was a thing, and we quarrelled about this. I had a feeling that she did not give me enough space.... I felt that she tried as much as possible to break my own new friendships with other people, with both men and women. I felt that she personally wanted to choose my friends (Unpublished autobiography).

An important aspect of becoming rooted in a new settlement is to find an open space, to be safe enough with the environment to be identified as an individual who is not the same as before. It sounds as it a person living through the processes of alienation in culturally strange life-situations needs more personal freedom than when living in a community which is relatively stable and whose rules are known and followed. During the first moments after arrival the newcomer may become "adopted" by the only person she or he knows because in this way the couple feels safe enough to make the decision to keep the contact alive when settling down in a new country:

> My girlfriend and I lived one and a half years in isolation from everyone else. She had only one friend and I did

> not speak Finnish. I noticed that it is common for Finnish people not to speak much. I wanted basically to write.... My co-habitant wife did not want to deepen her acquaintanceship with her workmates because she did not want me to feel even more discrimination. It was an enormous mistake. Almost always we had no chance to meet other people; we did not exchange any ideas with other people. We got lost in our own labyrinths (Unpublished autobiography).

Male immigrants may have culturally traditional expectations concerning the behaviour of a good wife. These expectations may not be fulfilled by a modern female person who expects the man to take care both of himself and his personal friends. In this case it does not seem that the wife behaves like the owner of her husband. The following description includes such aspects of indifferent attitudes on the part of the Finnish wife that care-giving tends to lack completely:

> I have a good friend here in Finland, a Kurd whom I have known for a long time. One day he wanted me to visit his house. It was a small, beautifully furnished apartment. He had been married to his Finnish wife for five years and they had two children. The wife opened the door and we went in. Without saying a word she settled down in a corner and started to leaf through magazines.... Time passed and we started to feel hungry, of course. As a matter of fact, when I expected to have something served, my friend's wife went to the kitchen and prepared something for herself without thinking it necessary to serve anything to me or her husband. Then she took the children and went out. I was more and more surprised. Ashamed my friend said: "I am so sorry. I have been married to her for five years without being able to teach her how to welcome guests and how to prepare and serve meals for guests." Even more, I have not seen the day that she would prepare a meal for me or to sit down at the table with me (Unpublished autobiography).

This may be an exceptional case. It includes, however, the

aspect of how the concept of equality — perhaps at its worst — can be interpreted. In other words, if women and men take care only of their own affairs, they cannot expect services to be provided by the other, and the individual man can be confronted with "modern" responsibilities that would otherwise be regarded as the duties expected of a traditional housewife. But can we say that the behaviour described above is culturally typical of Finland any more than in some other country? Hospitable behaviour towards guests has been characteristic of human culture in general and it is difficult to imagine that female representatives of the older generations would have behaved in that way. But it is also true that there are fewer and fewer Finnish men who open the door for a female person or express any other traditional compliments related to the sex of the person in question.

Agreement about how family life should be organised is one of the basic conditions for starting the construction of a stable home nest. The everyday order of a member community must be internalised for the individual to feel home. But I do not regard this alone as the basis of the reconstruction of the identity of a displaced migrant. In this sense it is meaningful how the autobiographer — who came to Finland for personal reasons, at least partly as an adventurer — describes his rooting within the new situation. After wondering long enough about the curious habits and other things that differ from everything he has learned earlier in his life, and after experiencing so much alienation so many hard and loneliness, he is ready to draw this conclusion:

> I started, at last, to think by myself that my staying in this distant country — so different from the country where I was born — was like a voluntary exile. But it was also a convenient way for me to distance myself from the ghosts of the past; in this way I could learn to know them better.... It became clear to me that my roots were situated inside me, notwithstanding the place where I happen to be at some moment on this planet (Unpublished autobiography).

This is an important aspect of any discussion of the relations between alienation and identification. It is also true that those wanderers who are totally homeless cannot even be alienated because they have no place to refer to as the starting point of their alienating experience. The writer of the quotation cited above helps us to see that the journey undertaken by a migrant is metaphorically as much a journey within oneself as it is a journey in the external world. A very important aspect, also included in the process of overcoming alienation, is concerned with how to make a home in order to become oneself, how to be able to choose freely, how to make friends with new people, how to be with the nearest people in the changed life-conditions and, step by step, how to feel familiar among those who were once the strange neighbours at the moment of arrival. It is most meaningful to become rooted within oneself in order to construct a habitat which will influence the ways in which the identity is constructed after flying in the liminality. In his memoir-novel *The Enigma of Arrival* (1987), V.S. Naipaul ponders on how everything in the surroundings of a migrant seems to have been immovable and stable as long as he or she has settled down enough to see the continuous change in the environment and its inhabitants.

The children of immigrants represent multicultural continuity and new possibilities for the identity of border-crossers. An autobiographer who came from Mexico describes this aspect of globalisation in a touching way:

> I was reluctant to have children without feeling deep love. I thought I knew that they would suffer from that situation later in their lives. But basically I was afraid of the responsibility which is included in stable commitments. I lived for quite a long time in Finland as if unconsciously inside my own culture and my own language. But now (after having a child at last) I think, honestly, that I am a world citizen and I feel how I belong both to Mexican and to Finnish culture. My son enjoys the privilege of double citizenship and he will be bilingual, which is a privilege in itself (Unpublished autobiography).

This message is also made evident by a Vietnamese autobiographer who has married a man from Somalia. Both of them settled down in Finland as refugees. They stayed to make a family here. She writes: "I look at our daughter. Her eyes are brightening. I want to give her the possibility of growing up like other Finnish children, with love. We are people who have got a chance to provide a healthy self-confidence and an acceptance of differences as a present to our children" (an unpublished autobiography).

Discussion

The border-crossings of migrants are discussed in this article by taking the distance or liminality between the local identification and the placeless alienation of a traveller into consideration. It is evident that, insofar as cultural identities are fixed to certain localities, boundaries tend to be formed between familiar and foreign social bodies. But when people desire or are forced to move from their place of birth to live in foreign environments and to settle down in strange communities they inevitably become conscious of the demands which this situation makes on the need for change or permanence in their selves. They have to try either to live closed within their fixed past which has been transferred with themselves to their new location or they have to expose themselves to the demands of the changing social and cultural identity. Demands such as these are increasing in the present world. Bauman (1993: 234) aptly suggests that it is less and less possible to live and breathe in a society like an encapsulated shell, although only this is a guarantee of a safely-rooted, solid identity.

People who are moving towards an openness of societies learn that the differences between cultures are not necessarily barriers separating people but also gateways to new connections, although they are also signals of complexity, as Iain Chambers (1994: 18; see also Ahponen 1996: 179) points out when discussing the experiences of migrants. After starting to be on the move, people will never be as deeply rooted anywhere as those who always stay situated in the same locality. But even cosmopolitans cannot live without local ties. The question of what glocality means is important in a globalising world. Global contacts and social groups are formed in new ways between people who meet each other only in the mediascape. Glocality is concretised in encounters between the old residents of local communities and newcomers who try to leave their alienating experiences behind them. Those who decide to stay and settle down need to reconstruct their identities for them to be applied in cultural practices under the new circumstances. They have to dissociate themselves from the ghosts of their past and to find out how the roots of identity grow internally, and how they can be encouraged to feel home again. In the best case they will enrich the community through their own contributions, so that the demand for social complexity, flexibility and tolerance become better understood. Their presence may make the members of that community conscious of the need for humanity in circumstances which are risky but safe enough to allow opportunities for growing up with healthy self-confidence and acceptance on the part of people of different appearance.

The autobiographical data illustrates very well the experiences of border-crossings and boundaries which are necessarily encountered in the journeys of migrants. Insofar as the life-stories sent to this autobiography competition are evaluated as research material, their composition can be seen to be quite heterogeneous when one case is compared with another. Certain episodes are emphasised, depending on the intentions of the authors and how the instructions given by the organisers of this competition have been understood. Certain experiences are regarded as personally or culturally worth telling, while some facts that would make the context clearer are forgotten or otherwise left out of the story. As is so often the case with autobiographies, childhood and youth are emphasised most. This tends to prove the significance of this period for the construction of identity with roots in a childhood family, a neighbourhood, community and the natural environment of early age.

At their best, the autobiographies of immigrants enrich our awareness of how social and cultural barriers are experienced and how boundaries can be crossed in concrete ways. It is impressive, even touching, how skilfully the best stories have been written, and how clearly the most significant phases of the migrant's journey are remembered, described and evaluated. But even the memories of wanderers are not fixed or stable, and the life-situation at the time of the writing process influences the way in which the experiences are interpreted:

> I became conscious of this writing competition two days before the period given for authors was to expire. My text must be short and pithy because I have no more time...to write about forty years in my life.... I have to tell my experiences in forty pages to be accepted in this competition. Therefore, I have to talk about four years in one and half hours and in three pages. This writing seems to be a marathon, as if the goal could be reached after three kilometres and I had three minutes time left, therefore I have to write three years of my life quicker than light (Unpublished autobiography).

For a storyteller it is important to find somebody who is willing to spend a moment to listen to the story. Even an opportunity to give a voice to an immigrant and to represent travellers who are making themselves at home influences the intention of writing and the enthusiastic way in which this task would be fulfilled. It can be seen as a sign of the importance of being identified and becoming less alienated.

REFERENCES

1. Empirical material:

Autobiographical stories submitted for the writing competition organised in 1997 for immigrants into Finland by the Department of Sociology and Social Psychology at the University of Tampere, together with the Advisory Committee for Affairs of Refugees and Migrants and the Finnish Literature Society. The stories are preserved in the archives of the Finnish Literature Society in Helsinki. The published anthology *Sama taivas, eri maa* is a selection of the stories. Special thanks are due to Dr. Laura Huttunen for arranging me the possibility to use unpublished material, and to Ms Eila Rantonen, Phil.Lic., for her practical assistance.

2. Literature:

Ahponen, Pirkkoliisa 1996: Cross the Border, Confront Boundaries. Problems of Habituality, Marginality, and Liminality. In Feyer, Felix ed.: *Alienation, Ethnicity, and Postmodernism.* Westport, Connecticut and London: Greenwood Press.

Ahponen, Pirkkoliisa. 1998: Alienation in the Finnish Culture. In Kalekin-Fishman, Devorah ed.: *Designs for Alienation.* Jyväskylä: SoPhi.

Ahponen, Pirkkoliisa 1999: On Discriminated Incipient Heroes — Or Prosperous Heroines. In Ahponen, Pirkkoliisa ed.: *Women's Active*

Citizenship. Studies in Social Policy. Joensuu: University of Joensuu. Department of Social Policy.

Ahponen, Pirkkoliisa and Josef Langer 2000: The reconstructed ideological boundaries after the fall of the Iron Curtain: Austria and Finland in the EU. In Ahponen, Pirkkoliisa and Pirjo Jukarainen ed.: *Tearing Down the Curtain, Opening the Gates.* Jyväskylä: Sophi.

Ahponen Pirkkoliisa 2001a: *Kulttuurin pesäpaikka. Yhteiskunnallisia lähestymistapoja kulttuuriteoriaan* [The nest of culture. Social approaches to culture theory]. Helsinki: WSOY.

Ahponen Pirkkoliisa. 2001b: Kodittomuuden marginaalissa [On the margins of homelessness]. In Suutari, Minna ed.: *Vallattomat marginaalit. Yhteisöllisyyksiä nuoruudessa ja yhteiskunnan reunoilla* [Powerless margins. Communalities in youth and the margins of society]. Helsinki: Nuorisotutkimusverkosto, Nuorisotutkimusseura.

Bauman, Zygmunt 1990: Modernity and ambivalence. In Featherstone, Mike ed.: *Global Culture. Nationalism, Globalization and Modernity.* London: Sage.

Bauman, Zygmunt 1992: *Intimations of Postmodernity.* London and New York: Routledge.

Bauman, Zygmunt 1993: *Postmodern Ethics.* Oxford and Cambridge: Blackwell.

Blumer, Herbert 1949: *Critiques of Research in Social Sciences I: An Appraisal of Thomas' and Zanieki's The Polish Peasant in Europe and America.* New York: Social Sciences Research Council.

Braidotti, Rosi 1994: *Nomadic Subjects. Embodiment and Sexual Difference in Contemporary Feminist Theory.* New York: Columbia University Press.

Castells, Manuel 1996: *The Rise of the Network Society.* Vol. 1: *The Information Age.* Cambridge: Blackwell.

Castles, Stephen and Davidson, Alasdair 2000: *Citizenship and Migration. Globalization and The Politics of Belonging.* Basingstoke, Hampshire and London: Houndsmill.

Chambers, Iain 1994: *Migrancy, Culture, Identity.* London: Routledge.

Denzin, Norman 1989: *Interpretative Biography.* Newbury Park, London and New Delhi: Sage.

Featherstone, Mike 1990: Global Culture: An Introduction. In Featherstone, Mike ed.: *Global Culture, Nationalism, Globalization and Modernity.* London, Newbury Park and New Delhi: Sage.

Horowitz, Irving Louis 1996: The Strange Career of Alienation: How a Concept Is Transformed without Permission of Its Founders. In Geyer, Felix ed.: *Alienation, Ethnicity, and Postmodernism.* Westport, Connecticut and London: Greenwood Press.

Jaakkola, Magdalena 1994: Puolalaiset Suomessa [The Polish in Finland]. In Liebkind, Karmela ed.: *Maahanmuuttajat* [The immigrants]. Helsinki: Gaudeamus.

Laclau, Ernesto and Mouffe, Chantal 1985: *Hegemony and Socialist Strategy. Towards a Radical Democratic Politics.* London: Verso.

Liebkind, Karmela 1994 ed.: *Maahanmuuttajat* [The immigrants]. Helsinki: Gaudeamus.

Naipaul, V.S. 1987: *The Enigma of Arrival.* Viking: Harmondsworth.

Roos, J.P. 1987: Life Stories in Social Changes: Four Generations in Finland. In Roos, J.P. and Andrzej Sicinski: *Ways of Life in Finland and Poland. Comparative Studies on Urban Populations.* Aldershot, Brookfield: Avebury.

Thomas, Williams I. and Florian Znaniecki 1958 (1918-1920): *The Polish Peasant in Europe and America.* New York: Dover.

PART FIVE

New Media Technology and Cultural Identity

14

Globalisation: A New Name for Imperialism in the Name of Modernisation and Telecommunications, and its Ramifications for those Involved in Literary Studies

MATTI SAVOLAINEN

In order to prevent misunderstanding and misinterpretation, some caveats are necessary. First, I write as someone who has been trained in the field of literary studies and who may have some expertise with certain areas of that discipline. Stepping outside this legitimised ground may seem to some of my colleagues a hazardous and futile move but I am going to make it anyway. I tie this move in with Edward Said's notion of the amateur, a lover of different and even conflicting knowledges, and his critique of the certified and institutionalised expert, who knows his or her own speciality inside out but who knows or cares to know very little of the bigger picture (Said 1996: 76-83). Professionalism and the cult of the expert has often resulted in what Gayatri Spivak has called "the sanctioned ignorance" of the theoretical elite (Spivak 1999: Preface). This kind of larger perspective advocated by these two theorists may well be something that we urgently need in this day and age.

Second, by "globalisation" I mean here the coming-together of the world in a single place. Through jet-travel and telecommunications the world has "shrunk" and everything takes place all over the world almost simultaneously. This, by necessity, echoes with Marshall McLuhan (1964, 1968), even though his position is marred by his unacknowledged eurocentrism and his lack of consideration of the economic factor. Globalisation is also a spatial concept-metaphor with the temporal dimension virtually erased, which may tempt the analyst to sidestep or belittle the historical antecedents of the process of globalisation or at least make him or her look at them from a shorter perspective than is necessary. Globalisation is generally taken to embrace at least the following notions: the redefinition of national sovereignty or an independent nation state; the growth of a market (market economy) within and between states; the collapse of the Soviet Union (and the Eastern Socialist Block in general); and global movements such as Greenpeace and environmental organisations of various kinds (e.g. Alasuutari & Ruuska 1999: 17-26). Other kinds of humanitarian and/or emancipatory movements might be added here, from the animal rights movement to the women's movement and the global partnership advocated by many indigenous peoples.

We can argue that there are in fact phenomena functioning in the world right now whose global effects we cannot escape, such as the global warming of the climate, the AIDS epidemic, the 24-hour stock exchange, and of course the multinationals (Alasuutari & Ruuska 1999: 53). There are grounds for excluding the Internet from the list (Korhonen 2000; Pöppönen 2002; but see Kupiainen in this volume). I do not deny that the Internet can be very helpful in creating a sense of community and developing and maintaining common social and political agendas among diasporic people, for example, but it is quite obvious that the prevalent (mostly western and metropolitan) discourse of information super highways for all is a distortion of facts.

Third, globalisation today is a name for a certain concept or idea, a signifier that we want to nail down to a fixed signified. It is part of a discursive practice, a configuration of names, with its displacements and deferrals. The name itself carries traces of those who have invented and introduced it, and both of these processes most likely took place in the affluent West or, in current parlance, in the affluent North. Like all names of this range and magnitude, globalisation is not ideologically innocent (see Menchú 2001; Annan 2001).

After these preliminaries I shall launch upon the rather pompous title of my paper, ponder upon its consequences and give a reading of a story by Mahasweta Devi in the context adumbrated above. In order to answer to the question of what ramifications this part of my endeavour may have for literary studies I shall briefly consider two points: the notion of global culture at the end of the twentieth century and the reinscription of the notion of world literature. These excursions are meant to connect the thematic of ethical encounter to the contemporary literary and cultural studies practice.

Configurations of Names

The civilising mission of historical imperialism legitimised the plunder and exploitation of non-western and non-white territories. This activity had an immense impact on the development in Europe, especially Britain. According to Vandana Shiva, the destruction of the Indian textile industry and Indian agriculture, the slave trade from Africa and the genocide of the indigenous North American people were the preconditions for the economic growth of the centres of modern industry in Britain (Shiva 1991: 26). The profits gained from the colonies were, to a great extent, the initial capital that set the wheels turning in the process of what we call the industrial revolution in England.

I will argue that the process of historical imperialism continues today in the guise of globalisation and transnational information systems. Aijaz Ahmad has claimed that by the 1960s and even the mid-1970s the process of decolonisation and a considerable expansion of socialist bases in many of the poorer countries were still going on, but that without any doubt the winner in the struggle between imperialism and socialism has been imperialism. This has meant the historically unprecedented growth, unification and technological power of capitalism itself, with its fully globalised circuits of production and circulation, with its increasing modernisation of travel, transport and communication technologies and concomitant far-reaching consequences for the international division of labour (Ahmad 2000: 34-35; 191-192). In the overall financialisation of the globe the subaltern groups in the Third World and the new urban subproletariat in the West are the losers, especially the subaltern women. Gayatri Spivak's focus has insistently been on the gendered subaltern, whether they are the tribal women in the fringes of the modern state of India or the Bangladeshi women working in sweatshops in the East End of London. Or we can think of the Latinos/ Latinas who cross the Mexican/US border illegally to LA and Southern California and eke out their living with low pay and without security. If we ignore or underestimate the subaltern today, we continue to support the imperialist project — in the name of modernisation and development, in the interest of globalisation (Spivak 1999: 290). The contemporary internal division of labour — the North/South configuration — is a displacement of the divided field of nineteenth-century territorial imperialism (ibid.: 274). In discursive practice the name of imperialism has been erased and substituted by globalisation, which has become the fashionable catchword, the new legitimate ruler, even the discursive tyrant.

The mostly invisible and silenced subaltern or sub-proletariat forms an integral part of the postindustrial and late capitalist New World Order. They have their allotted place in the North/South division in which the North equals Europe and North America, and the South equals the so-called Third World (as a result of the collapse of the Soviet Union, parts of Eastern Europe belong to the South). Historical territorial imperialism has been displaced by neocolonialism and new globalisation. This is especially so when the situation is perceived from the perspective of the poor, the marginalised, the disfranchised.

By the turn of the second millennium the discourse of developed/underdeveloped or technologically advanced/ backward was replaced by the division between the north and the south. At the present juncture we do not hear so much about sustainable development, and even when we do, we should seriously suspect the undercurrents in its evocations. Vandana Shiva reminds us that development, sustainable or otherwise, is not universally benign. Development often deprives politically weak communities of access to resources and steals resources from nature in order to generate growth for the privileged in society (Shiva 1991: 10). In the acerbic words of Gayatri Spivak, the general ideology of global development is "racist paternalism..., its general economics capital-intensive investment, its broad politics the silencing of resistance and of the subaltern" (Spivak 1999: 373).

In the official language of the United Nations the slogan "Women in Development" has been replaced by "Gender and Development" where, once again, woman is the loser, at least when it comes to the so-called Third World. Closer to home, looking at the practice of literary studies, we notice that Third World Literature and postcolonial literature have almost come to be conflated with First World Literature — what we are in fact studying are works by cosmopolitan, European and North American educated academics and intellectuals who write in hegemonic western languages and publish in London, Paris and New York. As Aijaz Ahmad puts it, Third World literature comes to us not directly or autonomously but through grids of accumulation, interpretation and relocation governed from the metropolitan countries. Even as we open ourselves up to the widest possible range of global cultural productions, it is best to keep in view the coercive power of the very channels through which we have access to those productions (Ahmad 2000: 44). In the fields of literary and cultural studies in the West there is a crying demand for "native informants" who are supposed to represent the "authentic" or "original" voice of the other, domesticated and commodified for Western consumption (Spivak 1999: Preface; see also Spivak 1988: 256).

Mahasweta Devi and the Ethical Encounter

To illustrate my argument here I will take a brief look at a story by Mahasweta Devi, published in a collection of stories *Imaginary Maps* (1995) and translated from Bengali and prefaced by Gayatri Spivak. The story is called "Pterodactyl, Puran Sahay, and Pirtha"; it is about 100 pages long and tells about the confrontation between modern India and the situation of the tribals. The Pterodactyl is a prehistoric bird which has a key position in the story; Puran Sahay is a journalist who comes to write a story about the tribals for a mainstream Indian newspaper; and Pirtha is a remote area, ravaged by famine and destitution, on the outskirts of modern India.

The tribals, or the Adivasi, comprise about eight per cent of the Indian population; the estimate of their numbers ranges from fifty to sixty million people. The tribals are the "original" or indigenous inhabitants of India, but when the Aryan-speaking peoples took the land, especially after India became independent in 1947, the tribals were pushed aside into areas where the soil cannot support them easily and where they live in a state of almost constant malnutrition, where health care, schools and other services are insufficient or non-existent. The tribals are darker in complexion than other Indians, and some Hindu castes have considered them even lower in the hierarchy than the "untouchables" (Ludwig 1990: 17-20).

The story itself is relatively simple in structure and characterisation, but we should refrain from applying Western aesthetic standards to assess its value. Its power lies elsewhere, in its worldly context (Said 1983), in the dimension that ultimately touches the relation between the global and the local. The story is basically about the initiation of Puran Sahay, the journalist, into an understanding of the tribals' plight. He begins to see how some government officials, contractors, businessmen and even pimps continue to exploit the tribals as work-force, how they ruthlessly grab the money that is supposed to contribute to their benefit, how they literally steal their lands.

Like the Native Americans, the tribals used to believe that land and forest and rivers belong to everyone, and, since several tribal groups have had no sense of private property, their right to their dwelling-places has been ignored (Devi 1995: x). The building of dams, the exploitation of forests for industrial use, large-scale mining and energy-intensive agriculture have changed all that. The tribals suffer because the natural base of their survival economy has been destroyed. In contrast to their considerate and respectful use of natural resources that has sustained and supported their traditional way of life, the modern market economy with its ideology of development and growth tends to shatter the intricate ecological system through massive and wasteful use of the resources. In addition, the profits do not go to the tribals. In fact, the globalisation process functions in ways in which local resources increasingly move out of the control of local communities and even national governments into the hands of international financial institutions (Shiva 1991: 336).

The story documents with meticulous care the social and cultural injustice that the indigenous tribals have been exposed to, and we may find Mahasweta Devi's didacticism somewhat excessive. One is perhaps reminded of a type of socialist realism rampant in the Soviet Union in the 1930s and onwards. Yet Puran, the modern journalist, is our mediator and co-traveller. What is the lesson that he is going to draw from this experience?

Puran has a mysterious encounter with the Pterodactyl, a bird with webbed wings and a body like a giant iguana. First he can see it drawn on the wall of a tribal abode and later looks for it engraved in stone in a secret cave, but he also experiences its presence in a dream-like state in which the prehistoric bird, a symbol and representative of the soul and wisdom of the tribals' ancestors, tries to communicate something to him. Puran's experience with the Pterodactyl is one of mystery, incomprehension and non-communication, reminiscent perhaps of the experience in the Marabar Caves in E.M. Forster's *A Passage to India* (1924), a paradigmatic illustration of the confrontation of East and West, mystery and modern rational thinking. My reading is triggered by certain similarities between the treatment of the cave and the concomitant dream-like atmosphere in the confrontation of the "mystery" in both Forster and Mahasweta Devi. In Forster's novel, Mrs Moore is terrified by the echo in the cave whereas Miss Adela Quested, in fact, imagines that she has been sexually assaulted by Dr Aziz, their Indian host, in the darkness of the cave. To follow this line of reading, in Mahasweta Devi's story the exploitation of the tribals can metaphorically be perceived as a collective rape. Even though Puran represents modern and westernised India, he realises that the mystery of the Pterodactyl will escape him and he cannot approach it and the stories around it with technological means, with the use of camera and tape-recorder. But is it possible to grasp without romanticising and exoticising something that goes beyond the scope of Western rational thinking?

Puran decides *not* to write a story about the Pterodactyl because that would divert readers' attention away from the pressing problems of the tribals: famine, malnutrition, exploitation. He wants to work *for* the tribals, not in the sense of developing and modernising them but working *with* them, learning from them, especially learning from their ecologically sound attitude to their environment. Their survival or sustenance economy is a viable option even in the modern world, at least with some modifications and adaptations. Hugh Brody's *Maps and Dreams* (1981), a study of the Beaver Indians in British Columbia, Canada, provides a convincing parallel. Brody points out that the renewable resource economy of the Beaver Indians today is modern, resilient and viable and in no way defunct. In the hegemonic market economy system, living off the land in general, or by hunting, trapping, fishing, picking berries etc. is associated with poverty, but it may in fact be a shift from such harvesting and a way of life that creates the conditions of poverty.

The dominant ideology of development should not, however, have the upper hand, because development in the Western sense equates development with economic growth, economic growth with expansion of the market economy, modernity with consumerism and non-market economies with backwardness (Shiva 1991: 24). In the process of contemporary growth and development, the gains accrue to one section of a society or nation while the economic and ecological costs are born by the rest. And naturally, the idea and practice of the international division of labour and the North/South configuration loom large in the background.

At the risk of generalising, I want to say that Mahasweta Devi's story explores and illustrates the possibility of an ethical encounter in which the object of ethical action is neither an object of benevolence nor of paternalism, for here responses flow from both sides. It is a two-way traffic. As Gayatri Spivak puts it, "ethical singularity" means responsibility and accountability, and it can exist only between equals (See Devi 1995: xxv, 211). In the last page of Mahasweta Devi's story we can look into Puran Sahay's mind when he ponders: "Only love, a tremendous, excruciating, explosive love can still dedicate us to this work when the century's sun is in the western sky, otherwise this aggressive civilization will have to pay a terrible price, look at history, the aggressive civilization has destroyed itself in the name of progress, each time" (ibid.: 196). In facing the impossibility of communication we must learn "love", which, in Gayatri Spivak's formulation, is "a simple name for ethical responsibility-in-singularity" (ibid.: 200).

Mahasweta Devi and Gayatri Spivak point to the idea of learning *from* the indigenous peoples, especially from their more balanced use of natural resources and respect for land and animals *without* romanticising or museumising them. I do not insist that we should look for a magic key to our global problems in the Fourth World nations, but we should more carefully turn our ears to the systems of knowledge and habits of relating to the environment that the natives of North America, the tribals in India, the Sami in Northern Scandinavia and many other indigenous peoples have developed over the centuries (Helander and Kailo 1999; Gunn Allen 1998). It is interesting to note that the terms "ecology" and "economy" are both rooted in the same Greek word *oikos* or "household" (Shiva 1991: 30). It is paradoxical and tragic that their later development has taken such divergent routes. Indeed, how do we tend to our global household?

Decentred Dictionary, Reinscribed Literature

To conclude, I will discuss two points that take the issue of globalisation from the sphere of economics and environmentalism into the field of cultural and literary studies. Here I should be more at home and within the confines of my own discipline. Undoubtedly my position is to some degree mediated and even determined by my institutional location in a small literature, art and anthropological studies department in the technologically oriented University of Oulu in northern Finland, geographically on the outskirts of Europe.

My first point is to ponder upon the question of what we mean by "global" culture. My test case will be *The Dictionary of Global Culture*, edited by Kwame Anthony Appiah and Henry Louis Gates Jr (1996). On the back cover we read: "Wide-ranging and informative, this reference work is the first authoritative overview of global culture to emphasize the achievement of the non-Western world". This is thoroughly admirable and praiseworthy, and we definitely need a de-centring of many taken-for-granted assumptions and conceptualisations, whether they have to do with "Europe" or "the West", race, gender or nationality.

In their introduction the editors claim that in their attempt to broaden the cultural spectrum to global dimensions they have placed some of the achievements of Western culture alongside those of many other (non-Western) cultures and traditions: "...in preparing the new generations for a culture that is more global, it is essential for them to learn about William Shakespeare as they learn about Wole Soyinka from Nigeria, Murasaki Shikibu from Japan, Rabindranath Tagore from India". Appiah and Gates go on: "As we in the West develop a more global culture, we do so in the context of Western traditions: we do so because an understanding of other cultures enriches, without displacing, our own" (Appiah and Gates 1999: xi).

It is obvious that the editors identify themselves with the West and clearly state that their context continues to be in the West. The idea is to take what is interesting or useful for them but the centre of gravity remains in the West: these other traditions and cultures never displace our own. The honesty of the editors in stating this is admirable: Perhaps they are right; it may be that the position one inhabits is the only position from which one can look at something outside that position. Yet I remain somewhat uneasy about the stance, because it seems to overstep or disregard the requirement of ethical singularity advocated by Gayatri Spivak and illustrated by Mahasweta Devi. It seems as if in cultural terms globality has come to mean something similar to what has happened with evocations of multiculturalism. In the liberal and well-meaning discourse on multiculturalism, its social and political consequences are not always fully realised, and it may be that once the fervour for multiculturalism has waned, we may find ourselves in a society still predominantly grounded in Western, middle-class culture, with a few added flavours and exotica (see also Jonsson 1993).

I quite agree with the contributions that many African American artists and intellectuals have made and that their work deserves to be foregrounded. The Harlem Renaissance of the 1920s with its poets and musicians has been an important event in American cultural history, but are each four or five figures mentioned so important "globally" that they deserve separate treatment? It seems to me that at least some of the entries in the dictionary are included there more because of an American sense of political correctness than for their global significance. As for the notion of Europe and European culture advocated by the editors, it might be added that Europe also has its marginal peoples and small cultures. Finland has been deemed "global" through two entries: the *Kalevala,* the Finnish national epic, and Sibelius, the composer, who has for many a very strong national character. In addition to these, I might think of Edith Södergran, our foremost modernist poet, and perhaps Alvar Aalto, the architect and designer. Iceland might have been included because of its heroic sagas from the Middle Ages and Estonia for Arvo Pärt, the internationally acclaimed composer. Why is Willa Cather relevant "globally" whereas Edith Södergran is not? But it is somewhat silly and futile to start picking out individual names and saying "Why this?" and "Why not that?" There is no end to that road. Yet my suspicion grows that some things that are deemed "global" are global because they have a globality from the American perspective, and that they have some connection with or relevance for the US or that one of their advantages is the simple fact that they have been written in English.

In addition to the *Kalevala* and Sibelius, I am tempted to add that there is a third entry that touches upon Finland. It is an entry about the Sami (or the Lapps), an indigenous people who live in northern Scandinavia, in Norway, Sweden, Finland and Russia. The concern with "political correctness" goes the opposite way here or is somewhat askew, because the dictionary talks about the Lapp (the Lapps), and the designation "Sami", which is the term that the Sami themselves prefer to use, is not even mentioned. Some of the Sami today would feel offended if they were called Lapps. In the same book the Inuit are correctly called the Inuit, not the Eskimo.

My second point is connected with rethinking the term "world literature". The term *Weltliteratur* dates from Johann Wolfgang von Goethe, for whom world literature did not mean an established list of "great" authors that everyone should know. Goethe's idea was more modest in nature. As

Schrimpf puts it, Goethe felt that after the ravages of the Napoleonic wars Europe needed authors in various countries and nations who would make an attempt to notice and understand each other, and if they did not wish to love another, they would at least learn how to tolerate one another. Goethe was very enthusiastic about various measures which would connect and improve communication and trade between different nations and religions (the plan to build the Panama Canal was one of the projects that inspired the poet). It was the free trade in ideas and feelings, particularly articulated in literature from folk songs to *belles lettres* that was to contribute to the well-being of all mankind (Schrimpf 1968: 9-14; 44-50). This is a project of cosmopolitanism in the sense of peaceful and respectful confrontation, tolerance and mutual understanding between nations. Goethe was not advocating universal conformity nor was he supporting the idea of great books of the West, or the world at large (see also Prize 2000: 213-227).

Homi K. Bhabha's suggestion for the reinscription of Goethe's notion of *Weltliteratur* is useful in this predicament. Bhabha suggests that the study of world literature today might be "the study of the way in which cultures recognize themselves through their projections of 'otherness'"; in this day and age "transnational histories of migrants, the colonized or political refugees...may be the terrain of world literature" (Bhabha 1994: 12). The displaced, the exiles, the diasporics — we have several names for these people who cross linguistic, cultural and national borders. Toni Morrison, Assia Djebar, Salman Rushdie and Michael Ondaatje would qualify for this group but Elias Canetti, who has lived in Vienna and London and writes in German, and the recent Nobel-prize winner Chinese Gao Xingjian, working today in Paris, would also be representatives of world literature in this sense. Bhabha has maintained that "unhomeliness", the condition of extra-territorial and cross-cultural confrontations, is a paradigmatic colonial and postcolonial condition. To be unhomed, that is, displaced from one's "original" place of birth and linguistic and cultural environment, does not necessarily mean that one is homeless. Bhabha's coinage resonates with Freud's *unheimlich* (usually translated as "uncanny" in English): the postcolonial, diasporic or exilic moment is exactly the moment when the things left behind and voluntarily or involuntarily forgotten come to the surface and demand to be accounted for (Bhabha 1994: 9-10). At that moment we are at the core of cultural difference. If Goethe in his time was more concerned with the relations and exchange of ideas between Germany and France or Germany and England, the postcolonial intellectuals, writers and artists of today are deeply immersed in coping and negotiating with the whole complex issue of cultural difference between the First and the Third Worlds.

I would like to emphasise that world literature in this reinscribed sense is not only postcolonial literature as it has taken root in academia — meaning literature mainly published in English. Nor is it only literature written and published in some other imperial languages such as French, Spanish, Portugese or Russian. I think indigenous languages should have a fair share in this constellation (granted the difficulties of translation and costs of publication) (cf. Spivak 1988: 267-268), especially in situations when new literatures in indigenous or even formely suppressed national languages are being created or recreated, strengthened and invigorated. The efflorescence of Sami literature in Scandinavia since the 1970s is a good example and the reinvigoration of the Baltic literatures after the collapse of the Soviet Union provides another. Introducing Mahasweta Devi to Western audiences is part of the same global phenomenon.

To achieve "transnational literacy" as advocated by Gayatri Spivak (1999) or to employ "counterpuntal reading" or "counterpuntal perspective" as promulgated by Edward Said (1993) requires a great deal of work in the form of actually finding and unearthing alternative or even silenced sources of information, and using those in a balanced way and disseminating that information to others; it also requires a constant vigilance and self-reflection of our complicity with the formation of the resultant information. One becomes global by giving weight to the local but, at the same time, also by paying attention to the larger perspective, picking out exclusions and teasing out parallels and comparisons. Our practice as literary and cultural studies critics is to subscribe to an ethics of knowledge, an enterprise for which Puran Sahay in

Mahasweta Devi's "Pterodactyl" provides one possible model. We should also acknowledge the fact that faced with the machinery of communications technology and transnational capital our failures often outweigh our victories.

REFERENCES

Alasuutari, Pertti & Petri Ruuska 1999: *Post Patria. Globalisaation kulttuuri Suomessa* [Post Patria. The Culture of Globalisation in Finland]. Tampere: Vastapaino.

Ahmad, Aijaz 2000 (1992): *In Theory. Classes, Nations, Literatures*. London: Verso.

Allen, Paula Gunn 1998: *Off the Reservation. Reflections on Boundary-Busting, Border-Crossing, Loose Canons*. Boston: Beacon Press.

Annan, Kofi A. 2001: Miten globalisoituminen saadaan palvelemaan köyhiä [How Globalisation Can Work for the Poor]. *Suomen kuvalehti*. 1/2001. 144-145.

Appiah, Kwame Anthony and Henry Louis Gates Jr. ed. 1999 (1996): *The Dictionary of Global Culture*. London: Penguin Books.

Bhabha, Homi K. 1994: *The Location of Culture*. London and New York: Routledge.

Brody, Hugh 1988 (1981): *Maps and Dreams. Indians and the British Columbia Frontier*. Vancouver and Toronto: Douglas & McIntyre.

Devi, Mahasweta 1995: *Imaginary Maps. Three Stories by Mahasweta Devi*. Translated and introduced by Gayatri Chakravorty Spivak. New York and London: Routledge.

Forster, E.M. 1967 (1924): *A Passage to India*. Harmondsworth, Middlesex, England: Penguin Books.

Helander, Elina & Kaarina Kailo ed. 1999: *Ei alkua, ei loppua. Saamelaisten puheenvuoro* [No Beginning, No End. The Sami Speak]. Helsinki: Like.

Ludwig, Klemens 1990: *Vainotut kansat. Kansallisten ja uskonnollisten vähemmistöjen kirja*. Translated by Marketta Helevä, Tuija Kokko, Leena Kristola ja Jaakko Anhava. Helsinki: Painokaari. (Original in German: *Bedrohte Völker, Ein Lexikon nationaler und religiöser Minderheiten*, 1985.)

Jonsson, Stefan 1993: *De andra. Amerikanska kulturkrig och europeisk rasism*. [The Others. The American Cultural Wars and European Racism.] Stockholm: Norstedts.

McLuhan, Marshall 1965: *Understanding Media. The Extensions of Man*. New York: McGraw-Hill.

McLuhan, Marshall 1968: *War and Peace in the Global Village*. (With Quentin Fiore.) New York, London, and Toronto: Bantam Books.

Menchú, Rigoberta 2001: Oikeuksia alkuperäiskansoille. [Rights to Indigenous People] *Helsingin Sanomat*. August 9, 2001.

Korhonen, Johanna 2000: Enemmistö puuttuu verkosta. [The Majority is Missing from the Net.] *Helsingin Sanomat.* September 8, 2000.

Pizer, John 2000: Goethe's "World Literature" Paradigm and Contemporary Cultural Globalization. *Comparative Literature.* 52:3. 213-227.

Pöppönen, Hannu 2001: Digitaalinen kuilu erottaa rikkaat ja köyhät. [The Digital Divide Separates the Poor and the Rich.] *Helsingin Sanomat.* April 1, 2001.

Said, Edward W. 1996 (1994): *Representations of the Intellectual.* New York: Vintage Books.

Said, Edward W. 1993: *Culture and Imperialism.* London: Chatto & Windus.

Schrimpf, Hans Joachim 1968: *Goethes Begriff der Weltliteratur.* Dichtung und Erkenntnis 5. Stuttgart: J.B. Metzlersche Verlagsbuchhandlung.

Shiva, Vandana 1991: *Ecology and the Politics of Survival. Conflicts over Natural Resources in India.* New Delhi, Newsbury Park and London: United Nations University Press and Sage.

Spivak, Gayatri Chakravorty 1988 (1987): *In Other Worlds. Essays in Cultural Politics.* New York and London: Routledge.

Spivak, Gayatri Chakravorty 1999: *A Critique of Postcolonial Reason. Toward a History of the Vanishing Present.* Cambridge, Ma. & London: Harvard University Press.

15

Digiwars: Notes on the Mental and Moral Dimensions of the Digital Revolution

PASI FALK

What is all this talk about "Network Society" — by Manuel Castells (1996) and many others? Obviously something crucial is taking place, something that is more or less directly linked to the ongoing digital revolution in the realms of information processing and transfer. It is creating new modes of communication which tend to change the structure of commerce both in the wider and in the narrower sense of the word: both in everyday social interaction and in economic transactions ranging from e-business to global financial markets. However, the digital revolution will not turn matter into mere bits or the world into pure virtuality or life into just another artificial construction, as the boldest bionic scenarios — populated with cyborgs, replicants and the like — and some other extreme versions of constructionism are suggesting.

Nevertheless, the digital information theory and practice, research and technology are not just tools for doing things differently and better, or for producing more sophisticated and accurate (scientific) knowledge of this or that. It is essentially more than that: it shapes the very notion of knowledge and it does this especially in a way that strengthens the link between knowledge and control. Such thinking is in certain contexts taken to such extremes as to provoke the question: is it realistic or rather based on an illusion of omnipotence? And furthermore, in case symptoms of such an illusion are detectable, where should we look for the conceptual tools for its explanation and interpretation?

Whether to label such symptoms "digital hubris" is justified or not, these phenomena do exist and there are several good reasons for locating their core or source in the rapidly growing digital communications complex — both as a mode of knowledge production (by means of digital information processing) and as various technological applications, from PCs and mobile phones to the global digital network.

In what follows I shall present some preliminary formulations and tentative interpretations of these symptoms, starting from the grass-roots level of mobile phones in social interaction and moving on to the Internet and its effects on both social and economic transactions. The mental dimension is primarily outlined in the realm of mobile phone use, while the moral dimension will play a prominent role in the latter topic of networked social and economic transactions.

The mobile phone or, in German, the "Handy" (the Finnish "kännykkä") is not just a technologically superior version of the telephone turned wireless and mobile — especially since its digitalisation into GSM and subsequent further innovations identified by abbreviations like WAP, GPRS and UMTS — but an element of the whole digitally networked communications complex and increasingly closely linked to other devices responding to codenames such as PC, Net and Web. At present, the personal Handy — to date used by over 80 per cent of Finns — is being loaded with functions that take the device very close to the mobile personal computer (laptops and palm-PCs).

Nevertheless, whatever new functions are attached to it — such as GPS (global positioning system) in some new models, which turns the device into a personal navigator — the mobile phone will probably remain first and foremost a communicator and, as such, especially a means of one-to-one communication (as speech and text). Thus the mobile phone will keep its place within the continuum of distanced one-to-one interaction, as a step further from mail, telegram and conventional telephone. On the other hand, the parallel digitalisation of the mass media — both as a net supplement and as a stand-alone version — will blur the distinction between personal communication and mass media consumption as the latter is turning interactive, allowing the delivery of individually designed mass media packages.

At present, all these personal devices are integrating into elements of a digital communications complex, aptly characterised by the term "network". This complex seems to question some of the basic conventional distinctions such as public/private, local/global and even the distinction of presence/absence as the network reaches a real-time global scale. In the following, I will formulate some preliminary notes on the mental dimensions of these trends especially in the context of mobile phone use, even though much of what will be stated here also applies to computer-mediated interaction modes, from e-mails to real-time chat (and IRC) sessions.

The "mobile" Mind

Unquestionably, the mobile phone deserves its popular German nickname: it is a handy tool indeed. In the same way that the club was an empowered extension of the caveman's arm, the handy mobile phone is an extension of the modern (hu)man's voice — it reaches far and at the speed of light. As such it acts as an extension of the body. It is a useful and rational tool that has already saved many lives, for example. On the other hand, the mobile phone is also an extension of the self insofar as it moulds and changes our relationships to others. At first sight, it seems to strengthen the "handyman's" individuality. After all, the device is more personal than the PC and it accompanies its owner almost everywhere she or he goes. The handy phone extends the individual freedom of its user and opens up new possibilities of action, most directly within the realm of communication.

However, the use of the mobile phone may involve a less obvious aspect, as a sort of unnoticeable supplement on top of the characteristics strengthening the user's autonomy: symptoms of an illusion of control accompanied with a kind of dependency. These mental dimensions are aptly formulated in a recent advert of the Finnish telecom company, "Elisa Communications". The slogan reads as follows: "I want to be everywhere with everyone, now and forever". The slogan characterises the mobile phone user as a caricature-like figure, and not without reason. It might just be the case that handy use promotes a kind of on-line mentality that tends to regard its users not merely the tool itself but also the other party of the communication relationship as an extension of his or her self. I am not proposing that the relationships with others are thus made purely instrumental. Rather, the possible effect is considerably less evident, being overshadowed by the hyper-social message of the advert. The on-line mentality is rather characterised by a kind of connectedness dependency that actualises itself when one fails to get through to the other. Some preliminary but unsystematic interviews and personal experience have revealed that such not-getting-through situations tend to evoke irritation of a tone that could be verbalised into reasoning of the following kind: why isn't the other one there for me just now when I need him or her, not necessarily for some instrumental use (e.g. the extreme case of getting help in an emergency) but for the contact itself. Thus the on-line mentality is characterised by impatience and the fear of being left alone. Consequently, the apparent message of the slogan may be reformulated as follows: "I want everybody (relevant to me in one way or another) to be within reach when and wherever I have a need for the other, or actually, for the contact itself".

The changed configuration tends to redefine the innocent personal communication tool into an omnipotent device ensuring the continuity of one's self "always and everywhere" with the help of available contacts. Thus the need to be connected overrides the duality of presence and absence, turning the latter into an on-line social presence that marginalises the capability of being alone and enduring separation and waiting, that is, the essential capability that develops in the process of individuation.

Saying this does not imply a normative understanding of individuality where independence is equated with the ability to manage without social relationships. Such a monadic stance would merely repeat the illusion of individual freedom as absolute omnipotence. Nevertheless, even such weak signs of the mental effects of the new communications technology outlined above may prove to be significant from a wider communication-cultural perspective. After all, these effects concern the very elementary structure not only of communication but of social interaction and of relating to others. The signs of the mental and moral dimensions of the digital revolution are more visible and articulated within the broader network perspective.

Net Market and/or Net Village?

The digital communications complex is linked ever more closely to the international market. On the one hand, the net develops into a central realm of economic transactions, from financial markets to retail net stores. On the other hand, a growing portion of goods are turning digital: computer applications, games, music and videos.

This tendency is not only about the market economy invading and utilising digital networks as a new and more effective means of realising the familiar economic interests. The brand-new digital communications complex actually changes the very dynamics of the market economy. Economic communication going net accelerates into an unprecedented velocity approximating the magic limit of global real-time. The simple but highly abstract money language fits perfectly into the digital universe. After all, money is an abstraction in a practical form and from the technical point of view it is nothing other than digital information — both in the older sense of the numerical and in the contemporary systemic sense referring to the basic level of binary on/off calculus. Both money and information are purely relational entities, lacking any stable essence beyond their relational and dynamic stance: there is neither information nor money without communications or commerce.

Thus, economic transactions and especially the financial markets have no problem in adapting to the net world — except for some minor practical matters. Or, as a columnist in a Finnish economic journal (*Taloussanomat*, May 2000) put it while envisioning in overtly optimistic tones the future of a globally integrated network stock exchange: the practically limitless power of digital computer technology will eventually make the world economy more stable and manageable, "provided that certain security issues are dealt with in a satisfactory way".

Such visions of a high-tech and high-speed new global economy are necessarily relativised by the reality principle of contemporary material production which, in spite of becoming more and more computer-aided — a tendency that applies to both distribution (computerised logistics) and marketing (computerised consumer demand monitoring) — is still bound to the confines of material inertia. Material objects move at best at the speed of sound, or a bit faster, and will continue to do so unless the "teleport" technology — envisioned in David Kronenberg's updated version (1986) of the classical science fiction horror film *The Fly* (1958) — one day pushes logistics to the light-speed level of electronic information transfer.

In other words, the great expectations of the liberated and integrated world markets rely in the last instance on the magical digital toolbox. It may be too early to tell whether such optimism is mere hubris or not. Nevertheless, one should be cautious when moving towards such conclusions. There are certainly signs that tend to contradict such optimism: recent history has already witnessed the first computer-generated — or at least computer-aided — stock exchange collapse, the "Black Monday" of 1987, caused by a widely-used computer application programmed to launch the sale of downward stocks at a certain critical level; a sort of computerised panic reaction.

Another genre of great expectations looks forward to the rise of a globally networked hyperdemocracy based on the rhizome-like, non-hierarchical structure of the Internet. These visions — mainly critical of the commercialisation of the net — involve a more or less vaguely outlined social utopia involving a radically individualised democracy based on the principle of free (net) speech or expression instead of free markets. It is a kind of interactivated and consequently democratised version of the global village (McLuhan), where every netizen has her or his own PC, homepage and voice serving as the democratic single vote applicable in whatever virtual community one joins and, eventually, in the globalised democratic political system to come. Such a vision might be characterised as a utopian version of the "digital hubris" opposing the perfected global market model, yet sharing with it an emphasis on individual freedom. For free trade people the emphasis is on good old utilitarian principles, while free speech people are looking forward to the empowerment afforded by grass-roots-level social interaction, peer-to-peer mutuality, communities and sub/countercultures.

Hence, both visions eventually rely on the individualised morals of a one-to-one (social) relationship mutually acknowledging the separateness and sovereignty of the two parties. Of course, this is a rule that in the real world is supplemented with a number of exceptions. Nevertheless, it remains a rule as long as the normal practice is closer to commerce than robbery, and closer to conversation — even heated verbal dispute — than raw violence. Both visions may be regarded as yet another variation on the "Great Narratives" of the Enlightenment, those that were declared dead not so many years ago, especially by François Lyotard (1984). Both versions of the progressivist narrative rely on new digital technology and both celebrate the dramatic shift from mechanical extension to digital intension as an opening up of the information highway which is taking us all towards a better — if not perfect — tomorrow.

But this is where the ways part. For free-traders, the highway or freeway is about market economy reaching its perfection as a real-time global system. For free-speakers, it is about reaching the ultimate limit of individual freedom and, consequently, about democracy in a substantial sense — with some utopian flavouring. However, the programmatic differences between these two stances tend to develop into a severe opposition of two camps that define the divide of good versus bad (guys) according to the principle of inversion. For free-traders, the hackers — in the original non-pejorative sense referring to computer and programming specialists and freaks (e.g. Himanen 2001) — crackers and other "anarchistic" nerds are parasites, sociopaths or downright criminals who belong to the same category as computer virus distributors, while they themselves represent the law-respecting constructors of a better economy.

From the free-speakers' perspective, the constellation is turned upside down: the bad guys simply want to make a profit, build up and guard monopolistic empires and take over the free, non-hierarchical space of the Internet with the purpose of turning it into a vast market. Fighting against all forms of "capitalist" suppression, concentration and commercialisation, these good guys defend the Internet as a realm of voluntary individual relationships, reciprocity and sharing — thus promoting all forms of togetherness (e.g. virtual communities) as well. Such an idea of social interaction, sharing and exchange lies far beyond the confines of economy — narrowly defined as a system based on mass production and the money-commodity exchange. Rather, it is a kind of moral economy that incorporates many of the characteristics of the pre-modern or archaic economies of reciprocal exchange or gift systems.

As community/society-constituting principles, such moral economies are less economical and more social than our modern Western market economy. In other words, in the former the instrumental aspect of relationships — guided by economic interests and thus giving primacy to the subject's relationship to objects (money and commodities) — is subsumed to the relationships' function of maintaining and reproducing the network of relationships, that is, the community and society itself. As distinct from the former, the market economy places economic interests in primary position. This does not overthrow the economy's role as an organising principle. In fact the globalisation of the market economy proves precisely the opposite. However, the nature of these primarily economic networks is fundamentally different from the former — as different as the broader social principle of reciprocity is from the principle of equivalent exchange based on money-commodity transactions. Yet the alternative moral economy of the free-speakers also seems to involve a more economic principle of exchange, barter, in which the economic interest plays a role but only in relationships with use-values and thus without the mediation of money. As will be shown below, the communicational dynamics of the Internet promote this pre-modern form of commerce as well.

DigiWars — Episode 2

It is certainly a rude oversimplication to depict the battles of the Digital Galaxy according to the mythical scheme of Star

Wars as a fight between free-traders (the darksiders?) and free-speakers (the brightsiders?). The overall configuration is very fluid indeed and involves a whole range of intermediate positions between opposite poles. Nevertheless, there are some good reasons for holding on to this stereotypical dichotomy as a heuristic thinking tool.

One of the less important reasons is the fact that some variations on this mythical scheme have gained significant visibility in the media over the last few years. In particular, the personified version of Bill Gates versus Linus Torwalds — or, in terms of companies and operating systems, Microsoft and Windows versus Linux — was given high visibility, first in *Time* magazine and then in countless newspapers, a few years ago. The world's richest ex-nerd or hacker Bill Gates and his Microsoft empire stood for the "dark forces" of monopolistic economic power, while Linus Torvalds and the operating system bearing his name, Linux, represented the new social and economic order celebrated by the software circles of free-speakers and many others critical of the overly concentrated and monopolistic software industry. In other words, we have here the "bad guy versus good guy" constellation in its purest form: the former primarily makes money while the latter offers his creation to mankind free of charge, as a gift. And what makes the bad guy's situation even worse is his role as an ex-hacker turned not merely cold capitalist but also traitor to "the hacker ethic", to borrow the title of a recent pamphlet by one of the free-speakers' spokesmen, Pekka Himanen (2001).

However, some more important and interesting aspects of this mythical scene have been revealed through an analysis of the emerging tensions and contradictions that lie behind the stereotypic dichotomy, as it were. These tensions and contradictions are linked both to the basic characteristics of digital products and the specific modes of communication not only made possible but also nurtured by the Internet. The former of these links may in the long run prove to be a considerable, if not fatal, problem for the commodity economy, while the latter might offer some hope for those looking forward to a new free-interactionist economic order.

Obviously, the complete range of mass-produced products today or tomorrow cannot turn digital, even though the digitalisation of production processes is an almost endless project. Yet the range of digital products proper now grows faster than any other product category and will probably continue to do so for quite a long time. After all, the digitalisation of the "old" informational products has just started, while the production of novel digital products — programmes, games, music, video — keeps growing exponentially.

Why should this be a problem for the commodity economy? In a certain sense, industrial mass production reaches its ultimate limit in the digital product — and actually goes beyond the limit of conventional mass production: it is no longer a question of producing a copy of the original but of producing identicals based on a prototype, mass products that are simultaneously both originals *and* copies, or original copies. Someone else — a dishonest rival or a pirate producer — could of course steal or copy your idea and prototype, and put up a production line for forgeries (in the legal sense) or copied original copies, but this someone would still need a production plant for this illegal business. However, with digital products, every copy is an exact clone of the copied original — be it the original copy or the prototype. They are all simply identical through and through: mere 0s and 1s in certain combinations. This being the case, the mass-(re)production of digital products still requires some kind of production plant, but such an arrangement concerns only the volume of (re)production, not the technology needed. The technical equipment is again identical with consumer electronics where the whole range of digital products are used or consumed.

If we now shift the focus from mass-producers — be they legal or illegal — to the mass of digital product consumers, we will realise that the last difference between production and consumption — now also including reproduction — is erased. In other words, every consumer of digital products and digital technology is a potential reproducer, and when looking at the volume of the realisation of this potentiality, even the difference between organised mass production and consumer reproduction loses its significance. Of course, the producers of commercial digital products do everything in their power to prevent such abuse, but as it appears, the fight against individual consumer pirates is doomed to fail. All electronic locks preventing copying will be opened and all safety codes cracked. To find the reasons for this scenario — which is nothing less than a crisis of the commodity — we have to (re)turn to the net.

The Internet is the primary realm for both the circulation of digital products and the different — mutually contradictory — transactional and interactional practices by which the circulation is implemented. The commercial party (free-traders) is developing secure procedures for selling and buying goods which in the case of digital products remain fully within the confines of the net: both money and the product circulate in a digital form. This is conventional commerce turned digital. The other party (free-speakers) — if we still stick to the stereotypical dichotomy — follows a different logic. It is much more difficult to define, not least because this other party is in fact a heterogeneous continuum ranging from true representatives of hacker ethics through various subcultures — crackers (code breakers and distributors) being only one example of many — to ordinary net-minded people, usually from the younger generations. As heterogeneous as this other party is, the people still share the following characteristics: they may be involved in economic transactions as e-shopping consumers, but the interactional social relationship is kept clear of business, even though these contacts may involve economic aspects, especially in the pre-modern forms of reciprocal exchange and barter. The point is, however, that these economic aspects are subsumed to the principles of interactional reciprocity: people exchange and share words, ideas, opinions and even their digital possessions.

The last category of items exchanged and shared is, of course, the critical one, especially from the commercial party's point of view and perhaps even from the perspective of the commodity economy at large. From this perspective, the escalation of a private-consumer-based exchange of digital products looks like the dystopian vision of a piratical economy threatening to ruin the market economy. All efforts to bring the emerging barter economy under control seem to fail, partly because of the half-professional crackers who always find a way around the security systems and distribute their knowledge freely in the net. Crackers are the active fighters in the battle against commodity economy, whatever the true motivation of their activity may be. But should the rest of the heterogeneous continuum be managed, that is, all the other people who just keep on doing as they have done before, according to the elementary principles of social interaction: exchanging, sharing, borrowing, lending, giving and receiving? Everything goes on as usual — except that it takes place in the placeless virtuality of the net. Precisely this makes the crucial difference.

Borrowing and lending books, records — to simplify my argumentation I will use the music industry as a paradigmatic example but the same applies to other digital products — and whatever among friends and within other local social groups is part of what is called social interaction. The technological innovation that made copying possible — the recording of music on cassette decks — did not significantly alter these practices, because it was integrated into the old local exchange and sharing practice as just another element. And the same applies to the present digital cloning, as well — as a social practice of local groups. The producer party already had some problems with the music cassettes, but nothing that could not be solved with agreements on some fees and taxes. On the other hand, the quality difference between the original and the copy was still significant. Today, the producers are much more nervous about the difference between the original and the copy fading away, but the local social practice would still not be considered an overwhelming problem. The real threat — for the producers and especially the big record companies — is located in the net. For smaller companies and independent artists, net circulation has opened up the way for new opportunities. Let us take a closer look at how this threatening situation is taking shape.

What the free-speakers praise and defend as the basic idea of the net — free interaction and communication in whatever sporadic or more lasting forms these take place — is actually modelled on the local social interaction patterns, including all the forms of reciprocity referred to above. On the other hand, strange things happen when the local model is transferred into the virtual (non)place of the net. The transformation is not about the local turning global or the private turning public. It is something more complicated because these bipolar dualities become blurred in the communicative dynamics of the net. Relating to these blurred distinctions the communicative dynamics are realised in a whole range of types: local groups duplicating and expanding their interaction patterns into the net; new groups with shared ideas and interests born in the net and staying there, or, perhaps occasionally becoming flesh and blood in real-world meetings; groups on open stages, others in private chambers and all the traffic between discussions and one-to-one secret conversations, within and between groups. Furthermore, the stuff of sharing and exchanging is not merely words but also things — just like in the local setting. There is one difference, however: only digital things move in the net as easily as — or even more so — tangible things at the local level. When we focus on the circulation of digital things or products, business (in the original non-economic sense of the term, used, for example, by Robert Burton in his *Anatomy of Melancholy*, 1621, and others) goes on as usual.

Thus the ingredients of a big clash between the differing and opposing interests of the two parties are at hand. A whole range of questions then arises. How can this escalating interactionist process be controlled? Is it morally condemnable? Should it be criminalised? Or simply, what can and should be done, if anything? Well, something is being done: the court case in the US against Napster, an organised community that was distributing music free through its website. Here the music industry seems to have a good case: at least they have something (the website) and someone (those running it) to be sued. However, something else has already taken place on the other side, as it were. The circulation (exchange, sharing) format has changed from a localisable website based system to one based on peer-to-peer links (p2p). Anybody interested may download — for free, of course — one of the many programmes which bring together those willing to share and exchange digital products according to the basic rule of reciprocity.

Now the circulation has neither centre nor operator: there is neither a web site nor those running it. The network exists only when at least two peers are around in the net using the program, or better, when at least two computers are activated in the p2p-network — and only for so long is this condition met. So, even though anybody can join the network — as a user or a spy, it makes no difference — the network itself exists only in the form of discrete and private transactions or communicative actions between peers. Consequently, all control measures are rendered impotent because there is no way to target the legal action, no one to blame.

On the other hand, something essential is missing from these circulation systems compared with the "real life" local interaction scheme. Even though the inner circle of the p2p networks maintains a two-channel contact — both as an exchange and sharing connection and as chatting — the majority uses only the former which in itself is an anonymous connection. Thus the personal relationships are actually pushed into a secondary position or eliminated altogether. Only the formal procedure of "give and take" remains an automatic procedure that takes place primarily between the computers. So, there is no need to romanticise these networks as the vanguards of the global gift economy to come. Nevertheless, the problem persists not only for the free-traders but all those worrying over the fate of the commodity economy. And questions arise.

Should the authorities proceed to criminalise the basic dynamics of social interaction itself, both inside and outside the net? Mission impossible1. Perhaps they should get rid of the net altogether? Mission impossible2 — besides, the net is the great project for reaching an even greater future in the free-traders' blueprints.

On the Possibility of "nethics"

We are facing an insoluble dilemma and simply have to learn to live with it, because there is no technical, political or legal means to stop the process. All measures to gain control evoke counter-measures, resulting in an endless series of metamorphoses of the basic formula of social interaction, unless a new ethical attitude, a new morality somehow appears, or to put it more exactly, if the ethics already present in the basic formula of interaction — the principle of reciprocity — are somehow elevated to a more general level. While interviewing a youth involved in music circulation networks, I began to ponder on such a possibility: he had a moral principle of reciprocity — substantial rather than formal — according to which he was prepared to pay for the music he really liked, provided that the band was not one of the big (= rich) ones "owned" by the big record companies. In other words, after downloading for free his favourite music he was still willing to buy the CD from the record shop, not according to the principle of equivalent exchange but according to the principle of reciprocity, as a gesture of gratitude.

However, there are at least two other symptoms (and possibly more) in the net that could point to the direction of the former case. Here I will briefly present these two. The first takes us back to the mythical figures of the Digi Wars, more precisely to the "good guy" Linus Torvalds and the Linux project — the project that has been considered the strongest sign for the arrival of the era of hacker ethics by the free-speakers (Himanen 2001). As is known, the project of developing a Unix based operating system was launched by Linus Torvalds as a private enterprise "just for fun", as the originator himself puts it in his book that bears this title (Torvalds and Diamond 2001). In other words, in the beginning there was no organised project, only the fun of doing; this was shared first within rather limited hacker networks and later throughout the whole Internet, incorporating tens of thousands of developers. It became a project but never a strictly organised or hierarchical one. Anybody could join in and everybody had access to its data from the source code onwards. Linux was the first major example of what was called the "open source" principle of hiding nothing from anybody. The only ethical rule for working on Linux was to render the results or versions as accessible as the previous ones. As a sub-rule to the former was the acknowledgment of the authors of the versions used in developing the new one — a principle of reciprocity familiar from the academic world.

It may be premature to declare the dawn of a new era of "hacker ethics" replacing the old "protestant" one (Max Weber) on these grounds, as Pekka Himanen (2001), in his overromanticised interpretation, tends to do. Nevertheless, the success story of Linux — having succeeded in integrating its product into the commercial realm as well — certainly shows that things can be done otherwise and that ethical rules play an essential role in doing so. Furthermore, the Linux experience provides evidence for yet another blurred distinction, that between work, hobby and entertainment.

The second symptom also points to hackers, only now to those involved in smaller projects and mainly working alone. These software developers create — obviously mainly for fun — small, more or less useful applications to be used as such or in connection with certain bigger commercial applications. They distribute their digital products freely in the net, not as freeware, usable without any obligations, but as shareware with an appeal to the potential user's moral sense in the following form, for example: "If you find this application useful, please send me $10 and help me to go on with my work and provide you with updates". Then again, there is no need to rush to hasty conclusions; this is hardly a sign of a shareware economy to come. Nevertheless, it is interesting to note that the young boy was prepared to fulfil a similar moral obligation even without an appeal. The possibility is — possible.

REFERENCES

Castells, M. 1996: *The Rise of the Network Society*. Cambridge, Mass.: Blackwell.

Dreyfus, H.L. 2001: *On the Internet*. London, New York: Routledge.

Himanen, P. 2001: *The Hacker Ethic. And The Spirit of The Information Age*. London: Secker & Warburg.

Humphrey, C. and S. Hugh-Jones ed. 1992: *Barter, Exchange and Value*. Cambridge: Cambridge University Press.

Lyotard, J.-F. 1984: *The Postmodern Condition*. Minneapolis: University of Minnesota Press.

Markham, A. 1998: *Life Online*. Walnut Creek, CA: AltaMira Press.

Mauss, M. 1967: *The Gift. Forms and Functions of Exchange in Archaic Societies*. New York: Harvester.

Negroponte, N. 1996: *Being Digital*. New York: Vintage Books.

Shields, R. ed. 1996: *Cultures of Internet*. London: Sage.

Torvalds, L. and D. Diamond 2001: *Just for Fun*. New York: Harper Collins.

16

Internet, Translocalisation and Cultural Brokerage in the Pacific

JARI KUPIAINEN

Technologies have enabled men to land on the moon 30 years ago. Millions of dollars have been spent on that. But, no rural people have ever benefited from the historic landing on the moon. Again, sophisticated arms and deadly warheads are on the rise in every superpower nation of our planet. The victims of this are certainly the most remote rural people. This brings nothing, but sorrow, misery and disharmony.

The only recent technology that helps the rural populace is the Internet. It brings people close to each other. It brings the world close to our door steps and makes the universe small and within our reach. It makes us understand that despite our remoteness we are still part of the one global society. We support PFNET and stand to salute the programme well done.

— From a statement on the Information Society, by the community of PFnet Silolo, Malaita [Solomon Islands]. (People First Network 2003)

Introduction

Surprisingly little attention has been paid to the fact that Internet applications such as email, Internet Relay Chat (IRC, "chat") and the World Wide Web (WWW) have become central in communications between many indigenous, ethnic and minority communities in the less-developed countries around the world, although other means of communication do exist in addition to these new media. This development may be seen to parallel the emergence of information and communication technology (ICT) in the technologically more advanced and wealthier countries, so that the advances in ICT have been adopted by many indigenous peoples and communities as a product of the international distribution of ICT. This technological adaptation has been especially noticeable in those technologically advanced countries that administer indigenous minorities within their areas. For instance, indigenous peoples of the USA, Canada, Australia, New Zealand and many European countries have been at the forefront of endorsement of the Internet in a variety of intra- and intercommunal uses and as channels of information distribution. The first websites of indigenous communities appeared in the Internet soon after the World Wide Web became available to the public in 1991, and especially with the introduction of the graphic Internet browser Mosaic in 1993.

The total number of Internet connections escalated throughout the 1990s and continues to grow, yet these new connections have been predominantly made in and among the technologically most advanced countries, while Internet connectivity in most African and Asia-Pacific countries has remained low. This trend has provoked critical commentary in the media to the effect that digital development and the Internet profit only the affluent societies, while the poor countries become increasingly marginalised in the world economy. In other words, the increase in Internet connections is seen as widening the digital divide between the rich and poor, between the economically-technically advanced countries and the less-developed.

This argument deserves closer — and also anthropological — scrutiny, but here I will address only certain aspects of the "digital divide" and bypass issues such as the globalising digital economy. My concentration, in other words, will be on some of the more positive effects of the distribution of ICT around the world. It is, however, necessary to ask questions about whether the situation of the digital development is indeed so bleak, clear-cut and apparent, and about the direction in which things are proceeding. According to the Internet survey company Nua Ltd., in September 2002 there were 605.6 million Internet connections worldwide. Of those, North America and Europe (182.67 M + 190.91 M, respectively) accounted for 373.58 million connections while the rest of the world combined had 232.02 million, or 38% of the total number of connections (Nua 2002). However, it is worth pointing out about these figures the fact that in 1998 the corresponding percentage for the rest of the world was 21.25% (Nua 1998). In China alone, the number of Internet users escalated 50% from 2000 to 2001, or from 22.5 million to 33.7 million in single year (China Internet Network Information Centre 2002). Such figures do not exclusively support claims that the Internet is growing only in technologically advanced countries and not elsewhere.

The so-called digital divide should be understood as a dynamic process that is changing its character in favour of a more complex setting, where practically all countries now have some kind of access to the Internet and other communication technology, but different regions proceed at different paces towards a more comprehensive penetration of this new technology. This complexity typically emerges as a formation of local and regional centres — or hubs — of information and communication technology used in distributing and channelling connections elsewhere in their surrounding regions. Normally, capital and regional cities have developed in this way, but various micro-level programmes and projects are notably diversifying the local processes, and a simple centre-to-periphery model of globalisation processes is clearly inadequate for describing the emerging situation. Even though rural areas and poorer regions remain on the margins of these ICT-developments, net cafés and email stations have recently surfaced in the most surprising and remote of places around the world, and satellite/solar technologies facilitate connections practically anywhere. The question of Internet access is rapidly becoming one of relative access and saturation once the issue of absolute access has largely been solved. In addition, the rhetoric of the widening digital divide is being swiftly shifted toward talk of digital opportunities and of digital bridges connecting the poor and the rich.

Cultural Brokerage and Internet Accessibility

The increase in Internet connectivity in the wealthier countries can be interpreted in terms of saturation or of already well-connected societies become even more connected via the Internet. In contrast, the increase in Internet connections in poorer countries needs to be viewed in terms of general accessibility. There is a significant difference here between the idea of saturation and the idea of general accessibility. Certainly, the increased access and use of the Internet in the wealthier countries will have its own local social repercussions, but that is not my primary focus here. Also, in the poorer countries, where the skills of reading and writing are not shared by all adults and where access to the necessities such as food, clean water, electricity and telephones is not at all self-evident, hi-tech Internet applications may at first sight sound irrelevant, unrealistic, and filled with meaningless techno-hype.

Distortions resulting from remote perspectives and positions are, however, equally apparent. Over the past few years I have been monitoring a number of indigenous societies in Melanesia and Polynesia that are presently attempting to catch up with modernisation processes and the hi-tech advances in communications. Many of these local communities have, to a notable extent, maintained their traditional lifestyle and customs, while modern education and modernisation also influence the lifestyles of younger generation and the urbanising section of local societies. In such settings, *de facto* access to the Internet involves only a very few members of the local communities, while for most others the very idea of such techno-advances is largely irrelevant — at first sight. In fact, the few locals who have access to the Internet have often quickly developed into important resource persons and cultural brokers in their communities. Today, they channel much of the intra- and inter-communal communications that take place between community members at home and abroad, as well as relations between the different communities and with the authorities.

Put simply, if one Internet connection exists in a population of one thousand, this does not indicate that only one member actually uses it while the others are excluded. More often, the case is rather the opposite. The person with Internet access becomes an intermediary and the cultural broker for the rest of the community by sending emails on behalf of relatives and other members of the community, or finding information for them, or putting up communal websites to represent the entire community, or becoming the intermediary who is contacted from abroad to pass on messages to the community, and so on. Thus, the one Internet connection in the community becomes multiply utilised by many, and the direct consequences resulting from this connection involve the larger community. What matters from the communal point of view is that, if one individual has the access, then all have it through that person because of communal solidarity and feelings of obligation towards relatives. In this sense, this single available Internet connection also influences those communal members who do not have electricity, or do not know how to read and write, or how to use computers. This is very much a question of *communal access* to the Internet in the absolute sense of the term.

Even limited and only periodical access to the Internet is access, and such access may have a dramatic importance for the whole community in terms of agency over its own affairs (see also Mele 1999). This agency can be observed in several contexts: amongst individuals communicating with each other, amongst families and clusters of relatives, and in villages, towns and provinces, and at national and international levels. It influences human relationships, medical care, education, trade and business, media, travel, military, politics, diplomacy and conflict resolution, international aid, church, religion, NGO activity, and numerous other almost unimaginable fields of social and individual life. In other words, the influences of ICT and the Internet operate and are present in the everyday of larger numbers of people around the world than the bare statistics may otherwise indicate. This is something that anthropologists and other researchers need to monitor more carefully.

Recent years have seen a swift and dynamic distribution of the new ICT and other technology around the world, and the planet is covered with various satellite and other technologies that facilitate connections practically everywhere. While this largely takes place in the primary context of "money talks", these technologies quickly find their ways into the global markets and to consumers. As usual, the less wealthy consumers manage simply with older and second-hand models, copies, or self-constructed versions and other such strategies. Significantly, this does not happen unidirectionally, from the factory to the table. For example, Linux and the open source code, Simputer, and other such inventions are convincing testimony that an individual or local invention can produce massive effects in the course of time and in ways that have global coverage. A basic condition for the emergence of such inventions has been the community of individuals who develop and design them, yet this community has been geographically diverse, with its members living and working all-around the world. This is one of the revolutionary consequences of the Internet.

Speaking of agency, these Internet-enabled means of communication provide powerful channels for political lobbying and expressing the community's viewpoints to the outside world, and they are frequently utilised in this way. Many indigenous communities have been able, through the Internet, to join forces with other indigenous communities elsewhere in the world, and international organisations such as the Society for Threatened Peoples, Cultural Survival, Survival International, Unrepresented Nations and Peoples Organization (UNPO), International Work Group for Indigenous Affairs (IWGIA), NativeWeb and many others have been able to boost their activities and lobbying precisely *because* of these technological advances. The organisations in question are actively utilising the Internet in their operations and information distribution, but increased accessibility to the Internet has also introduced into these organisational activities a growing number of indigenous peoples and communities across the world, people who live in isolated locations and rural areas remote from centres and are often subject to government and military harassment. For instance, the monitoring of human rights violations has recently become an increasingly real-time and comprehensive activity in many remote corners of the world, a factor which may indicate very concrete improvements from the point of view of a local society subject to such violence. The Internet has not, of course, not wiped out inequality or politically motivated violence in the world, but it has greatly increased the speed with which the world is informed about such incidents, which until recently would often go unnoticed for extended periods of time.

The Internet and Social Networks in Migration

We may now turn to the influence of the Internet in local and communal networks of communication. Of central importance in this regard is the problematic related with migrants and their home societies. Through the Internet migrants have found powerful channels for maintaining their family and communal relations at home, and there have emerged locally important and regular social networks based on the Internet that surpass geographical, generational and social distances, and connect an increasing number of communal members on a daily or regular basis without regard to their location.

The island states of Oceania are largely characterised by the notably high numbers of immigrants living outside their home islands, especially in Australia, New Zealand and the United States. This is true to the extent that from a quarter to 90 per cent of the population may be living elsewhere. Such societies, for instance Samoa, Tonga, Fiji, Cook Islands, Niue, Tokelau and Kiribati, extend nowadays over a wide geographical area with great distances between the community members. The maintenance of cultural identity is usually central to these migrants even in their new locations, and the strong sense of communality and a distinct ethnic identity has persisted despite the assimilating pressures of their host societies (e.g. Friedman 1994; Siikala 2001). Among the migrants, email communication has often become vital in their daily activities, and email is used actively and regularly in efforts to stay in contact with the home community and with other communal members who have migrated elsewhere. News of family affairs travel fast and efficiently in both directions, and local arrangements can be conveniently organised from a distance by using email.

In his analysis of the elite class in the Kingdom of Tonga in 1980, George E. Marcus (1998: 137) speaks of the

> international dimension of contemporary Tongan social organization...[which is] a consequence of a historically

> subordinate and peripheral integration into a world system where Tongan elite formation has depended on the development of international family networks, yielding a kind of parasitic access to resources and opportunities in richer localities. These networks represent diversified economic activity which increases the degree of autonomy and flexibility of groups of individuals in relation to both local and overseas political and economic institutions.

Marcus published his analysis originally in 1980, when the varied impact of ICT in the case of the Tongan elites was far less pronounced. Since then, Tonga has become an active player in promoting new communication in the Pacific and especially in Tonga, not only by selling their Internet domain suffix *TO* to international operators but also by establishing ICT companies such as the Shoreline Communications founded by Crown Prince Tupouto'a to build up both wireless and a fiber optics net infrastructure in the country, or the government-owned Tonga Communications Corporation, which in 2001 took over the national telecommunications business that had been managed by the (British) Cable and Wireless, or the Tongasat company established by Princess Pilolevu Tuita to promote satellite technology in communications (see e.g. Braun 2001). Such actions appear to correspond with Tongan concerns to emphasise modern telecommunications not only in business but also in terms of the "internationally distributed" Tongan society.

Recent ICT developments indicate that the diverse geographical locations of communal members and their absence from home are becoming decreasingly important in the daily management of communal affairs (see also Ginsburg et al. 2002). In fact, the Internet has *reconnected* the communal members residing overseas with their home relatives and communities in ways that are efficient, fast, often reasonably cheap or free and that contain elements of real involvement in the management of communal affairs. Indeed, telephones existed before the Internet, and regular mail was in operation, but email has revolutionised the ease and cost with which many migrants maintain their communal ties with home, and it has also revolutionised the level of influence the overseas migrants can have in the management of local affairs. Little research has yet been conducted in this area, but a recent study from Trinidad clearly supports these observations and points to the rapid process of Internet utilisation among Trinidadian migrants in reconnecting with their home communities (Miller and Slater 2000; Miller 2002). Email and chat applications in particular have emerged as a central means in this process, and net cafés and other access points provide opportunities for resident Trinidadians to keep in touch with their migrant relatives on a regular basis. This has in practice extended the active Trinidadian community into a wide geographical area far surpassing the island context, where distances are not that important but the commitment to communal affairs is.

The concept of virtuality is often associated with forms of communication that utilise the Internet and cyberspace, yet an underlying connotation of "not-real" or "quasi" is also identified with this concept. Thus, to speak about "virtual communities" existing in the net tends to produce the default expectation that these virtual communities in cyberspace are somehow not real, or that they do not have causal effects in the real world outside the net (see also Wellman 1997). Such notions are misleading and often erroneous in the context of migrant communities. It is evident that migrants using email and chat are motivated by far more concrete and functional goals than simply passing their leisure time when they participate in the affairs of the home community through the net. Rather, these connections produce multiple direct and indirect consequences in the everyday lives of migrants and in their home community. In these contexts, the "virtual community" should rather be seen partly as an extension of existing forms of communality. But it also transforms particular aspects of the "older" communality in ways that result from the basic character of electronic communication (see also Jones 1998).

Translocalisation and the Net Environment

Particularly in the context of migration we may talk of *translocalisation*. By translocalisation I mean the processes by means of which migrants in their host societies build up new forms of locality and communality based partly on their own cultural backgrounds and partly on the opportunities and sociocultural contexts of the host society in ways that interconnect the different localities. The concept of translocalisation is an analytical attempt to focus on those (contemporary) processes of identity formation that involve aspects of migration and the international distribution of members relevant to identity. Translocal commitment to a particular locality is one aspect of a personal identity which also consists of other, often equally or more relevant, levels of that identity. Translocalisation should be regarded as a looser process of identity formation than, say, ethnicity or cultural identity because the primary identification of translocality occurs through a place that is most often geographic in character, though not always — certain communalities clearly without a geographic basis nevertheless exist in the Internet, and the "geographical" locality of such communities is the net, cyberspace. However, commitment to a locality frequently translates as a commitment to a cultural or ethnic identity, and becomes conceptualised, operationalised and treated as such in the social everyday of its bearers (see also the discussion of "virtual ethnicity" in Poster 1998 and of "neo-tribalism" in Maffesoli 1996). Such social settings are also my primary focus here.

A commitment to a locality and its cultural identity may indeed result from a "melting" of the two into each other, yet analytically they need to be kept separate. In comparison with cultural and ethnic identities, a translocal identity also allows for the inclusion in the relevant community of those members who would otherwise be marginalized in terms of ethnicity or cultural identity: spouses of different cultural backgrounds, bi- or multi-cultural children born in migration, intercultural friends and activists promoting goals relevant to the community, and so on. For example, anthropologists who have fieldwork-based relationships with the communities they study become involved in and become members of that translocal community, which is also, in part, constructed and established through such interactions.

In translocalisation processes, the role of the Internet is becoming increasingly central. Information technology applications provide migrants with concrete means and vehicles to overcome geographical locality and extend communality into the Internet. In such settings, translocalisation refers to processes where the limits of geographical locality appear to be secondary, and the community in practice becomes established as a combination of members of the origin community and its migrants scattered across the world. Thus, translocalisation consists of processes in the migrant communities *and* in the origin community. Membership in translocal communities is not decided according to the geographical location of its members but according to the activity of its members in maintaining social relationships even in the changing circumstances of international migration. In analysing locality, a key element would be the question of presence, or proximity. Translocalisation processes involve the idea of establishing socially relevant and effective presences, proximities and agency across a distance while these processes are simultaneously motivated to maintain the community and also its cultural identity.

In translocalisation the clusters of migrants and their origin community maintain a network of regular or even daily interaction, which occurs despite the actual locations of its members. Ethnicity studies in migrant communities have paid little attention to such networks of migrants and their home communities from the point of view of locality lacking a single definite geographical basis. Such aspects of migrant ethnicity and cultural identity have been more or less bypassed or ignored in most migration studies until very recently, and the Internet contributes increasing complexity to this question. What, indeed, is the locality of a migrant community nowadays when an increasing number of overseas migrants find it easy to participate through means provided by the ICT in the daily affairs of their home community?

Such developments in the Internet environment indicate certain revisions in the ways in which social scientists have been accustomed to treat social networks and communality. Nevertheless, certain existing analytical ideas and models appear applicable in the present problematic. The American sociologist Mark Granovetter (1974, 1982) has analysed social networks as composites of various strong and weak ties connecting the members to each other. Usually the weak ties are established between persons of different backgrounds, whereas the so-called strong ties refer to primary relationships among relatives, family members and good friends. Granovetter has emphasised the importance of the so-called weak ties in social networking, and these weak ties refer to connections between friends and relatives across geographical distances and to casual relationships that actualise only infrequently. Despite the relative weakness of such interrelationships, these weak ties often appear crucial in the contexts of migration, social mobility and agency, as analysed empirically by Granovetter. Within this context of social networking models we may say that Internet access obviously adds a significant dimension to the maintenance of strong as well as weak ties. In fact, the migration setting tends to transform the primary strong reciprocity ties of home into weak ties since regular contact with home is frequently hard to maintain from abroad. Thus, we can see here the potential of the Internet from the perspective of social networking models (see also Kollock and Smith 1999; Wellman 1997).

Web-assisted Communities

The Internet is noticeably influencing the practical everyday forms of communal identity maintenance across the world. An important forum in this identity work has been the World Wide Web, where websites have appeared not only to advertise the local community in support of the tourism industry but especially to provide channels of social networking across distances. Such sites often contain local databases, bulletin boards for messaging, discussion groups restricted to community members, even genealogical charts which people can use in tracing their history and relationships, chat-sections, and many other features. A pioneering successful example in the Pacific to encourage communal interaction and migrant networking in the Internet has been the Rotuma website, maintained by Professor Alan Howard of the University of Hawai'i. Drawing on his more than thirty years of research into Rotuman culture in the northern Fiji Islands, Howard established the Rotuma website in 1995. Since then, the website has proved central to Rotuman social life and through it there has emerged a translocal virtual community of migrant Rotumans who utilise the site in their regular management of Rotuman affairs. The content providers in the site are mainly the Rotumans themselves, with Professor Howard and Dr. Jan Rensel managing the site and adding Rotuma-related archive materials and manuscripts (among many other things) in digital format, with a view to establishing a Rotuman digital library available to all Rotumans in the website. As Howard (1999: 161-162) notes:

> The fact that so many Pacific Islanders are willing to allocate a significant portion of their resources to sustaining relations with geographically distant friends and relatives indicates a commitment to maintaining cultural communities in the face of formidable obstacles. The sheer volume of remittances in the form of money and gifts that emigrants send home is remarkable testimony to the power of that commitment. My argument, however, is that letters, repetitive visits, and telephone calls are not, in themselves, enough to sustain internationally scattered communities in the long run. Cheaper, more frequent communication is required, and it is becoming increasingly available to Pacific peoples via the Internet.

Howard is right in this. Letters, occasional visits home, or infrequent telephone calls are not enough to maintain communities across distances, and this has been amply evidenced by the assimilation of numerous ethnic minorities into their new host societies as a result of migration. Nowadays, the "melting pot" metaphor associated with migration is transforming into the "salad bowl" metaphor — indicating that although groups share the same physical environment of the host society, the ethno-cultural characteristics and identity of the group are being systematically upheld. From this perspective we can see that the Internet is a powerful tool for identity maintenance in migration, and it contributes towards the group's ability to maintain its communality and social networks across distances. The virtual communities that have emerged through the Internet should be regarded as real, actual formations that concretely produce causal effects in the lives of its members, both abroad and at home.

I have thus far referred to developments in the less-developed countries, and projects executed with limited resources, yet wealthy countries have also been developing corresponding net applications for their own purposes. Such projects have frequently been set up with major investments and institutional and/or business resources to contribute to the overall development of the digital society. For example, the Irish solution to the international distribution of Irish people is worth pointing out. Since the mid-1990s, the Dublin-based Internet research and consulting company Nua Ltd., together with Telecom Ireland, has been building and developing a comprehensive web database and on-line community of Ireland and the Irish. The site is called Local Ireland (http://local.ie/), consisting of a large database of matters and locations Irish, intended to serve the millions of Irish immigrants and their decendants abroad as well as the Irish in Ireland. The site is a serious attempt to establish a comprehensive on-line Irish community in the Internet, and the site contains extensive data on the cultural traditions and the whole of Irish society. Among its various features, the Local Ireland website also contains extensive genealogical databases that Irish users can utilise in tracing their family backgrounds and "roots" from abroad. People can contribute their own genealogical data to these genealogy databases and also search for their relatives. According to Gerry MacGovern (personal communication), the NUA's former CEO, the genealogy site has been especially popular among the many Irish migrants living in North America, Australia, and elsewhere. The data located in the Local Ireland website is, as with the Rotuma website, provided essentially by the locals, the ordinary Irish themselves. The role of the NUA is basically to maintain, develop and organise the data which people send them.

Translocalisation, Cultural Brokerage and Social Development in Melanesia

The geographical and territorial communality is being extended to cyberspace, yet this does not mean that the Internet should be treated as a mere technical extension of already existing social networking (Jones 1998: 6-9). Rather, the social content of translocalisation processes, in the present context, is that the Internet is opening up altogether new modes and forms of communality which do not necessarily follow the same models, structures and hierarchies as local communities based on the physical proximity of its members. The dynamics of such networking and communality can easily reverse customary hierarchies, and class and gender differences among its participants, and a closer analysis of the relationship between territorial and cyberspace-assisted communality amongst a given group of people is clearly needed. Such a study would probably reveal tensions and conflicts of authority that challenge traditional or customary aspects of the existing social structure. Nevertheless, such "structural" differences between community members often seem to disappear with surprising ease in the context of cyberspace when people email and chat in the net or when they participate in email discussion lists. Many of the formalities and manners of face-to-face conversation are simply not there — even though other manners involving "netiquette" may exist — and the "relative anonymity" of the net environment levels its participants to more-or-less equal electronic identities. How these "electronic identities" operate in the actual social world and how this "electronic dilution of real-world status" relates with the social everyday are questions that would require fresh ethnographic research for them to be properly addressed.

If we take into account the emerging role of the cultural brokers who channel email and other electronic communication locally — in the Pacific or elsewhere — it is often evident that the traditional status hierarchy of the community appears to be of secondary importance in the actual management of such affairs. Instead, the commitment and skills of the cultural broker in her or his contribution to the management of messaging in communal affairs are important, not the age, gender or social status of the person. Those capable of managing and using computers and ICT will be employed in such situations, not necessarily those with the most "culturally suitable" backgrounds. Usually those who work in offices and with more education tend to emerge as central in this brokerage, but teenagers and younger adults seem to gain the upper hand as the "new class" of local (and cultural) resource persons. Frequently, but not always, the cultural broker is assisted by the surrounding community (or a patron) to sponsor the computer or other such technology and services, or these become established locally by businesses, government bodies, international programmes and NGO projects, even by a military presence, thus opening for the broker the necessary operating channels alongside their own activities.

The nation-state of the Solomon Islands in the southwestern Pacific consists of a broad Oceanic archipelago of some 100 populated islands with almost as many languages and cultures. From 1892 until Independence in 1978, the region was known as the British Solomon Islands Protectorate. Postcolonial times have brought mixed blessings to the nation-state since then. The country has experienced deep economic troubles throughout its existence and problems have more recently culminated in civil war and ethnic crisis, which have continued to be acute since late 1998. The fighting has concentrated between groups from two of the main islands, Malaita (with the largest population) and Guadalcanal, where the capital city of Honiara is located. The crisis has centred on the question of Honiara where Malaitan, but also other local migrants have been moving in and establishing their own "urban villages" throughout the period of independence, taking over increasing areas of lands from Guadalcanal landowners for their houses (e.g. Kupiainen 2000: 128-137). The years since 1998 have seen the capital city of Honiara turn into a lawless battle-zone with severe damage to the infrastructure, the government and the business services. The national economy is practically bankrupt and large numbers (over 20,000 out of the estimated total of 80,000) people have fled Honiara to their home islands during the ethnic crisis, as the conflict is labelled in the national media. Despite this unfortunate setting, certain ICT services have been more or less operational throughout the crisis years.

In the Solomon Islands, the Rural Development Volunteers Association together with the United Nations Development Programme and the Solomon Islands Government's Rural Development Division (RDD) of the Ministry of Provincial Government and Rural Development in January 2001 launched the People First Network (*Pipol Fastaem* Network) project with the aim of bringing email and Internet to rural areas throughout the country. The PFNet is an email system based on robust technology using a laptop computer with modem, short-wave radio and solar power panel. Its central hub is the Honiara Internet Café, which functions as the central email post office in the country from which outgoing and incoming emails are distributed to their destinations, thus channelling the rural email station mails across the country and abroad. The PFNet is currently building a network of a total of 25 rural email stations in the different islands and provinces. At the moment of completion of this article, nine of the planned rural email stations are already in operation: Sasamungga (Choiseul 11-10-2001), Pirupiru (Ulawa 13-3-2002), Kati (Temotu Province 11-5-2002), Sigana (Isabel Province 25-5-2002), Vanga (Kolombangara, Western Province 11-8-2002), Silolo (Malaita 9-9-2002), Kia (Isabel 22-10-2002), Hutuna (Rennell 3-3-2003) and Pelau (Ontong Java 23-4-2003). The rural community email stations are locally managed, local operator-assisted and accessible to everyone. Thus, one does not need to know how to read or write because the operators can provide typing assistance at a nominal price. The network of email stations has already proven a local success, and its impact has been noticed internationally. In early 2002 the PFNet was selected among the fifteen finalists in a worldwide competition organised by the International Institute for Communication and Development. More recently, the PFNet was selected as one of the finalists competing in the Stockholm Challenge International Communication Technology competition, 2002.

The PFNet statistics collected by the personnel from the Honiara Net Café reveal that 82% of the emails sent from the rural email stations were sent elsewhere in the country, mostly to Honiara, and that 42% of all mails sent were addressed to friends and relatives, by far the most popular reason for sending mails (PFNet 2002). In addition, in the Honiara Net Café the statistics reveal that the primary use for computers was, for 18%, the reason to stay in touch with friends and relatives inside the country, and for 54%, to stay in touch with friends and relatives living abroad. Such figures emphasise the fact that the primary motive (the combined 72% of these statistics) for using the Internet among Solomon Islanders is to stay in touch with friends and relatives living elsewhere.

Conclusion: Addressing the Digital Everyday?

It is evident that the social and cultural impacts of the Internet are significantly more complex than might be expected from looking at the bare statistics of net connectivity in the world today. Moreover, these processes are currently proceeding at an accelerated pace in most places, and they are highly dynamic. Massive changes in the coverage and distribution of ICT around the world have taken place in a very few years, and sometimes these transformations appear to be extreme — from the "coconut wireless" and talking drums to the Internet and mobile communication, as the case may be. Yet the more things change, the more they stay the same. Social networking and communication between relatives, friends and neighbours are as important social factors locally as ever, and where the new communications technology has been introduced it seems to have been employed especially to serve this function: to improve the *existing* social networks of in-group communications. This is probably a central motivation in the local acceptance of new technologies: to improve something in the existing social situation — in this case, the opportunity to communicate.

However, each society and culture adopts a different strategy in introducing ICT locally, and experiences vary notably. From the Chinese attempts at censoring net traffic to the wholeheartedness of Finland in its aspirations and constructions of a digital society, such processes happen in specific social and cultural contexts. With regard to the global spread of ICT, many may feel that "there is something going on but I don't quite know what it is", and such a view is, analytically speaking, justified. Little is actually known of such processes but speculation abounds, especially among business consultants and political spin doctors. There is an immediate need for more empirical research to address and focus on the everyday of this digital revolution in the many different social and cultural contexts around the world.

REFERENCES

Braun, Josh 2001: Tonga: Unplugged. There's a Techological Revolution Going On and It's not where You Think. *The Daily Nexus*. 6 November 2001. http://www.dailynexus.com/science/2001/1693.html. 9 June 2003.

China Internet Network Information Centre: http://www.cnnic.net.cn/develst/rep200201-e.shtml. 9 June 2003.

Ginsburg, Faye, Lila Abu-Lughod and Brian Larkin ed. 2002: *Media Worlds. Anthropology on New Terrain*. Berkeley: University of California Press.

Granovetter, Mark S. 1974: *Getting a Job. A Study of Contacts and Careers.* Cambridge, Ma.: Harvard University Press.

Granovetter, Mark S. 1982: The Strength of Weak Ties. In Peter W. Marsden and Nan Lin Ed.: *Social Structure and Network Analysis.* London: Sage.

Howard, Alan 1999: Pacific Based Virtual Communities: Rotuma on the World Wide Web. *Contemporary Pacific.* 11:1. 160-175.

Jones, Steven G. 1998: Information, Internet, and Community: Notes Toward an Understanding of Community in the Information Age. In Steven G. Jones ed.: *Cybersociety 2.0. Revising Computer-mediated Communication and Community.* London: Sage.

Kupiainen, Jari 2000: *Tradition, Trade and Woodcarving in Solomon Islands.* Finnish Anthropological Society and Intervention Press. Helsinki and Höjbjerg.

Maffesoli, Michael 1996: *The Time of the Tribes. The Decline of Individualism in Mass Society.* London: Sage.

Marcus, George E. 1998: *Ethnography through Thick and Thin.* Princeton (NJ): Princeton University Press.

Mele, Christopher 1999: Cyberspace and Disadvantaged Communities: The Internet as a Tool for Collective Action. In Marc A. Smith and Peter Kollock ed.: *Communities in Cyberspace.* London and New York: Routledge.

Miller, Daniel 2002: The Fame of the Trinis: Websites as Traps. In Christopher Pinney and Nicholas Thomas ed.: *Beyond Aesthetics: Art and the Technologies of Enchantment.* Berg: Oxford.

Miller, Daniel and Don Slater 2000: *The Internet. An Ethnographic Approach.* Oxford: Berg.

Nua 1998: http://www.nua.ie/surveys/analysis/graphs_charts/1998graphs/location.html. 9 June 2003.

Nua 2002: http://www.nua.com/surveys/how_many_online/index.html. 9 June 2003.

PFNet [People First Network] 2002: http://www.peoplefirst.net.sb/General/ICafe_Stats.htm. 9 June 2003.

PFNet [People First Network] 2003: http://www.peoplefirst.net.sb/. 9 June 2003.

Poster, Mark 1998: Virtual Ethnicity: Tribal Identity in an Age of Global Communications. In Steven G. Jones ed.: *Cybersociety 2.0. Revising Computer-mediated Communication and Community.* London: Sage.

Rotuma website: http://www2.hawaii.edu/oceanic/rotuma/os hanua.html. 9 June 2003.

Smith, Marc A. and Peter Kollock 1999: Communities in Cyberspace. In Marc A. Smith and Peter Kollock ed.: *Communities in Cyberspace.* London and New York: Routledge.

Wellman, Barry 1997: An Electronic Group is Virtually a Social Network. In Sara Kiesler ed.: *Culture of the Internet.* Mahwah, N.J.: Lawrence Erlbaum Associates, Publishers.

PART SIX

Defining Cultural Identity Through Literature

17

Using and Refusing America: "America" as a Way of Creating Modernity and National Identity: A Case Study of a Finnish-Swedish Detective Novel from 1916

KRISTINA MALMIO

One particular aspect strikes me when I am reading newspapers in Finland today: changes seem to be taking place in Finnish society that, at least on the discursive level, have something to do with America. To put it another way: changes in Finnish society are often articulated, discussed and measured in relation to discourse on "America", a collection of cultural images related to the United States of America. America is used as the "natural" object of comparison, as a measuring stick when discussing economics, culture, democracy, mentality, beauty, wealth or the development of Finnish society. The first example that comes to mind is from a song by a popular band called Hassisen Kone whose words, symptomatically I think, asked "Is America heaven, is God living there?" (1980). When I start looking for similar examples from contexts chosen at random, I soon find out that they are numerous and occur in all kinds of texts and media. The following were found in an editorial article in a newspaper devoted to financial news and from the "yellow press" and they compare Finland and America in an attempt to create a vision of the future:

> We Finns relate negatively both to success and failure. Envy and malice are always our guests. I hope that our attitudes on this point become more American, although I otherwise don't appreciate the American way (Ritvos 2000: 3; translation K.M.).

> The whole world is becoming America. Lately especially in Finland we have, taken huge steps towards the Heaven of Blockheads. The Finns have been forced to confront conflicts of a very American type, for example the increasing inequality that is a result of more wealth. One comical contradiction strikes me as especially American. Incredibly beautiful women are obtaining silicone implants at the same time as people are very concerned about food containing preservatives. The more remarks that are made about preservatives on the packaging of fast foods, the more frightened people become (Vienonen 2001: 9; translation K.M.).

In the daily newspaper *Helsingin Sanomat* the manager of a trade and industry research centre expressed the view that "During the current rich years, people's relationship to wealth has changed totally in Finland. Nowadays wealth is openly strived for. Finnish society has become Americanized" (Alkio & Möttölä 2001). A publisher in Helsinki rejected the "constant songs on literature's direction towards entertainment and ongoing angloamericanisation" as nonsense (Hämäläinen 2000). In the same day's newspaper a Finnish researcher declared that Finland has now become the laboratory of the future, watched by the Americans and "even others" (Lahdenperä 2000).

America seems to be (one of) the constant measures of trends in Finland, the object of idealisation and rejection, admiration and contempt, even mistrust. It is as if there was a constant competition going on, a small country in northern Europe chooses a rival that is impossible to defeat. Is this typical of the way the Finnish national identity is structured? No matter what, different disciplines seem to use America in quite similar ways.

"America" in Finland has a long history, and already in the 1850s the Finnish cultural elite discussed American democracy with admiration in the Finnish press (Salo 1988: 63). Finnish emigration to the USA, beginning in the 1870s, also had its effect on the perception of America in Finland, especially among the "lower" social classes (Salo 1988: 74). I am looking here for the image of America in literature at a very contradictory time in Finland, the 1910s, a time that was characterised by ongoing modernisation, the striving towards national independence and the rise of a domestic popular literature. What interests me is how the relationship between America and Finland is articulated in the detective and adventure novel *Guldgruvan* (The Goldmine), written in Swedish in Finland in 1916. *Guldgruvan*, with the subtitle "a detective and adventure story", was published in 1916, when the dissemination and influence of American culture was increasing (Virtanen 1988: 501). The protagonist of this novel is a young man called Olle Björck. He is in a state of debasement, lazy, drinks a lot, is fat and unathletic. Olle has a crush on an independent and athletic young woman, Greta Spangen. Suddenly Greta disappears mysteriously and it is Olle's task to find her. The novel falls into two parts. The first part consists of solving the mystery surrounding Greta's disappearance; finding out why the evil American, Mr. Briggs, has kidnapped her. The second part describes the adventures and fights that Olle is forced into when trying to free Greta and capture Mr. Briggs. *Guldgruvan* tells the story of the transformation of a Finnish-Swedish flâneur, *dagdrivare*, into an American hero, a story that is told twice as it is revealed — *mise en abyme* — that some thirty years earlier Greta's father had also been sent to America to become a better man, to be cured of his alcoholism, laziness and extravagance.

The questions I pose here are the following: What do "America" and "Finland" signify in *Guldgruvan*? What are the uses of "America"? What is said about Finland by using America? I will then link the representation of "America" in *Guldgruvan* to the cultural situation in Europe and especially in Finland in the 1910s and to the deepening impact of America in European and Finnish culture (Virtanen 1988: 501). At the end of the article I will also discuss whether the use of the image of present-day America bears any similarities to its use in 1916.

The period 1891-1917 has been called "the breakthrough of Americanness" (Virtanen 1988: 243). The new American foreign policy with its imperialistic interest in the world outside America and the increasing modernisation in the European countries increased the interest in "Americanness" and American culture, apprehended as modern and democratic (Virtanen 1988: 246, 289). In the 1910s, the economic and cultural impact of America on Europe and on the world economy was deepening. America was about to become the leading world economy, which would make it possible for the USA to dominate European and world economy and politics (Salo 1988: 27, 33). America was, and is still, seen as the paradigmatic example of modernisation and capitalism, rationalism, efficiency, hedonism and technology (Björkin 1998: 255).

Finland in 1916: A Part of Russia turns toward America

Theories of modernity have emphasised the importance of a new apprehension of time and place as a characteristic feature of modernity (e.g. Berman 1982; Giddens 1990; 1991; Koivisto 1992; Karkama 1990; Rojola 1995). In 1896 the phrase "Time is money" was included for the first time in the collection of the archives of Finnish folk poetry of the Finnish Literature Society (Knuuttila 1992: 109). In spite of political events — that is, the ongoing World War I, in which Finland was involved as a part of the Russian Empire, and Russian policy in Finland during the years after 1900, which caused intellectuals to turn inwards and made it difficult to openly express opinions — between the years 1890 and 1917 the country was economically and socially becoming modern and international (Virtanen 1988: 437-438).

Finland became familiar with popular literature slowly in comparison to other countries in Europe. The international entertainment culture started to stabilise as late as at the end of the nineteeth century (Knuuttila 1992: 111). This lateness was due to several factors: the country's peripheral position on the map, the fact that two languages were spoken in Finland (Finnish and Swedish), and the censorship laws that the Russian Empire invoked several times in the nineteeth century and at the beginning of the twentieth century to keep Finland under control. In addition, the efforts of the book-publishers and booksellers on behalf of the cultural development of the nation made them unwilling to support popular entertainment and popular books. The emphasis was on informative and educational literature (Salo 1988: 48).

The writing of adventure stories, detective stories, and

other novels labelled by the critics as "popular" was on the whole scarce at this time. In fact, Finnish and Finnish-Swedish popular literature was actually being created by the authors and in the discourse of the critics from the end of 1910s and with increasing intensity in the 1920s (Malmio 1999: 290; 2000: 161-163). The writer's decision, then, to write in a genre that was apprehended as an international product and an invention of the modern world (Sundholm 2000: 175), already bears the connotations of "change" and "modernity". In 1909 Olaf Homén wrote a review of foreign detective novels translated into Swedish. He touches on the genre's relation both to America and to modernity when writing on the history of the detective novel genre: "although the detective novel seems to embody a considerable part of the actual spirit of our age, it certainly is not the modern, Americanized Western world that invented the detective novel genre" (Homén 1909: 212).

In Finland, in the nineteenth century certain stereotypical ideas concerning America were already visible in newspapers. Democracy, economic wealth and cultural poverty were associated with America (Salo 1988: 74-75, 115). Hanne Koivisto has analysed the reactions of the Finnish cultural circles to an increasing Americanisation in the 1920s (see also Björkin 1998: 10-11, 42-44, 52). She asks what was understood by the conception of "American", how American culture arrived in Finland and what kind of reactions American jazz, films and popular literature aroused (Koivisto 1992: 39). According to Koivisto, the Finnish attitude to America was neutral right up to 1917 (see also Virtanen 1988: 478-479). On the basis of the number of American popular novels published and films shown in Finland, it is possible to see a clear orientation towards America in the 1920s, Koivisto declares (Koivisto 1992: 58). American films were shown in Helsinki soon after the turn of the century, and in the 1910s American films were shown on a regular basis (Virtanen 1988: 472-473). Koivisto mentions the year 1916 as the breakthrough of American films in Finland (Koivisto 1992: 51). Koivisto shows that between 1870-1918 the amount of American literature translated into Finnish was only four per cent of the total amount of literature translated, while between the years 1919-1928 the corresponding figure was 17 per cent (Koivisto 1992: 47-48). American detective series, for example the Nick Carter books, were translated into Finnish from 1907 onwards and they were popular both here and in other parts of Europe (Virtanen 1988: 472).

I find Koivisto's article very informative, but I disagree with her on two points. First, she writes that "[a]t times American culture even showed up in Finnish novels" (Koivisto 1992: 43; translation K.M.). When reading popular texts from the 1920s written in Finland, however, it seems to me that I bump into America in different forms in most of the texts I am working with: for example, Gabriel Sanden: *Money*, with its subtitle "An American Novel" (1916); Gabriel Sanden: *Konsul Carlings hundår* [The Years of Struggle of Consul Carling] (1919); Lennart Wikström/Henning Söderhjelm: *Mångmiljonärens randstadsresa* [A Millionaire's Journey to the Border States] (1920); Elsa Soini: *Jumalten ja ihmisten suosikit* [The Favourites of Gods and Men] (1926); Olli Karila/Niilo Pärnänen: *Kultakuume* [The Gold Fever] (1926); Valentin/Ensio Rislakki: *Herra MacKee matkustaa Suomessa* [Mr. MacKee Travels in Finland] (1929) (see also Salo 1988). America takes many different forms in the texts. Writers use America, on the one hand, as a vehicle for transformation and modernisation, while on the other hand, America is shown as something utterly strange and as something that brings forth the Finnish identity. Second, Koivisto argues, that "It can thus be seen that the United States caused strong reactions in Europe. This also concerned the Finns. However, they seldom strived to analyse or explain Americanisation but, instead, attempted to relate it to the changes in culture and the democratisation of society" (Koivisto 1992: 47; translation K.M.). I will attempt in the following to interpret the different ways in which America is represented in the fictional texts as attempts to analyse and explain America, and also to relate it to changes in culture, an activity that *Guldgruvan* exemplifies very well.

Guldgruvan, a Story Written under Disguise

The author of the novel, Lennart Wikström, a penname for Henning Söderhjelm, was at the time a doctor in psychology working at the library of the University of Helsinki. Söderhjelm was active on two cultural fronts, on the one hand in activities with a high status and, on the other hand, writing stories that the contemporary critics labeled as popular novels. He also published scholarly articles, detective and popular novels, appeared as one of the editors of *Arena*, a cultural journal in 1916-1920, and was also a member of a group of young Finnish-Swedish authors, called *Dagdrivare-gruppen* (Flâneur group), active in 1907-1917. The novels written by the *Dagdrivare* writers represented young male heroes who felt spiritually ill and dreamt of a life full of health, vigour and strength. The novels told stories of outsiders wandering through the streets of Helsinki, killing time at fashionable restaurants, unable to find a place for themselves in society, and full of despair (Ciaravolo 2000: 47, 49). The popular novels Söderhjelm wrote were written, according to Olof Mustelin (1991: 57), "in an ambivalent mood". In 1914, after Söderhjelm had written a collection of parodies of the detective novel together with two friends, Söderhjelm's publisher urged him to continue this activity, but the writer was worried about his reputation in the academic world, if it became publicly known that he "had a curriculum vitae that was in the mind of the public consciousness full of detective novels" (Mustelin 1983: 49).

The few reviews of *Guldgruvan* welcomed the book as one of the first examples of domestic popular literature. H.N. (short for Holger Nohrström) wrote in *Hufvudstadsbladet,* a major Finnish-Swedish newspaper, that Finland had not produced much in the way of detective novels, but this novel could be seen as a "promising effort to replant this appreciated genre in Finnish soil" and closed his review with the remark that the book was very suitable for reading in a hammock (Nohrström 1916; see also Sundholm 1999; 2000).

America: Setting Story, Time, Place and Protagonist in Motion

Finland and America are compared and contrasted in *Guldgruvan.* The atmosphere of Finland at the beginning of the novel is characterised by melancholy, stillness and a lack of future prospects. Greta asks if it would be possible for Olle to reform himself because of her love for him, but he describes himself as a person who has already thrown away several years of his life and the heritage of his parents by drinking and doing nothing. Olle is a representative of a "lost generation", a self-conscious parody of a *dagdrivare* protagonist. Consequently, the romantic story is not enough to motivate him. Söderhjelm himself wrote in 1910 an article on the reasons why the Finnish-Swedish "youth of today" was passive, critical, pessimistic and slack. He argued that it was due to a loss of ideals to fight for, the current political situation, the fragmentation of the world, the modern subject and science, and the situation of the Swedish-speaking population in Finland. He described the contemporary mood as that of "an exhausted world" (Söderhjelm 1910: 155). This is the background of the *dagdrivare* phenomenon and the protagonist Olle.

The discussion between Olle and Greta takes place in the garden of an old house, in a place full of peace, quietness and the presence of history. Greta then disappears, and Olle, the passive and dull flâneur, becomes willy-nilly the protagonist of a detective story. Olle's first contact with America occurs when he is trying to discover the circumstances surrounding Greta's disappearance. An eyewitness whom Olle interviews has seen "men in uniforms, a steamship, somebody taken prisoner." Olle draws the following conclusion: "It was all too magnificent to be domestic. ... There was no doubt about it that it all smelled of America, yes, it gave off a strong smell of America" (Wikström 1916: 29-30). Some pages later he declares: "America has run away with her" (Wikström 1916: 33). At this point in the story, "America" is huge, magnificent and anonymous, a way of acting in a manner familiar from adventure stories and films. America intrudes into Finland and kidnaps a young woman who, besides being Olle's beloved, is the story's link to America and money. Greta has been born in America and she is the heiress to a goldmine. The connotations of America-in-Finland are wealth, villainy, technology, motion and fiction. When the evil Mr. Briggs threatens Olle with a gun, he tells Mr. Briggs that his way of treating his guest is "too American" (Wikström 1916: 53).

Olle's transformation from a flâneur to a detective starts with Greta's disappearance. America-in-Finland gives Olle a task and starts immediately to transform Olle and the time and place around him. A flâneur's relation to time and place is the opposite of a detective's. He has no goal, no hurry, no task, no direction and he is certainly not rational. On the other hand, a detective's time is structured around a task and a logical method. In order to find Greta and foil Mr. Briggs' evil plan, it is necessary for Olle to be at the right place at the right time. To catch a rich American villain who has at his disposal the best technological means presumes that one must also use all available modern technological vehicles when moving from one place to another (cars, steamships, trains, boats and elevators are used during the adventure), modern technology for communications (telephone, telegraph) and the clock. Söderhjelm, who himself, rather ironically, wrote a review of the book he had published under a pseudonym, calls this feature "technical romanticism" and argues that it is typical of the genre (Söderhjelm 1916: 151). He also argues that it is the law of genre models that forces the story to leave Helsingfors and travel to America, "the natural scene of action as far as thrillers are concerned" (Söderhjelm 1916: 151).

Olle travels to America, the "country of remarkable modernities" (Wikström 1916: 79) on an Atlantic steamship, described as huge, luxurious and comfortable, reading books on America because he feels himself "as poor in exact knowledge as he was rich in very wonderful stories" (Wikström 1916: 77). In America Olle soon finds out that "over there" it is impossible to behave in relation to time in a Finnish way, for the fictive America is the country of action and decision-making. The way the story represents time becomes increasingly precise and forces the hero to react ever more quickly. Olle starts to enjoy speed, action, efficiency, cars and rapid change. The first person Olle meets in New York is a detective working at Pinkerton's, "the most famous detective office in the world" (Wikström 1916: 80). Mr. Bangs tells Olle to wait for five minutes, and Olle notices that he returns after four minutes and fifty seconds! (See also Boëthius 1989: 105). *Guldgruvan* holds out a fantasy in which America is the place of pure modernity and where modernity is something pleasurable.

The separation of time and space, which is typical of modernity, is, according to Anthony Giddens, one of the explanations of the extreme dynamics of modernity (Giddens 1990: 17-21; 1991: 16-17). In pre-modern societies "when" was almost universally either connected with "where" or identified by regular natural occurrences: "The invention of the mechanical clock and its diffusion to virtually all members of the population, a phenomenon which dates at its earliest from the late eighteenth century, were of key significance in the separation of time from space" (Giddens 1990: 17). What makes *Guldgruvan* so interesting is that at the same time as it describes a modern standardised "empty" time, this time is connected to a specific space and place, America. Olle's life in Finland is not regulated by the clock or a timetable. In this novel time is not separated from place, yet.

America: Olle's Identity Changes

At the beginning of the story in Finland Olle declares: "I am a FLÂNEUR" (Wikström 1916: 7), but the transformation that America sets in motion becomes even more complete when Olle comes in contact with the atmosphere in New York. There, it is as if his "whole nervous system had been created anew so as to be able to receive a stronger current" (Wikström 1916: 101). He wants to keep on moving all the time, to be quick in his decisions and actions. He has become slim, he has now "sharp features, forceful jaws and a burning energy in his eyes", which make him look American (Wikström 1916: 116).

Olle is transformed into a fictional type with a long history in European literature. Lars Wendelius points out that Americans in Swedish prose fiction, travel books and popular scientific accounts at the end of the 1890s "are depicted outwardly in a remarkably uniform way. In particular, their slimness, the marked features of the face, and sharp eyes are all accentuated" (Wendelius 1982: 42). Efficiency, precision and hard work, materialism, energy, and cold-bloodedness were common features in the representation of the typical Yankee, according to Wendelius.

Mats Björkin has noticed that, after the First World War, America was regarded in two ways, as "the modern society par excellence on the one hand, and as the place of resistance against the decadence of the post World War Europe on the other" (Björkin 1998: 295). In *Guldgruvan* America clearly has both these functions. Olle is transformed from a domestic flâneur to a foreign detective and from a Finn to a Yankee. Earlier he was pasty, with a brushlike moustache of indefinite colour that gave his mouth a touch of weakness, and his posture was bad. The narrator identifies these as "national features", common to many in Finland (Wikström 1916: 118), and they connotate unhealthiness, ugliness, being neither masculine nor desirable. As a Yankee, he regains a masculine identity, and he starts to act like a "man". He only uses his European knowledge when it is needed to deceive Mr. Briggs.

Berman asks what kind of people the permanent revolution of modernity creates. His answer is:

> Modern men and women must learn to yearn for change: not merely to be open to changes in their personal and social lives, but positively to demand them, actively seek them out and carry them through. They must learn not to long nostalgically for the "fixed, fast-frozen relationships" of the real or fantasized past, but to delight in mobility, to thrive on renewal, to look forward to future developments in their conditions of life and their relations with their fellow men (Berman 1982: 95-96).

The rapidity and large number of comic changes of identity that Olle undergoes can be read almost as a parody of the eagerness to change that Berman describes. In addition, the protagonist's very identity is fictional, even bound to place and time. It is dependent on the demands of the situation, totally transformed when the protagonist, who belongs to one genre, the flâneur novel, enters another genre, the detective novel, and the place and time of that genre. Even comments on language support the ease with which his identity is transformed. Exchanging his "Helsingfors slang for that of Brentwood is not difficult at all", Olle notices happily (Wikström 1916: 115).

At the end of the story, Olle rejects the American mentality, its individualism, materialism and straightforwardness, and chooses a life as an author instead. Olle and Greta are on board a ship leaving America. Greta is happy about Olle now being a man of action, but Olle says:

> Poor Greta, that is an illusion I am forced immediately to break. When I stand here looking at the country of my transformation, I understand better than ever that I am not created for action. I have done it because I love you. But from now on I am not going to work or act anywhere else than at my desk. I hate this hurried, exciting life that is called American but is likely to become the life of the future. I am happy not to be an American man of action (Wikström 1916: 255).

In *Guldgruvan* this American modern time is temporarily deflated, or at least its victory is postponed, but this is only a short-term setback. The story s message is that the future is going to be American. Olle s friend in Finland, a businessman, dreams of the day in the future when his huge ice-breakers will keep the passage from America open to Finland round the year (Wikström 1916: 39-40).

The last that Olle and Greta see of America and the last words in the book are the text of an immense advertisement selling polish, an ironic or comic comment on the content and form of the American future. And indeed, the passages from America to Finland are today open day and night, all year round, both mentally and physically.

America-in-Finland, Finland-in-America: The Dialectic of Globalisation?

In *Guldgruvan* the relation to modern time and place is contradictory. On the one hand, one must travel to America to become rational, masculine and modern; on the other hand, time and place in the story are already immaterial, or global , if you like. The story emphasises this several times. While sitting on a chair in Denver, Olle notices that the chair is similar to the one he has sat on in Helsinki, the whisky he is drinking is the same, and the man sitting opposite him, his manners and the suit he is wearing all remind Olle very much of his meeting two weeks earlier with a businessman in Helsinki. He thinks a thought that he then repeats several times: How small the world is! (Wikström 1916: 88), The world is no doubt small indeed! (ibid.: 98), It is wonderful how small the world is! (ibid.: 115). I find this an interesting fictional description or example of what Giddens calls the dialectic of the global and local", that is typical of globalisation (Giddens 1991: 22). On the material level, then, America is already in Helsinki. On the level of one's mentality, however, one has to get in touch with all of America, the centre of modernity, in order to change definitely.

Roland Robertson (1990: 19) calls the years 1880-1925 a "crucial take-off period" of globalisation, and, indeed, the way the relationship between America and Finland is described in *Guldgruvan* can be seen as a part of an ongoing globalisation or an example of what Robertson calls miniglobalisation (ibid.: 21). A characteristic feature of the take-off phase of globalisation is, according to Robertson, "the thematization of ideas concerning national and personal identities" (ibid.: 26-27). This thematisation of identity takes place in Wikström's novel in a dialectic movement between the two contradictory poles of Finland and America.

The fictional America of *Guldgruvan* also contains — surprisingly or not — a Finland or a miniature of Finland. One could ask whether this can also be seen as an aspect of the dialectic of globalisation. The restless pursuit of Mr. Briggs that drives the story leads to a place where the conflicts that Mr. Briggs' avarice has produced are finally solved. It is a place in Colorado that consists of a goldmine and a house once owned by Greta's father. The house is an exact copy of a modest Finnish farmhouse and a picture of history, a representation of Finnish time and place, a miniature of Finland before modernisation. The narrator describes the setting: "It was a Finnish country house that slumbered in the quietness of a winter night, tranquil and peaceful and common place." And Greta's uncle says to Olle: "It is like being at home" (Wikström 1916: 229). At the centre of a story written in Finland according to international genre models, the hero finds Finnish domestic economic history and the literary ideal of the Finnish national literature. The house must be seen in relation to the Finnish immigration to the USA that started in 1860-1880, with 1902 as the peak year (Engman 1997: 31-35). By "literary ideal" I mean here the agrarian realism admired by the critics, the endless representations of people, ordinary peasants, as a means of shaping a national identity (Jokinen 1997: 7).

What kind of a place is, then, Finland-in-America in *Guldgruvan*? It is a place of history, truth, authenticity and pre-modern times. The house can be related to certain nationalistic ideas concerning the Finnish-Swedish people. The parliamentary reform that took place in Finland in 1906 changed the political structures in a very fundamental way. The status and significance of the previously dominant Finnish-Swedish upper class decreased radically and this development led to a movement in which the upper classes turned towards the Finnish-Swedish people in order to unite the Finnish-Swedish population and in this manner to guarantee some of its former status.

America: Rationality and Entertainment

The ambivalent attitude towards America, seeing it at the same time as an ideal and as a threat in Finland in the 1920s, has been noticed by other researchers of Finnish modernity (Immonen, Mäkinen & Onnela 1992: 14). This attitude is visible in *Guldgruvan*. On the one hand, America is embodied in the mean and uncivilised Mr. Briggs, whose houses are copies of European originals and who is obsessed with money. On the other hand, America is described as a large country in which it is possible to do things in a magnificent way, and, for example, regain one's lost masculinity. Everything that America has touched is described as big, luxurious, modern, comfortable and foreign, although at the same time familiar, because the representation of America has its roots in American films and popular stories.

In *Guldgruvan* America is, as I have shown, a vehicle of transformation. The time and place of America is used in the novel as a means for discussing national cultural identity, but also as a vehicle for change related to the ongoing modernisation of Finnish society and creating a domestic popular literature. The confrontation between Olle and Mr. Briggs can be interpreted as a representation of the overall cultural situation in Europe and Finland in relation to America and a fictional staging of the ongoing processes of globalisation.

The intensive Americanisation of Europe began after the First World War, (Björkin 1998: 10-11; Koivisto 1992: 40; Paavolainen 1990: 34-35) but English intellectuals were already discussing the threats of Americanisation in the nineteenth century (Strinati 1995: 22). The significance of the foreign, especially American, mass-market publishing and film industry became more and more obvious in Europe in the 1910s (Bradbury and McFarlane 1976: 60). Björkin (1998: 63, 71) describes America as a double face consisting of rationality and entertainment. This is indeed what *Guldgruvan* is about. At the level of the narrative, a displaced European gains his lost rationality, health, and masculine identity in the American atmosphere. He learns to work, earn money and fight. On the level of reading the novel in a hammock, as one reviewer recommended, America makes good reading — it is an entertaining combination of a popular story with the pleasures of the vicarious rationality and action experienced during the story. America can also be seen as escape, a turning of one's back on a Russian Empire already in the process of falling apart, with the Finnish people hovering between solidarity and national strivings (Paasivirta 1988: 16). Moreover, the story is a portrayal of a cultural situation in which Finland is becoming modern and the entertainment industry is starting to transform the cultural scene in Finland by its mere presence. In *Guldgruvan* America is a synonym for change, modernity and a measure of extreme otherness, positive and/or negative. The word "America" is used not only to articulate change, but also to create it.

The subsequent 1920s were a decade in Finnish history that has been described in economic and commercial terms (Tarkka 1980: 33), a time that very much reminds me of present-day Finland with its ongoing privatisation of the public sphere and a liberal economy that gives business a free hand, since, as one hears, "otherwise Finland is not going to manage in the global economic competition". Today, as in the 1920s, everything is measured in financial terms. It is ironic, however, that Finland has embraced only the globally oriented materialism that America represents, not the energetic and positive mentality that might make that system psychologically bearable. The atmosphere that alters Olle in America has not yet arrived in Finland; on the contrary, it seems that we have developed a quite unique combination of an American-inspired free liberal market economy and our own melancholy and pessimistic mentality.

Not long ago I turned on the television and listened to a debate on media and politics. I heard the MP Liisa Jaakonsaari say: "The Finnish media have lately developed in an American direction in setting the political agenda ..." (Jaakonsaari 2001).

REFERENCES

Alkio, J. & M. Möttölä, 2001: Suomalaisia yrityksiä myytiin maailmalle laman jälkeen halvalla. [Finnish companies were sold cheaply to the world after the economic depression]. *Helsingin Sanomat*. 8 January.

Berman, M. 1982: *All that is Solid Melts into Air. The Experience of Modernity*. London and New York: Verso.

Björkin, M. 1998: *Amerikanism, bolsjevism och korta kjolar. Filmen och dess publik i Sverige under 1920-talet*. [Americanism, Bolshevism and short skirts. The film and its audience in Sweden during the 1920s.] Stockholm: Aura Förlag.

Boëthius, U. 1989: *När Nick Carter drevs på flykten. Kampen mot 'smutslitteraturen' i Sverige 1908-1909*. [When Nick Carter was driven away. The battle against 'dirty' literature in Sweden, 1908-1909.] Gidlunds.

Bradbury, M. and J. McFarlane ed. 1976: *Modernism. 1890-1930*. Pelican Guides to European Literature. Harmondsworth: Penguin Books.

Ciaravolo, M. 2000: Dagdrivare och Runar Schildt. In Clas Zilliacus and Michel Ekman red.: *Finlands svenska litteraturhistoria II. Andra delen: 1900-talet* [Finnish-Swedish literary history. Part 2: The 19th Century Helsingfors]. Stockholm: Svenska litteratursällskapet i Finland & Bokförlaget Atlantis.

Engman, M. 1997: *Norden och flyttningarna under nya tiden*. [Nordic countries and emigration in the Modern era]. København: Foreningerne Norden.

Giddens, A. 1990: *The Consequences of Modernity*. Cambridge: Polity Press.

Giddens, A. 1991: *Modernity and Self-identity. Self and Society in Late Modern Society*. Cambridge: Polity Press.

Hassisen kone 1980: *Muoviruusuja omenapuissa*.[Plastic roses in an apple tree.]

Homén, O. 1909: Detektivlitteraturen. [Detective literature]. *Argus*. 22. 212-214.

Hämäläinen, T. 2000: Kustantaja sopeutuu markkinoihin. [A publisher adapts to the market]. *Helsingin Sanomat*. 23 December.

Immonen, K., K. Mäkinen & T. Onnela 1992: Kaksikymmenluku — oliko sitä? [The 1920s – did it exist?]. In Tapio Onnela ed.: *Vampyyrinainen ja Kenkkuinniemen sauna. Suomalainen kaksikymmenluku ja modernin mahdollisuus*. [The vampire woman and the sauna of Kenkkuinniemi.

The Finnish 1920s and the possibility of modernity]. Helsinki: Finnish Literature Society.

Jaakonsaari, L. 2001: *A-talk*. TV 1. 25.4.2001.

Jokinen, K. 1997: *Suomalaisen lukemisen maisemaihanteet.* [The ideal Finnish landscape of reading]. Jyväskylä: University of Jyväskylä, Centre for Contemporary Cultural Studies.

Karkama, P. 1994: *Kirjallisuus ja nykyaika. Suomalaisen sanataiteen teemoja ja tendenssejä.* [Literature and modernity. Themes and tendencies in Finnish literary art]. Helsinki: Finnish Literature Society.

Knuuttila, S. 1992: Massakulttuurin maihinnousu. Miljardien kulttuuri. [The disembarkation of mass culture: The culture of billions]. In Jukka Tarkka ed.: *Suomi 75. Itsenäisen Suomen historia 4: Kekkosen aika* [Finland 75. The history of independent Finland Vol. 4: The Kekkonen era]. Espoo: Weilin & Göös.

Koivisto, H. 1992: Kaksi Amerikkaa. Suomenkielisten kulttuuripiirien suhde amerikkalaisuuteen 1920-luvulla [Two Americas. The way the Finnish cultural circles related to Americanity in the 1920s]. In Tapio Onnela ed.: *Vampyyrinainen ja Kenkkuinniemen sauna. Suomalainen kaksikymmenluku ja modernin mahdollisuus.* [The vampire woman and the sauna of Kenkkuinniemi. The Finnish 1920s and the possibility of modernity]. Helsinki: Finnish Literature Society.

Lahdenperä, J. 2000: Pesukone mittasi sivistystahtoa [The washing machine measured the will to education]. *Helsingin Sanomat.* 23 December.

Malmio, K. 1999: Älykästä sukkeluutta ja reipasta realismia –1920-luvun ajanvietekirjallisuus. [Intelligent witticism and quick realism — The popular literature of the 1920s]. In Lea Rojola ed.: *Suomen kirjallisuushistoria 2: järkiuskosta vaistojen kapinaan* [Finnish literary history — From a belief in rationality to the revolt of the impulses]. Helsinki: Finnish Literature Society.

Malmio, K. 2000: Finlandssvensk populär litteratur 1900-1940. [Finnish-Swedish popular literature, 1900-1940]. In Clas Zilliacus and Michel Ekman ed.: *Finlands svenska litteraturhistoria 2. Andra delen: 1900-talet.* Helsingfors, Stockholm: Svenska litteratursällskapet i Finland, Bokförlaget Atlantis.

Mustelin, O. 1983: *En förläggare och några av hans författare. Kring Holger Schildts förläggardebut 1913-1917* [A publisher and some of his writers. On the debut of Holger Schildt as publisher]. Helsingfors: Svenska Folkskolans vänner.

Mustelin, O. 1991: *Holger Nohrström, biblioteksman och forskare, publicist och översättare* [Holger Nohrström, a librarian and scholar, publicist and translator]. Helsingfors: Levnadsteckningar 12, Skrifter utgivna av Svenska litteratursällskapet i Finland, nr. 571.

Nohrström, Holger /H.N./ 1916: En sommarbok [A book for the summer]. *Hufvudstadsbladet.* 28.5.1916.

Paasivirta, J. 1988: *Finland and Europe. The Early Years of Independence 1917-1939.* Peter Herring ed. Helsinki: Finnish Historical Society.

Paavolainen, O. 1990 (1929): *Nykyaikaa etsimässä. Esseitä ja pakinoita.* [In search of modern times. Essays and causeries]. Esipuhe Ritva Hapuli, Katriina Mäkinen, Paula Paavolainen, Kari Immonen. Helsinki: Otava.

Ritvos, P. 2000: Yrittäjän arvostus [The appreciation of the entrepreneur]. *Kauppalehti Optio.* 19 October.

Robertson, R. 1990: Mapping the global condition. Globalization as the central concept. *Theory, Culture, and Society.* 7. 15-30.

Rojola, L. 1995: *Varmuuden vuoksi. Modernin representaatio Volter Kilven Saaristosarjassa* [For safety's sake. The representation of modernity in Saaristosarja by Volter Kilpi]. Helsinki: Finnish Literature Society.

Salo, Tiina 1988: *Suomalaisen seikkailukirjallisuuden Amerikka-kuva vuosina 1918-1939* [The picture of America in Finnish adventure literature, 1918-1939]. Unpublished Master's thesis. University of Turku, Department of Cultural History.

Strinati, D. 1995: *An Introduction to Theories of Popular Culture.* London and New York: Routledge.

Sundholm, J. 1999: *Populärt berättande och offentlighet. Sujett, excess, den sociala detektiven och den privata familjen* [Popular narration and the public. *Sjuzet,* excess, the social detective and the private family]. Åbo: Åbo Akademis förlag.

Sundholm, J. 2000. Den klassiske detektivromanen [The classic detective novel]. *Finlands svenska litteraturhistoria. Andra delen: 1900-talet.* Helsingfors, Stockholm: Svenska litteratursällskapet i Finland, Bokförlaget Atlantis.

Söderhjelm, H. /H.S./ 1910: De unga [The youth]. *Argus.* 17. 152-155.

Söderhjelm, H. 1916. I bokhandeln [In the bookshop]. *Finsk Tidskrift.* Augusti 1916:II. 151-152.

Tarkka, P. 1980: *Otavan historia. Toinen osa: 1918-1940.* [The history of the Otava publishing company. Part 2: 1918-1940]. Helsinki: Otava.

Vienonen, M. 2001: Silikoni & säilöntäaine [Silicon and preservatives]. *Ilta-Sanomat.* 16 February.

Virtanen, K. 1988: *Atlantin yhteys. Tutkimus amerikkalaisesta kulttuurista, sen suhteesta ja välittymisestä Eurooppaan vuosina 1776-1917* [The Atlantic connection. A study of American culture in Europe in 1776-1917]. Helsinki: Finnish Historical Society.

Wendelius, L. 1982: *Bilden av Amerika i svensk prosafiktion 1890-1914* [The representation of America in Swedish prose 1890-1914]. Uppsala: University of Uppsala, Department of Literary Studies.

Wikström, Lennart/Henning Söderhjelm 1916: *Guldgruvan. Detektiv- och äventyrsroman* [The Goldmine. A detective and adventure novel]. Helsingfors.

18

"What Do You Think of Indian Feminism?": The Problematics of Indian Feminisms[1]

JOEL KUORTTI

When one considers feminism in the Indian context, several issues can be brought to the fore. In this article, I will first look briefly at the traditions and history of feminine ideals and activism. From these I move on to look at the work of one outspoken critic of feminism, Madhu Kishwar. After that, I outline the views on feminism held by seven Indian English women writers, and, finally, I present a discussion of the importance of ideological critique.

Background

Among the issues related to the questions about feminism in India there are the traditions concerning women and the movements that have aimed at changing women's status throughout history. In the beginning, figuratively, there is the goddess in her multiple personifications.

In the Vedas, we find thirty-three gods, while the theophanies of the goddesses such as Usas, Sarasvati and Aditi are left undeveloped (Khanna 2000: 82). The Earth Goddess as the principle of life emerges in the Atharva Veda as a universal mother goddess. This element of motherhood will attach itself permanently in the imagery of the goddess.

Further on in the literary tradition several goddesses emerge and the all-pervasive image of the goddess is strengthened. The Upanishads, the Mahabharata and other hymns describe Uma, Aniruddha, Durga, Kali, and other goddesses. The all-pervasiveness gets its most common definition in the idea of *Shakti*. Shakti, derived from Sanskrit "shak" (power, energy, ability), is the abstract principle that "denotes a divinity in female form or the active power of a male deity personified as his wife or a consort" (Khanna 2000: 85). In Shakti the multiplicity of the proliferating forms of the goddess are unified into "an indivisible Feminine principle" (Khanna 2000: 86).

Later on, the idea of the mother goddess develops towards the national image of Bharat Mata, or "Mother India", later re-utilised for nationalist purposes. In the religious and nationalist political revival of the mid-nineteenth century, writers, thinkers, artists, and politicians increasingly used Bharat Mata in their articulation. Gayatri Sinha describes the force of the image as follows:

> For ordinary women as those participating in the 1930s salt *satyagraha,* Bharat Mata became a source of both emulation and liberation. In her solitary state outside the codes of conduct of goddess as consort, and wedded to the ideal of freedom, Bharat Mata must have been in the vanguard of an idealized feminine modernity (Sinha 2000: 119).

In the more recent political scene, Bharat Mata imagery has been appropriated especially by Indira Gandhi ("India is Indira, Indira is India": B.K. Borooah, quoted in Sinha 2000: 61). Other women politicians have subsequently been able to use the dynamics of image-making which Indira Gandhi established, among them Jayalalitha, Sonia Gandhi, and Mayavati (Sinha 2000: 121). On the contemporary popular level, cinema and television have proved to be productive in recreating and intensifying the goddess imagery. It is thus clear that there are strong traditional female ideals in India. These are a living part of the culture, especially among the rural majority living in villages and small towns. Another perhaps even more portentous dimension related to the background of feminism in the present context of women's issues in India is activism.

In her study of the history of women's movements, *The History of Doing. An Illustrated Account of Movements for Women's Rights and Feminism in India, 1800-1990* (Kumar 1998), Radha Kumar outlines major trends within women's activism from the nineteenth century to the 1990s. To sum up briefly, women participated in male-dominated movements (e.g. nationalist, Tebhaga and Telangana movements but they also organised their own campaigns: "the communist-led food campaigns of the nineteen-forties, Chipko, the anti-alcohol and anti-price-rise movements of the nineteen-seventies" (Kumar 1998: 3). For the present purposes, we need only to recall that there are numerous grass-root-level organisations working for the improvement of women's working conditions and their health, educational, economic, family, and social status.

Continuing from this brief traditional/historical review of the background, the question in this article is: "What do you think of Indian feminism?" What I would like to consider in this essay, are the several ways in which activists, thinkers, writers, and theorists have tried to tackle the issues of feminism in India. Underlying my excursion is my research on Indian women writers and the question: how do women see the changing status of Indian women? Quite naturally, feminism as one of the most important frameworks with regard to such changes in women's issues needs to be discussed. But since the 1980s, many women's rights movements have been accused of being "westernized, upper-class and urban, and therefore ignorant of, and unsympathetic to, traditional 'Indian' society" (Kumar 1998: 159). Lila Abu-Lughod (1998: 25), too, in the Middle Eastern context, warns against uncritical acceptance of "the terms of the upper-middle- and middle-class women involved in most feminist projects" as one gets "caught up...in nonsensical notions like 'retraditionalization'". The two dimensions of ideological spaces for women outlined above — the traditional and the activist — seem to collide when one begins to talk about feminism.

A Critic of Feminism: Madhu Kishwar

In 1999 Madhu Kishwar, the editor of *Manushi: A Journal about Women and Society*, published a collection of essays from *Manushi*, titled *Off the Beaten Track. Rethinking Gender Justice for Indian Women* (Kishwar 1999). In the book Kishwar emphatically declares her horror of "isms" and explains, for example, why she is not a feminist. The most relevant article in this regard, "A Horror of 'Isms': Why I Do Not Call Myself a Feminist", was originally published in 1990 but in the version included in the book it is revised and updated. The work for women's justice, equality and freedom that Kishwar has done for more than two decades in *Manushi* since 1978 has had the result, as one critic has commented, that "her popular image has always been that of a firebrand feminist" (Mukerji 2000). Kishwar herself is very adamant on this score. From the beginning, she wanted that *Manushi* should *not* be called a feminist journal and she says that she has hardly ever used the word (Kishwar 1990: 273).

There is thus a tug-of-war between her being seen as a feminist and her own refusal to be called one. One result of this has been that not infrequently feminists have reproached her for betraying important issues. But what in fact are Kishwar's reservations concerning feminism? How does someone who was once called the high priestess of Indian feminism and the Germaine Greer or the Kate Millet of India justify her criticism of feminism? To begin with, in her article Kishwar criticises established ideologies or "isms" in general for not being able to maintain their idealistic agendas. What is done in the name of a given "ism" is repeatedly an adulteration of the original ideal. In her opinion, such ideologies as Marxism, Leninism and Maoism are time- and culture-specific and they do tend to get ossified. Movements with a less personified make-up such as feminism, humanism and anarchism share the aspect of culture-specificity and they are also prone to institutionalisation. With feminism, Kishwar decries "the intellectual regimentation demanded in the name of solidarity with the women's movement" (1990: 268).

Linked to this general distrust in ideologies is Kishwar's emphasis on individual choice. She criticises the individualistic foundation of feminism because it has resulted, in the West, in the atomisation of society. However, she readily grants individual women the right to determine how they live their lives. In an interview she has said: "My business is not to tell women what is good for them" (Severn 1995). Furthermore, Kishwar in her "inherent mistrust of authoritarian structures" (Kishwar 1990: 282) denounces all forms of statist approaches to social reform. The way in which the feminists have tried to get laws passed and implemented for example on pornography is for her not acceptable since it arms, as she says, the "very corrupt and criminalized state machinery with even more repressive powers" (Kishwar 1990: 274). One recent issue in which Kishwar and *Manushi* have been vocal against legislative methods and for moral responsibility concerns the constitutional amendment, the Women Reservation Bill that has been debated in the parliament, Lok Sabha, since it was introduced in December 1999. In the January-February 2000 issue of *Manushi* there was an alternative to the Bill in which the topic is discussed from the moral rather than juridical point of view (Narayan et al. 2000: 5-13).

Kishwar's reservations are not, however, only on the level of institutional criticism. Her even more stringent critique concerns Western feminism but the critique Kishwar offers is not against it as such: "in the western context", she says, "the word 'feminism' evokes many positive associations" (Kishwar 1990: 276). Neither is she vocal in accusing "First World" feminists of intervening in Indian affairs. Her criticism is aimed at the way in which Western feminism has been adopted in India. For example, Debashish Mukerji comments that "[i]nstead of the usual targets of feminists, the 'patriarchal society', Kishwar's ire seems to be directed at the West, and Indian feminists who have been overly influenced by it" (Mukerji 2000). This is true indeed. Kishwar understands feminism first of all as a very culture-specific phenomenon that emerged in the West and benefited the societies there in making them more equal and democratic. But she does not think that the objectives of feminism are universal. In her opinion, Indian traditions such as the goddess worship and feminine *shakti* provide Indian society with a far more suitable blueprint for voicing women's issues (Kishwar 1990: 276).

In Kishwar's perception, Indian feminism is metropolitan, elitist, statist, patronising and dependent on funding from international agencies. The missionary zeal of such feminists to engage in development projects has not improved the status of women. So, for example, in her critique of capitalism within development, Maria Mies comments that "[i]ntegrating women into development [has] only increased women's work load" (Mies 1994: 115). Similarly Kishwar sees that not only has feminism been ineffective in accomplishing changes but it has in fact witnessed a decline in the status of women, as the statistics on rape, domestic violence and so on clearly showed, for example, in Indian media reports around International Women's Day in 2000. Kishwar's conclusion is that one should not, in consequence, force foreign concepts into practices where they are not applicable.

Together with her general mistrust of feminism's potential for effecting change, Kishwar thinks the Indian "feminist establishment" uses "their pro-poor rhetoric" to advance their own ends (Kishwar 1990: 268 and 287). For her, the popularity of the so-called Third World feminism is a sign of this. She laments bitterly:

> These days, to declare oneself a third world feminist is to open the gates of many career opportunities which otherwise would not come your way — research grants, fellowships, teaching assignments, invitations to international conferences, project funds, and so on. You are at once admitted as a member of the intellectual elite of the world. In the last decade, with the various international funding agencies promoting feminism in third world countries, to be identified as a third world feminist has become a very lucrative proposition indeed (Kishwar 1995: 182).

In the academic environment we inhabit today, these issues cannot be passed over lightly. This problematic is in fact something that has been embedded in the research project of which this article is a part and which concerns Indian English women's writing. It has, indeed, been funded by the *Development* Studies Subdivision of the Finnish Academy. In the following I will draw attention to some aspects that I have encountered when interviewing writers for my research in India.

Women Writers and Feminism

Several features frame Indian English women's writing. There is, first of all, the linguistic anomaly: although English is a prestigious link language of administration and higher education, only a small minority speaks it (less than three per cent of the population). As English is primarily the language of the educated urban middle and upper-class elites, literature written in English in India is both marginalised and, at the same time, emphasised. One fact attesting to this is the international fame of many Indian authors such as Jhumpa Lahiri, Arundhati Roy, Salman Rushdie, and Amitav Ghosh.

Women writing in English in India (and in the Indian diaspora) do not form a coherent group. They come from various cultural (Hindu, Muslim, Sikh, others), linguistic (Hindi/Urdu, Tamil, Kannada, others), and geographical (urban and rural, India and abroad) backgrounds. The wholesale identification of women writers as feminists does not work either. Thus, Mridula Garg, a Hindi writer, claims the following:

> Can the novels written by women in India really be called feminist, or are they merely novels written by writers who happen to be women? If by feminist writing we mean texts that project a unique world-view different from the historically accepted world-view of men, then most writing by women in India cannot be called feminist. It is definitely a step in the direction of feminist writing inasmuch as it looks at woman as a unique class (Garg 1991: 418).

In order to probe into this writing and its variety, it was the aim in my research to locate writers from a variety of backgrounds and to let them voice their opinions on their work and its relevance on women's issues. I also wanted writers with different careers, so there are writers with only one volume as well as those more established. In addition, they are writing both prose and/or poetry.

All the seven writers, five novelists and two poets, whom I interviewed expressed reservations as to either the use of the word feminism in the context of their writings or, in more general terms, feminist discourse. There are a couple of issues to consider here. The first issue relevant to the topic came up in discussion with Shashi Deshpande. Deshpande is one of the leading women writers in English in India, although her career has been building up only slowly, despite her numerous publications.

While artistically differentiating from feminism, Deshpande understands feminism in India as activism rather than theory. She suggests: "It's not theory. It's not Simone de Beauvoir;

it's not Germaine Greer, or anything. Some people will read these, but what changes is activism" (Deshpande 2001). Where Kishwar criticises Indian feminism for both relying on (Western) theories and adopting statist strategies, Deshpande acknowledges the achievements in legislation. Although she does not view the changes in society too optimistically in general, there seems to be some hope. As she says: "what has really changed is the awareness that these things have to be taken into account" (Deshpande 2001). Through this awareness the changes become possibilities rather than ideals.

She also talks about the second issue: the difficulties involved in getting published abroad. An extremely small proportion of Indian women writers is known outside their language communities, be the communities larger or smaller. This is, of course, a more universal problem facing marginal language groups all over the world, but this is true even of Indian English writers, although they travel more easily across geographical distances. Wanting to eschew the title of a feminist writer, Deshpande still knew that, whether it was Finland, the United Kingdom or the USA, "only a feminist publisher would publish" her (Deshpande 2001). Her writing began from the realisation of "what it was to be a woman in this country", but she does not want to be labelled a feminist (Deshpande 2001). In many of her novels, although to Deshpande's dismay they are almost invariably in academic analyses viewed from a feminist perspective, the themes are multilayered, even more so in her later novels. For example, in *A Matter of Time* the narrator is a man named Gopal.

Similar regrets are expressed by the novelist Shama Futehally, whose novel *Tara Lane* was understood by one critic as a feminist novel (Dimri 1998). Futehally says that she "wouldn't call it feminist at all" (Futehally 2003). While the novel attests to an awareness of certain limitations within a woman's life, it is an observer's awareness. Futehally concludes her comment by clearing her story of all feminist leanings: "I would say it's a story, a human story. The minute you say feminist or socialist or anything, you get into trouble" (Futehally 2003). In such a situation, women writers have to juggle between different pressures, as Ranjana Harish (2000: 107) comments: "in the absence of any well-defined theory of tradition of women's writing in male culture, women writers often invent strategies to cope with two opposite pulls — their creative urge [...] and their need for acceptance in a patriarchal set-up".

The existing circumstances in the literary establishment have very much determined, defined, and confined women writers. One result has been writing that mainly follows the traditional realist mode of prose. Another one, as Jasbir Jain points out, is competition between women for male attention. In order not to be confined within this vicious circle, Jain (1991: 38) reckons, "women need to look at themselves not as exceptions to the feminine norm but as the norm itself".

For her part, Deshpande laments that the needs for change are not equally understood between men and women. She says: "Women are moving, there's much more awareness among women [...]. But I think men are not moving fast enough" (Deshpande 2001). In contrast, the poet Lakshmi Kannan who thinks it is vital to write also about men, whatever the feminist agenda might say, comments that "men are changing, and they have to be registered. Recorded. Created artistically in our work. That is my belief. There are a few of us doing that. Despite what feminists, some of these strident feminists who have this one way of understanding, [say]" (Kannan 2003).

With the importance of writing about men, here Kannan refers to that kind of regimentation among feminists, which Kishwar also took up above. This third kind of issue is a common objection that the writers whom I interviewed felt, a reluctance to yield to established feminist representations.

In similar vein, Githa Hariharan talks about her novel *The Thousand Faces of the Night* (Hariharan 1992). At the end of the novel, the story of the rebellious Devi and her mother Sita does not reach a neat conclusion (Hariharan 1992: 139). Hariharan comments on this: "Some feminist readers asked me for instance, 'Where is the feminist revolution?' And my answer of course was that I was not trying to make any sort of a blueprint for action" (Hariharan 2001). Shama Futehally affirms this sentiment from her own perspective: "if that's what you want well why have literature, write a pamphlet" (Futehally 2003).

It is not only in their writing that writers sense an alienation from certain feminist ideas. For example, the novelist Anuradha Marwah-Roy tells about having come up against other kinds of problems. With regard to the divorce process she is going through, she has found it difficult to argue why she does not want to give up her right to motherhood. When her novels *The Higher Education of Geetika Mehendiratta* (1993) and *Idol Love* (1999) could be seen as statements on the rights of women, her stance, then, on the custody of her children bears witness to a clash between Indian tradition and feminism. She says: "Some activists feel that insistence on custody only hinders divorcing women. It's so exhausting to convey to them that for me motherhood is a privilege, not a responsibility" (Marwah-Roy: forthcoming).

Shama Futehally also comments on this breach between tradition and feminism, on one hand, and between oneself and feminism, on the other:

> Sometimes one kind, a wrong kind of feminism makes you a little nervous about admitting...[t]hat the birth of a child, or...marriage [is] extremely important.... There is a certain tendency within feminist thinking that makes you nervous about admitting that. You think it might be misunderstood. That somehow you are putting yourself in a subordinate position but I'm not doing anything of the sort, I'm just acknowledging something which is humanly very, very important to me (Futehally 2003).

What these examples show perhaps most clearly is that the writers are both conscious of the call to be politically correct and reluctant to forego their personal views either in their writing or in their views. This reluctance applies to poetry as well as to fiction. The poet Sujatha Mathai asserts that in writing a poem, the text is primary. A political programme, she says, "can never be poetry. Because if it comes so consciously, it can never become a poem.... I mean, if I was consciously thinking of a text it obviously wouldn't become a poem. It would become an essay" (Mathai: forthcoming).

One last aspect to be drawn from the interviews is expressed by Kannan, who argues, in much the same way as

Kishwar, that feminism has not succeeded in India. There has even been a deterioration and backlash in the status of women. Kannan describes Indian feminism as "strident, shrew feminism that in *my* view is very stereotypical. Feminism that's just counterproductive — it's a whole lot of noise" (Kannan 2003). The hope for change for her is mixed with huge obstacles. She understands that reality "*is* changing. For the better. Though there are the peripheries, the pockets. Rural India has not changed" (Kannan 2003). Shashi Deshpande, too, senses stagnation within the process of change: "For most of the women, especially the women in the villages, life has not changed at all" (Deshpande 2001).

The issue here has been the reservations some Indian authors have expressed about the applicability of feminism in the Indian context. It is not necessary to accept these at face value but it is, nevertheless, essential to be aware of these debates. I experienced this when in the course of the interviews when, while I was referring to the Indian feminist critique of the Indian society and women's issues, one of the interviewees said to me: "But you wouldn't know, Joel. You wouldn't know" (Singh: forthcoming).

Critique of Ideology

Criticism of development, feminism, postcolonial studies and ideologies in general is a worthwhile effort when we are shuttling between unequally equipped cultural spaces. In my opinion, such criticism is as important as the shuttling itself. The universalist feminist agenda has been eroded and, as Francoise Lionnet (1997: 1) puts it, there is a call for "*comparative* feminist criticism". This stems to a large extent, she claims, from "the alienated status of the feminist postcolonial writer" (ibid.: 27). I would agree and argue that this may partly be seen from the discussions of Indian writers presented above.

This discussion by no means covers the whole field. Indian, not to say "postcolonial feminism", is a wide issue. The term postcolonial feminism — or alternatively, "third world feminism" — is both widely used and heavily criticised (e.g. Harding and Narayan 1998; Jain 2000; John 1996; McClintock, Mufti and Shohat 1997; Minh-ha 1989; Mohanty and Alexander 1997; Narayan 1997; Rajan 1993; Suleri 1992). In a situation where even a traditional critic may attest that, unlike in the Western countries, "[i]n the third world countries, feminism has a very different set of concerns" (Srivastava 1996: 13), it is of importance to take issue with the ways feminist critique is applied in the postcolonial situation.

Here, instead of a conclusion, I would like briefly to introduce a handful of possible approaches. To begin with, a booklet has been produced by an important Indian women's press, Kali for Women. The booklet, *Some Questions on Feminism and Its Relevance in South Asia* (Bhasin and Said Khan 1999) was originally published in 1986. In this booklet, Kamla Bhasin and Nighat Said Khan approach the issue in a question-answer format covering a whole variety of themes. From my point of view it is also a fairly convincing book. Bhasin and Kali have also recently published another study booklet, *Understanding Gender* (Bhasin 2000). Together with the earlier one, it provides a challenging contrast with Kishwar's position, both of which are deeply rooted in the everyday lives of Indian women. The Kali booklets provide straightforward arguments as to why feminism is indeed relevant in India and in South Asia in general.

In her recent article on postcoloniality and Third World feminists, Ulla Vuorela recognises the discourse on the problematic connection between the issues of development, feminism and cultural criticism. She refers, for example, to such well-known critics as Trinh T. Minh-ha, Gayatri Spivak and Chandra Talpade-Mohanty, who in the 1980s started up a debate on postcolonial feminism (Vuorela 1999: 18-9, 27). There are quite a few of these critics now, and in the present context I would like to draw attention only to two more recent and highly topical publications. First, there is Chilla Bulbeck's *Re-Orienting Western Feminisms. Women's Diversity in a Postcolonial World* (1998). She challenges the hegemony of Western, that is, in the present case, Anglophone feminism, and tries to provide a more comprehensive and diverse understanding of feminism. Another book, Irene Gedalof's *Against Purity. Rethinking Identity with Indian and Western Feminisms* (1999), is similar in its aim to delineate the variety within feminist discourse.

What do you think of Indian feminism? As far as the actual changes in women's issues in Indian society are concerned, the question is not of importance. Only when we begin to consider issues such as solidarity and identification do we need to think about what feminism actually means, and what in particular it means in the context of India. Some approaches have been developed around Gayatri Spivak's (1993: 3) idea of "strategic essentialism", of the kind Gita Rajan outlines in her analysis of Suniti Namjoshi's "double vision" as an Indo-British border intellectual (G. Rajan 1997: 90). There are, however, no easy solutions between the universalist and the localist, the individualist and the communalist, or the constructivist and the essentialist approaches. Indian feminism could be anyone of these.

We could even try to do without feminism altogether, or replace it with some other term, such as the one introduced in the context of African and Afro-American women by Alice Walker: "womanism" (Walker 1984). Whatever our practical or ideological answer might be in the end, I applaud all the approaches as they show how differently things can be thought about. To conclude, I should like to quote Francoise Lionnet (1997: 188), who expresses a similar wish: "I think the only way out of that fundamentalist feminist impasse is, and will continue to be, through the awareness of the multicultural, multiracial dimensions of various strands of feminism inside and outside the academy."

NOTE

1. This article is based on papers given at two seminars, "Cultural Identity and Its Glocal Manifestations" at the University of Joensuu, 14-16 September 2000, and the "Gender, Development and Post-Colonial Theory" seminar at the University of Helsinki, 25-29 September 2000. Thanks are due to Erkki Sevänen, Jopi Nyman and John A. Stotesbury in Joensuu and to Ulla Vuorela, Mari Korpela and Anu Hirsiaho in Helsinki. I would like to extend special thanks to Durre Ahmed, Fawzia Mustafa, Mahmuda Islam and Raisa Simola for discussing the matters and for their valuable comments.

REFERENCES

Abu-Lughod, Lila 1998: Introduction: Feminist Longings and Postcolonial Conditions. In Lila Abu-Lughod ed.: *Remaking Women. Feminism and Modernity in the Middle East.* Princeton: Princeton University Press.

Bhasin, Kamla 2000: *Understanding Gender.* New Delhi: Kali for Women.

Bhasin, Kamla and Nighat Said Khan 1999 (1986): *Some Questions on Feminism and Its Relevance in South Asia.* New Delhi: Kali for Women. 2nd ed. revised by Kamla Bhasin.

Bulbeck, Chilla 1998: *Re-Orienting Western Feminisms. Women's Diversity in a Postcolonial World.* Cambridge: Cambridge University Press.

Deshpande, Shashi 2001: Women Are Moving: Years of Silence Came to an End. Interview with Joel Kuortti. *Kunapipi* 23:2. 145-166. Reprinted in Kuortti 2003: 26-56.

Dimri, Jaiwanti 1998: Voicing Women's Experiences in *Tara Lane.* In Naresh K. Jain ed.: *Women in Indo-Anglian Fiction. Tradition and Modernity.* New Delhi: Manohar.

Futehally, Shama 2003: Women Will Find Ways of Breaking Out. Interview with Joel Kuortti. In Joel Kuortti: *Tense Past, Tense Present. Women Writing in English.* Kolkata: Stree. 66-94.

Garg, Mridula 1991: Metaphors of Womanhood in Indian Literature. *Alternatives.* 16:4. 407-424.

Gedalof, Irene 1999: *Against Purity. Rethinking Identity with Indian and Western Feminisms.* London and New York: Routledge.

Hariharan, Githa 1992: *The Thousand Faces of the Night.* New Delhi: Penguin.

Hariharan, Githa 2003: The Double Burden: The Continual Contesting of Tradition and Modernity. Interview with Joel Kuortti. *Journal of Commonwealth Literature.* 36:1. 7-26. Reprinted in Kuortti 2003: 101-125.

Harish, Ranjana 2000: Male Culture, Female Strategies. In Mohan Ramanan and P. Sailaja ed.: *English and the Indian Short Story. Essays in Criticism.* Hyderabad: Orient Longman.

Harding, Sandra and Uma Narayan ed. 1998: *Border Crossings. Multicultural and Postcolonial Feminist Challenges to Philosophy 2.* Bloomington: Indiana University Press.

Jain, Jasbir 1991: The Feminist Perspective: the Indian Situation and Its Literary Manifestations. In Jasbir Jain: *Problems of Postcolonial Literatures and Other Essays.* Jaipur: Printwell.

Jain, Jasbir 2000: Positioning the 'Post' in Post-Feminism: Reworking of Strategies. *Critical Practice.* 7:2 (June). 32-47.

John, Mary E. 1996: *Discrepant Dislocations. Feminism, Theory, and Postcolonial Histories.* Berkeley: University of California Press.

Kannan, Lakshmi 2003: I Could Never Stop Writing Poems. Interview with Joel Kuortti. In Joel Kuortti: *Tense Past, Tense Present. Women Writing in English.* Kolkata: Stree. 180-191.

Khanna, Madhu 2000: The Idea of Shakti. In Gayatri Sinha ed.: *Woman/ Goddess. An Exhibition of Photographs.* New Delhi: Multiple Action Research Group.

Kishwar, Madhu 1990: A Horror of 'Isms': Why I Do Not Call Myself a Feminist. *Manushi.* 61. Reprinted in Kishwar 1999: 268-290.

Kishwar, Madhu 1995: When India 'Missed' the Universe. *Manushi.* 88. Reprinted in Kishwar 1999: 173-191. Also available at http://www.umiacs.umd.edu/users/sawweb/sawnet/beauty.html (7 May, 2003) and http://www.freespeech.org/manushi/beauty/beauty.html (7 May, 2003).

Kishwar, Madhu 1999: *Off the Beaten Track. Rethinking Gender Justice for Indian Women.* New Delhi: Oxford University Press.

Kumar, Radha 1998 (1993): *The History of Doing. An Illustrated Account of Movements for Women's Rights and Feminism in India, 1800-1990.* New Delhi: Kali for Women.

Kuortti, Joel 2003: *Tense Past, Tense Present. Women Writing in English.* Kolkata: Stree.

Lionnet, Francoise 1997: *Postcolonial Representations. Women, Literature, Identity.* New York: Cornell University Press.

Marwah-Roy, Anuradha 1993: *The Higher Education of Geetika Mehendiratta.* New Delhi: Disha.

Marwah-Roy, Anuradha 1999: *Idol Love.* New Delhi: Ravi Dayal.

Marwah-Roy, Anuradha 2003: Stories Can Never Be Told to the End Completely. Interview with Joel Kuortti. In Joel Kuortti: *Tense Past, Tense Present. Women Writing in English.* Kolkata: Stree. 135-148.

Mathai, Sujatha 2003: Because of the Unbearable Pain. Interview with Joel Kuortti. In Joel Kuortti: *Tense Past, Tense Present. Women Writing in English.* Kolkata: Stree. 199-218.

McClintock, Anne, Aamir Mufti and Ella Shohat ed. 1997: *Dangerous Liaisons. Gender, Nation, and Postcolonial Perspectives.* Minneapolis: University of Minnesota.

Mies, Maria 1994: 'Gender' and Global Capitalism. In Leslie Sklair ed.: *Capitalism and Development.* London and New York: Routledge.

Mohanty, Chandra Talpade and M. Jacqui Alexander ed. 1997: *Feminist Genealogies, Colonial Legacies, Democratic Futures.* London and New York: Routledge.

Mukerji, Debashish 2000: Volte-face, What? Books: Madhu Kishwar, *Off the Beaten Track. The Week.* 6 February. Available at http://www.the-week.com/20feb06/life1.htm#1 (7 May, 2003).

Narayan, Jayaprakash, Dhirubhai Sheth, Yogendra Yadav and Madhu Kishwar 2000: Enhancing Women's Representation in Legislatures: an Alternative to the Government Bill for Women's Reservation. *Manushi.* 116. 5-13.

Narayan, Uma 1997: *Dis/locating Cultures/Identities, Traditions, and Third World Feminism.* New York: Routledge.

Rajan, Gita 1997: (Con)figuring Identity: Cultural Space of the Indo-British Border Intellectual. In Gisela Brinker-Gabler and Sidonie Smith ed.:

Writing New Identities. Gender, Nation, and Immigration in Contemporary Europe. Minneapolis: University of Minnesota Press.

Rajan, Rajeswari Sunder 1993: *Real and Imagined Women. Gender, Culture and Postcolonialism.* London and New York: Routledge.

Severn, Jennifer 1995: Words with Madhu Kishwar, Indian activist, writer and publisher. Available at http://www.freespeech.org/manushi/mk-intvu/mk-intvu.html (7 May, 2003).

Singh, Mina 2003: The Past is This Wonderful Creation. Interview with Joel Kuortti. In Joel Kuortti: *Tense Past, Tense Present. Women Writing in English.* Kolkata: Stree. 154-171.

Sinha, Gayatri 2000: Woman/Goddess. In Gayatri Sinha 2000 ed.: *Woman/Goddess. An Exhibition of Photographs.* New Delhi: Multiple Action Research Group.

Sinha, Gayatri ed. 2000: *Woman/Goddess. An Exhibition of Photographs.* New Delhi: Multiple Action Research Group.

Spivak, Gayatri Chakravorty 1993: In a Word: Interview. In Gayatri Chakravorty Spivak: *Outside in the Teaching Machine.* New York: Routledge.

Srivastava, Sharad 1996: Feminism & Feminist Movements. In Sharad Srivastava: *The New Woman in Indian English Fiction.* New Delhi: Creative.

Suleri, Sara 1992: Woman Skin Deep: Feminism and the Postcolonial Condition. *Critical Inquiry.* Summer. 756-769.

Trinh T. Minh-ha 1989: *Woman, Native, Other. Writing Postcoloniality and Feminism.* Bloomington: Indiana University Press.

Vuorela, Ulla 1999: Postkoloniaali ja kolmannen maailman feministit [The postcolonial and the third world feminists]. In Jaana Airaksinen & Tuula Ripatti ed.: *Rotunaisia ja feministejä. nais- ja kehitystutkimuksen risteyskohtia* [Women of race and feminists. Crossroads of women's studies and development studies]. Tampere: Vastapaino.

Walker, Alice 1984: *In Search of Our Mothers' Gardens.* San Diego: Harcourt Brace Jovanovich.

Wisker, Gina 2000: Writing by Women from the Indian Sub-Continent. In Gina Wisker: *Post-Colonial and African American Women's Writing. A Critical Introduction.* Houndmills and London: Macmillan.

19

Imagining Transnationalism in Bharati Mukherjee's *Leave It to Me*

JOPI NYMAN

Introduction

Within the globalised world of transnationalisms, post-colonialisms and mobile postmodern identities a particular genre of migrant literature has emerged. Although migrancy and exile have always been central in literary production in general and modernism in particular, as the examples of Joseph Conrad, James Joyce, Thomas Mann, Richard Wright and Bessie Head show, more recent postcolonial writing by authors such as Salman Rushdie, Caryl Phillips and Emine Sevgi Özdamar, seeking to cross cultural, linguistic and national boundaries, has called into question our fixed understandings of the issues of home, identity and nation. As a sign of this development, critics have begun to pay attention to the cultural effects of increased migrancy, including the emergence of diasporas, hybridised cultures and the visibility of cultural difference in formerly culturally homogeneous sites. According to Stuart Hall (2000: 215), globalisation may aim at homogenisation "but it cannot control or saturate everything within its orbit" and thus produces "unintended effects", that is, "subaltern formations and emergent tendencies", diverse and hybrid cultural forms. In addition to the migrant writing under consideration in this essay, such forms range from British Asian cinema (Roscoe 2000) and the emergence of Francophone rap (Huq 2000) to the Latino / a reinvention of Los Angeles urban space (Davis 2000). Though generated by globalisation, these forms may, at least occasionally, function as sites of resistance and critique, "constructing a third space beyond existing political, social and cultural binaries" (Bromley 2000: 1).

One author particularly relevant to these hybrid imaginings is the contemporary Indian/Canadian/American novelist and short story writer Bharati Mukherjee (b. 1940), whose fictions rewrite the traditional migrant's story, imagining new spaces. Born in India, and with degrees from various Indian and North American universities, since the 1970s Mukherjee has written a number of critically acclaimed novels and short stories exploring the problem of constructing (im)migrant subjectivity in various fictional settings, ranging from seventeenth-century India to contemporary cosmopolitan circles. A key figure in contemporary South Asian American writing, though controversial as a result of her fascination with America, in her texts Mukherjee often redefines the process of (im)migration as a translation and as a new opportunity for the individual, a view articulated by the protagonist of her novel *Jasmine*: "Nothing was rooted anymore. Everything was in motion" (1989: 152). Summing up the transformative aspects of Mukherjee's narratives, Jennifer Drake argues that in them

> people and nations scatter and gather. Assimilation is cultural looting, cultural exchange, or a wilful and at times costly negotiation: an eye for an eye, a self for a self. People mix with gods and goddesses, or become gods and goddesses, reincarnating, translating narratives of coherence. Translated men and women make nations metaphorical, imagining homes in the cracks between nostalgia and frontier dreams. Violence roams, Kali's bloody tongue. *Mayflower* claims it can't save anyone; we're all immigrants, strangers in a strange land (1999: 60).

While several critics have found Mukherjee's project worthy and liberating in its appraisal of multiplicity (Drake 1999: 82) and its ability to rupture the homogenising process of globalisation (Bromley 2000: 20-26), some aspects of her writing have also proved problematic to the scholarly community because of her apparently unproblematic appraisal of migrant identity as a site of agency and glorification of the American self-constructed in her texts (see Knippling 1993; Pfeil 1994).

Towards Transnational Identities

In this essay I will problematise such simple readings of the "emotional paralysis of exile" (Nelson 1993: x) by reading the presence of transnationalism into Mukherjee's most recent novel *Leave It to Me* (1997) in the context of recent postcolonial theorisations of home and migrancy. I will argue that this novel, a prime example of hybridity in its themes and narrative strategies, maintains the idea of home, the signifier of individual and national identity, yet rewrites it in a more flexible manner, as is the case in more traditional immigration narratives. In so doing, I am aligning myself with scholars finding more opportunities than problems in her writing. The constant reconstruction of identity is shown in the novel's main character Devi Dee, "originally" Debby DiMartino, the child of an American hippie mother (Clear Water Iris-Daughter alias Jess DuPree) and her Indo-European serial killer guru, who is adopted as a baby by an Italian American family from an Indian orphanage run by Catholic nuns. Seeking knowledge of her past and of her parents' story, that is, her identity, Debby/Devi, a 23-year-old SUNY-Albany graduate, takes different lovers, explores different worlds and finds herself amidst the San Francisco entertainment industry. It is there that she locates, and loses, her parents, when a massive earthquake destroys the city. Thus, my reading of the novel seeks to show how Mukherjee decentres the fixed identities of modernity and replaces them with an idea of transformation as home.

Contemporary developments and cultures of diaspora redefining our understanding of home and identity are directly related to the emergence and strategies of transnational, neocolonial capitalism. Transnational corporations, in the view of Masao Miyoshi (1993: 736), are no longer tied to any home nation: they are "adrift and mobile, ready to settle anywhere and exploit any state including its own, as long as the affiliation serves its own interest". Miyoshi projects a vision of a world in which transnational corporations operate globally, unattached, independent of the nation-state. For Miyoshi (1993: 741-747), transnationalism is mainly negative, replacing national rootedness with corporate identity, increasing thus homogeneity and devaluing the local.

However, as the view of Stuart Hall quoted in the introduction of this paper shows, the processes of globalisation are not that simple: not all locals become passive CNN watchers. This is also the view of Arjun Appadurai (1990: 295), who calls for separation between the terms "Americanisation" and "homogenisation": "at least as rapidly as forces from various metropolises are brought into new societies they tend to become indigenized in one or other way: this is true of music and housing styles as much as it is true of science and terrorism, spectacles and constitutions". While aware of the negative effects of globalisation, its "riots" and "refugee-flows", Appadurai also pays attention to its brighter sides, including, for example, "the expansion of many individual horizons of hope and fantasy" and "the growth of a wide range of progressive, transnational alliances" (Appadurai 1990: 308). Thus, globalisation and increased networking allow for the movement of ideas and the formation of "transnational linkages", as the feminist critics Inderpal Grewal and Caren Kaplan (1994: 13) call them in the introduction to their collection of essays. It is their view that transnational feminist practices, interethnic coalitions, alliances and networks crossing and transcending national and ethnic lines reconstruct sites where home can be located.

While the migrant experience may also be a tragic one, especially in the case of refugees, theorists of the migrant experience have also argued that the experiences of mobility and in-betweenness may transform from the sense of exile and not-being-home to a more positive experience, generating hybridity (Bhabha 1994) or syncretism (Canevacci 1992). Here it should be emphasised that the theorists of hybridity argue that it is not only the marginalised migrant who changes but also the dominant culture or the coloniser. Stuart Hall indeed points out that the term denotes a process, "the cultural logic of translation", not "the mixed racial composition of populations" (Hall 2000: 226). Hybrid, often hyphenated identities (such as British-Asian or Chinese-American), are, as John McLeod (2000: 219) points out, "perpetually in motion, pursuing errant and unpredictable routes, open to change and reinscription".

If transnationalism is understood as the cultural logic of global capitalism, Mukherjee's novel telling of boundary crossings and international networks reveals a number of the effects of transnationalism on people and their fates. The main character, Debby, originally named Faustine after a typhoon, and adopted by a "normal" Italian American family (which makes her an object of international adoption trade) and renamed, is embedded in the globalisation of culture since (and before) her birth. As the novel gradually unfolds, her real parents represent transnational networks peculiar to the 1960s and early 1970s. Her "Bio-Mom" is a Berkeley-educated American hippie who deserts her child in India, and her "Bio-Daddy" a man of many transnational identities, a guru-turned-killer and a grandson of a Pakistani who settles in Indochina. She is the product of changing names and national affiliations. Upon killing her mother, whose confession has put him into jail for murdering a number of Western tourists, he tells Debby the family story:

> Because my father, Yves Haque, ran the Snow White Pedicab Company of Saigon. Our surname — your name — was spelled H-a-q-u-e by then. H-a-q to H-a-q-u-e was strictly an economic decision. A penniless man makes his way out of Peshawar or someplace equally filthy, and peddles cigarettes, chewing gum, dirty cards in *Indochine* cities. Ib Haq was an okay moniker for that man. His son upgrades Haq to Haque, buys himself a Eurasian whore for a wife, and makes what living he can driving pedicabs on the crowded streets of Saigon. Haque's son, yours truly, Americanizes his name to H-a-w-k, and procures for GI's to-die-for dreams. A procurer is not, repeat not, a pimp. We're talking imagination on the grand scale, Miss Dee. If you can supply satiety, there'll always be appetite (1998: 219; italics original).

Not only does the transforming family name reflect the colonial history of South East Asia but the passage points to the logic of globalised capitalism where arms traders and other sinister businessmen operate beyond, and regardless of, national identification, as Hawk's words reveal: "The war was great, especially since Vietnam wasn't my real homeland" (1998: 219).

In addition to the Haq/Hawk family, Debby is connected with transnational capitalism through her employer and lover Frankie Fong, a Chinese actor and producer of internationally marketed serialised kick-boxing films who figures as a successful businessman in the first section of the novel. Debby's particular position in this business is an example of how global capitalism does away with place-related work. She works in telemarketing selling Elastonomics, "manufactured in Asia by Fong Home Products" (Mukherjee 1998: 19), which facilitates her particular identity play. As an effective salesperson because of her sexy voice, she constructs identities and localities to satisfy her customers' wishes for exotica and romance. Though she is located physically in a former Schenectady mall with fifty telemarketing colleagues, her callers believe in her individual identity and think that she inhabits spaces more romantic than their own frustrated everyday spaces in suburbia. Instead of realising that she is physically located in gloomy upstate New York, they think that she is in "Florida or in California. Sleepless in Jersey told me he heard surf in my voice. *Three o'clock in the morning out here in East Orange, babe. Just midnight where you are, I bet*" (Mukherjee 1998: 21; italics original). The callers, unaware of her rootedness, allow her to test the fluidity of her identity:

> The surprise for me was that my callers were romantics. They believed in me, not in salvation through Elastonomics. They begged, *If I call you back, how do I know I'll get you?* I made them effortless promises. Just ask for me, Helena. Or depending on the mood of the day, Staci, Traci, Eva, Magda, Desiree. Some nights I tried out thirty personas. My lies paid off. Loverboys and couch potatoes parted with bucks. What did they expect from me? Phone sex passing itself off as self-improvement, a date once they got in shape? *Sounds good, Roger! You never know, do you, Dave? Expiration date?* (Mukherjee 1998: 21; italics original).

Here Debby's more mobile sense of identity is pitted against the commodification of human relationships in the late-capitalist

USA and the fixedness of the lives of her clientele. The quasi-personal relationship between the telemarketer and the client acquiring gymnastics equipment is merely economically structured, as her phrase-like inserts in the passage above show. The multiple names that Debby uses, and the diverse ethnicities referred to, point to more general readings of the role of ethnicity in Mukherjee's fiction where different (ethnic) narrative voices are often utilised. According to Victoria Carchidi (1995: 94), "Mukherjee feels free to speak for other nationalities and backgrounds because they are her natural subject as an American writer, and the many colored strands of people's lives are the quintessentially American experience". More significantly, Debby's action also shows what Jennifer Drake sees as a central facet in Mukherjee's construction of the Americanisation narrative: "she and other immigrants are 'Americans' — a metaphor/process/state of mind that signifies transforming selves, transforming the nation" (Drake 1999: 67). Indeed, it is Frankie Fong who induces transformation in Debby, generating a change that challenges her naturalised American identity: "The charm of Frankie Fong started out as the charm of foreignness, of a continent I couldn't claim but which threatened to claim me" (Mukherjee 1998: 36).

In the process of transforming, Debby, aware of her status as an adopted child, finds in Frankie a family story she feels is missing from her own life. The DiMartino grandfather's roots in Italy are not for her. Her sister Nicole may consider "Cousin Gino, the only DiMartino who's done time in a state penitentiary, as Jesse James with a Sicilian twist" (Mukherjee 1998: 64). What Debby prefers is a romanticised transnational narrative such as that of Frankie's father's life in hotels and nightclubs, a nostalgic fantasy of a colonial upbringing in imaginary Singapores and Shanghais, places that are "hot, loud, smoky, full of cheats and drugs and whores; the nightclubs were always places of viciousness and degradation and carnality" (Ibid.: 27). The Asian history which Debby is "robbed of" (Ibid.: 27) through her insertion into the DiMartino family is one of a romanticised colonialism and colonial culture, a representation constructed in countless films and other representations of exotica and nostalgia. The work of imagination becomes evident when Debby, speaking of Frankie, tries to accommodate her biological mother in the narrative:

> He lingered on the books he'd devoured in libraries of faded hotels with colonial names, the Imperial, the Nelson Arms, the Lord Curzon. Had these same hotels been my backpacking mom's haunts? He'd self-educated himself, he confessed, on Dorothy Sayers and H.E. Bates, on leatherbound sets of Dickens, Bennett and Galsworthy. I'd never heard of any of these authors except Dickens, but I could feel my fingertips touching Moroccan-leather spines, could see the sparkle of gold dust rubbing off in my hands (Mukherjee 1998: 27).

As Debby seeks identification with Frankie's Indiana Jones-like fantasy of Asia, she problematises her position as one of the DiMartinos, who now become "aliens" (Mukherjee 1998: 27). Not only does she recognise her difference but considers herself a stranger: "Who are you when you don't have a birth certificate, only a poorly typed, creased affidavit sworn out by a nun" (Ibid.: 16). This problematic doubleness and the subsequent need to locate herself motivates her to discover more about her own story, which can also be seen in her adolescent poem in which she posits herself as a dog that she once saw in the local animal shelter: "Take me, love me, shelter me, my barking said" (Ibid.: 17).

The novel's transnational dislocations are not limited to the stories of Debby, her biological parents and her lovers, but they also include those of other characters whose presence contributes to Mukherjee's attempt to redefine America. Upon entering California in her search for parents, Debby enters the prime site of globalising and postcolonialising America inhabited by immigrants, freaks and refugees with roots in such places as Somalia, Vanuatu, Belgium and Serbia. This postcolonial space is supplemented in the novel with another California, the California dream of the Pacific, hippies and Hollywood immortalised and commodified in contemporary culture and exported as US popular culture all over the world. This California is what Japanese tourists want to see when visiting the sacred sites of the Haight, the centre of the 1960s San Francisco hippie movement. The replacement of the original hippies with the homeless of today does not trouble the tourists, coming in their buses to meet a SUNY graduate performing as a latter-day hippie: "I could do a little camera posing, change my down-on-my-luck or what-a-shit-country-we-live-in sob story and squeeze wads of sympathy cash out of fat-cat tourists" (Mukherjee 1998: 70). The commodification of the California lifestyle can also be seen in such references as the description of Madame Kezarina, a "pay-per-prediction prophet" with a "Hate-me Hand" to be stuck with "voodoo pins", a "Vishnu Foot" to be rubbed (Ibid.: 52).

Fantasies of California

Indeed, as Madame K shows, it is not only Debby who performs but the whole city, and its older generation appears to be imitating its (and their) former, allegedly authentic days of glory. For instance, Ham Cohan, Debby's film-producer lover and a former action film hero who has specialised on American remakes of Frankie Fong's films, tells her about 1968 when the whole commune left the city to live in Napa to "coworship...at Baba Lalji's feet" (Mukherjee 1998: 114). Similarly, film crews come to the Haight to reconstruct its past, forcing modern cars leave the streets, thus making the 1990s Haight a nostalgic performance of a 1960s San Francisco. California is also the space that shows best the ironies of globalisation. It can be seen as one example of what Appadurai (1990: 299) refers to as mediascapes, globally available "image-centered, narrative-based accounts of strips of reality...out of which scripts can be formed of imagined lives". As a commodity and signifier of the American lifestyle, California is the object of the desire of all third-world consumers. As a geographical space its boundaries are heavily patrolled against illegal aliens seeking to cross its borders. Emphasising Mukherjee's project of transforming America and Americanness, she allows Debby to share a meal with a Somali medical student (who praises the end of the Western civilization), his four wives and numerous children: "In his world the aliens had already landed and their children were going to college" (Mukherjee 1998: 189). This new immigrant critiques the "infidel" American values, yet claims that "I work harder, I earn dollars, I'm a family man" (Ibid.: 191), thus voicing the basis of the American dream and showing the power of its pull. Not surprisingly, the narrator inserts an ironical comment on the Somali's reproduction of American rhetoric, comparing his family-centred values to those of a 1950s American sitcom: "*Father knows best*" (Ibid.: 190). Yet the view of the Somali resembles Mukherjee's definition of the new American which she has voiced in an essay reflecting on her own naturalisation ceremony, where the transformation of the immigrant and also of America is emphasised: "These new Americans are not willing to wait for a generation or two to establish themselves. They're working for themselves and their children, of course, but they're not here to sacrifice themselves for the future's sake" (Mukherjee 1988: 28). Hence, the new immigrant, while preaching the end of America, also spreads the gospel of a new America where the old and the new are fused, the old immigrant de-Europeanised, as is also shown in the case of Debby replacing her Italian roots with Asian connections.

The novel explores the Golden State's transnational status and refers to it as a space of hybridity and mixing cultures. The hybridity of the novel's postcolonial and multilingual California assists the protagonist to reconstruct herself. As she puts it herself upon entering the state of California, "Debby DiMartino died and Devi Dee birthed herself on the Donner pass" (Mukherjee 1998: 62). This entry is narrated in the novel as a migrant's entry into any nation she does not belong to, complete with the role of the customs officer played by a Fruit Inspector checking Debby's Corolla for non-California vegetables. The "Fruit Buster" (Ibid.: 62), "Asian, but not Chinese" (Ibid.: 63), welcomes Debby into California, thus countering her (or any immigrant's) fear that "*I'm a disgrace to California, I deserve to be turned away*" (Ibid.: 62; italics original). What is peculiar to the novel's hybrid California is that it resembles Debby's America but is not quite the same. Rather than the more traditional cultural fantasy of white America, this space, though preserving its (stereotypical) association with fresh air and post-1960s liberalism, is referred to as "Asia" by Debby (see Ibid.: 67), who recognises San Francisco's multicultural character. In Homi Bhabha's terms, this is the unhomely (*unheimlich*) Third Space, the existence of which "challenges our sense of the historical identity of culture as a homogenizing, unifying force, authenticated by the originary Past, kept alive in the national tradition of the People" (Bhabha 1994: 37). In the following, Debby describes her encounter with the Third Space where tradition and the fixity of signs disappear, reconstructing her identity: "A lot of people reminded of people I'd known, like we'd all drifted west till we'd run out of land, and then'd started to mutate a little, like salmon on their way back to spawn, getting a little cruder, a little uglier, on the way to die" (Mukherjee 1998: 71). The same is true of her identity as perceived by others: both Chinese and Indian males occupying marginal positions consider Debby as one of their own, showing that her position is not fixed but fluid and mobile. Not only do they provide her with access to many stories but her fluidity functions as a critique of essentialist appeals to authentic ethnicity. She becomes someone lost and found:

> Some days in Chinatown, strangers claimed me as fellow-lost. In a Chinese restaurant while I was stoking up on the all-you-can-eat, a waiter mumbled something in a soft, gloomy voice, then hovered for an answer I couldn't give. In a McDonald's an Indian man who looked like a student blurted to me, "Wanna catch a new Amitav?" (Mukherjee 1998: 66).

This hybrid space of the contemporary metropolis with its global links is what Debby makes her home. Yet her identity is not so much place-related as it is connected with the opportunities that this space provides her with, allowing her to function in a community she finds more rewarding and enriching than that of her sister's aspirations to a middle-class life in the New York City. The hybrid urban space is able to accommodate a plethora of conflicting stories and lives, yet it is precisely this multiplicity that attracts Debby and allows her to perform a variety of identities: the hippie, the lover of a producer, the arsonist and the killer: "pick the one that *feels good*" (Mukherjee 1998: 212; italics original). Catholicism changes into non-Western and New Age religions, combining "love and profit, charity and sex, faith and ecology, space and time" (Ibid.: 69). This syncretic space is liberating to Debby: "I felt free; I was free" (Ibid.). Her behaviour confirms what Roger Bromley has found central in fictions of diaspora. In his view they "speak of, from and across migrant identities and develop narratives of plurality, fluidity and always emergent becoming" and "seek to renew severed links between the conflicted, diasporic 'self' and the collective, to shape a critically imagined solidarity, a healing, out of discursive rupture" (Bromley 2000: 2). And indeed, this is what the Third Space of hybridity makes possible for Debby. While her attachments with others, including the Stoop Man, the private eye Fred and the Vietnam Vet Loco Larry, are of a temporary nature, as such they are peculiar to the conditions of diaspora and allow the marginalised subject to critically reflect on the dominant. As she puts it herself,

> It seemed totally natural to identify with dropouts, to step around cops, to look out for scanners and closed-circuit monitors. All that shrapnel of cherubic faces, all those brandings and tattoos looked cool, though not for me. The Haight's lesson was: Nothing in appearance or behaviour need cost a drop of dignity. I didn't look jobless and didn't feel homeless. No sour odor of dim futurity (Mukherjee 1998: 69).

As the passage suggests, the existence of the Third Space and hybridity works against the feeling of homelessness. Here the meaning of home is also more metaphorical than literal, signifying issues such as solidarity and community. It is the aim of the following section to discuss in greater detail the role(s) allotted to home in the novel.

Refiguring Home in the Transnational World

When Debby announces her liking of the Haight, it is of interest that her words refer to it as her home: "My space, my turf, my *homeland*" (Mukherjee 1998: 68; italics original). Regardless of the fact that she attempts to cut loose from her old self, the idea of home follows her on her journey to the hybrid spaces of the contemporary global city. Yet David Morley, writing in particular of the media in his book *Home Territories: Media, Mobility and Identity*, argues that in postmodernity "traditional ideas of home, homeland and nation have been destabilised, both by new communication technologies which routinely transgress the symbolic boundaries around both the private household and the nation state" (Morley 2000: 3). Indeed, it is apparent that the trope of home may be used in different ways, not only to signify nostalgic Heimats and mythic homelands, sacred sites and shared place-related histories (see Smith 1991). Biddy Martin and Chandra Talpade Mohanty have distinguished between two forms of feeling, two "modalities", as they put it:

> "Being home" refers to the place where one lives within familiar, safe, protected boundaries; "not being home" is a matter of realizing that home was an illusion of coherence and safety based on the exclusion of specific histories of oppression and resistance, the repression of differences even within oneself. Because these locations acquire meaning and function as sites of personal and historical struggles, they work against the notion of an unproblematic geographic location of home (Martin and Mohanty 1988: 196).

Thus home is not only a nationalist trope but a multi-accented one. Memories of homelands and home places may provide minority cultures with opportunities to resist dominant discourses and to negotiate cultural identity. With particular reference to African American culture, bell hooks defines the home place as a "site of resistance and liberation struggle" (1990: 43). Similarly the trope is significant in narratives of migration. The narrated subjects are constantly located in places which, since they are often understood as not-home, force the subject to reconstruct her identity and to reflect on issues related to home and community, as the subject may become an Other, an intruder, a foreigner who, to use the words of Julia Kristeva (1991: 95), is "the other of the family, the clan, the tribe". Yet Otherness is only one part of the migrant's identity, an identity that is, as Sarup points out, constantly changing. According to Sarup, the long road to the other place changes the subject: "identity is changed by the journey; our subjectivity is recomposed. In the transformation every step forward can also be a step back: the migrant is here and there" (Sarup 1994: 98), constantly seeking to (re-)locate herself.

Here Mukherjee's novel is of particular importance, as it describes a number of journeys that change the identities of her characters. When they cross cultures and worlds and construct ever different narratives of self, it is no surprise that the significance of home transforms into one that does not gain its meanings in particular localities. The treatment of nations and borders in Mukherjee's novel can be seen to criticise, if not to recast, our understanding of home. Debby does not seek security and fixedness. For her, as for the constantly changing Jyoti/Jasmine/Jazzy/Jase/Jane of the earlier novel *Jasmine*, transformation is imagined in terms of home, or *vice versa*. "Location" is, to quote Caren Kaplan (1996: 168), "a part of travel" that "entail[s] movement or multiplicity rather than stasis and singularity". This emphasis on movement is so much in the core of the novel that Debby refers to it as her world-view: "Who but a foundling has the moral right to seize not just a city, but a neighbourhood, and fashion a block or two of it into home? When you inherit nothing, you are entitled to everything: that's the Devi Dee philosophy" (Mukherjee 1998: 67).

Although the position is definitely self-centred and unashamedly individualist, like that of Jasmine in *Jasmine* (1989), it follows from her hybrid position between her cultures and their histories. While the adoption distinguishes Debby from the DiMartinos, it also provides her with a double perspective and multiple opportunities. Indeed, while Debby is raised as a middle-class Italian American in upstate New York, her growing awareness of the significance of adoption subverts the idea of the fixedness of home and identity, pointing to their constructed nature and stressing the fact that postmodernity as a general cultural condition allows for temporary attachments and strategic essentialisms, rather than universal truths and grand narratives. It is here that the significance of Mukherjee's project emerges. As her characters possess, to use Stoneham's words (2000: 85), "a double voice — a hybrid tongue which articulates the language of the self and the other", they politicise the postmodern and show that the sites constructed may function as locations of critique. "Balance", or compromise, is not enough:

> Debby DiMartino is a lie. Whoever my parents intended for me never existed. That unclaimable part of myself is what intrigues me, the part that came to life in a desert village and had the name Baby Clear Water Iris-

> Daughter until it was christened in a Catholic orphanage. That's the part I want to remember. But there's another part I try to keep secret, the part that sings to moons and dances with stars. With everything I've done, I've tried to find a balance. It's just that Debby DiMartino has no weight, no substance. I had to toss her out (Mukherjee 1998: 10).

As Debby considers herself "a lie", the novel represents identity and home as changing constructs that can be remade; life-narratives are then adopted. Like Debby, but to a much lesser extent, her sister Angie DiMartino re-makes herself in New York, physically and linguistically, by abandoning her "Hudson Valley accent, hair color, clothes, muscle tone and skin" (Mukherjee 1998: 18). The novel constantly emphasises the construction of identity, as can be seen in Frankie Fong, whose childhood homes vary depending on his mood: "born in.... Hong Kong or maybe in Manila or Surabaya" (Ibid.: 25), everywhere rather than in one fixed location. Fong's romanticised stories of his growing up in brothels and opium dens are contrasted with Debby's initial insecurity about her own past: "I was a garbage sack thrown out on the hippie trail" (Ibid.: 13) unable to "claim" an Asian childhood (see Ibid.: 27): "What are you when you have nightmare and fantasies instead of dates and statistics? And, in place of memory, impressions of white-hot sky and burnt-black leaves" (Ibid.: 16). In other words, Debby yearns for a home she has never had, thus countering the view presented by Gail Ching-Liang Low's article on Mukherjee where she comments on Mukherjee's attempts to distance herself from "authentic" traditions. Unlike many other postcolonial authors, she argues that "Mukherjee seemed not to be concerned with preserving cultural identities" (Low 1993: 9). Yet the home in *Leave It to Me*, figured in narrations of fantasy pasts and spaces to be claimed, is not so much a place-related one as it is an ability to transform and to claim home. In so doing, the text writes against the rhetoric of assimilation reproduced in American discourses on immigration and allows Debby to function as a site of resistance to the more conservative doctrines. Her home is not that of Clint Eastwood or the bestseller writer Stark Swann, shown reading his novel which reproduces mythic

American family values and homecomings, complete with horses and images of the West:

> *Sometimes, like when the Fate's croupier fixes the throw, and the suety slob in the white suit pockets your dice, and Lawman Lance weighs in with low blows, and the burned-out bimbo you saved from rape runs off with the finicky florist from Sacramento, there's only one way to go: just suck it in and spur your tired mare on the hot, dusty, cruel trail home, 'cos there's a sweet, sad-eyed woman waitin' for you by the kitchen stove, a loving woman who knows you and cares for you, a real woman who understands you so well she doesn't shackle your ankles to the bedpost but gives her blissful womanhood to you of her own accord and for as long as you need and want her to, and who senses when to step aside, and lets you go without tears, and weeps only after the dust's blown...* (Mukherjee 1998: 161-2: italics original).

The idea of redefining home and reconstructing identity recurs throughout the novel. Since the self-constructed in this process is a mobile one, Debby's task of searching for her biological parents cannot be seen as the adopted child's simple attempt to locate her biological parents. When Debby tells Mrs DiMartino that "[i]t's not about us" (Mukherjee 1998: 50), she leaves unsaid that it is basically about "psychic legacies" (Ibid.: 52). Here it is important to remember that her adoption is a transracial one in which a white family has raised a child of mixed-race parentage, and so to reconstruct herself she needs to confront her racial history, a history containing recurrent memories of India, its landscape and life in the orphanage. This task redefines the meaning of home and makes Debby a racially constituted postcolonial subject. This supports my reading of the novel and emphasises the transformation of her naturalised middle-class American identity with ideological constructions of home and family into a much more problematic position in the margins of a racially constituted US society. She describes herself as "that dark, ghost, *thing*" (Ibid.: 239; italics original). In the process, Debby, while finding her parents but not a family, has to confront what Martin and Mohanty (1988: 196) call the sense of "'not being home'", the illusory character of domesticity.

This can also be seen in her recognition of the functions of the local animal shelter, a space that she has figured as a form of home. The pound, as her family calls it, is not "an alternate lodging between loving homes" (Mukherjee 1998: 13); it is also a place where unwanted animals are eliminated: "No one ever told me they gassed puppies and kitties" (Ibid.: 13). To leave Schenectady is then only to immerse fully in the adoption by imagining being adopted by America. As I will argue, in the end it is only the imagination of nation, the mythical America with transformative powers, that may take over the role of the home.

From Family to Nation

The abolition of the conventional idea of finding home and family is emphasised in the final section of the novel, where Debby's serial murderer father, Romeo Hawk, a look-alike of "Valentino and Nureyev and Adonis" (Mukherjee 1998: 213), kills her mother Jess and decapitates her mother's lover Ham. As an act of revenge, Debby, like her namesake the goddess Devi, "with the will to save and the strength to kill" (Ibid.: 5), commits parricide. In so doing, she performs both as a kick-boxing actor and as a supernatural goddess, and fights against both evil and demons. While the death of Ham in particular is tragic, that of Romeo is a liberating moment imagined in the novel by drawing on Indian mythology. The use of myth transforms the ending into a new beginning by representing an earthquake (the Big One) destroying San Francisco as an act of "the Cosmic Spirit smil[ing] on its daughter goddess" (Ibid.: 6). The Pacific Ocean opens up and swallows the houseboat with the bodies, saving the protagonist from "waist chains, handcuffs, leg shackles" (Ibid.: 239). The novel's opening and ending are connected: the prologue's images of the Cosmic Spirit "creating, preserving, breaking and re-creating the cosmos as always" (Ibid.: 6) and of the fight between the Buffalo Demon and Devi, the "Warrior Goddess [who] wipes demon blood off weapons and puts them away for the next time they are needed" (Ibid.), hint at the final struggle between Debby and her father.

Thus the mythological elements of the novel subvert an understanding of home as a fixed (spatial or cultural) location and promote transformation, imagining the construction of identity as a never-ending process. The destruction of San Francisco is not the final end of the Western civilization but a call for, and a sign of, the reconstruction of Americanness, both individual and cultural. In Mukherjee's narrative the adopted will make the nation their home; as Debby puts it herself: "not *I was adopted*, but *I am adopted*, meaning I want you to know that we've both invented ourselves" (Mukherjee 1998: 33; italics original). By claiming San Francisco as her home, Debby enters, and rewrites, the American dream, fulfils Jasmine's mission, and penetrates the heart of the American dream, transforming it into her home. In this sense the novel ends up by drawing on the master narrative of America as the immigrant's promised land, thus resembling earlier writings by immigrants who have made America theirs, as is the case in the texts of the Jewish immigrant Mary Antin and the Basque American writer Robert Laxalt. The representation of the new immigrant claiming an identity in the (new) home cannot but boost Mukherjee's project of claiming a position in America. However, given the way in which the novel links the rhetoric of home with that of Americanisation, the novel lays itself open to conservative readings emphasising the fixity of Americanness. Mukherjee, however, is not promoting such an option, but through constant makings and remakings of identity she shows the mobility and fluidity of her transnational home and locates her characters in transforming spaces where fixed identities (national, cultural, racial) are challenged and shown to be ideological constructs.

While America remains *the* location for the construction of identity, in Mukherjee's writing it becomes a re-imagined global space, not the unified nation-state which it has pretended to be. Although the solutions imagined in Mukherjee's *Leave It to Me* can be seen as individualist, her cultural dialogues do not aim at traditional liberal solutions content with recognising mutual worth. Instead, they seek to change both the "immigrant" and the "host", and re-imagine the identity of America in a new way. In so doing, her novel can be read in the context of a gendered rewriting of national identity where, as Norma Alarcón, Caren Kaplan and Minoo Moallem (1999: 10-12) have argued, the link between nation and woman as its icon is disrupted. It is through such counter-performers as Debby/Devi, who cannot be easily accommodated in the traditional model of nationhood urging the subject to be either inside or outside it, that the power of the nation state and its emphasis on normativity is criticised. In other words, in the figure of Debby/Devi, Mukherjee shows that the nation's pedagogy, regardless of its emphasis on totalisation, can be rewritten and counter-performed, resulting in a new conception of nationhood where femininity is active and able to resist the hegemonic masculinity of the nation state.

REFERENCES

Alarcón, N., C. Kaplan and M. Moallem 1999: Introduction: Between Woman and Nation. In C. Kaplan, N. Alarcón, and M. Moallem ed.: *Between Woman and Nation. Nationalisms, Transnational Feminisms, and the State*. Durham: Duke University Press.

Appadurai, A. 1990: Disjuncture and Difference in the Global Cultural Economy. In M. Featherstone ed.: *Global Culture: Nationalism, Globalization and Modernity*. London: Sage.

Bhabha, H. 1994: *The Location of Culture*. London: Routledge.

Bromley, R. 2000: *Narratives for a New Belonging. Diasporic Cultural Fictions*. Edinburgh: Edinburgh University Press.

Canevacci, M. 1992: Image Accumulation and Cultural Syncretism. *Theory, Culture & Society*. 9. 95-110.

Carchidi, V. 1995: 'Orbiting': Bharati Mukherjee's Kaleidoscope Vision. *MELUS*. 20. 91-101.

Davis, M. 2000: *Magical Urbanism. Latinos Reinvent the US City*. London: Verso.

Drake, J. 1999: Looting American Culture: Bharati Mukherjee's Immigrant Narratives. *Contemporary Literature*. 60. 60-84.

Grewal, I. and Kaplan C. 1994: Introduction: Transnational Feminist Practices and Questions of Postmodernity. In I. Grewal and C. Kaplan ed.: *Scattered Hegemonies. Postmodernity and Transnational Feminist Practices*. Minneapolis: University of Minnesota Press.

Hall, S. 2000: Conclusion: The Multi-Cultural Question. "In B. Hesse ed.: *Un/Settled Multiculturalisms. Diasporas, Entanglements, Transruptions*. London: Zed.

Hooks, b. 1990: *Yearning. Race, Gender and Cultural Politics*. London: Routledge.

Huq, R. 2000: Living in France: The Parallel Universe of Hexagonal Pop. In A. Blake ed.: *Living through Pop*. London: Routledge.

Kaplan, C. 1996: *Questions of Travel. Postmodern Discourses of Displacement*. Durham: Duke University Press.

Knippling, A.S. 1993: Toward an Investigation of the Subaltern in Bharati Mukherjee's *The Middleman and Other Stories* and *Jasmine.* In E.S. Nelson ed.: *Bharati Mukherjee. Critical Perspectives.* New York: Garland.

Kristeva, J. 1991: *Strangers to Ourselves.* London: Harvester Wheatsheaf.

Low, G. Ching-Liang 1993: In a Free State: Postcolonialism and Postmodernism in Bharati Mukherjee's Fiction. *Woman: A Cultural Review.* 4. 8-17.

Martin, B. and Mohanty, C.T. 1988: Feminist Politics: What's Home Got to Do with It? In T. de Lauretis ed.: *Feminist Studies/Critical Studies.* London: Macmillan.

McLeod, J. 2000: *Beginning Postcolonialism.* Manchester: Manchester University Press.

Miyoshi, M. 1993: A Borderless World? From Colonialism to Transnationalism and the Decline of the Nation-State. *Critical Inquiry.* 19. 726-751.

Morley, D. 2000: *Home Territories. Media, Mobility and Identity.* London: Routledge.

Mukherjee, B. 1988: Immigrant Writing: Give Us Your Maximalists! *The New York Times Book Review.* 28 August: 1. 28-29.

Mukherjee, B. 1991: *Jasmine.* London: Virago.

Mukherjee, B. 1998: *Leave it to Me.* London: Virago.

Nelson, E. 1993: Introduction. In E.S. Nelson ed.: *Bharati Mukherjee. Critical Perspectives.* New York: Garland.

Pfeil, F. 1994: No-Basta Teorizar: In-Difference to Solidarity in Contemporary Fiction, Theory, and Practice. In I. Grewal and C. Kaplan ed.: *Scattered Hegemonies. Postmodernity and Transnational Feminist Practices.* Minneapolis: University of Minnesota Press.

Roscoe, J. 2000: From Bombay to Blackpool: The Construction of Indian Femininity in *Bhaji on the Beach.* In R.J. Crane and R. Mohanram ed.: *Shifting Continents / Colliding Cultures. Diaspora Writing of the Indian Subcontinent.* Amsterdam: Rodopi.

Sarup, M. 1994: Home and Identity. In G. Robertson, M. Mash, L. Tickner, J. Bird, B. Curtis-Barry and T. Putnam ed.: *Travellers' Tales. Narratives of Home and Displacement.* London: Routledge.

Smith, A. 1991: *National Identity.* Harmondsworth: Penguin.

Stoneham, G. 2000: 'It's a Free Country': Visions of Hybridity in the Metropolis. In A. Bery and P. Murray ed.: *Comparing Postcolonial Literatures. Dislocations.* London: Macmillan.

20

Reiterating a Massacre: Sharpeville and After

JOHN A. STOTESBURY

An Apartheid Tragedy

At Sharpeville, a "native" township to the south-west of Johannesburg, on 31 March 1960, sixty-nine people, all of them black South Africans, ranging in age from 12 to 58, were shot dead by South African policemen. Those who died, and the larger number wounded, were (in the main) participants at a demonstration staged around the local police station by the Pan-Africanist Congress (PAC), a political movement more exclusively "black" than its principal rival, the African National Congress (ANC). They were protesting against increasingly draconian apartheid legislation that eventually obliged all blacks to carry their passbooks at all times in public. A standard popular work such as J.D. Omer-Cooper's *History of Southern Africa* adds the detail that at Sharpeville "most were shot in the back" and "in addition 180 people were wounded" (Omer-Cooper 1987: 209). The South African historian T.R.H. Davenport cites the same official figures, adding that this "was not a calculated massacre like the slaughter of Indians at Amritsar in 1919, but a panic reaction" (Davenport 1987: 395). Davenport's term for the event, and also for police killings of black protesters at Langa, near Cape Town, on the same day, is that it was a "tragedy" (Davenport 1987: 396), a description which in retrospect can be regarded as something of an understatement.

In more recent times, and writing from a post-apartheid vantage point, the Johannesburg-based political historian Philip

Frankel has contributed further vital statistics on the shooting. Its duration, he suggest, was probably 15 seconds, though it may have extended to 30 seconds (Frankel 2001: 130, 146). Estimates of the number of rounds fired range from the semi-official "several hundred" (Frankel 2001: 130) to a more credible official total of 1344 (Frankel 2001: 117). At the same time, while the casualties cited in most history books are those already mentioned, Frankel sheds fresh light on gruesome but largely verified accounts which tell about the police, both white and black, bludgeoning some of the wounded to death, while the people of Sharpeville also concealed the fate of some of the victims, for fear of state retribution for their participation in the demonstration (Frankel 2001: 150-153). Thus, Frankel's fresh study of the event tends to restore detail to the historical account where mythologisation had predominated.

In the aftermath of what swiftly came to be known both locally, in South Africa, and around the world as the "Sharpeville Massacre", Sharpeville became "the essential reference point for world attitudes towards the South African system" (Frankel 2001: 213). Like many other commentators, Omer-Cooper (1987: 209) adds that Sharpeville "marked a major turning point in popular attitudes to the South African situation in the Western world". Frankel's account uses a similar term, "watershed" (Frankel 2001: 2), to describe the massacre's global political impact, while its effect on South Africa has been termed a "national trauma" (Troup 1972: 386). In the context of this description, it may be important to recall that although the event clearly was traumatic, the trauma made its impact on a time-scale that took a further thirty years to come to political fruition with the freeing of Mandela and the liberation of the democratic process in the 1990s.

In the decades that followed, the massacre was used for a variety of political purposes. In Frankel's reading of the secondary resources, "Most of what little exists is hagiographic, repetitive, polemical or designed to serve one or another political agenda on the part of the major role players on the South African stage in the past forty years" (Frankel 2001: 248). Since Frankel's primary agenda is to establish a more accurate "history" of the atrocity, its causes and impacts, such resources have only a relatively minor significance for his study. My own interest in Sharpeville is, however, more restricted in its aims and has an alternative purpose: to explore the discursive process through which the local, historical event that occurred in 1960 in Sharpeville became identified — swiftly, repeatedly, and on a global scale — as the "Sharpeville Massacre". Since the details, repeatedly cited in the mainstream histories, have started to waver and shift, the problematic of this process becomes apparent in the extent to which, as Frankel's fresh examination of the historical events has revealed, the accepted "facts" of the event can be proven unreliable.

Frankel's approach has involved discarding the mythologisations of the history of Sharpeville, which he considers to have made it "virtually impossible to dissect [Sharpeville] in a way that enhances our understanding of South Africa" (Frankel 2001: 10). In contrast, my own approach, with its focus upon the processes through which the mythologisation of the event has worked, intends to take Frankel's investigation forward by attempting to gain an understanding of the globalisation of the local event implicit in that process of mythologisation. To serve this purpose, I intend to present a handful of discursive representations of Sharpeville, each of which can be considered ideologically "biased", and then to discuss the nature of their contributions to the globalised gaze that Sharpeville has attracted in the years since the historical massacre. For the sake of a degree of focus, the three sources selected here for particular attention were all produced in the three years leading up to Mandela's release in 1990.

Spectacular Remembrance

In terms of its visible nature, what caused the Sharpeville massacre to assume such lasting political and historical significance might, initially, be defined in terms of *spectacle.* I draw here on the generality of Guy Debord's theorisation of spectacle published in English translation as *Society of the Spectacle* (1987 [the French original was first published in 1967, first English trans. 1970]), in which he argues that "the spectacle is the present *model* of socially dominant life" (Debord 1987: no pagination; section 6, original emphasis), that is, "not a collection of images, but a social relation among people, mediated by images" (Debord 1987: section 4). This would appear to be particularly apposite for the present analysis, as is Debord's delineation of the process of analysis appropriate to the spectacle:

> To describe the spectacle, its formation, its functions and the forces which tend to dissolve it, one must artificially distinguish certain inseparable elements. When analyzing the spectacle one speaks, to some extent, the language of the spectacular itself in the sense that one moves through the methodological terrain of the very society that expresses itself in the spectacle. But the spectacle is nothing other than the *sense* of the total practice of a social economic formation, its *use of time*. It is the historical movement in which we are caught (Debord 1987: section 11, original emphases).

In a more recent critique of Debord's Situationism, Régis Debray has suggested that there is a tendency in Debord's model towards too complete a degree of abstraction, ignoring the "prior digestion of substances":

> It allows one neither to think through the effective realities it designates, nor to criticize to the very roots what it denounces. For where there is no *careful discernment* of the articulations and turning points in the development of a process, no scrutiny of the joints and chinks in the armour, there can be no intellectual *purchase* on the concrete course of things (Debray 1995: 137, original emphases).

Hence, I would argue after Debray that while spectacle may potentially be used to refer to any kind of memorable "concrete" event in history, within the extreme colonial context represented by apartheid the term is inevitably associated with the memorialisation of events through the individual and collective memory of pain, shock, political and physical oppression, and trauma in all of its manifestations. In effect, through its repeated presentation in visual and verbal forms across the range of communicative media — television, radio, the press, and subsequent reproduction in polemical accounts — the brutal killing and wounding of several hundred local residents of Sharpeville obtained a world-scale, globalised audience to a massacre that was, perhaps, "modest" in its actual proportions (compared, say, with Amritsar) but also one that has come to represent a significant moment in the global memory of apartheid. The photographic images of the dead and wounded form a section of our collective "spectacular" memory in much the same way as do those of the naked, napalm-burned Vietnamese girl fleeing a US air raid, the moment of non-judicial execution of a Viet Cong captive by a Saigon police chief, and the skeletal inmates of concentration camps, be it in Belsen, Auschwitz or Serb-controlled territory in a disintegrating Yugoslavia. Apartheid, in the over-familiar litany of state-inflicted brutality, has supplied and, despite its legal cessation in 1994, continues to supply memorial images of its own practices. Such images seem likely to remain vital long after the demise of their immediate, contemporary instigators and witnesses, both within South Africa and in the wider world.

A number of interrelated problems arise from the ways in which "narrators", or "cultural producers", have treated the colonial history of South Africa. My specific concern here is with what the South African scholar Njabulo S. Ndebele has written about the "representation of spectacle" in his essay "The Rediscovery of the Ordinary" (first presented as a public lecture in 1984). The essay, which is passionately Marxian in style and intention, is worth quoting at length:

> The history of black South African literature has largely been the history of the representation of spectacle. The visible symbols of the overwhelmingly oppressive South African social formation appear to have prompted over the years the development of a highly dramatic, highly demonstrative form of literary representation. ...It is the manifest display of violence and brutality that captures the imagination of the spectators. ...Everything in South Africa has been mind-bogglingly spectacular: the monstrous war machine developed over the years; the random massive pass raids; mass shootings and killings; mass economic exploitation the ultimate symbol of which is the mining industry; the mass removals of people; the spate of draconian laws passed with all the

> spectacle of parliamentary promulgations; the luxurious lifestyle of whites; servants, all encompassing privilege, swimming pools, and high commodity consumption; the sprawling monotony of architecture in African locations, which are the very picture of poverty and oppression. The symbols are all over: the quintessence of obscene social exhibitionism (Ndebele 1991: 37).

Ndebele's intention is to focus upon what might be termed the last resort of the *black* South African writer. He claims that the colonial impact of apartheid was so massive, so grotesque, that only by resorting to simplistic, hyperbolic literary representations of the "real" world of South Africa could black writers hope to achieve the desired impact of protest. Ndebele (1991: 45) cites, for example, the fiction produced by the exiled mixed-race Cape Town writer, Alex la Guma, which achieve their effect through representing the "glaring contrasts" in South African society. Much of La Guma's writing works through the simplicity of allegory at the same time as depicting the violence of South African life, and as Ndebele points out, their discursive impact is achieved precisely through their obviousness. Although such narrative strategies may, by Western standards, appear to be crude and unartistic, the contingency of their origins in the black South African experience also marks the emergence of what Ndebele identifies as a new artistic convention which "will validate itself in terms of its own primary conventions; in terms of its own emergent, complex system of aesthetics" (Ndebele 1991: 44).

Here, however, my intention is to appropriate Ndebele's vision of the South African spectacular and in the light of Debord's and Debray's theorisations of spectacle to expand its application to a more selective range of texts. At the same time, my discussion will not lose sight of Ndebele's primary focus, which is upon the grotesqueness of what has always been visible in South Africa's colonial culture. In a general sense, however, and in a way which is complicated by our Western perspective, Ndebele's evocation of the representational spectacle of the colonial experience becomes increasingly problematic. On the one hand, it invites us to gaze imaginatively upon the spectacle; but then it also demands our critical analysis of our own voyeuristic act of gazing.

Although there can be little space here to examine the colonial and postcolonial gaze as such, I intend to return to certain aspects of its impact towards the end of this paper.

South African history is crowded with spectacle of a kind that has made it peculiarly open to scholarly and pedagogical scrutiny as well as to literary and other narrativisations. Events that have been appropriated in particular by the popular fictions of colonialist narratives include the landing at the Cape in 1652 of the first Dutch settlers under the leadership of Jan van Riebeeck; the exit, under the pressure of British rule, of the Voortrekkers from the Cape into the Southern African interior in the early nineteenth century and their violent clashes in later years with the Zulus led by Chaka and Dingaan; and the discovery of diamonds at Kimberley in the 1860s and gold on the Witwatersrand in the 1880s. These in turn resulted only a decade later in the conflict of the Anglo-Boer War, which itself was ironically reversed in the establishment after 1910 of Afrikaner-dominated white governments under the ostensible power of the British Empire. But the most profound image of all, unleashing violent change and disruption, has undoubtedly been the spectacular defeat of the pro-British Empire Prime Minister, Jan Smuts, in the parliamentary elections of 1948, leading immediately to the installation of the first apartheid government. The rather more circumscribed event which I have chosen to focus on, however, is "spectacular" in all senses of the word, both popular and academic: the massacre at Sharpeville. Sharpeville, as I intend to demonstrate, remains one of the key sites of South African memory for its impact on the domestic decolonising process, but also for the critical attention that it attracted in the outside world, a centrality that has led to repeated discursive representations in South African history and culture.

A second point of reference, given the interest of this paper in the process of *memorialisation* of a historical event as traumatic as Sharpeville has proved to be, is to the work of Pierre Nora, who himself draws on earlier studies by Maurice Halbwachs into the relationship between the retention and preservation of *memory* and the social creation of *history*. The aspects of Nora's now familiar deliberations on the conflict and contradictions between his *lieux de histoire* (sites of history) and *lieux de mémoire* (sites of memory) which appear to be most pertinent to the present study are contained in his article "Between Memory and History: *Les Lieux de Mémoire*" (Nora 1989). Towards the end of the article, Nora suggests that

> If we accept that the most fundamental purpose of the *lieu de mémoire* is to stop time, to block the work of forgetting, to establish a state of things, to immortalise death, to materialise the immaterial..., it is also clear that *lieux de mémoire* only exist because of their capacity for metamorphosis, an endless recycling of their meaning and an unpredictable proliferation of their ramifications (Nora 1989: 19).

As the detail of this paper will attempt to illustrate, the massacre at Sharpeville in 1960 may be regarded as exemplary of Nora's formulation. In the four decades since the event itself it is apparent that there has come to exist, on the one hand, an official "history" that was established to a major extent by an inquiry conducted by the South African apartheid régime in the succeeding months. Then, on the other hand, there also exists a constantly diminishing pool of individual "memories" that have formed and still form a significant part of the "history" of the massacre, but which undoubtedly also contain a considerable amount of mythologisation or "urban legend" (Frankel 2001: 148). As Nora indicates, however, "Among history books, only those founded on a revision of memory or serving as its pedagogical breviaries are *lieux de mémoire*" (Nora 1989: 21).

In an important sense, it would seem productive to link up Nora's formulations with the various conceptualisations of the spectacle. If, as Nora theorises, sites of memory are locations where history and memory coincide problematically in order to "crystallise" and retain memory of an iconoclastic event or episode, then the recovery of memory of the historical event is no longer straightforward. Memories, as Nora claims, are "moments of history torn away from the moment of history, then returned; no longer quite life, not yet death (or forgotten), like shells on the shore when the sea of living memory has receded" (Nora 1989: 12). To simplify: contained in Nora's idea is the notion that although particular historical events may always be remembered, we are liable to give them fresh meanings which inevitably transform them from the area of historical factuality. Such sites of memory are invariably specific to the culture producing them, which helps to explain why so much postcolonial literature is concerned with the reconstruction of historical moments. At the same time, as evidenced, for example, by Frankel's recent exhaustive study of Sharpeville, there is a powerful postcolonial desire to reconstruct memory in ways which will bypass the accumulated layers and deceptions imposed historically by slavery, discrimination and racism. My present treatment of Sharpeville will, nevertheless, attempt to emphasise the colonial discursive process, in the belief that only through recalling that process can its future potential for repetition be lessened.

As already mentioned, where the present investigation intends to locate its focus is on sources whose selectively structured representations of Sharpeville render them more labile, possibly less dependable than conventionally "historical" discourse, and visibly more "polemical" — and hence in a variety of ways more subversive — than any scholarly history of the event. Their genres also vary: from the popular colonialist adventure novel (Wilbur Smith 1987, *Rage*), to the cinematic feature film (*Mandela* 1987, directed by Philip Saville), and to a partially journalistic "history" (Allister Sparks 1990, *The Mind of South Africa*). It is not assumed, however, that each of these narrativisations of Sharpeville will have been received by an identical audience, merely that as representations of the event they exist and function as participatory texts in the often discordant discourse that has grown up around the historical event. As such, their existence may nevertheless be regarded as potentially exemplary, despite their limited number and scope in the present investigation. Viewed on a broader scale, it may also be claimed that multi-generic discursive studies of this kind can be used to augment insight not only into the process of any historical process *per se* but also into significant aspects of the ways in which we continue to remember and subsequently historicise the events in question.

Three Texts

While Philip Frankel and the majority of his informants ultimately agree that the Sharpeville massacre was "not supposed to happen" (Frankel 2001: 17), he remains disturbed by the polemical confrontation between the various narrativisations of the event. What I intend to take up here is a single example (*Mandela* 1987) of what he terms the "politically adversarial, monochromatic and morally unambiguous stories" (Frankel 2001: 11-12) and to compare it with another single example (Smith 1987) of "the other version", which holds that "Sharpeville was precipitated by a violent and bloodthirsty mob who assembled before the police station with the clear intention of slaughtering its inhabitants" (Frankel 2001: 12). Frankel then also cites a third, "somewhere between" version of the Sharpeville story, which broadly premises the "'massacre as mistake' theory" (Frankel 2001: 12). This third version I assume to include a basic (if partial) outline of much of Frankel's own reading of the events, although the complexity of the evidence that he presents in his study of Sharpeville as a whole constructs colonialism and apartheid to contain rather more than passive elements in the eventual equation. The discursive example I have chosen to exemplify this third reading is by the South African journalist, Allister Sparks (1990).

Mandela (1987)

Mandela, a documentary feature film dramatisation of Mandela's life, was circulated in 1987, three years prior to his release but at a point when, under the premiership of P.W. Botha, the South African apartheid government had already commenced tentative negotiations with Mandela and the ANC, and Mandela was no longer imprisoned on Robben Island but under relatively comfortable conditions at Pollsmoor Prison, on the outskirts of Cape Town. Given subsequent global familiarity with the public persona of Mandela and that of his then wife Winnie, the film now appears poorly cast, its dialogue stilted, and its locations and storyline overly predictable. Despite the film's weaknesses, however, its representation of Sharpeville remains significant for the pattern of its adherence to — and, more strikingly, its deviations from — even the apartheid régime's officially-certified version of the events of 31 March 1960.

The duration in the film of the principal events of the day

extends to some 9½ minutes, and in Frankel's terminology, the cast of the film's message is indisputably "politically adversarial". This can clearly be seen in the contrast between the festive mood of the black protestors as they gather around the Sharpeville police station and the cynical manipulation of the truth by the Sharpeville police commander, who telephones headquarters in Johannesburg, blithely asserting the hostility of a 20,000-strong crowd wielding sticks and stones. In his assessment, the police station is "under siege". Police reinforcements arrive; the African crowd sings African songs; the police arm themselves. There is no hint of a police strategy other than a programmatic process of falsehood and the assertion of paramilitary superiority. The policemen file out of the station, lining up to face the African crowds on the other side of the perimeter fencing. The police chief utters two commands: "Aim! Fire!"; Africans fall dead, and continue to do so as they flee in terror, while the police continue to fire volley after volley, until the command to "Cease fire!" is issued. One or two policemen grin sheepishly, then move forward out of the police compound to begin the task of retrieving the dead and placing their corpses in orderly rows along a roadway near the station.

Thus, the melodrama contained in the familiar binary codings of white/black, colonised/coloniser, festive/fixated, good/evil, and so on becomes emblematic of this filmic (re)construction of the massacre as a whole. Perhaps the most striking aspects of this dramatisation are contained in its simultaneous exaggeration and simplification of the familiar. Where, for example, previous historical accounts of the massacre had already established with considerable reliability that the shooting went on for 15-30 seconds, its duration in the film is a full minute-and-a-half. In addition, the film represents the apartheid police force as totally culpable in the act of massacre: the police chief lies in order to have instant reinforcements sent from outside Sharpeville, and his command initiating the massacre remains uncontested and unmodified by anything other than the slightest of token hesitations on the part of a single, low-ranking policeman. Police power is portrayed as absolute and unquestioned. Nevertheless, while as spectators we recognise the deviations of this visual narrative from the probable "reality" of the historical events of the day, if we accept the liberal-humanist-liberationist view of colonialism and apartheid, then we are likely to concede that there can also exist a "reading" of the film's text with which we may concur. Its tendency to melodramatise events can readily be interpreted as a means to achieving its ends. The fact that not all of the film's spectators will view it from this perspective is not under debate — the film has readily signalled its own consistent reading of the composite text of colonialism and apartheid, and ultimately we are expected to concur that this is indeed the composite text, as the film powerfully insists, that can be identified as the root cause of the massacre at Sharpeville.

Wilbur Smith: *Rage* (1987)

The representation of Sharpeville in Wilbur Smith's popular apartheid thriller *Rage*, published in the same year as the *Mandela* film appeared, is more subtle, less readily deciphered or deconstructed, and more deeply embedded in the global propaganda war waged in the 1980s over the continuation of the apartheid state. Like much of Smith's fiction since the start of his highly successful career as a colonialist novelist in 1964 (see Stotesbury 1994), *Rage* personalises both apartheid in general and Sharpeville in particular, and it does so principally through narrating in the guise of a "family saga" a period of South African history that is indelibly associated with the introduction and entrenchment of apartheid, from the early 1950s to the mid-1960s (see Maughan-Brown 1990). In the case of the half-dozen or so pages covering Sharpeville (Smith 1987: 492-498), by means of personalisation of the Sharpeville police commander as an Afrikaner relative of the novel's anglophone South African protagonist, Shasa Courtney, *Rage* excels in its obfuscation of the perceived factuality of the historical event. Although, as Maughan-Brown (1990: 147) comments, Smith seems to have consulted as reputable a source as Tom Lodge's *Black Politics in South Africa since 1945*, Lodge's (1983: 210) account of the massacre is in fact as concise as most general history book accounts of Sharpeville tend to be. In Smith's defence, it must be recalled that this is indeed a fictionalisation of the massacre, and according to Smith himself, when questioned in interview about his treatment in *Rage* of the chronology of South African events, "History's an untidy old bag and you have to sort it out in fiction" (Stotesbury 1996: 78-79). Maughan-Brown's reading of this aspect is damnatory: "Wilbur Smith is not simply 'taking liberties' with history in the interests of dovetailing this history of South Africa with that of the Courtney family, he is deliberately manipulating and distorting history" (Maughan-Brown 1990: 147).

It would seem, then, that a fictionalised narrative of this kind may function within a *lieu de mémoire* such as Sharpeville by means of a process of replacing actual memory with ideologically-constructed "false" memories. While this suggestion may appear, at least superficially, to echo the charges laid by the Frankfurt School against mass culture for its apparent involvement in the creation of "false consciousness", my use of the notion of falsity is in relation to the attempt made in the text to manipulate not only memory of a past event but also its significance in the contemporary South African political confrontation between the past and a potential future. Clearly, a similar charge could well be laid against the production of the *Mandela* film, though for reasons which differ from those involved in Smith's *Rage*, where "History and fiction make a potent ideological combination" (Maughan-Brown 1990: 149).

Where this ideological manipulation is most obvious in Smith's Sharpeville is in his colonialist premise founded on the historically unresolved, racialised "tribal" struggle between the "natives" and what has frequently been termed the "white tribe of Africa", the Afrikaners:

> The sergeant beside [Lothar De La Rey, the fictionalised Sharpeville police commander] swore softly. "My God, just look at those black bastards, there must be thousands of them," and Lothar recognised in the man's tone his own horror and trepidation.
>
> What they were looking upon was the nightmare of the Afrikaner people that had recurred for almost two centuries, ever since their ancestors moving up slowly from the south through a lovely land populated only by wild game had met suddenly upon the banks of the great Fish river the cohorts of this dark multitude.

> He felt his nerves crawl like poisonous insects upon his skin as the tribal memories of his people assaulted him. Here they were once more, the tiny handful of white men at the barricades, and there before them was the black barbaric host. It was as it had always been, but the horror of his situation was not in the least diluted by the knowledge that it had all happened before (Smith 1987: 492).

Given the repetition yet again of the colonial myth of a pre-colonial African landscape devoid of human inhabitants, what emerges from the episode as a whole is the narrative identification of whites with "tribal" *memory* and blacks with "tribal" *behaviour*. In this process, the stereotypical associations of the signifier "tribal" shift between "group, communal, social" on the one hand and "barbaric, uncivilised, savage" on the other, with the latter signification coming to rest, inevitably, on the blacks.

While the blacks fill the hours prior to the massacre with an accretion of "dark" tribal behaviour — chanting, eddying and pushing, humming "fierce fighting songs", rumour-mongering, cheering, growling, surging, and (a typically Smithian touch) emitting "the odours of hot African bodies" — the whites try with increasing desperation to exercise their understanding of "calm". When, therefore, the tension peaks and panic shooting breaks out from amongst the ranks of the Afrikaner police, it does so with no command having been issued by Lothar De La Rey:

> There was a loud and jarring sound close behind him that Lothar did not at first recognise. It sounded as though a steel rod had been drawn rapidly across a sheet of corrugated iron. Then he heard the other terrible sounds, the multiple impact of bullets into living flesh, like ripe melons bursting open from blows with a heavy club, and he shouted, "No! Oh good Christ, no!" (Smith 1987: 497).

The collective terrors of his own tribal group then overwhelm Lothar, and against his own will he participates in the shooting by firing off the contents of his sten gun, only then, after a quasi-sexual release of the seeds of death, reasserting the self-control of the "civilised" man over his own fears to order a cease-fire. The episode concludes, bathetically, piously, mock-liberally, with a reverse-perspective utterance that echoes Christ's "Father, forgive them, for they know not what they do": "'Oh, God forgive me. What have we done?' he choked. 'Oh, what have we done?'" (Smith 1987: 498).

Allister Sparks: *The Mind of South Africa* (1990)

Allister Sparks's approach to the site of memory represented by Sharpeville differs radically from both previous texts. Again embedding Sharpeville in a larger study of South African history, Sparks proffers to his readers a decentred, multivocal text. His Sharpeville is prefaced by Sipho Sepamla's elegiac verse:

> in a flash
> of the eye
> of gun-fire
> like spray flayed
> they fled they fell
> the air fouled
> the minute fucked
> and life fobbed
>
> our heads bowed
> our shame aflame
> our faith shaken
> we buried them for what they were
> our fallen heroes and our history
> (Sepamla, qtd. in Sparks 1990: 233)

The remainder of Sparks's brief memorialisation of Sharpeville is taken up with an account of one of its survivors, Michael Zondo, a local schoolteacher: "He remembers the day well" (Sparks 1990: 233). Drawn by curiosity rather than political engagement, Zondo joins the crowds assembling around the police station:

> At 1:50 exactly, Zondo recalls, there was a commotion at the gate over to his right. ...Suddenly, as he was looking at this, Zondo heard a chattering noise in front of him.

> "Brains", he murmured, shaking his head in a vague way that conveyed a sense of disbelief still, after twenty-nine years. "I just saw brains. Skulls were bursting open in front of me" (Sparks 1990: 234).

For Zondo, in Sparks's re-narration of Sharpeville, the massacre is spectacle, its immediate impact a scarcely-perceived leg-wound: "I saw some kids from my class. They started shouting, '*Tichara othunswe! Tichara othunswe!*' which is Sisotho for 'Our teacher has been shot'" (Sparks 1990: 234), and it concludes with a brief account of the continuation of Zondo's life under apartheid, which has included no promotion throughout the rest of his teaching career.

Critical Challenges

How, then, in the present do we conclude this process of viewing and re-assessing the globalised spectacle of apartheid exemplified by these mythologisations of the Sharpeville massacre? Or as the South African academic Michael Chapman asked in the period immediately after the release of Mandela, "How in a society where contexts overwhelm texts do we proceed as critics and educators?" (Chapman 1991: 7). A number of provisional conclusions present themselves, but nothing that is solid or reassuring. A large challenge to this kind of analytical investigation has been issued by an informed critic of white South African representations of colonial violence such as Rosemary Jane Jolly. As critical, no doubt resistant, but also voyeuristic spectators of representations of a violent history in which others have suffered from an obvious atrocity, we are, Jolly argues, "in a position of privilege: [we are] not involved in the scene that constitutes [our] subject" (Jolly 1996: xi). But at the same time Jolly then proceeds to an aspect of the critical dilemma that may be rather more problematic from our own (possibly white, liberal, European) perspective: "This position is, at the same time, rendered genuinely unenviable because of the spectator's tendency to repeat violations that stem from his or her response to the scene of violation" (Jolly 1996: xi).

If, however, we attempt to reject her speculation over our own inescapable (Western) involvement in global oppression and atrocity, in what meaningful way — if any — can we then respond to the colonial spectacle of violence? Do we distance ourselves from the pain by "aestheticising" our emotional responses, explaining them away in terms of conventional "catharsis", for instance, and thus end up with a response which can only be defined in terms of intellectual pleasure? Or do we enter into the full spirit of the horror by regarding it as an aspect of modern gothic which thus permits us to "share" in the pain endured by others, or, indeed, by the Other? Is this kind of vicarious experiential identification any more "real"?

At the same time, we are indeed obliged to remember that such sites of memory as Sharpeville are of rather more profound significance to those others who were closer to the historical moment. To what extent, then, is our remote "participation" in or witnessing of such moments similar to the voyeuristic pleasures to be gained from pornography? As Jolly also suggests, as witnesses we are likely to have no desire to be "trapped as spectators in a vision of horror" (Jolly 1996: xiv), but conventional literary or textual analysis does not necessarily liberate us from such entrapment. The spectacle cannot simply be experienced and then condemned: it certainly requires analysis and comprehension. But above all, it requires that we understand our own starting-point, and where the source of the violence is actually to be found — perhaps within our own local cultural identities rather than in those of people whom we conventionally regard and label as beyond our own experience, as a haphazardly "globalised" Other. Another version of an answer may also be found in the concluding remarks of Chapman's soul-searching article (Chapman 1991: 11): "When a student comes to me and says, I want to write on so-and-so, I might be impelled to ask why. For whom are you writing? For what purpose? What has your writing got to do with restructuring identities in this country? Is your writing progressive in intent, liberating in purpose? What do these questions about literature have to do, finally, with ideas of justice and compassion in a post-apartheid South Africa?"

REFERENCES

Chapman, Michael 1991: The Critic in a State of Emergency. *Kunapipi*. 13:1-2. 1-11.

Davenport, T.R.H. 1987: *South Africa. A Modern History.* Third edition. Toronto: University of Toronto Press.

Debord, Guy 1987 (1970): *Society of the Spectacle.* No place [UK]: Rebel Press. Originally published in 1967 as *La société du spectacle.*

Debray, Régis 1995: Remarks on the Spectacle. *New Left Review.* 214. 134-141.

Frankel, Philip 2001: *An Ordinary Atrocity. Sharpeville and its Massacre.* Johannesburg: Witwatersrand University Press.

Jolly, Rosemary Jane 1996: *Colonisation, Violence, and Narration in White South African Writing. André Brink, Breyten Breytenbach, and J.M. Coetzee.* Athens, Ohio: Ohio University Press.

Lodge, Tom 1983: *Black Politics in South Africa since 1945.* London: Longman.

Mandela 1987: Prod. Richard Bamber. Dir. Philip Saville. Videocassette. USA. TVS.

Maughan-Brown, David 1990: Raising Goose-Pimples: Wilbur Smith and the Politics of *Rage.* In Martin Trump ed.: *Rendering Things Visible. Essays on South African Literary Culture.* Johannesburg: Ravan Press.

Ndebele, Njabulo S. 1991: The Rediscovery of the Ordinary: Some New Writings in South Africa. In *Rediscovery of the Ordinary. Essays on South African Literature and Culture,* by Njabulo S. Ndebele. Fordsburg, Johannesburg: Congress of South African Writers.

Nora, Pierre 1989: Between History and Memory: *Les Lieux de Mémoire. Representations.* 26. 7-25.

Omer-Cooper, J.D. 1987: *History of Southern Africa.* London: James Currey.

Smith, Wilbur 1987. *Rage.* London: Heinemann.

Sparks, Allister 1990: *The Mind of South Africa. The Story of the Rise and Fall of Apartheid.* London: Heinemann.

Stotesbury, John A. 1994: Smith, Wilbur (Addison). *Encyclopedia of Post-Colonial Literatures in English.* 2. London: Routledge.

Stotesbury, John A. 1996: Popularising Late-Apartheid South Africa: An Interview with Wilbur Smith. *Teaching and Learning* (University of Joensuu). 2. 73-88. Available online: http://www.geocities.com/sriramna/Wilbur_Smith_Interview.html.

Troup, Freda 1975 (1972): *South Africa. An Historical Introduction.* Harmondsworth: Penguin.

21

Afterthoughts: Notes on the Politics of Cultural Identity

JARI KUPIAINEN

Around the time of our conference "Cultural Identity and Its Glocal Manifestations" in the year 2000, the topic of cultural identity was a flourishing one. Diverse indigenous, ethnic and cultural groups, communities and minorities were busily engaged in projects designed to promote their distinctiveness and specificity amidst the encompassing pressures of economic and media globalisation. In analytical discourse, the concept of glocal was in the process of emerging as a new catchword to account for many of these processes where local and more international elements of identity were mixing and melting together and composing emergent identities operational in the contemporary condition. Since then the world has seen a deep surge towards cultural and religious fundamentalism and absolutism, produced especially by the terrorist attacks in the USA and its aftermath in the Eurasian continent, most notably the wars in Afghanistan and Iraq. At the time of writing these "afterthoughts" in 2003, the prospects for diversifying cultural identities and multiculturalism look gloomy indeed. Whatever "shock and awe" the military operations in Iraq and elsewhere may have produced, it seems apparent that the processes of multiculturalism and cultural diversification of recent decades will face a major challenge as a direct consequence of the emerging polarisation between Christian fundamentalists and Islam.

In this *post scriptum* my attempt is to reflect on some of the recent political developments in the world, in terms of the analysis of cultural identity processes, and I will also point towards perspectives and ideas that may prove fruitful in terms of future research into these topics. It would seem that the positions of culture — and cultural identities — within international politics and state apparatuses are approaching a certain fundamental crossroads, where "culture" or "cultural identity" may diminish into mere aesthetic decoration placed atop various communities and societies in the world. All countries and societies are today entangled within one worldwide network of "flows", or ethnoscapes, technoscapes, finanscapes, mediascapes and ideascapes as Arjun Appadurai (1990) has labelled them. Although local reactions to and strategies for managing these "flows" and "scapes" will remain as diverse as ever, the point is that all are responding to either the same or similar questions, issues and matters — parallel to and simultaneously with each other. What this actually means for local cultural identity processes remains to be studied further.

What used to be celebrated as cultural diversity, involving attempts at establishing cultural identities as autonomous units in contemporary social formation, has now come face to face with the disheartening reality of polarising political processes, reflected in expressions such as "the axis of evil" or "coalitions of the willing", as American military rhetoric addresses these questions these days. Suddenly, the world seems to be shifting towards bi-polar visions where one is either "good" or "bad", or "a friend" or "against us". Under the current circumstances cultural identity — when it articulates identities different from the mainstream society — appears to be assuming a pronounced political character whenever it is expressed in public.

We may, however, notice that cultural identities appear to be taking quite the opposite turn: they are becoming tacit. In other words, cultural identities are — at least in certain societies — in the process of turning clandestine and going underground. Expressing your distinctive identity is fast becoming dangerous in some countries, and to strive for cultural autonomy in such places would mean that you are fast heading for trouble. Moreover, self-conscious and distinctive cultural identities may be seen to carry a challenge to the mainstream culture and society because they frequently organise themselves into activist and action groups, that mainstream society (or its authority bodies) and media consider suspect. In this tightening international situation, attempts at cultural diversification become treated increasingly as political confrontation by state apparatuses that see cultural diversity as a "security risk". Cultural separatists or radicals easily become labelled as potential terrorists, as sympathisers undermining the authority of the state — at least in the eyes of the military and police authorities. For them, cultural distinctiveness is not a virtue but a vice.

In the current situation it will be useless to attempt to figure out what exactly will be the general future of cultural identities in the global condition. Nevertheless, we may try to formulate questions and research issues to reflect upon the social and structural changes in cultural organisation that are currently taking place. One such issue has been brought to prominence by the sociologist Scott Lash in his recent book (2002; see also Lash and Urry 1987), where, among other issues, he analyses "disorganizations". For Lash, disorganizations demonstrate the "decline of organized capitalism" as "a decline of organizations and a rise in individualism...[they] entail a rise in certain forms of sociation that are non-organizational, indeed often non-institutional" (Lash 2002: 39). With disorganizations, Lash is not only referring to certain recent developments in business culture (typically represented by the loose hierarchies and operating modes of the new media and IT businesses), but also to structural shifts in the compositions and operating modes of socio-cultural formations, movements and subcultures. According to Lash, we are facing a new phase of social development where networks, personal relationships in the midst of global formations, anti-hierarchies, the distancing from geographical places, and various anti-mainstream values characterise the new trends.

At least in certain respects we may consider the cultural identities of today as "disorganizations". Cultural identities remain communal and collective, they are shared, and there exists a community relevant to the identity, but it is less evident that a cultural identity should still be associated with a particular ethnicity or with a particular place. Increasingly, and particularly boosted by international migration, the relevant community may be dispersed around the world, or it may emerge as a composite of members of different ethnicities, as would be evident in the context of, for example, workplace cultures. Or it may be void of a definite centre or basis, as the case may be with certain Internet-based communalities and "cultures".

Often, a particular cultural identity can be at least partially adopted by anyone interested or committed enough. In these terms, a cultural identity would appear as a social performance rather than essentia, not unlike Judith Butler's ideas (1990) about performing gender. To paraphrase Butler, you perform your gender and likewise you perform your cultural identity. Both are social constructions. There is one caveat, here, though: in Butler's analytical framework the eventual decision-maker in determining what is to be involved in "performing one's gender" is the individual. It is a matter of individual choice to reflect, in one's performances, the norms and conventions of the surrounding society in whichever way one decides, either confirming to them or distancing oneself from them. Although this performance *always* takes place in a specific socio-cultural context and is firmly situated in place and time, the emphasis is on the individual.

It is a commonplace these days to refer to diverse sorts of emergent groups and collectives as "cultures" and to their identifying markers as "cultural identities", but it would be wise to remember that at the core of "culture" in its anthropological definitional sense is the idea of an ethno-cultural group and nation. Of these, especially the traditions and lifeways of indigenous peoples may be highlighted as cultures *par excellence*. Indigenous peoples in the contemporary world are also the most vulnerable to extinction, and more often than not they are subject to systematic oppression and marginalisation by mainstream society. It would be an insult to present ideas to these peoples about how they might be "performing their cultural identity" amidst ongoing genocide or army harassment. The world's indigenous peoples struggle for recognition and survival amidst the processes of modernisation, economic globalisation, international media, industry, tourism, government and NGO activities, urbanisation, and mainstream school education. Frequently their health and life expectances are far below those of the mainstream population, and their social situation is depressing. Current education systems have ascertained that colonial and world languages are replacing local indigenous languages efficiently and comprehensively all-around the world, so that the long-cherished richness of the world's linguistic diversity is fast turning into a travesty, one hiding systematic assimilation politics and cultural eradication. Students and researchers of cultural identities need to acknowledge the profound consequences related to these processes.

In terms of research practice, this signals the end to studies directed mainly by the interests of Western academia and its theoretical concerns that ignore the interests of local communities. Increasingly, the object of study has become the subject of negotiations between local communities and the researchers, and the researcher has to include aspects of communal interest in the study, or formulate the study in terms of issues also of interest to locals. It is becoming evident that cultural and indigenous communities want researchers who are willing and able to operate as partners for the community to promote communal goals and the community's practical interests in the wider world.

Linda Tuhiwai Smith's (2002, 1) words may serve here as a conclusive warning:

> From the vantage point of the colonized, a position from which I write, and choose to privilege, the term 'research' is inextricably linked to European imperialism and colonialism. The word itself, 'research', is probably one of the dirtiest words in the indigenous world's vocabulary. ...It galls us that Western researchers and intellectuals can assume to know all that is possible to know of us, on the basis of their brief encounters with some of us. It appals us that the West can desire, extract and claim ownership of our ways of knowing, our imagery, the things we create and produce, and then simultaneously reject the people who created and developed those ideas and seek to deny them further opportunities to be creators of their own culture and own nations. It angers us when practices linked to the

last century, and the centuries before that, are still employed to deny the validity of indigenous people's claim to existence, to land and territories, to the right of self-determination, to the survival of our languages and forms of cultural knowledge, to our natural resources and systems for living within our environments.

REFERENCES

Appadurai, Arjun 1990: Disjuncture and Difference in the Global Cultural Economy. In Mike Featherstone ed.: *Global Culture. Nationalism, Globalization and Modernity*. London: Sage.

Lash, Scott 2002: *Critique of Information*. London: Sage.

Lash, Scott and John Urry 1987: *The End of Organized Capitalism*. Cambridge: Polity Press.

Butler, Judith 1990: *Gender Trouble. Feminism and the Subversion of Identity*. New York: Routledge.

Smith, Linda Tuhiwai 2002 (1999): *Decolonizing Methodologies. Research and Indigenous Peoples*. London, New York and Dunedin: Zed Books and University of Otago Press.

Contributors

Pirkkoliisa Ahponen. Department of Social Policy, University of Joensuu, Finland.

Pasi Falk. Department of Sociology, University of Helsinki, Finland.

Marja-Leena Hakkarainen. Department of Comparative Literature, University of Turku, Finland.

Kaija Heikkinen. Karelian Research Institute, University of Joensuu, Finland.

Joel Kuortti. English Department, University of Tampere, Finland.

Jari Kupiainen. Centre for Media Culture, University of Joensuu, Finland.

Mikko Laaksonen. Department of Comparative Literature, University of Turku, Finland.

Ilkka Liikanen. Karelian Research Institute, University of Joensuu, Finland.

Kristina Malmio. Department of Nordic Literature, University of Helsinki.

Tuomas Martikainen. Department of Comparative Religion and Folkloristics, Åbo Akademi University in Turku, Finland.

Stein Roar Mathisen. Finnmark College, University of Alta, Norway.

Jopi Nyman. Department of English, University of Joensuu, Finland.

Matti Savolainen. Department of Literature, University of Oulu, Finland.

Rien T. Segers. Department of Culture and Business Administration, University of Groeningen, The Netherlands.

Erkki Sevänen. Department of Cultural Research, University of Joensuu, Finland.

John A. Stotesbury. Department of English, University of Joensuu, Finland.

Pekka Suutari. Department of Cultural Research, University of Joensuu, Finland.

Juri Talvet. Department of Comparative Literature, University of Tartu, Estonia.

Ilya Utekhin. Department of Ethnology, European University at St. Petersburg, Russia.

Rein Veidemann. Department of Literature, University of Tartu, Estonia.